PRAISE FOR *RETHINKING SUPPLY CHAIN*

'Bram DeSmet has done it again! In *Rethinking Supply Chain*, he creates highly needed clarity by unravelling relevant phenomena at play in the supply chain field. DeSmet builds on the strong foundations of his earlier concepts like the Supply Chain Triangle, adding the urgent topics of resilience and sustainability to the supply chain equation. There is plenty of food for thought here for business leaders and for the wider supply chain community. Highly recommended reading.'
Ed Weenk, Senior Associate Professor, EADA Business School Barcelona

'A captivating exploration of the dynamic world of supply chain management that we need in today's environment. Drawing from his extensive experience and unwavering commitment to the field, Bram DeSmet offers invaluable insights into building a strategy-driven, sustainable and resilient supply chain. From the strategic trade-offs between service, cost and cash to the incorporation of sustainability and resilience, this book provides a comprehensive framework for navigating the complexities of modern supply chains.'
Eric Wilson, Director of Thought Leadership, Institute of Business Forecasting and Planning

'By fundamentally reconsidering the well-entrenched foundations of our approach to supply chain management and adapting them to the realities of a world that needs to more seriously consider the social and environmental impacts of our businesses, Bram DeSmet provides us with a playbook for success in the 21st century.'
Jonathon P Karelse, CEO, Northfind Management and author, *Histories of the Future*

'Sustainability has been part of the strategy agenda for quite some time, but managers struggle to link their sustainability initiatives to the strategic plans of their company. *Rethinking Supply Chain* shows that sustainability can and should be added and integrated into your strategy and supply chain management. Bram DeSmet has succeeded in translating this complex topic into clear, easy-to-understand models that are insightful and practically relevant for every strategy and supply chain manager.'
Kurt Verweire, Professor of Management Practice in Strategy, Vlerick Business School

'While the Covid-19 pandemic highlighted the need for robust supply chains to navigate disruptions in the market, few people pointed out the close connection between improved supply chain planning and a company's health. Bram DeSmet's latest work illustrates that supply chains are most effective if they are purpose-driven. Indeed, supply chains should never be designed and operated without company strategy in mind. Another invaluable addition to the literature.'
Dr Harpal Singh, CEO, Arkieva

'Another great contribution by Bram DeSmet on supply chain strategy. In an era where businesses increasingly see that their success is based on their supply chain capabilities, there is a high need to think strategically about matching demand and supply. In his new book, Bram DeSmet does an excellent job in integrating two contemporary trends to his earlier frameworks: resilience and sustainability. Nothing less than required reading for all supply chain professionals and all board members who are looking for a strategic perspective on their organization.'
Jack van der Veen, Professor of Supply Chain Management, Nyenrode Business University

'By reading this book, you will understand how strategy driven and sustainable supply chains can create sustainable stakeholder value in times of high volatility and business disruptions. Bram DeSmet explains the different value choices of companies leading to different value propositions and trade-off decisions. The new integrated value planning and execution model is groundbreaking for any effective business and supply chain management of the future.'
Frank Vorrath, Vice President, Supply Chain Services, Danfoss Climate Solutions

'As we enter the age of uncertainty, it is vital that all organizations step back and rethink their supply chain strategy. The ideas explored in this book will provide practical support for managers and others who seek to ensure that their supply chains will be fit for purpose in the years ahead.'
Martin Christopher, Emeritus Professor of Marketing and Logistics, Cranfield University

'As someone who has been in the industry for years, I can confidently say that *Rethinking Supply Chain* is not just an educational tool but a compelling call to action. It urges managers and leaders at every level to rethink, reinvent and revolutionize supply chain strategies for a more efficient, sustainable and globally

competitive future. Whether you're a seasoned supply chain veteran looking to update your knowledge or a novice in the industry, this book holds valuable insights and practical advice that will undoubtedly guide your strategic and operational decisions.'
Mourad Tamoud, Chief Supply Chain Officer, Schneider Electric

'How should companies align their business strategy with their supply chains in today's turbulent world with geopolitical tensions and ongoing disruptions? And how should decision-makers make the right trade-offs between cost, service, cash and sustainability? Bram Desmet is on a journey to find practical answers to these strategic questions. In *Rethinking Supply Chain*, he provides readers with actionable tools and exercises to face the future with more resilience and sustainability.'
Martijn Lofvers, CEO and Chief Trendwatcher, Supply Chain Media

'In his new book, Bram DeSmet has significantly expanded the scope of supply chain design and operations by including sustainability and resilience as part of the central core. He also takes traditional S&OP thinking to a new elevated level by introducing the concept of Integrated Value Planning and associated metrics. These additions to the theory and practice of supply chain management will surely lead to a material improvement in decision-making at the operational level.'
John Gattorna, Global Supply Chain Thought Leader and author

'Taking integrated business planning to the next level requires more than functional knowledge, senior management communication skills and entrepreneurial thinking. In his new book Bram DeSmet shows both a framework and practical examples to make the right decisions in today's business reality with growing complexity, increasing volatility and the need for rethinking supply chain strategies for more resilient, social and sustainable solutions.'
Rüdiger Fuchs, Supply Chain Director, PPF Group

'The Covid-19 pandemic made supply chains a mainstream topic. Since then the discipline has not only attracted significant additional interest, but also resources from multiple areas. In this book, Bram DeSmet shows how to evolve a supply chain into a multi-dimensional model, providing a consistent and clear value-adding framework as basis for decision-making in an increasingly disrupted world.'
Dirk Holbach, Chief Supply Chain Officer, Henkel Consumer Brands

Rethinking Supply Chain

Build a Strategy-Driven, Sustainable and Resilient Supply Chain

Bram DeSmet

Publisher's note

Every possible effort has been made to ensure that the information contained in this book is accurate at the time of going to press, and the publishers and authors cannot accept responsibility for any errors or omissions, however caused. No responsibility for loss or damage occasioned to any person acting, or refraining from action, as a result of the material in this publication can be accepted by the editor, the publisher or the author.

First published in Great Britain and the United States in 2024 by Kogan Page Limited

Apart from any fair dealing for the purposes of research or private study, or criticism or review, as permitted under the Copyright, Designs and Patents Act 1988, this publication may only be reproduced, stored or transmitted, in any form or by any means, with the prior permission in writing of the publishers, or in the case of reprographic reproduction in accordance with the terms and licences issued by the CLA. Enquiries concerning reproduction outside these terms should be sent to the publishers at the undermentioned addresses:

2nd Floor, 45 Gee Street
London
EC1V 3RS
United Kingdom

8 W 38th Street, Suite 902
New York, NY 10018
USA

www.koganpage.com

Kogan Page books are printed on paper from sustainable forests.

© Bram DeSmet, 2024

The right of Bram DeSmet to be identified as the author of this work has been asserted by him in accordance with the Copyright, Designs and Patents Act 1988.

ISBNs

Hardback   978 1 3986 1600 4
Paperback   978 1 3986 1598 4
Ebook   978 1 3986 1599 1

British Library Cataloguing-in-Publication Data

A CIP record for this book is available from the British Library.

Library of Congress Control Number

2024936575

Typeset by Integra Software Services, Pondicherry
Print production managed by Jellyfish
Printed and bound by CPI Group (UK) Ltd, Croydon CR0 4YY

To my beloved parents for their dedication to my brothers and me.

CONTENTS

List of figures and tables xii
About the author xviii
Foreword xix
Preface xxiii
Acknowledgements xxvi

Introduction 1

01 The sustainable triple triangle: balancing people, planet and profit 5
Introduction 5
Get ready for the 5D or fourth generation supply chain 6
The Supply Chain Triangle 8
Balancing the triangle is about optimizing value as measured by the return on capital employed 12
From one to three triangles: the profit, the people and the planet triangle 23
Offshoring in the 1980s: impact across the three triangles 28
The Triple Triangle of people, planet and profit 29
Linking supply chain with ESG: the quadruple ESG triangle 32
Conclusion 42
Endnotes 42

02 The sustainable supply chain 'zone': the social foundation and the environmental ceiling 44
Introduction 44
Doughnut economics 48
The Sustainable Supply Chain 'Zone' 50
The supply chain diamond, square, pyramid? Costing for externalities? 65
Three models to describe the fourth generation 5D supply chain 75
Conclusion 77
Endnotes 77

03 The resilient supply chain 79

Introduction 79
The Covid paradox 81
Volatility: external drivers 82
Volatility: internal drivers 88
Resilience: service, product, supply chain and organization design 98
Resilience: sensing, shifting, steering 119
Conclusion 121
Endnotes 122

04 The need for a sustainable and resilient fourth generation supply chain 125

Introduction 125
The impact of a lack of resilience 126
From second to fourth generation supply chain capabilities 129
From second to fourth generation capabilities: strategic planning and design perspective 131
From second to fourth generation capabilities: tactical planning perspective 144
Conclusion 153
Endnotes 154

05 Strategy-driven: sustainable and resilient – supply chain design 156

Introduction 156
Recap: the strategic value proposition 157
Extending the strategic value proposition with sustainability and resilience 164
Recap: the strategy-driven supply chain 168
Strategy-driven sustainable and resilient supply chain design 176
Conclusion 192
Endnotes 192

06 Including circularity, segmentation and scenario management 195

Introduction 195
Strategy-driven circular supply chain design 196
Segmenting markets and supply chains 205
Preparing for uncertainty using scenarios 211
Strategy-Driven Supply Chain Maps 224
Cross check second versus fourth generation strategic supply chain design capabilities 231
Conclusion 232
Endnotes 233

07 Our evolving supply chain ecosystem and the new concept of Integrated Value Planning 235

Introduction 235
Modelling the supply chain and business ecosystem 239
The lack of integration in planning processes and systems 243
The long road to integrated planning 249
Integrated Value Planning or IVP 251
Conclusion 270
Endnotes 271

08 Implementing Integrated Value Planning through an eight-stage maturity model 272

Introduction 272
The Integrated Value Planning process 274
The Integrated Value Planning dashboard 278
Strategy-Driven Integrated Value Planning 283
The drag of functional organizations and functional silos 287
Cross functional balance and the Chief Value Planning Officer 290
Organizing for complex and dynamic environments 293
Conclusion 303
Endnotes 304

Conclusion 305

Index 307

LIST OF FIGURES AND TABLES

Figures

Figure 1.1 From a 1D to 5D supply chain, from first to fourth generation supply chain 6
Figure 1.2 Traditional imbalances in the Supply Chain Triangle 9
Figure 1.3 The Supply Chain Triangle during Covid-19 10
Figure 1.4 The Supply Chain Triangle during Covid versus post Covid 12
Figure 1.5 Balancing the Supply Chain Triangle equals optimizing the ROCE 13
Figure 1.6 The H&M version of the Supply Chain Triangle 17
Figure 1.7 The H&M methodology built around the Supply Chain Triangle 18
Figure 1.8 Example case: offering customers products from a secondary warehouse 20
Figure 1.9 Example case: offering customers products from a secondary warehouse – order of magnitude 21
Figure 1.10 Broader evaluation criteria of scenarios 22
Figure 1.11 The Supply Chain Triangle as the Profit Triangle 24
Figure 1.12 Three triangles feeding our supply chain and operations 25
Figure 1.13 The People Triangle 27
Figure 1.14 The Planet Triangle 27
Figure 1.15 The impact on the three triangles of offshoring in the 1980s 29
Figure 1.16 The Triple Triangle: profit, planet, people 31
Figure 1.17 Linking supply chain with ESG: The Quadruple ESG Triangle 33
Figure 1.18 The non-profit Supply Chain Triangle 34
Figure 1.19 The Social Triangle leading for MSF 35
Figure 1.20 The environmental and social triangle leading for Greenpeace and Tony's Chocolonely 36
Figure 1.21 Balancing the Non-Profit Supply Chain Triangle at MSF 38
Figure 1.22 Governance rules in the Quadruple Triangle of MSF (www.msf.org) 39

List of figures and tables   xiii

Figure 2.1	The Sustainable Supply Chain 'Zone' 51
Figure 2.2	The Sustainable Supply Chain 'Zone': Example metrics and regulatory frameworks 54
Figure 2.3	The environmental ceiling at Vandemoortele 61
Figure 2.4	The social foundation at Vandemoortele (to be rotated left) 62
Figure 2.5	The Supply Chain Triangle within its social foundation and environmental ceiling at Vandemoortele 63
Figure 2.6	The Supply Chain diamond, square or pyramid 66
Figure 2.7	The Danfoss Supply Chain Triangle and how it supports the business objectives of profitable growth while driving a strong cash flow 69
Figure 2.8	The 2023 strategic objectives for the Danfoss Supply Chain 71
Figure 2.9	The 5D strategy-driven supply chain at Danfoss Climate Solutions 72
Figure 2.10	The 2024 strategic objectives based on the 5D strategy-driven supply chain model 73
Figure 3.1	External and internal drivers of volatility 84
Figure 3.2	Consumer Price Index (CPI), per cent change from year ago, for 2010–2023 85
Figure 3.3	Federal funds effective rate, in per cent, for 2010–2023 85
Figure 3.4	Consumer Price Index (CPI), per cent change from year ago, for 1948–2023 86
Figure 3.5	Federal funds effective rate, in per cent, for 1954–2023 86
Figure 3.6	Major hurricanes in the North Atlantic, for 1960–2022 90
Figure 3.7	Major hurricanes in the North Atlantic, for 1851–2022 90
Figure 3.8	Lagging and bias in traditional forecasting methods 92
Figure 3.9	Repeated disruptions leading to actual sales as a poor predictor of future sales 93
Figure 3.10	Leading indicators as a way to understand what is driving the actual sales 93
Figure 3.11	Project timeline for leading indicator forecasting at Solvay 94
Figure 3.12	Historical sales and turning points in the Automotive Resin sales for the Americas 95
Figure 3.13	Leading indicator forecast versus sales rep forecast for Automotive Resin for the Americas 95
Figure 3.14	Underlying trend in the leading indicator forecast versus sales rep forecast for Automotive Resin for the Americas 96

List of figures and tables

Figure 3.15	The value chain or 'bubble' analysis for Automotive Resin 97
Figure 3.16	Drivers for resilience 100
Figure 4.1	The impact of a lack of resilience 127
Figure 4.2	Volatility and a lack of resilience clashing at the heart of the triangle 128
Figure 4.3	Fourth generation supply chain 130
Figure 4.4	Traditional bike supply chain 137
Figure 4.5	Assemble-to-order bike supply chain 140
Figure 4.6	Assemble-to-order bike supply chain with full control of the component supply towards the tier 1 assemblers 141
Figure 4.7	Alternative way of collaborative planning and information sharing for the ATO supply chain 142
Figure 5.1	The seven value drivers from Crawford and Matthews 158
Figure 5.2	Linking the strategy model of Crawford and Matthews with Treacy and Wiersema 160
Figure 5.3	Example output of strategic positioning survey 162
Figure 5.4	Example output of strategic positioning survey – split per department 162
Figure 5.5	Example output of strategic positioning survey – dominance of value drivers 163
Figure 5.6	The extended nine value drivers from Crawford and Matthews + sustainability + resilience 164
Figure 5.7	Sustainability leadership as a fourth option in the world of Treacy and Wiersema 165
Figure 5.8	Strategy-driven supply chain design in seven steps 169
Figure 5.9	The old 'consumer electronics' versus the new 'experience electronics' value proposition 173
Figure 5.10	Strategy-driven sustainable and resilient supply chain design in seven steps 177
Figure 5.11	Schematic overview linking dynamic capabilities with business models and strategy 186
Figure 5.12	The strategic diamond at Siemens 187
Figure 5.13	Siemens supply chain diamond: example end-to-end mapping 188
Figure 6.1	Strategy-driven circular product and supply chain design in seven steps 200
Figure 6.2	Strategy-driven market and product/supply chain segmentation 207
Figure 6.3	Including scenario management in our Strategy-Driven Sustainable and Resilient Supply Chain Design 217

Figure 6.4	Blank Strategy-Driven Supply Chain Map	226
Figure 6.5	Strategy-Driven Supply Chain Map illustrating impact of expanding the product portfolio	227
Figure 6.6	Strategy-Driven Supply Chain Map illustrating reinforcing impact of lead time decisions	228
Figure 6.7	Strategy-Driven Supply Chain Map illustrating impact of a sustainability-driven decision	229
Figure 7.1	The evolving CPG ecosystem	237
Figure 7.2	Modelling the supply chain and business ecosystem – guided by Rummler and Brache, 1995	240
Figure 7.3	Integrated Value Planning as a need for managing the 'system'	244
Figure 7.4	Fragmented silo optimization as witnessed by the software systems in use	246
Figure 7.5	The five stages of the Gartner S&OP maturity linked to the Supply Chain Triangle	249
Figure 7.6	Integrated Value Planning or IVP	252
Figure 7.7	Four steps to get to Integrated Value Planning (IVP)	253
Figure 7.8	Integrating financial planning and supply chain planning	259
Figure 7.9	Information flows with the sales, marketing, product and resource plan	264
Figure 7.10	Integration of key customers and key suppliers into our planning process	267
Figure 7.11	Integration of sustainability metrics into all of our planning processes	269
Figure 8.1	The monthly Integrated Value Planning (IVP) Cycle	276
Figure 8.2	Fixing a new 'ambition' or budget every six months	277
Figure 8.3	The Integrated Value Planning (IVP) dashboard	279
Figure 8.4	The Integrated Value Planning (IVP) dashboard – example metrics	280
Figure 8.5	Impact of less accurate forecasts on the Integrated Value Planning (IVP) dashboard	281
Figure 8.6	Strategy-Driven Integrated Value Planning	283
Figure 8.7	Functional metrics and responsibilities in a traditional organization chart	289
Figure 8.8	Functional metrics leading to imbalance in the triangle, the social foundation and the environmental ceiling	289
Figure 8.9	Functional metrics and planning processes leading to imbalance in the triangle, the social foundation and the environmental ceiling	290

Figure 8.10	Complementing functional metrics and planning processes with cross-functional metrics and planning processes to improve balance 293
Figure 8.11	From five to eight maturity stages and from S&OP to Integrated Value Planning – 1 297
Figure 8.12	From five to eight maturity stages and from S&OP to Integrated Value Planning – 2 299

Tables

Table 2.1	Key financials of Vandemoortele NV, as taken from the integrated report of 2022 56
Table 3.1	Base supply chain for fashion company – output in units 104
Table 3.2	Base supply chain for fashion company – sales and cost price 105
Table 3.3	Base supply chain for fashion company – output in Euros 105
Table 3.4	Higher margin supply chain for fashion company – output in units 106
Table 3.5	Higher margin supply chain for fashion company – sales and cost price 107
Table 3.6	Higher margin supply chain for fashion company – output in Euros 107
Table 3.7	Flexible supply chain for fashion company – output in units 109
Table 3.8	Flexible supply chain for fashion company – sales and cost price 110
Table 3.9	Flexible supply chain for fashion company – output in Euros 110
Table 3.10	Business case and theoretical payback with base supply chain 112
Table 3.11	Actual payback with base supply chain 113
Table 3.12	Business case and theoretical payback with flexible supply chain 115
Table 3.13	Actual payback with flexible supply chain 116
Table 3.14	Comparison of theoretical payback with actual payback in base and with flexible supply chain 118
Table 4.1	Strategic planning and design capabilities in a second versus fourth generation supply chain 131
Table 4.2	Tactical planning capabilities in a second versus fourth generation supply chain 145

Table 6.1	Local factors and driving forces for our focal decision on how to conquer the city 212
Table 6.2	Four example scenarios for our focal decision on how to conquer the city 213
Table 6.3	Four example scenarios for our exercise on what the future supply chain will look like 215
Table 6.4	RECAP – second versus fourth generation strategic supply chain design capabilities 231
Table 8.1	Four basic organizational environments according to Henry Mintzberg 294
Table 8.2	Tactical planning capabilities in a second versus fourth generation supply chain 302

ABOUT THE AUTHOR

Dr. Bram DeSmet is an adjunct professor at the Vlerick Business School, where he is part of the Competence Centre of Supply Chain and Operations. He is also a visiting professor for the Beijing International MBA programme at Peking University where he teaches quantitative subjects like statistics and decisions sciences. Bram is also the CEO of Solventure, a consultancy the helps companies turn their supply chain into a competitive edge. Before that Bram was a partner in Strategy, Supply Chain and Operations at MÖBIUS Research and Consulting.

Bram's research interests are in the domain of strategy, supply chain, finance and sustainability. He combines academic research with practical applications. He is the author of two previous books *Supply Chain Strategy and Financial Metrics* (2018) and *The Strategy-Driven Supply Chain* (2021), both published by Kogan Page. He obtained his PhD on the topic of multi-echelon inventory optimization and applied it at companies like Agfa-Gevaert and Daikin Europe. Within Solventure, he is developing AI-based supply chain intelligence solutions.

With this book Bram hopes to contribute to the field of sustainable supply chain strategy. Bram appreciates your thoughts and feedback. He can easily be reached via his contact page on LinkedIn or via his personal website www.bramdesmet.com.

FOREWORD

Welcome to our new normal and new world of global reset, volatility, disruptions, emerging technologies and major shifts of global power. The magnitude and frequency of disruptions in the last few years have increased dramatically. Supply chains have been under an extreme pressure test caused by the Covid-19 pandemic, geopolitical tensions and wars, climate change and natural catastrophes, cyberattacks and major supply chain constraints. At the same time, the political, monetary and economic conditions to reach our climate goals are changing. The world is also changing to overcome the huge debts compiled over many years through the zero or near-zero interest rates driven by the quantitative easing monetary policies that have led to massive printing of money, resulting in big political and social conflicts within countries. At the same time, we are at the peak of some major shifts in the global trading world. We should anticipate a new era of statecraft where government intervention plays a more pervasive role in global trade flows causing further pressure on supply chains. The impact of climate change is very visible to everyone, and more and more countries, governments and companies are committed to take actions within their own control, their trade flows as well as within their economic ecosystems. Governments are taking more control by creating more environmental and social regulations and conditions addressing the global risk on all stakeholders and the planet. For many companies, Environmental Social and Governance (ESG) has become the license to operate. It has created a new global playing field and competitive advantage for them to sell their products to their customers. At the same time it allows to attract more capital from major investor firms or at lower interest rates through green bonds to re-invest the capital into their business to sustain their value creation in the long-term.

During the Covid-19 disruption, companies adapted quickly from a just-in-time lean management supply chain strategy into a just-in-case supply chain strategy to protect themselves against major losses in value. An end-to-end total value with risk management has become part of the toolbox for an effective global supply chain management in companies. To effectively deal with future disruptions and the given volatility in global markets, companies are now forced to find new answers in their pursuit to create long-term value for their stakeholders.

In our past world managing a 3D supply chain, companies struggled immensely to balance the Supply Chain Triangle of Service, Cost and Cash, choosing became losing and by avoiding making deliberate and strategic trade-off decisions more value got destroyed than created. To find the right balance in future will become even more complex because of the environmental and social dimensions being added to the mix of strategic and operational choices and decisions to be made by companies.

Welcome to the next big supply chain transformation and evolution from the three dimensional supply chain into the new five dimensional supply chain. The 5D strategy-driven and sustainable supply chain will be the key competitive advantage for companies and their economic ecosystem where value can be planned and executed through an integrated value planning framework and execution model.

In his new book, Bram DeSmet reveals the timeless and universal forces behind this 5D supply chain transformation driven by some of the major global shifts and uses them to look into the future, offering practical principles and insights for companies to consider positioning themselves for what is ahead.

Building on his previous books, *Supply Chain Strategy and Financial Metrics* and *The Strategy-Driven Supply Chain*, Bram DeSmet introduces the five dimensional strategy-driven and sustainable supply chain framework through an integrated value planning model by demonstrating how the fundamental shift from a shareholder to stakeholder value creation model will impact companies and their supply chains in their pursuit of long-term value preservation.

He explains the global reset of the entire economic system, some of the triggers and inflection points such as the Covid-19 pandemic and the post-Covid consequences, the change and shifts in global power with major shifts towards stakeholder value creation and outlines the bigger picture of the business cycles. He shows the impact for companies based on their chosen strategy, value proposition, value capture and value creation modelled together with their strategy-driven and sustainable supply chains can create a competitive edge for their long-term value creation.

The reader will understand that we cannot disconnect major global mega trends and business cycles. Shifts in power within global markets all create their own dynamics, volatility and disruptions from a company's value proposition, supply chain strategies, integrated value planning and execution. All of this will force companies in the future to build different strategic and operational capabilities to create long-term stakeholder value. All five dimensions of the 5D supply chain within the Integrated Value Planning framework and model will be explained in detail. Readers will understand that strategy-driven and sustainable supply chains will be the most important strategic means to an end with that end being long-term value creation and value preservation.

Bram DeSmet's new book creates a breakthrough for companies to build a more strategic and operational understanding how strategy-driven, and sustainable supply chains are not just part of any business. Strategy-driven and sustainable supply chains enabled by a well-defined and chosen strategic integrated value planning and execution model are the businesses creating a competitive edge in the long-term.

Enjoy reading!

Frank Vorrath
Vice President Supply Chain Services
Danfoss Climate Solutions

Supply chain management as we know it today is still a relatively young discipline. Whilst there has always been a concern for the efficient movement and storage of goods to satisfy customers' demands in the most effective way, it is only recently that there has been a recognition of the importance of managing beyond the boundaries of the single enterprise to achieve these goals.

In the past when organizations were often vertically integrated and performed a multitude of activities in-house there was little need to worry too much about the interfaces with other entities in the supply chain, either upstream or downstream. Now however, the situation has changed dramatically. Because we have outsourced so many elements of our chains we have, as a result, significantly increased our dependence on others. Rather than being largely stand-alone businesses we are now part of a wider and more complex ecosystem.

A further challenge facing businesses today is the fact that we have moved from a world of relative stability to one which is much more turbulent and unpredictable. In these changed circumstances it is vital that we rethink our approach to the design and management of supply chains. So now, instead of a narrow focus on cost reduction and efficiency improvements, the priority has to be the enhancement of agility and resilience. A further concern for those charged with developing and implementing supply chain strategy is the requirement to ensure that supply chain decisions take account of the need for higher levels of sustainability and circularity.

All of these imperatives must be factored into the way we think about and manage supply chains. It is therefore timely that Bram DeSmet has made these issues the foundation for this book. Building upon ideas first presented in his previous books, DeSmet shows how it is possible to meet the challenges we face today whist still strengthening our competitive capability and ensuring long-term profitability.

As we enter this age of uncertainty it is vital that all organizations step back and rethink their supply chain strategy. The ideas explored in this book will provide practical support for managers and others who seek to ensure that their supply chains will be fit for purpose in the years ahead.

Martin Christopher
Emeritus Professor of Marketing & Logistics
Cranfield University, UK

PREFACE

As a preface to this book, let me answer a few of the questions I get from a number of people.

Why do I write books?

First, to become an expert. As a novice, you start by following courses. Once you've followed most of the courses, you start reading books and articles. Once you've read many books and articles, it is time to write your own book. It obliges you to structure your mind and your knowledge, to structure what you have learnt. As you discover later, it is only a snapshot, of where you are in your learning process. Through talking about the book and its subjects, at conferences, in lectures, with practitioners calling for help, you get asked many smart questions. They reveal things that are not clear in your head, and that get clarified as you look for the answers. You also meet people that took some of your ideas, and turned them into reality. That gives you the energy and the courage to write another book, and take another snapshot. It expands and deepens your knowledge and helps you become an expert.

Second, to contribute to the development of supply chain thinking. Supply chain is a young profession, compared to manufacturing, sales or finance. It's a profession in full evolution. With a whole generation of supply chain thinkers at the age of retiring (Martin Christopher, John Gattorna, Hau Lee, David Simchi-Levi to name a few) there is a gap to be filled. We miss role models and thought leaders in the field of supply chain. I want to deliver my humble contribution.

Third, books open doors. They give me the opportunity to teach about strategic supply chain management, which I love. They give me the chance to talk to leading supply chain professionals and engage with leading supply chain companies, which is a privilege and gives me the opportunity to work with the best supply chain talent, which is humbling. They bring me to places where I have never been, to talk about my passion. How fantastic is that!

Fourth, it is about giving back. I've received a lot from education and from all those authors that spent so much effort in writing their wonderful books. I have learnt so much, through working with such a diverse set of companies. I believe it is a duty, a privilege and a pleasure to give something back. Through writing this book, through giving guest lectures at universities and business schools, I hope to give back. Please reach out to me, I'm happy to support you and give something back.

Why did I write this book?

Ever since I first presented the Supply Chain Triangle of Service, Cost and Cash, people asked me how to incorporate sustainability. It took me two books to understand and clarify the relationship between strategy, finance and supply chain. Over the last three years I've studied how sustainability, a longer-term trend and requirement, and resilience, a more recent question and requirement, can be incorporated, or how existing models can be extended to include these aspects.

I also hope to contribute to the development of sustainability thinking. If supply chain is a recent discipline, sustainability is even more recent. As I was reading about sustainability, I got increasingly intrigued, and at times puzzled, by the lack of answers or the lack of coherence. By including sustainability, and resilience, in the strategic trade-offs of the company and the design of their supply chains, I hope to contribute to the development of sustainability thinking.

Where do I find the time to write books (when you don't even have the time to read one)?

It's probably a bit compulsive. Like some people find or make the time to run marathons or ultramarathons, I find or make time to write books. I spent around 70–80 days researching and writing in 2023. I probably spent a comparable effort researching and publishing some essays on LinkedIn in 2021 and 2022. Most of these days have been weekends and regular holidays, to manage the impact on my other roles.

I love the creative process, pushing the boundaries of my knowledge and imagination, pushing and challenging the boundaries of others, taking a different and more ambitious perspective and swimming against the current. The speaking, the teaching, and at times the inspiring, gives me the energy and the courage to continue. Writing a book probably is a bit like a marathon. It is as much a test of perseverance as of knowledge, like a marathon is as much a mental as a physical challenge.

And the people around me share the burden. My colleagues at Solventure, who grow the business when I'm away, physically or mentally, my family, who support me in spending a lot of what they would rightfully consider family time, and there is a circle of supply chain afficionados I interact with, through LinkedIn, or in a call, when I share essays, or visions, or send them drafts, and who share things with me like books or articles they think are relevant. Taking so much comes with a responsibility. The responsibility to deliver some good, something worth the energy all these people have indirectly put in.

What is next?

Through researching and writing this book I woke up to a new reality, with questions to be answered for myself. Where do I see my material impact? What is my purpose? What is my contribution to people and planet, beyond profit? And what about Solventure? Twenty years ago, I was trained myself at the Vlerick Business School in the Friedman doctrine, that dictates that creating shareholder value is the sole or at least primary objective of a business. Today, I've received a new compass, with a new social and a new environmental dimension, but I didn't receive a manual on how to use it. Today, I know I will have to unlearn some of the old practices, and learn some of the new, but I don't yet know which ones or what exactly. So next for sure is figuring out how this works and rethinking myself to become part of a sustainable world.

As I explained, writing a book is taking a snapshot. I hope to get as many questions as I got on the previous books, and to have as many interactions with leading supply chain professionals and companies. These will make my thoughts move on and they will develop new insights, which through the compulsory need to create new things, to give something back, to contribute to the development of supply chain thinking, will hopefully lead to another book, that could start the cycle over again. But let us start here, with the current snapshot. Let's explore it together, let's get in touch with each other and let's have a discussion on where we are and where this could go next.

ACKNOWLEDGEMENTS

There is a long list of people I would like to thank, with the biggest danger I forget someone as I'm rewinding the long journey that led to this result:

- Frank Vorrath, for being my long-time supporter and sparring partner, for making my life difficult (at times), for not giving me the 'mum-test'. I learn the most from the people that challenge me the hardest, you do exactly that.
- Martijn Lofvers, creative thinker, challenger, you invigorate me, as at times I invigorate you on where supply chain is as a profession and where it could go. We attack it with humour. We had plenty of laughter when we met online and in real life. Thank you for being a lighthouse in the world of supply chain.
- Dan Kogan, my compagnon de route, we've been pushing ideas and texts back and forth. You pick up ideas and bring them alive in engagements with customers and in trainings, you point me to relevant ideas, texts and books. You are carrying the flag of our strategy-driven institute from where we want to educate the world in the strategy-driven thinking. Your support has been immense.
- Jonathon Karelse, you provoke me and others. You help us cut through the myths and the misunderstandings of S&OP, you help us see a different, sometimes harsher but always more truthful reality, you inspire us and encourage us to take a different perspective.
- Ton Geurts, for being a long-time sparring partner and mentor. You keep triggering me with the sustainability question and agenda, you keep pushing the boundaries yourself. Please keep doing so.
- Johan Heyman, for being a long-time sparring partner, for triggering me with the sustainability question early on, for having an open mindset, for having a heart for supply chain and operations and for caring about the people that power them.
- Dr. Ed Weenk, for triggering me on sustainability, for the discussions and interactions on LinkedIn and via Teams, and for your excellent book *Mastering the Circular Economy*. You taught me a lot.

- Prof. Dr. Jack van der Veen, for your passionate reactions to my LinkedIn posts, for driving the interaction on where we are and where to go with the supply chain profession and for your authentic and honest opinions, views and concerns. You are a rock in the rough supply chain ocean.
- Martin Hendel, for picking up and spreading concepts like the Supply Chain Triangle through your work and books, for your passion about supply chain, for your seemingly endless energy, for being an inspiration to myself and many others. You are a practitioner, you actually do it, you are moving the real boundaries, kudos to you!
- Eric Wilson, for being an advocate of the Supply Chain Triangle, for your passion and enthusiasm for forecasting, planning and supply chain, for developing and advancing supply chain thinking, for being an advocate and a champion in the supply chain field.
- Dr. Harpal Singh, Dhiran Singh and Sujit Singh from Arkieva, for our exciting 15 year partnership, for immersing me in the world of advanced planning systems, and how technology makes a difference in running our complex supply chains, for caring about your people and partners and for being sustainable at heart.
- Prof. Dr. Ann Vereecke, for carrying the flag for operations and supply chain, for giving me the opportunity to lecture about these fascinating topics at our wonderful Vlerick Business School, and for giving me a stage.
- Prof. Dr. Kurt Verweire, for introducing me to the domain of strategy, for being passionate about strategy, about what it can do to a business when done properly, for making strategy tangible and concrete, and for inspiring me and many others.
- Dr.ir. Hendrik Vanmaele, for introducing me to the topic of supply chain management 20 years ago (you saved me from a career in IT), for providing me the opportunity to pursue a PhD in supply chain, and for supporting me in developing my professional career.

In preparation for the book, I gathered a number of supply chain professionals in five sessions of two hours. In each session, I introduced one or two concepts that I planned to include in the book. I then asked a question or gave an exercise, with which the group first interacted in smaller sector specific sections, then followed by a full group debrief. It was a validation whether 'the concepts make sense'. It was also about enriching the concepts by providing practical examples and by providing new insights. One of the

Acknowledgements

outcomes was putting sustainability more centre stage, as the stronger and longer-term driver for supply chain and business transformation. Chapters 3 and 4 also build heavily on the outcome of the work with this group, that I have called my 'executive book council'. So thank you so much for your energetic participation:

- Kyle Yonce and Yasser Bin Sabir from Clariant
- Usha Dasari and Holger Tewes-McCoy from Huntsman Polyurethanes
- Rob Sliter, Paul Bouvy and Jason Nofziger from Owens Corning
- Dirk Holbach from Henkel Consumer Brands
- Jeroen Dejonckheere from Ontex
- Alberto Lupano, Bijju Padmanabhan and Anupam Jain from Reckitt
- Piet Vandenbroucke from Curium Pharma
- Alex Van Ash, Risna Swart and Olivia Heering from GSK
- Stef Vermeiren, retired from J&J
- Johan Heyman, Filip Deruijck, Rob Jonckheere and Kathy Verledens from Barco
- Niels Behrensen, Frank Vorrath, Torsten Worm, Charlotte Dyhr, Havard Jorgensen, Stefan Schoettl, Jesper Bundgaard, Dan Bruun, Brian Markedahl and Roger Meijers from Danfoss Climate Solutions
- Mark Van Abeelen and Stefan Wischnewski from Ricoh Europe SCM
- Piao Jin, Stuart Whiting and Stephane Piat from Schneider Electric
- Sven Markert, Alexander Tschentscher and Udo Mayer from Siemens Smart Infrastructure

I have been lucky and privileged to work and exchange with so many companies on all of the struggles and difficulties addressed in this and my earlier books. I am so grateful that the following people and companies were willing to share their stories and their experiences, with their struggles and with their solutions. So thank you,

- Jesper Metz, Saki Sarker and Erika Linton from H&M
- William Vannier and Julio Victoria from MSF Belgium and MSF Supply
- Piao Jin from Schneider Electric
- Roeland Rombaut and Jeroen Verstraeten from Vandemoortele
- Frank Vorrath from Danfoss Climate Solutions

- Christian Backaert from Solvay
- Joeri Kuik from Media Markt Saturn
- Alexander Tschentscher and Sven Markert from Siemens Smart Infastructure
- Mark Van Abeelen from Ricoh Europe SCM
- Konstanze Knoblich from Infineon
- Dirk Leemans from Colruyt Group
- Martijn Lofvers from Supply Chain Media
- Alberto Lupano from Reckitt

I need to thank my many colleagues at Solventure, for growing the business, when I was away, and for keeping up with me when my thoughts were drifting away. Thank you all, for being as passionate about supply chain as I am. I learn from you every day. We're in this journey of moving the boundaries together. I want to thank our customers for putting their trust in us as their trusted supply chain adviser and partner. This is where we learn how difficult moving the boundaries is. I want to thank the many supply chain professionals with whom I have been able to exchange on their supply chain challenges and what I see as possible solutions. Each of those discussions has developed the insights shared in this book.

And last but not least, I want to thank my family, my wife Leen, and my kids, Matties, Julie and Emiel. I tend to excuse myself by saying it is not the quantity but the quality of our time that counts, though even that quality was probably not what you could rightfully expect. So thank you for giving me the freedom to do this, to pursue my passion. You have been an intimate part of this process and we have sacrificed a lot of our time together. I hope you will share some of my pride.

So where I may be the author, it is not just my work. It may have passed through my brain and fingers, but it is based on your triggers, questions, thoughts, examples and the support of each and every one of you. I am feeling blessed and grateful.

Thank you all so much,
Bram

Introduction

The world is changing. We must be, and are becoming, more sustainable. In his book *Cannibals with Forks*[1], John Elkington describes how in the 1970s environmental concerns were still something for activist groups like Greenpeace and were considered by most managers as something that was at odds with the free enterprise. In her book *Doughnut Economics*[2], Kate Raworth, explains how we can't go on like this. She describes how the fundaments of our economic thinking are too simplistic, a caricature of the complex world we live in, that we have built a doomsday machine, that we are addicted to growth as a cure for all pains, and that we have to rethink our economic fundamentals. In his book *Prosperity*[3], Colin Mayer questions the so called 'Friedman doctrine', which positions 'maximization of shareholder value' as the sole purpose of a (for profit) company. He clarifies that by not accounting for other sources of capital like social capital and environmental capital, we are maximizing financial shareholder value at the expense of these other sources of capital. He clarifies that if we're not accounting for the cost to restore the damage we do to our planet and our societies, any financial profits are simply overstated. So to be more sustainable, we need to think more holistically. We need to understand that as companies, we not only have a responsibility towards our shareholders, and their financial capital, but we have a responsibility for all forms of scarce capital, including social capital and environmental capital, and towards all stakeholders, including our people, our societies and the next generations, for which we need to preserve the planet. Mayer describes it requires a new form of governance, where the board of directors must look after more than just the interests of the shareholders, it needs to look after the interest of all stakeholders. That broader ambition and responsibility should be defined in the purpose of the company, and the board should act in the interest of that broader purpose. I will give examples on how that can be done, by talking about 'impact companies' like Tony's Chocolonely, for which '100% slave-free chocolate' is the purpose, and for whom financial results like growth and earnings before interest and taxes (EBIT) are a way to increase that impact.

Governments are active stakeholders in this process. The Green Deal in Europe and the Inflation Reduction Act in the US, are structuring and accelerating this change. In Europe the Corporate Social Responsibility Directive (CSRD) is forcing the disclosure of non-financial, social and environmental information. No more secrecy, no more hiding. Banks are introducing green financing, where interest rates are linked to your sustainability plans and performance, as it reduces their risk. It recognizes that social and environmental exposure can lead to a significant loss of financial value. Reading through all of this is changing and broadening my mindset, as an academic, as a consultant and as an entrepreneur. What is my material impact? On people, planet and profit?

The world is changing. It has become more volatile, and we need to become more resilient. Since 2020 we have confronted the Covid-19 pandemic, that led to massive shortages, disturbed demand patterns, increasing lead times and inflation. We have the war in Ukraine, that led to volatility in energy prices and to global shortages of wheat. We have seen the impacts of global warming, impacting crops and harvests and increasing the number of heavy storms disturbing our global supply chains. We had the Ever Given blocking the Suez Canal, the war in Gaza and we can expect more to follow. While 2010–2019 was a period of relative stability, since 2020, volatility has increased. The time between two events is getting shorter, with no time to recover, and their impact is getting more severe with more complex interactions.

If the world is changing, it is time to rethink and deploy what I will call the fourth generation supply chain. The first generation supply chain was simple, one-dimensional or service driven. We just expect the supply chain to deliver what is needed, no further questions asked. The second generation supply chain was about the AND-AND, AND deliver service, AND lower the cost. It was the dominant paradigm of the 1990s and the 2000s. With my previous two books, *Supply Chain Strategy and Financial Metrics*[4] and *The Strategy-Driven Supply Chain*[5], I introduced the third generation supply chain, which is three-dimensional (3D) as it is about managing service, cost and cash. It also introduces strategic trade-offs, the OR-OR. You can't have the gross margin of a product leader with the inventory level of the lowest price player. It's either one or the other. The fourth generation supply chain is five-dimensional (5D), it is about balancing service, cost and cash with social and environmental objectives. It makes sustainability and resilience an integral part of the strategic-tradeoffs and the value proposition, of the supply chain design, and of the supply chain planning and steering.

This book has two main goals. The first is to create a better understanding of why we need to move to the fourth generation supply chain. It is answering the 'why'. The second is to provide the tools to build the fourth generation supply chain. Which is answering the 'how'. I will do this while building on the work and the base concepts of my previous two books *Supply Chain Strategy and Financial Metrics* and *The Strategy-Driven Supply Chain*.

Chapters 1 and 2 are about including sustainability in supply chain by linking the work of John Elkington, the triple bottom line, and the work of Kate Raworth, doughnut economics, to our core Supply Chain Triangle of Service, Cost and Cash, one of the building blocks from my earlier books.

Chapters 3 and 4 are about studying and understanding the 'volatility' and 'resilience' aspect. Has volatility increased? What are the drivers? How can we measure it? How to build resilience? What about a lack of resilience? What is the impact? Can we define the needed fourth generation capabilities? Can we contrast them with the current, still dominant, second generation capabilities? Does a better understanding help us with the 'why'? Is it increasing the sense of urgency?

Chapters 5 and 6 are including sustainability and resilience in the strategic trade-offs and into what I will call 'Strategy-Driven: sustainable and resilient – supply chain design'. It will review questions such as, what does it mean to be at par/differentiate/dominate on sustainability and resilience? What is our target positioning? How does it impact the complexity and variability in our supply chain? The cost and capital employed? Our financial model? Chapter 6 will incorporate concepts such as circularity, segmentation and scenario management.

Chapters 7 and 8 introduce a new, fourth generation, vision for integrated planning, called 'Integrated Value Planning' or 'IVP'. It goes beyond the traditional 'Sales & Operations Planning' (S&OP) or 'Integrated Business Planning' (IBP), which are typical second generation capabilities. I will discuss the new IVP process, how to support executive decision making based on a new, more holistic IVP dashboard, how to balance the power in the executive team and organize for IVP success. I will introduce an eight-stage 'IVP maturity' model, that shows us the way, on how to get there step by step. Integrated Value Planning will make us more agile and resilient. Disconnects in planning processes create the inverse. Integrated Value Planning will make us more sustainable, by incorporating sustainability metrics and trade-offs into all of our planning and decision making processes.

I have tried to make the book interactive by providing plenty of exercises for you, to do with your executive team or a cross-functional group. It should allow you to apply the models to your specific situation, make it more tangible, deepen the learnings and the understanding, creating awareness, and helping you on the way towards a more sustainable and resilient supply chain.

I've tried to make it practical, by providing 21 named and anonymized case studies. They tell the stories of how real-life companies get stuck with old supply chain thinking, and how leading companies have taken some of the concepts and are using them to build more professional and more mature supply chains. This book has one foot in the literature and the theory, and another strong foot in practice.

It is with a combination of pride and anxiety that I present this book. I'm excited to share how my insights have evolved over the last three years. It feels like I woke up to a new reality I can no longer deny. I'm eager to share that and share some of that excitement. I'm also a little nervous and anxious. Will I meet your expectations? Is it clear, helpful, concrete, engaging, relevant? I hope it is fundamental, moving boundaries, providing deeper insights, connecting the dots. I hope it provides a vision on where supply chain could go, beyond what we knew or understood so far. It is with that mix of pride, eagerness and anxiety that I present you this book. So please do me a favour and let me know what you think. Please connect with me on LinkedIn and share your opinion. Let's engage in a discussion and keep building insights for better supply chains serving a better future, together.

Endnotes

1 J Elkington (1999) *Cannibals with Forks: The triple bottom line of 21st century business*, Capstone, Oxford
2 K Raworth (2017) *Doughnut Economics. Seven ways to think like a 21st-century economist*, Penguin Books, London
3 C Mayer (2018) *Prosperity: Better business makes the greater good*, Oxford University Press, Oxford
4 B DeSmet (2018) *Supply Chain Strategy and Financial Metrics: The supply chain triangle of service, cost and cash*, Kogan Page, London
5 B DeSmet (2021) *The Strategy-Driven Supply Chain: Integrating strategy, finance and supply chain for a competitive edge*, Kogan Page, London

The sustainable triple triangle: balancing people, planet and profit

01

Introduction

In this chapter, I recap the concept of the Supply Chain Triangle of Service, Cost and Cash, and I use it to illustrate the imbalances I have seen during and after the Covid-19 pandemic. I recap how the triangle links to financial metrics, which makes it in essence a 'profit' triangle. Both are treated in more detail in my previous books. I discuss how H&M uses the triangle as the foundation of its supply chain and as a compass to design, operate and control it.

Next, I introduce a People Triangle and a Planet Triangle, next to the Profit Triangle, to come to a Triple Triangle, as the equivalent of the triple bottom line. I use the Triple Triangle model to analyse the reasoning behind and the impact of the massive offshoring during the 1980s. I also explore the impact across people, planet and profit of the more recent reshoring trend.

Environmental-Social-Governance (ESG) seems to be a more recent terminology to describe sustainability thinking and practices. I extend the Triple Triangle to the Quadruple Triangle putting governance at the heart of the Triple Triangle. I use the case of Médecins Sans Frontières (MSF) to illustrate how the Quadruple Triangle works in explaining and designing non-profit supply chains.

I start this chapter by introducing how the inclusion of sustainability is a next step in supply chain thinking. I describe different generations of supply chain thinking and how we are currently moving into a fourth generation supply chain.

Get ready for the 5D or fourth generation supply chain

In this book, I will try to show that supply chain management as a discipline is in full evolution. One way to illustrate and better capture that evolution is to talk about how supply chain is shifting from a one-dimensional (1D) to a five-dimensional (5D) operation. Along these lines I can also introduce how we are evolving into a fourth generation of supply chains and supply chain thinking. The different steps are summarized in Figure 1.1.

In the past, the 'first generation supply chain', life was simple, you just (tried to) deliver what the customer asked. Supply chains were service-driven or 1D. In sales-driven and highly profitable companies this can still be the case. Supply chain is seen as a purely operational role, just there to deliver, a necessary evil, not expected to mingle or cause problems.

The supply chain thinking of the 1990s as exemplified in the books of Martin Christopher[1] and John Gattorna[2] was about the promise to increase service while reducing cost[3]. By connecting otherwise disconnected processes through S&OP (sales and operations planning), and by doing more thoughtful engineering and design of supply chains, for instance by implementing supply chain segmentation, we could do the AND-AND, AND more service, AND lower cost. Supply chain was equivalent to delivering more of everything and was providing the magical answer for companies

Figure 1.1 From a 1D to 5D supply chain, from first to fourth generation supply chain

1970–1980s 1st generation	1990–2000s 2nd generation	2010–2020s 3rd generation	2020+ 4th generation
1D SC Service-driven	2D SC Service & cost-driven	3D SC Service, cost & cash-driven	5D SC Sustainable supply chains
Just deliver what the customer wants	Improve service while reducing cost	Improve ROCE	Balance service, cost and cash with ESG

under pressure. Customers were ever more demanding. They wanted more service at a lower price, and the second generation supply chain was promising to deliver exactly that. The second generation supply chain was the 2D supply chain, one eye on service, one eye on cost, and improving on both at the same time.

Improving on service and cost has been and will always be possible, depending on your starting point and maturity level. Implementing the best practices from the second generation supply chain gurus allows us to deliver exactly that. There is a big problem, however. As supply chain has been delivering the AND-AND over the last two to three decades, their colleagues in marketing and sales or finance, have never been trained in trade-offs. Our service promises and the complexity of our product portfolio went up, but we all assume that at the same time we will be able to lower the costs and the inventories. The AND-AND has also kept supply chain away from the strategy table. Many strategy processes are pre-occupied with the 'business' or 'commercial' strategy. How will we grow the business, how will we compete. Even if it is about more service, we simply expect supply chain to deliver it at a lower cost. The second generation supply chain thinking has gridlocked supply chain into its current 'operational-tactical' position.

When I first introduced the Supply Chain Triangle in my 2018 book *Supply Chain Strategy and Financial Metrics*[4], without really knowing it, I introduced the 3D supply chain and the third generation supply chain thinking. What I brought to the table is fundamentally different from the above in two ways. The first is that I explicitly introduced the third dimension of cash (working capital), or more broadly the capital employed (working capital + fixed assets), and the resulting links to return metrics like ROCE. The second is, I explicitly introduced strategic choices, the OR-OR. You can't have the gross margin of Kroger or Carrefour with the inventory levels of Aldi or Lidl, it's either one OR the other. The Supply Chain Triangle basically ends the period of AND AND, and starts the period of strategic supply chain trade-offs, the period of OR-OR. As elaborated in more detail in my second book, *The Strategy-Driven Supply Chain*[5], to make the correct strategic trade-offs, we need supply chain at the strategy table. This third generation or 3D supply chain is pulling supply chain out of the 2D gridlock it has been in for 20–30 years.

And the world of supply chain moves on, at high speed, as in this book, merely six years after first introducing the triangle, we will be expanding from a 3D into a 5D supply chain. We need to understand the impact of our decisions on the environmental (4D) and social (5D) metrics and objectives we have put forward. Understanding that broader impact requires a further broadening of the interest, knowledge, skillset and involvement of the supply chain professional. The external pressure on understanding and managing the environmental and social impact of our supply chains is mounting fast. It will further increase the strategic relevance and impact of supply chain as a discipline. As such we are quickly moving into the fourth generation supply chains where we need to manage five dimensions: service, cost, cash, environment, society.

I will start this chapter by doing a recap of our Supply Chain Triangle, providing recent examples of how companies have been using it as a foundation to organize and steer their supply chain. Next, I will expand the triangle thinking to include environmental and social aspects and provide a new foundation for building and steering sustainable supply chains.

The Supply Chain Triangle

The Supply Chain Triangle captures the struggle in many companies to balance three, often conflicting, objectives: service, cost and cash. Cash in the narrow definition equals working capital, which equals the inventory plus the accounts receivable minus the accounts payable. When we add the fixed assets, the cash can be extended to the capital employed. In this book I will assume a thorough knowledge of these basic financial metrics. For a quick recap, I encourage you to read the 'accounting basics'. A free download is available from my website[6].

The original examples, illustrating the dynamics in the Supply Chain Triangle, are shown in Figure 1.2. Let's start at the top left. By sourcing in the Far East or producing in bigger batches, companies may be able to reduce the cost per unit but it typically comes at the expense of extra inventory. At the same time we become less responsive (because of the longer lead times) and we increase the service risk (think about what happened when the Ever Given blocked[7] the Suez Canal in 2021).

At the top right, when you are in a tender-driven environment, you may decide to improve your responsiveness by investing in extra 'peak' capacity. That should obviously be good from a service and sales perspective, but you'll have to spend cash (CAPEX) on investing in extra fixed assets and operating your assets in peaks is typically less cost efficient, which is negatively impacting the cost side of the triangle.

Figure 1.2   Traditional imbalances in the Supply Chain Triangle

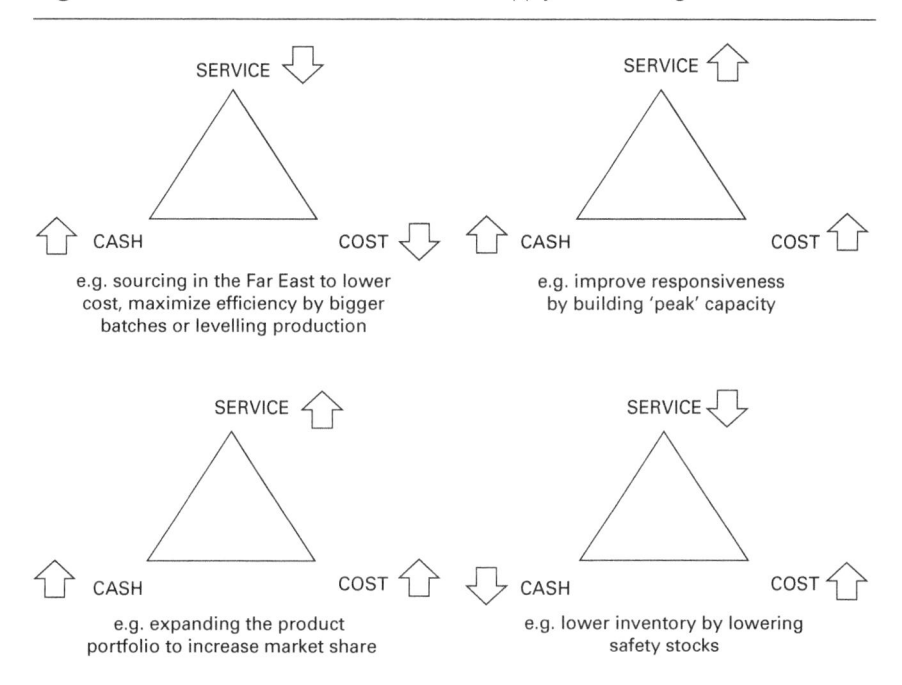

SERVICE ⇩ / CASH ⇧ / COST ⇩
e.g. sourcing in the Far East to lower cost, maximize efficiency by bigger batches or levelling production

SERVICE ⇧ / CASH ⇧ / COST ⇧
e.g. improve responsiveness by building 'peak' capacity

SERVICE ⇧ / CASH ⇧ / COST ⇧
e.g. expanding the product portfolio to increase market share

SERVICE ⇩ / CASH ⇩ / COST ⇧
e.g. lower inventory by lowering safety stocks

Continuing bottom-left, in general I see that people in sales and marketing are eager to expand the product portfolio. It improves service to the customer as it gives more choice. It will also be beneficial from a sales and a market share perspective. The insidious thing is that, when we introduce 20 per cent new products, the top-line is typically not going up 20 per cent. This implies that we create fragmentation, lose more time on changeovers, which will negatively impact the cost. If we want all these items to be available on stock, it also creates a long tail of more slowly moving products, which negatively impacts our stock rotation.

Finally bottom-right, every five years we witness companies in an 'inventory crisis' situation. They significantly miss their inventory targets and as a result have new and even more aggressive targets for the following year. They launch an inventory reduction programme with multiple projects. Purchasing will look at MOQs, supply chain will look at the safety stock settings, improve the forecast accuracy, and so on. Around March to April, the company realizes that out of say 10 projects only three have really started, as they lack the appropriate resources. Around June they realize that none of the projects are really bringing the benefits anticipated. By September, there is sheer panic and they resort to lowering the safety stocks in the planning system. By lowering the safety stocks in the planning, the inventory will go down, but service issues will appear all over the place, which leads to all kinds of operational firefighting. It is not what I recommend, but I have seen it many times.

Little did we know about the potential impact of unbalance in 2018, when I published my first book. At that time, the world was dormant, addicted to cheap and ample supplies, steady growth in many markets and low interest rates. The disturbances in the triangle were like ripples on a flat ocean. Little did we know how our world was going to be shook up by the Covid pandemic, that started at the end of 2019 and in multiple waves continued to disrupt the world for multiple years.

Figure 1.3 summarizes some of the effects. After the initial lockdowns, for many industries, the demand came back much faster and much stronger than anticipated. That quickly led to massive shortages of critical components, like micro-electronics, and key raw materials, sometimes even

Figure 1.3 The Supply Chain Triangle during Covid-19

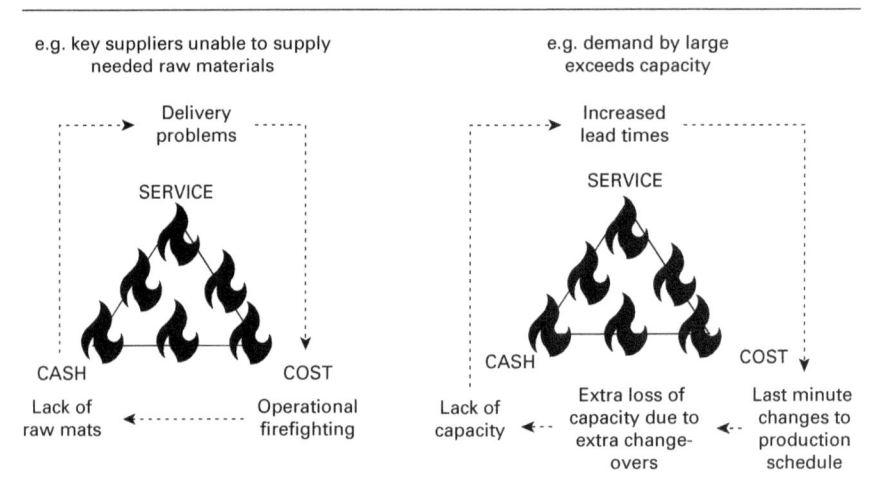

e.g. key suppliers unable to supply needed raw materials

Delivery problems

SERVICE

CASH — COST

Lack of raw mats ←------ Operational firefighting

e.g. demand by large exceeds capacity

Increased lead times

SERVICE

CASH — COST

Lack of capacity ←-- Extra loss of capacity due to extra change-overs ←-- Last minute changes to production schedule

and combine the above with

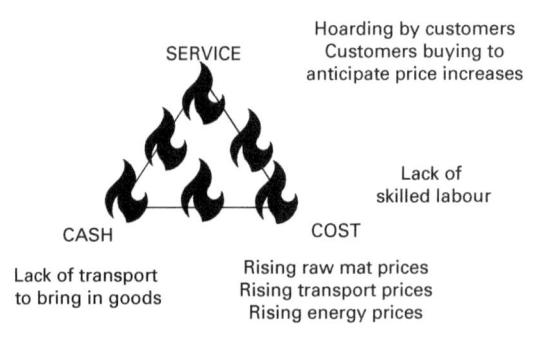

SERVICE

Hoarding by customers
Customers buying to anticipate price increases

Lack of skilled labour

CASH — COST

Lack of transport to bring in goods

Rising raw mat prices
Rising transport prices
Rising energy prices

packaging. That propagated down the chain and created delivery problems in virtually every product in every sector. Supply chains were on fire and a lot of operational firefighting was done, such as continuous changes to the production schedule based on the latest confirmed material availability, and last-minute expediting.

As companies, we were stretched way beyond our limits. Even if we had all the raw materials we needed, the demand was often largely exceeding our production capacity. There was a kind of craze in the market, customers buying 'just-in-case' instead of 'just-in-time'. The hoarding of customers was fuelled by anticipated price increases ('let's buy some more before prices go up'), and companies were improvising on how to deal with this. In many sectors the customer order lead times went up from a couple of weeks to a couple of months or over a year. It was more like 'showing their commitment' and 'trying to reserve their piece of the pie' rather than knowing what they would really need over that time-frame. What it implies is that, when the orders came into the operational horizon, there was still a lot of rescheduling to be done. We were rescheduling all the time, both from the demand side as well as from the supply side. We were not concerned about efficiency. We just tried to make the puzzle work.

And I could continue stretching. Even if we had all the raw materials and the capacity we needed, we probably lacked sufficient skilled labour, as some of our labour force was affected by illness, or we were lacking the drivers and the transport to get our products in or out. Or maybe we were lacking something else. The constraints were overwhelming and they were everywhere.

And when there is scarcity, prices go up. Prices of everything were rising. IMF figures[8] show the cost of shipping a container on the world's transoceanic trade routes increased seven-fold in the 18 months following March 2020, while the cost of shipping bulk commodities spiked even more. Though the price of everything was going up, companies were buying whatever they could at whatever price as they knew they were able to charge it to their customers who were also willing to pay whatever price to get their customer served. There was huge pressure on closing the service gap. Supply chains at this time were service driven, and companies were willing to make extra financial expenses and take on extra inventory or working capital risks to close the service gap.

And what goes up, must come down. So, in the second half of 2022, I saw many companies becoming concerned about a possible downturn in their markets. The shortages in the supply chain were increasingly resolved, lead times were being normalized and many industries saw a gradual slowdown in their demand. Instead of being service driven, we

Figure 1.4 The Supply Chain Triangle during Covid versus post Covid

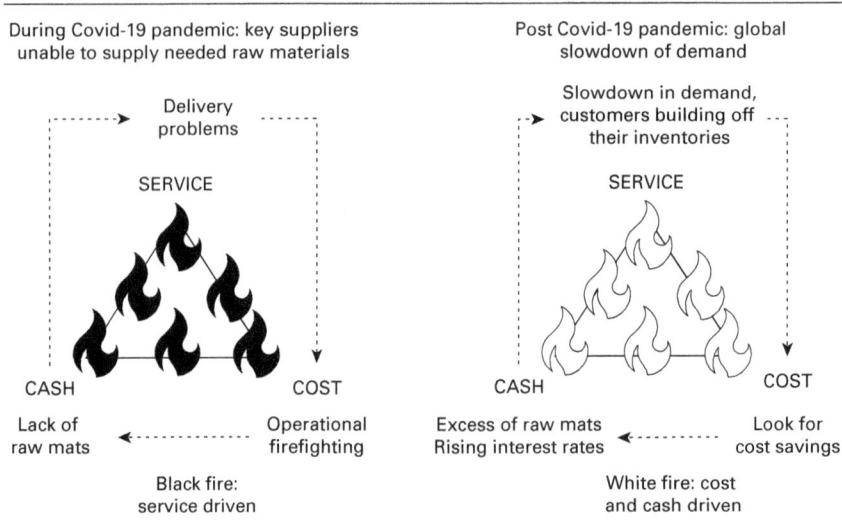

During Covid-19 pandemic: key suppliers unable to supply needed raw materials

Delivery problems

SERVICE

CASH — COST

Lack of raw mats ← Operational firefighting

Black fire: service driven

Post Covid-19 pandemic: global slowdown of demand

Slowdown in demand, customers building off their inventories

SERVICE

CASH — COST

Excess of raw mats ← Look for Rising interest rates cost savings

White fire: cost and cash driven

became cost and cash driven. Many of us were now trying to deplete the expensive overstocks that we had built up during Covid-19. That was adding to a further slowdown of the upstream demand, which was further reinforcing the cost and cash focus in companies focused upstream. At one of the companies I worked with senior executives were talking about rumours that their competitors were massively cancelling orders at their suppliers, and there was an intensive debate on whether they had to do the same. Decelerating a supply chain is as hard and can be as chaotic as accelerating a supply chain. It could be a white flame instead of a black flame but it equally puts the triangle on fire. I have illustrated those different flames and fires in Figure 1.4.

Balancing the triangle is about optimizing value as measured by the return on capital employed

When first using the triangle to explain conflicting priorities to companies, people asked me 'We understand and recognize the dynamics in the triangle, but is this not how companies work? Won't there always be conflicting objectives between sales, operations and finance? And will different departments not always speak a different language? And is the shifting focus between service, cost and cash indeed not linked to the economic cycles we go through?' Well, my answer is no, it is not just OK, or how companies should work. And yes, priorities can change throughout economic cycles, but to me it feels like many companies lack a proper understanding of how the different corners of the triangle connect, causing unintended harm to customers, employees and the financial results.

To understand why the balancing is important, in my first book, I took an investors perspective. As shown in Figure 1.5, service is basically a driver for the top-line. If we improve the service towards our customers, for instance by expanding our product portfolio, shortening lead times or increasing product performance, we expect to either sell more or to sell at a better price. However, as an investor, I'm concerned with more than just the top-line or a top-line metric like growth. At least in the long-run I would like to see a margin. Well, as illustrated in Figure 1.5, if I combine the top-line with the cost, I can get to a margin, for instance the EBIT. And even then, and this is where it becomes more tricky, as an investor I'm concerned with more than just the margin. The reason is the following. Assume that I have two companies generating 50 million of EBIT, the first requires 50 million of capital employed, whereas the second requires 100 million of capital employed. In which case I obviously prefer the first company. So, as an investor, I'm driven by what is the margin being generated over the capital employed, in financial terms, the 'return on capital employed' or 'ROCE', in spoken language it is the bang-for-the-buck. I invest 1 dollar (buck) in your company, what do you give me as a margin (bang) in return.

Figure 1.5 Balancing the Supply Chain Triangle equals optimizing the ROCE

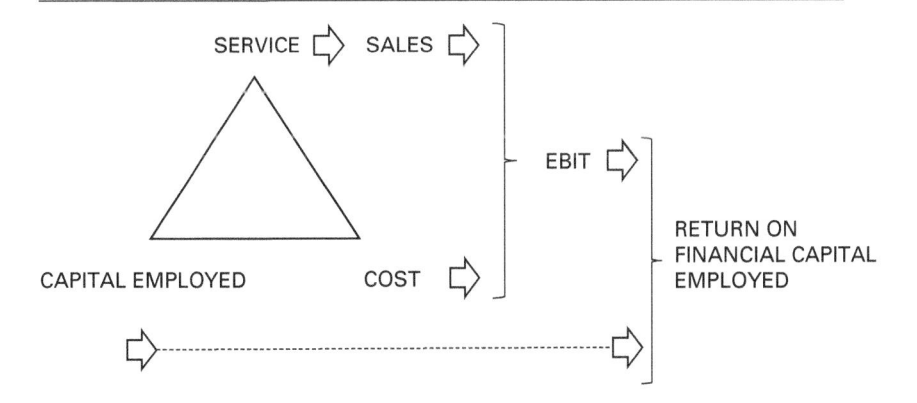

So balancing the Supply Chain Triangle is about optimizing the financial value we generate, as measured through the ROCE or the bang-for-the-buck. That implies that the balancing isn't optional, it is mandatory. It also connects supply chain and finance, both functions basically have the same objective, though I believe that is poorly understood on both sides.

In my previous two books I explored alternatives to EBIT as a margin metric and to ROCE as a return metric. In the outline I try to summarize why, still today, I am a fan of ROCE as a metric for supporting supply chain design and analysis. I tend to challenge supply chain managers that they should demand finance to measure them on ROCE, as opposed to individual and often conflicting service, cost and cash metrics.

Alternatives for ROCE

In *Supply Chain Strategy and Financial Metrics*, I analysed different alternative metrics for the margin in detail such as gross margin, EBITDA, EBIT and net profit. Gross margin is a good indicator of the strategy of the company, the more differentiating the position, the higher the premium a company can drive. That premium is needed to cover the higher costs and capital employed that are needed to drive that strategic positioning. The gross margin accounts for the cost of goods sold (COGS) but still excludes the sales, general & administrative (SG&A). As a 'bottom-line' metric I prefer EBIT over net profit as it includes all operational costs (cost of goods sold and the SG&A) while it excludes financial costs such as interest and taxes. As the D&A are relatively fixed, I'm less concerned with the difference between EBIT and EBITDA, and as EBIT leads to ROCE, I usually look at EBIT.

In my second book, *The Strategy-Driven Supply Chain*, I analysed alternative return metrics like the return on assets (ROA) and the return on equity (ROE). From a supply chain perspective I prefer ROCE over the other metrics as the capital employed is so tangible, it is the working capital plus the fixed assets, things that I, as a supply chain and operations professional, have a direct and material impact on. The ROE starts from the net profit (which includes the interest and taxes) and looks at the equity instead of the capital employed (which is influenced by my debt versus equity structure). ROE may be relevant from a financial perspective but is harder to control from a supply chain and operations perspective. I prefer to work with ROCE over ROA for the two following reasons. First, ROA, like ROE, calculates profitability based on net profit, whereas I prefer to work with EBIT. Second, if I can compensate an increase in receivables with an increase in payables, my ROCE (and my cash flow) will remain constant while my ROA will go down, as my total assets go up. Or vice versa, if I'm under pressure from my suppliers to reduce payables, my ROCE (and my cash flow) will remain constant, if I can compensate it with a reduction in receivables or inventory. My ROA in this case will go up, as my total assets go down. From my perspective, there is no real value creation in both situations. We're rather compensating short-term liabilities with short-term assets. ROCE reflects that 'status quo', whereas ROA would report value creation or value loss. Hence, I prefer to work with ROCE over ROA.

In the second book I also showed that ROCE and leverage together drive the earning per share (EPS). I got that as a question from a senior operations executive at Henkel. In a benchmark study of around 30 FMCG companies I could empirically show that ROCE and the debt-to-equity ratio (D/E) together explain most of the variance in the EPS. I had already theoretically shown you can inflate your ROE (or EPS) by increasing the leverage (amount of debt) as long as the net interest (interest after accounting for the tax advantage) is lower than the starting ROE. Though valuable, that is the easy part I would say. The harder part is improving the ROCE, which requires us to improve the mastery of the triangle. It will be very hard to get to a decent ROE or EPS starting from a bad ROCE. ROCE is like the 'physical' and 'material' foundation on which a healthy EPS is built. For further reference, I have made the benchmark study available for free download from my website.[9]

Case Study: H&M – the Supply Chain Triangle as a relevant part of the supply chain strategy, by Jesper Metz, Zaki Sarker and Erika Linton

H&M Group may not need a lot of introduction. It is a global fashion and design company with over 4,000 stores, in more than 70 markets and with online sales in over 60 markets.[10] All their brands and business ventures share the same passion for making great and more sustainable fashion and design available to everyone. Each of the brands, like H&M, COS, Weekday, ARKET, Afound, has its own unique identity. They complement each other and strengthen H&M Group, to offer customers unbeatable value and enable a more circular lifestyle.

The Supply Chain Triangle of Service, Cost and Cash, has become a relevant element for H&M, steering its supply chain. The triangle is a key starting point for the supply chain strategy team, for the supply chain performance management, and it will be an active working tool for general supply planning tasks.

As part of their work, the supply chain strategy team have aligned their own version of the Supply Chain Triangle, shown in Figure 1.6. It contains the necessary elements to generally answer over 90 per cent of the questions they receive. Traditional network optimizations are often focused on cost minimization only. They may look at operational costs like warehousing and logistics and at the required investments (CAPEX), but, for example, they will not try to model the impact on sales revenues, they take service as a constraint like 'all online customers/stores need to be delivered within x days'.

H&M's team has taken the triangle as a foundation to expand this traditional modelling. For instance, on the service side, they added questions like, what is the impact of customer lead time and reliability on the sales revenue? Can we model this from data? Can we test it in real life? Or what is the impact of throughput capacity on the year-end sales? Jesper Metz, Supply Chain Analytics & Modelling Manager, comments that:

> Even if we could not model the sales impact, at times we still went back to the stakeholders saying, just as an extreme example, "You'll need to increase the sales with 300 per cent if you want this to pay off". It is of course a mindset shift. From a modelling perspective service targets are rarely seen as hard requirements. We always model the impact on sales, and if needed we challenge the requirements and targets.

The traditional network design is also quite rough in the inventory modelling. It may make basic assumptions like we need 10 days of inventory for all items. Inspired by the triangle, the H&M strategy team started modelling the inventory in more detail, asking questions like, what is the inventory impact between different scenarios? The overall goal is always to evaluate scenarios not just on a cost level, but also on calculated sales revenues, on capital employed and as a result on the ROCE, exactly as introduced in Figure 1.5.

Figure 1.6 The H&M version of the Supply Chain Triangle

Impact on Revenue?
- Customer lead time & reliability
- Throughput capacity
- Product portfolio
- Availability
- Order flexibility
- Sustainability

Impact on Capital Employed?

Inventory
Fixed assets (CAPEX)

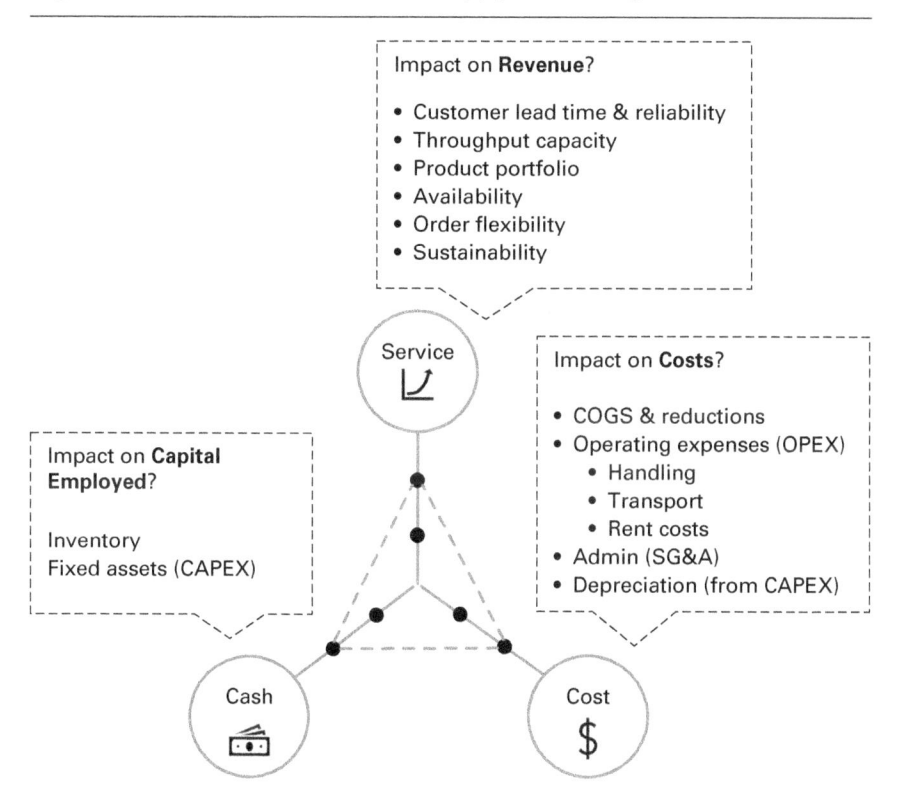

Impact on Costs?
- COGS & reductions
- Operating expenses (OPEX)
  - Handling
  - Transport
  - Rent costs
- Admin (SG&A)
- Depreciation (from CAPEX)

Service

Cash

Cost

Figure 1.7 shows the methodology the supply chain strategy team at H&M has built around the triangle. It starts with the overall strategy or hypothesis, and as Jesper Metz comments:

> It is also about helping to refine strategies overall, which may not always reflect all necessary trade-offs & effects along our supply chain. It is not uncommon to see aspirations of wanting and trying to improve all aspects at the same time. From the modelling approach, we can help the stakeholders to reveal the options and the necessary trade-offs.

The next steps in Figure 1.7 show how the H&M team models the impact of service scenarios on the sales, simulates alternative solutions from, for instance, a cost and inventory perspective, which allows it to compare scenarios from a P&L, a cash and a ROCE perspective. Another direct outcome from the modelling is which key metrics to monitor. Jesper comments that 'Once you know what the important drivers in the scenario are, for instance

Figure 1.7 The H&M methodology built around the Supply Chain Triangle

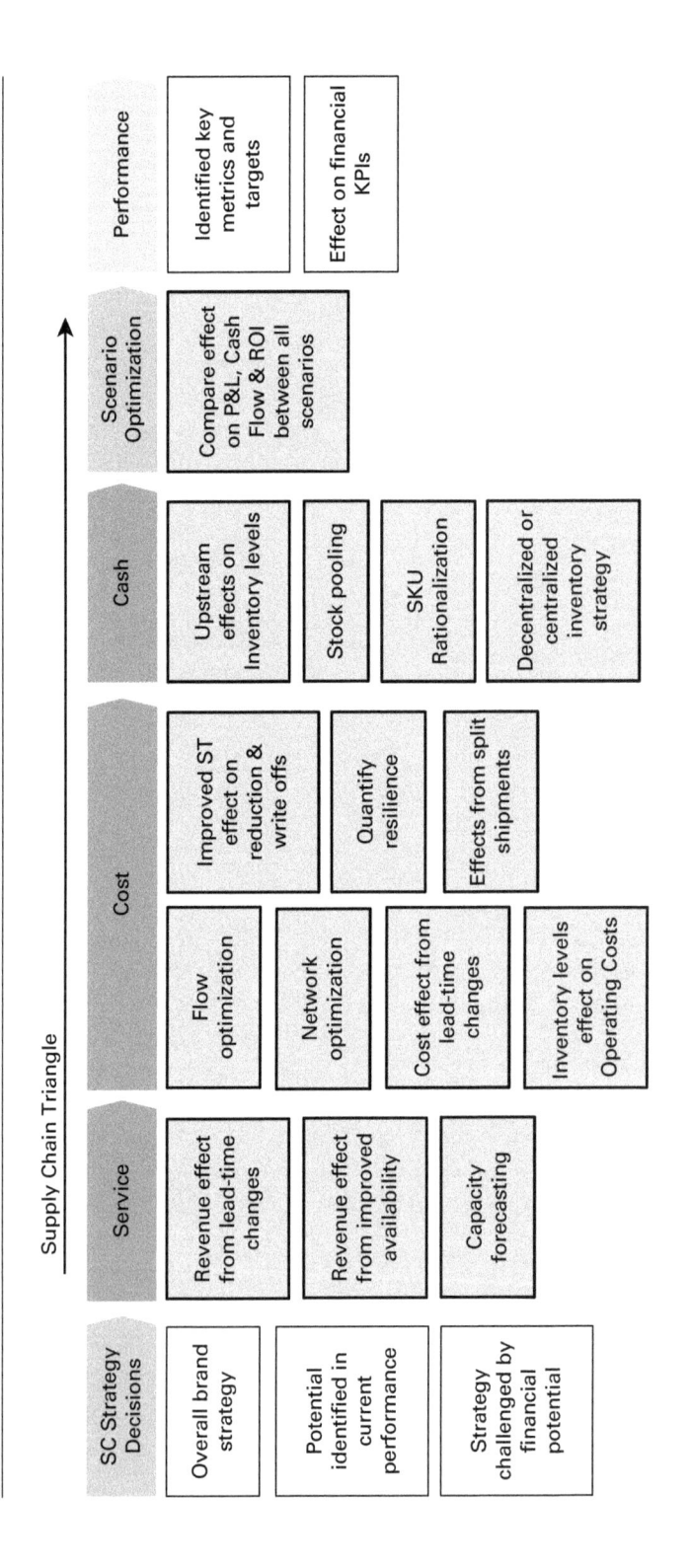

Supply Chain Triangle

SC Strategy Decisions	Service	Cost	Cash	Scenario Optimization	Performance
Overall brand strategy	Revenue effect from lead-time changes	Improved ST effect on reduction & write offs	Upstream effects on Inventory levels	Compare effect on P&L, Cash Flow & ROI between all scenarios	Identified key metrics and targets
Potential identified in current performance	Revenue effect from improved availability	Quantify resilience	Stock pooling		Effect on financial KPIs
Strategy challenged by financial potential	Capacity forecasting	Effects from split shipments	SKU Rationalization		
		Flow optimization	Decentralized or centralized inventory strategy		
		Network optimization			
		Cost effect from lead-time changes			
		Inventory levels effect on Operating Costs			

lead times, it is also immediately clear that this is a KPI you want to track and monitor from an operational perspective.' In other words, it becomes easier to create a clear connection between planned operational performance and calculated financial success.

Figure 1.8 shows an example, investigating whether it could be reasonable to allow online customers to shop from a secondary warehouse. Compared to the baseline scenario of doing nothing, this could potentially lead to a positive effect on the sales and the resulting gross margin. As we start having split parcels and will travel longer distances with corresponding CO_2 emissions, the operating cost could go up. The question becomes 'by how much' and what is the impact on EBIT? Next, the H&M team questions the inventory impact. If we allow ordering from a secondary warehouse, we expect inventories to go down. The question once more is 'by how much, what is the impact on the total capital employed (= working capital + fixed assets), and what is the impact on ROCE (Return On Capital Employed = EBIT/Capital Employed)?

While H&M cannot disclose details, an example output is shown in Figure 1.9. The conclusion is obvious in this example, as both EBIT is going up and capital employed is going down. Jesper Metz comments that 'When you see that in one of the scenarios, for instance, the increase in transport cost is the challenge to making the scenario attractive, you then start looking into alternatives to realize the intended outcome but at a lower cost level. This type of modelling is an iterative process.' The supply chain team also has the possibility to test the conclusions of the models in real life. Do we see the anticipated sales impact? Can we measure the expected cost increase and the inventory effect? A good model makes you more targeted in what to measure and how to evaluate these type of pilots.

One of the necessities for H&M was to introduce this way of evaluating scenarios at all levels. Jesper comments 'We included ROCE next to the more traditional investment metrics like NPV, in a broader scorecard'. That scorecard is shown in Figure 1.10. ROCE basically measures the value generation, whereas the NPV analyses the cash flows. Jesper comments that 'they tend to go in sync'. H&M also shows the impact on ESG, so that basically the three dimensions are used for comparing alternatives: value generation potential (ROCE), cash flow (NPV) and ESG impact (ESG score).

Where the use of the triangle may have started in the supply chain strategy, it has expanded into other areas like supply chain performance management. With a cross functional working group, H&M defined which metrics to

Figure 1.8 Example case: offering customers products from a secondary warehouse

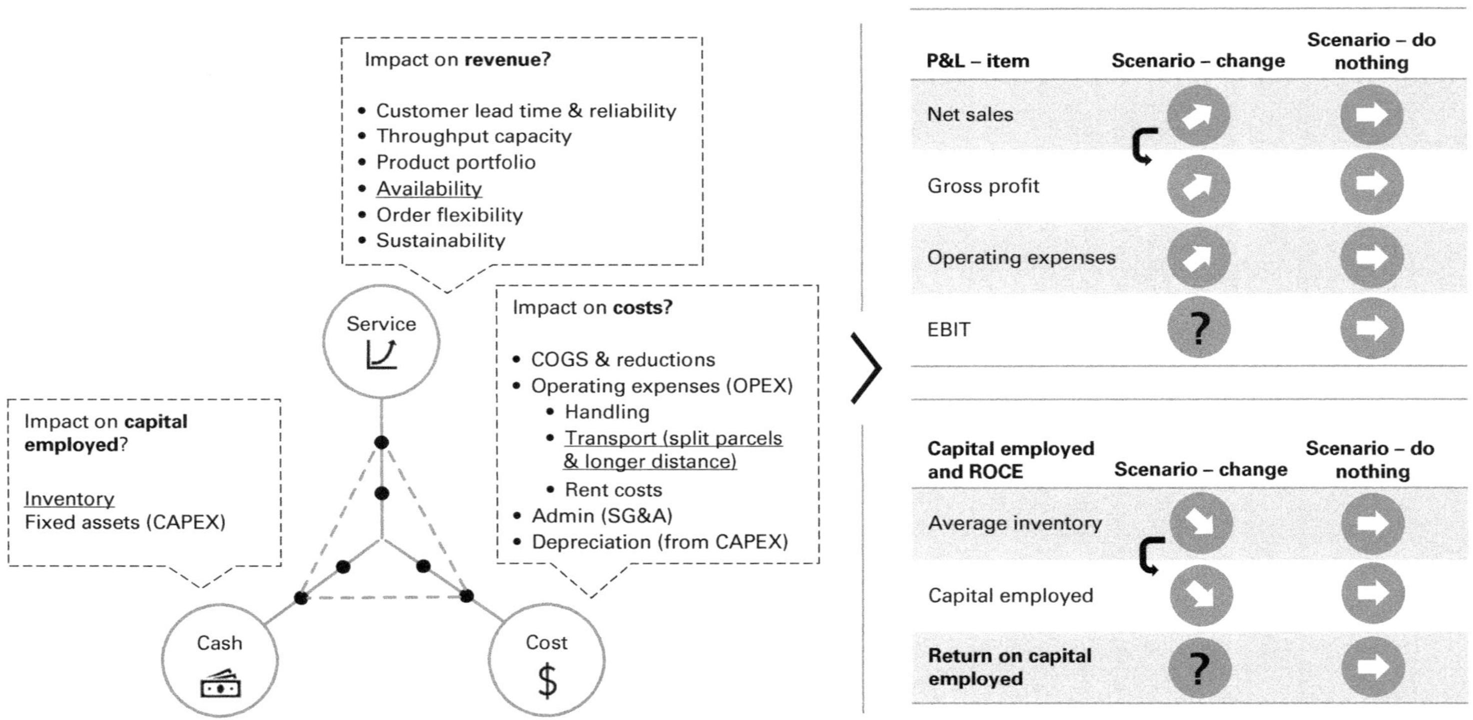

Figure 1.9 Example case: offering customers products from a secondary warehouse – order of magnitude

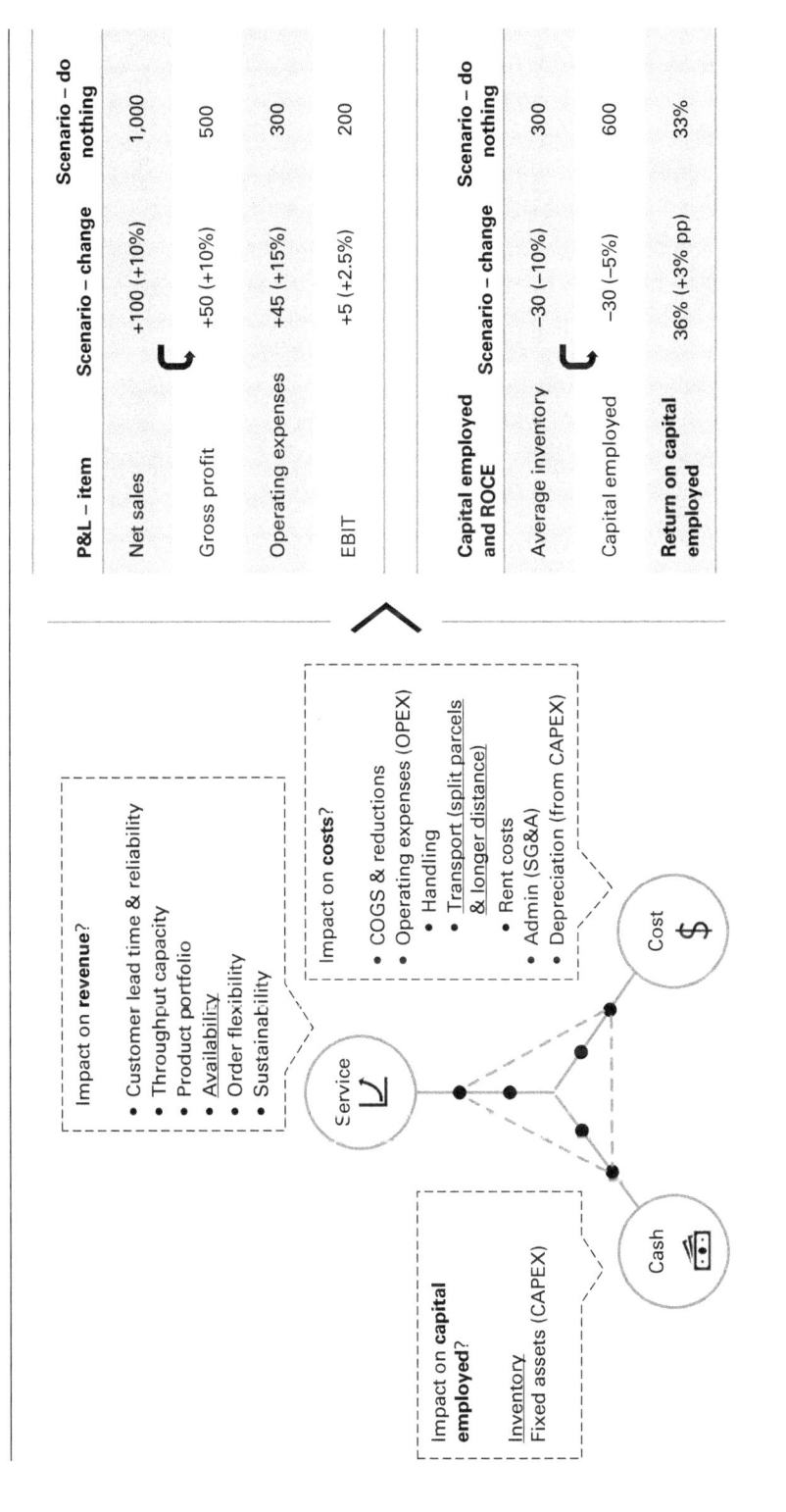

Impact on revenue?
- Customer lead time & reliability
- Throughput capacity
- Product portfolio
- Availability
- Order flexibility
- Sustainability

Impact on costs?
- COGS & reductions
- Operating expenses (OPEX)
  - Handling
  - Transport (split parcels & longer distance)
  - Rent costs
  - Admin (SG&A)
  - Depreciation (from CAPEX)

Impact on capital employed?
Inventory
Fixed assets (CAPEX)

Service — Cost — Cash

P&L – item	Scenario – change	Scenario – do nothing
Net sales	+100 (+10%)	1,000
Gross profit	+50 (+10%)	500
Operating expenses	+45 (+15%)	300
EBIT	+5 (+2.5%)	200

Capital employed and ROCE	Scenario – change	Scenario – do nothing
Average inventory	−30 (−10%)	300
Capital employed	−30 (−5%)	600
Return on capital employed	36% (+3% pp)	33%

Figure 1.10   Broader evaluation criteria of scenarios

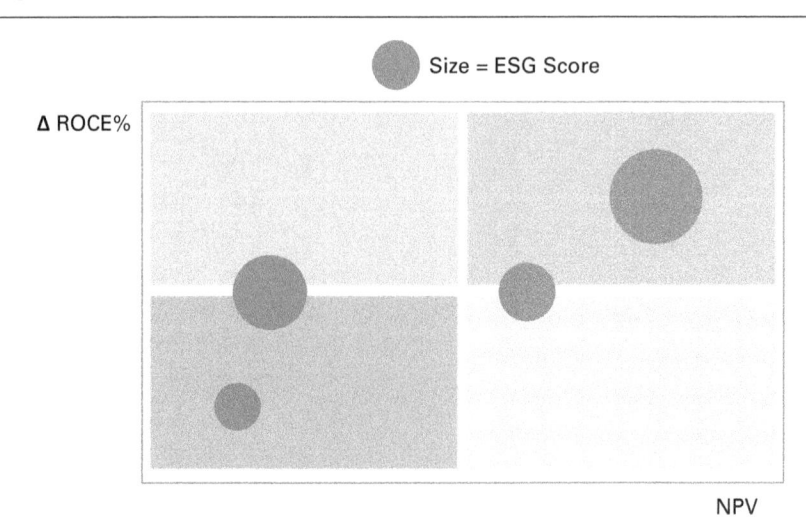

follow up on a monthly basis. The starting point was the triangle. To consistently report service and top-line, cost and bottom-line, and working capital metrics, into one single integrated overview. H&M also added sustainability metrics to complete what you could call their balanced scorecard. 'Showing this type of dashboards changes the mindset,' comments Zaki Sarker, Head of Supply Chain Performance Steering at H&M. Jesper Metz adds:

> We always show all the components in our strategic analysis. Even if there is no impact on inventory, we still show the inventory in the results to strengthen joint learnings and be clear about one direction and parameters. That is how you change the mindset towards more integrated thinking.

Zaki Sarker comments that 'Understanding the relationships between all of the metrics is naturally a challenge'. We of course strive to improve on all KPIs and exceed also our goals, but that's normally not possible since trade-offs must be made. That also means that the targets themselves need to reflect those trade-offs and balance within the triangle to be relevant. Which brought us to the topic of planning. Can we define planning scenarios and how these potentially impact service, cost and cash?

Supply planning is an independent function within H&M. The supply planning organization is the element responsible for optimizing the quantities produced, as well as how to steer the inventory end to end. In this type of function, you need some metrics on how you will measure its performance. 'Those metrics are defined around the Supply Chain Triangle,' comments Erika Linton, currently the global Head of Supply Chain Strategy and Design.

'There are also other areas where the triangle is the starting point,' continues Jesper Metz.

> There are a lot more connections to the triangle beyond strategic work. Take tech as an example: all steering logics and engines that control and optimize our inventory flow. It should normally not be about optimizing towards 1 variable here, and another there. Overall, it needs to be about steering towards the optimal balance between revenue, costs (profit) and inventory efficiency. So, in the end, also here, it's also about optimizing the Supply Chain Triangle.

'It has been a very interesting journey so far,' Erika Linton concludes. 'The compass is an accurate way to describe how we use the triangle. It has been helpful, inspirational, and foundational for us. It really supports us to make the most out of our supply chain organization.'

From one to three triangles: the profit, the people and the planet triangle

Ever since I started talking about the Supply Chain Triangle, people asked me 'how can we link it with sustainability'? It took me a while and two books to fully understand and document the Supply Chain Triangle and how it links to strategy. I'm now most happy to try and tackle the following two questions: 'What actually is sustainability?' and 'How does it link to the Supply Chain Triangle?'

One of the cornerstones of the sustainability literature is the book *Cannibals with Forks* by John Elkington.[11] Elkington describes how in the 1970s, environmental concerns were still something for activist groups like Greenpeace and were considered by most managers as something that was at odds with the free enterprise. The assumed best tactic for businesses at that time was to limit transparency and try to operate below the radar of these activist groups.

Elkington continues to describe how gradually the mindset changed, in multiple waves characterized on the one hand by environmental disasters (Bhopal, discovery of ozone hole above the Antarctic, Chernobyl, Exxon Valdez, Brent Spar) and on the other hand by initiatives of pressure groups and the UN (Stockholm Conference, Montreal Protocol, International Earth Day, Earth Summit Rio De Janeiro). He elegantly elaborates how, slowly but surely, companies changed their way of thinking, to become more inclusive about both environmental and social aspects.

Figure 1.11 The Supply Chain Triangle as the Profit Triangle

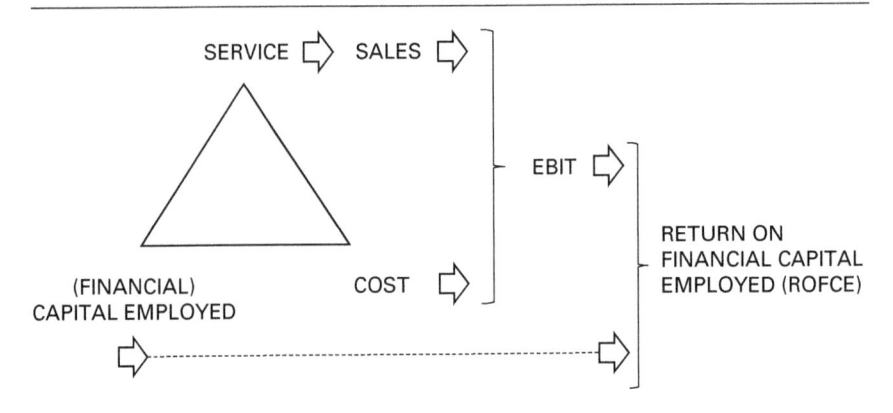

Elkington defines sustainability as 'the principle of ensuring that our actions today do not limit the range of economic, social and environmental options open to future generations'. He makes it concrete by introducing a 'social bottom line' and an 'environmental bottom line' next to the 'economic bottom line'. In his vision, sustainable capitalism and the sustainable corporation is managing, not just one, but the so-called 'Triple Bottom Line'. That Triple Bottom Line is commonly referred to as the 3Ps: people, planet, profit. It is a good starting point to make the connection with supply chain thinking through the Supply Chain Triangle.

First of all, when thinking about the triple bottom line, I realized that the Supply Chain Triangle is, in essence, a Profit Triangle, focused on the optimization of the financial profit, we generate on our financial capital employed, as is shown in Figure 1.11.

Next, I realized we can easily make the analogy for people and planet. As we use 'Financial Capital', in our supply chains, our manufacturing and distribution processes, we also use People Capital and Planet Capital. The People Capital, in the most direct form, are our employees, the people who work for us. Indirectly, it may be employees of our suppliers, or their suppliers, or it may be people working with our products, or the consumers consuming them. Through the individuals we may have an impact on their families, and more broadly the communities and societies they live in. As explained by John Elkington, companies increasingly understand they have a broader social responsibility, and they increasingly take care of it.

In our value chains, we also use Planet Capital, for instance in the form of land, water, air, fossil fuels or rare earth elements. In general, you could call it natural resources. One of the big questions in sustainability thinking is how to

Figure 1.12 Three triangles feeding our supply chain and operations

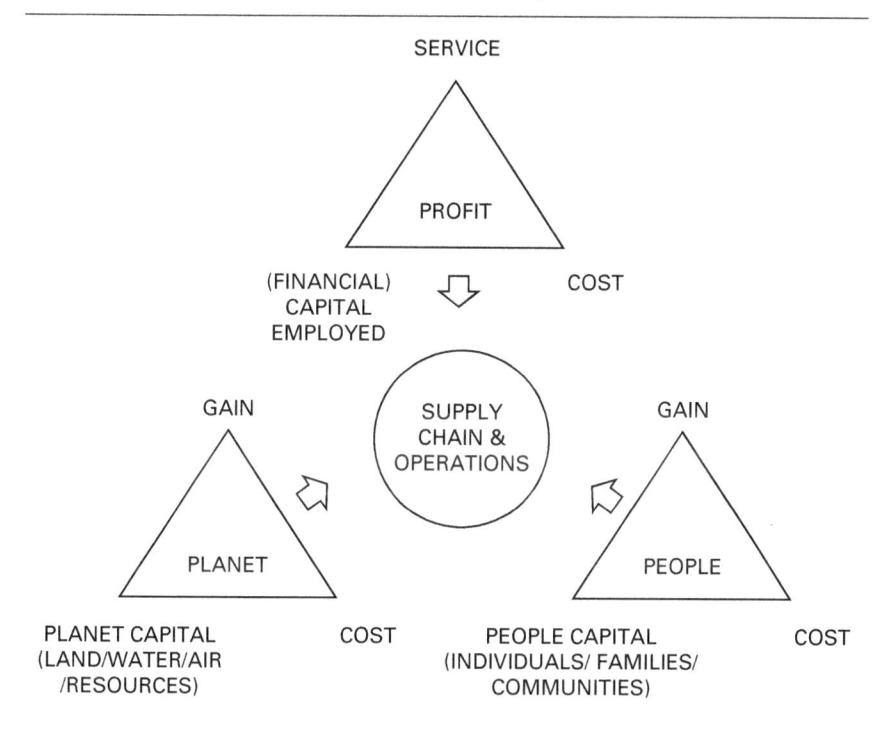

```
                        SERVICE
                          /\
                         /  \
                        /    \
                       / PROFIT\
                      /_____\
         (FINANCIAL)      ⇩        COST
          CAPITAL
          EMPLOYED

  GAIN          ┌─────────┐         GAIN
   /\           │ SUPPLY  │          /\
  /  \          │ CHAIN & │         /  \
 /    \    ⇨    │OPERATIONS│   ⇦   /    \
/PLANET\         └─────────┘        /PEOPLE\
/_____\                          /_____\

PLANET CAPITAL      COST      PEOPLE CAPITAL      COST
(LAND/WATER/AIR              (INDIVIDUALS/ FAMILIES/
 /RESOURCES)                      COMMUNITIES)
```

decouple economic growth from consuming ever more resources or Planet Capital. Without changing our approach, we risk to both kill and deplete our planet. Kill, for instance through global warming, which is the result of the accumulation of greenhouse gases we release in the atmosphere, and deplete, as we are using increasingly more fossil fuels and many rare earth elements that are inherently finite. So, in summary, as shown in Figure 1.12, our supply chains run on three types of capital, financial capital, people capital (humans) and planet capital (natural resources).

During the usage of any type of capital we incur costs to it, which decrease its amount, its quality or its value. Common people costs are stress, burnout, unhealthy working conditions, which can lead to increased absenteeism, longer-term illness and potentially death. As we are impacting the individuals, we may impact their families, communities or society as a whole. Common planet costs include the depletion of non-renewable energy sources, pollution of air (CO_2, NO_2), pollution of land (with a lot of recent discussions on PFAS[12]), pollution of water (by all sorts of fertilizers), destruction of biodiversity.

During the usage of the people and planet capital, we can also increase the amount, the quality or the value. I will call those gains. There are plenty of examples from a people perspective. Through providing people with work, we also provide them with an income, which can lead to economic prosperity, which in turn can lead to increased health conditions. Through interesting work, we can provide people with happiness, or even with a purpose. We can also provide people with training and personal development. All of these increase the quality and value of the People Capital.

In the Planet Triangle, instead of 'gains', more of the examples could rather be called 'cost avoidance'. We may try to reduce our usage of land, water, energy or other scarce resources, which slows down the pace at which these are being depleted. We may try to reduce the pollution of air, water and soil. Think about improved filtering of the waste waters we release back in our rivers or the capturing of the CO_2 emitted by our plants, as was recently announced by Arcelor Mittal.[13] We may also switch to alternative sources, for instance green electricity or electric vehicles for our city logistics. And by making our supply chains more circular, we can extend the lifetime of our products by reusing, refurbishing and redistributing them. That lowers the net new consumption of scarce resources. We can also try to recycle more materials instead of sending them to the landfill, which lowers the net new consumption of resources and reduces the environmental costs generated by landfills.

When looking for purer 'gains' in the Planet Triangle, as a company we may decide to plant more trees on the land we own, or we may contribute to reforestation programmes. Some of the bigger initiatives to 'add' to the Planet Capital may currently be driven by governments or NGOs. Think about the 'Nature Restoration Law[14]' which was recently approved by the European Parliament, and which will oblige member states to 'bring at least 30 per cent of habitats in terrestrial, coastal, freshwater and marine ecosystems that are not in good condition, into good condition by 2030'.

And just like we can calculate a 'net gain' or 'profit' in the financial triangle and a 'return on the financial capital employed', as shown in Figure 1.11, we can calculate net gains in the People and the Planet Triangles, leading to a return on the people capital employed, and a return on the planet capital employed. Those resulting People and Planet Triangles are shown in Figure 1.13 and Figure 1.14. Though measuring the return may be impractical for now, I believe it is important from a conceptual point of view. As we manage our supply chains, how are we getting the maximum out of the people, planet and financial capital we employ. That's what sustainable supply chains are about.

Figure 1.13 The People Triangle

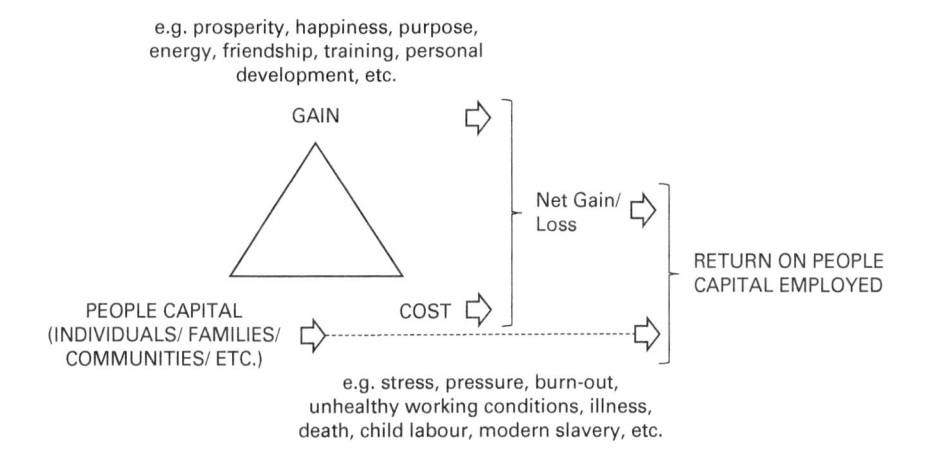

e.g. prosperity, happiness, purpose, energy, friendship, training, personal development, etc.

GAIN

Net Gain/Loss

RETURN ON PEOPLE CAPITAL EMPLOYED

PEOPLE CAPITAL (INDIVIDUALS/ FAMILIES/ COMMUNITIES/ ETC.)

COST

e.g. stress, pressure, burn-out, unhealthy working conditions, illness, death, child labour, modern slavery, etc.

Figure 1.14 The Planet Triangle

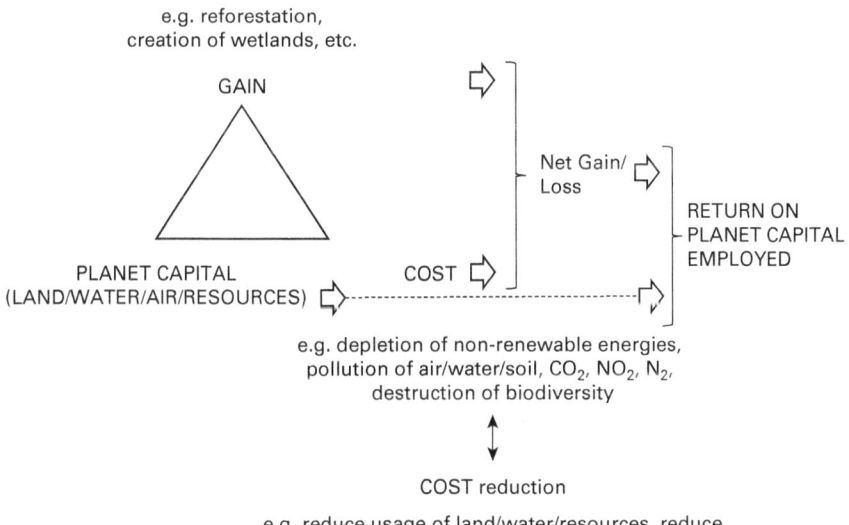

e.g. reforestation, creation of wetlands, etc.

GAIN

Net Gain/Loss

RETURN ON PLANET CAPITAL EMPLOYED

PLANET CAPITAL (LAND/WATER/AIR/RESOURCES)

COST

e.g. depletion of non-renewable energies, pollution of air/water/soil, CO_2, NO_2, N_2, destruction of biodiversity

COST reduction

e.g. reduce usage of land/water/resources, reduce pollution of air/water/soil, use of alternatives (renewable energy), circularity (reusing, refurbishing, redistributing, recycling)

Offshoring in the 1980s: impact across the three triangles

Now that I have created the individual triangles, I can start analysing the dynamics across the three triangles. For this, I borrow an example from Ed Weenk, from his book *Mastering The Circular Economy*[15]. He discusses the people and planet impact from the massive offshoring to China and Southeast Asia by European and American companies that took place in the 1980s.

This offshoring was driven by the Profit Triangle. The access to almost unlimited low cost labour gave an important cost advantage. It basically allowed companies to lower the price in mature markets for many products which gave a huge boost to consumption and to 'consumerism' in general. Instead of repairing consumer electronics it became common to dispose of them and just buy the latest greatest.

When looking at the financial capital (employed) impact of the offshoring, on the one hand, the longer lead times for production and cross-ocean transport required carrying more inventory. On the other hand, because the labour was so cheap, any increase in inventory was typically compensated by having less investments in expensive machines and automation. In Figure 1.15 I have assumed the net capital employed to go down leading to a triple positive effect on the return on capital employed: more sales, at a lower cost and with less capital employed.

The impact on the People Triangle was double. On the one hand, the creation of jobs for sure helped to reduce poverty in Southeast Asia. At the other hand, it led to a loss of jobs in the US and Europe, leading to whole regions such as the American Rust Belt where manufacturing closed, and leading to an increase in social problems.

From the perspective of the Planet Triangle, as we moved production into Southeast Asia, we can expect that environmental controls, especially in the early years, were less strict. So, it is fair to assume that the offshoring had an unfavourable impact on all kinds of pollution. As many more goods had to travel across the ocean, we also safely assume it had an unfavourable impact on the amount of CO_2 emitted.

As John Elkington explains, companies in the 1980s were primarily driven by profit objectives and were less concerned about the social or the environmental impact than they are today. Given the important financial gains from offshoring, it explains its massive use by companies in that era.

Figure 1.15 The impact on the three triangles of offshoring in the 1980s

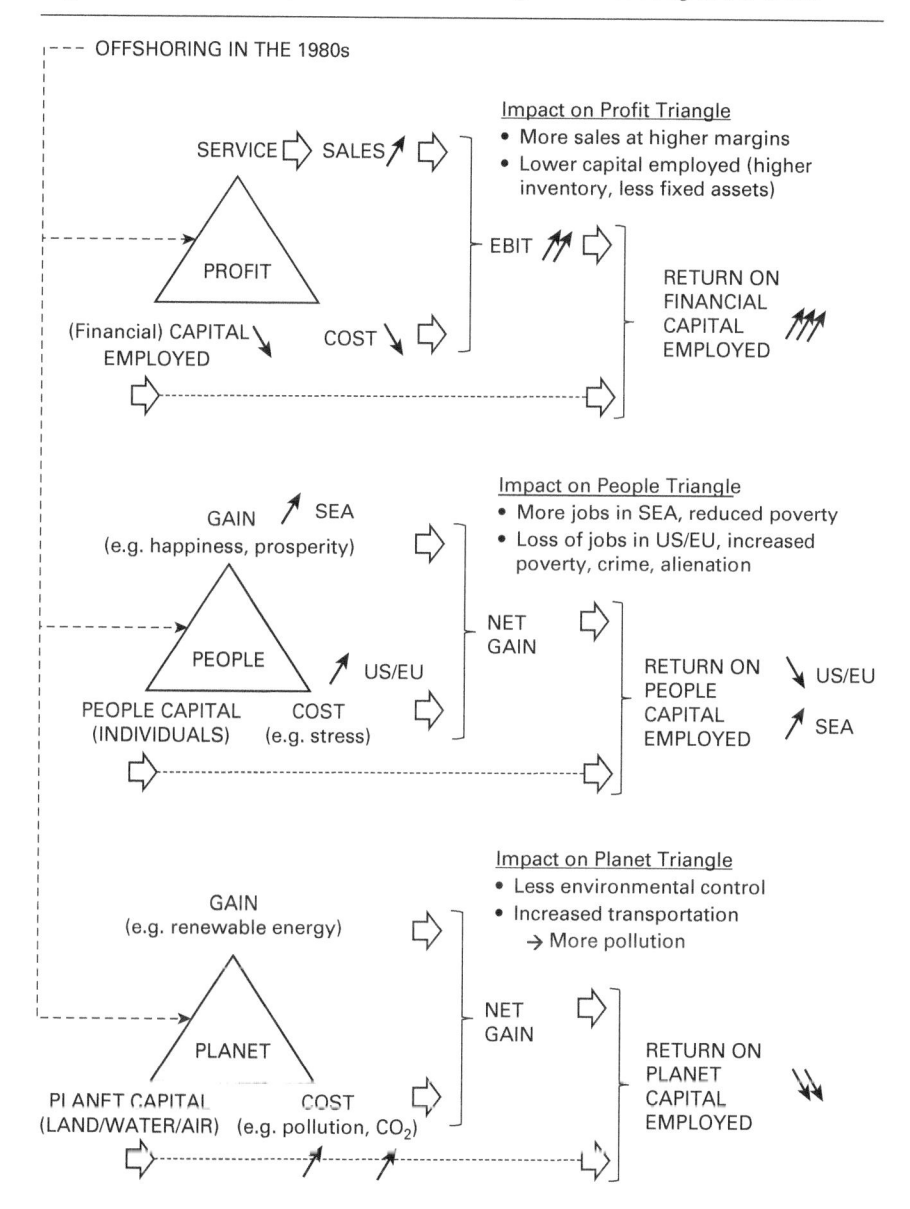

OFFSHORING IN THE 1980s

Impact on Profit Triangle
- More sales at higher margins
- Lower capital employed (higher inventory, less fixed assets)

SERVICE ⇒ SALES ↗

Triangle: PROFIT
- (Financial) CAPITAL EMPLOYED ↘
- COST ↘

EBIT ↗↗ ⇒ RETURN ON FINANCIAL CAPITAL EMPLOYED ↗↗↗

Impact on People Triangle
- More jobs in SEA, reduced poverty
- Loss of jobs in US/EU, increased poverty, crime, alienation

GAIN ↗ SEA (e.g. happiness, prosperity)

Triangle: PEOPLE ↗ US/EU
- PEOPLE CAPITAL (INDIVIDUALS)
- COST (e.g. stress)

NET GAIN ⇒ RETURN ON PEOPLE CAPITAL EMPLOYED ↘ US/EU ↗ SEA

Impact on Planet Triangle
- Less environmental control
- Increased transportation → More pollution

GAIN (e.g. renewable energy)

Triangle: PLANET
- PLANET CAPITAL (LAND/WATER/AIR)
- COST (e.g. pollution, CO_2)

NET GAIN ⇒ RETURN ON PLANET CAPITAL EMPLOYED ↘↘

The Triple Triangle of people, planet and profit

If we align with the thinking of Elkington, then in the 1970s and the 1980s, the only real concern was the Profit Triangle and little consideration was given to the people or the planet impact. Whereas for sustainable capitalism, and sustainable enterprise, a conscious and continuous balancing across the three triangles needs to be performed. Given the 'Triple Bottom Line' is such an iconic work, I thought it was natural to extend our model of the Supply Chain Triangle into the model of the 'Triple Triangle', as shown in Figure 1.16. The 'full' Triple Triangle takes the three triangles as shown in Figure 1.12 and then completes the individual triangles as shown in Figures 1.11, 1.13 and 1.14.

To understand the relevance of the 'Triple Triangle', let's apply it to the opposite example of offshoring: reshoring, an actual discussion in many executive teams and boardrooms. As a kind of 'hangover' from the Covid period, we suddenly seem to realize that we are overly exposed by a concentration of sourcing from China and Southeast Asia. As long as the supply is reliable, and the cost of transport is low, the offshoring works well. The Covid period has been a wake-up call in both aspects. Add to that the increased political tensions between China and the US, and it has caused companies to reconsider their options. In response to the experiences during the Covid period, there is an urge to make our supply chains more 'resilient'. We could say that resilience starts from the service side of the Profit Triangle. We want to be more resilient to ensure we can serve our customers and realize our growth plans. Regional sourcing and production are options considered to improve our resilience.

If we extend the analysis to the People Triangle, reshoring to the US or Europe is considered positive. It is bringing back jobs that have been 'lost' in the past, which politically is a popular argument. It will also be beneficial from a planet perspective, less kilometres travelled means less CO_2. Both are reinforced by legislation like the 'Inflation Reduction Act[16]' in the US. On the face the IRA is about boosting clean energy, reducing healthcare costs and increasing tax revenues. There are concerns in Europe however, that it is also a campaign to 'buy American[17]', as the Act contains requirements for local US or North American contents and production.

The big 'but' of reshoring is the financial impact. Local resources are expected to be more expensive. If we want to do the reshoring, we will need extra investments in local assets. Nevertheless, the double win on resilience and sustainability, together with the legislative push, seems to push companies towards the reshoring option. The reshoring question is probably the more current example of how thinking across the three triangles is needed to come to decisions today.

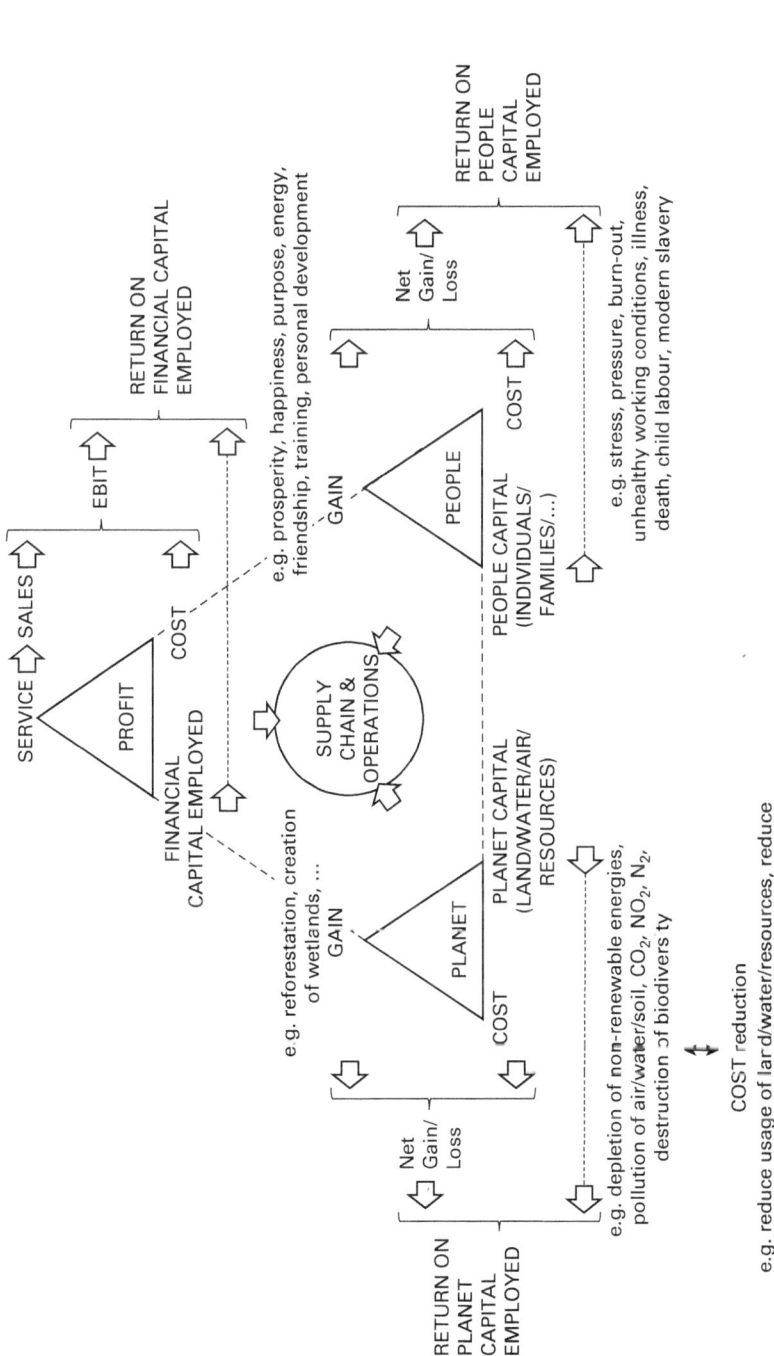

Figure 1.16 The Triple Triangle: profit, planet, people

Linking supply chain with ESG: the quadruple ESG triangle

Where the 'Triple Bottom Line' may be one of the fundaments of sustainability thinking, talking about 'people, planet, profit' seems to be less in vogue. The current talk is 'ESG' or 'Environmental, Social and (Corporate) Governance'. The term ESG is more heavily used in the context of (ESG) reporting/ratings/regulations and (ESG) financing/investing and has essentially taken over as the term to describe sustainability efforts within companies.

While planet and people easily translate into environmental and social, ESG more explicitly adds the 'G' or the 'Corporate Governance', which includes factors such as corporate structure, board composition, business ethics and anti-corruption. According to the World Economic Forum,[18] Corporate Governance predates environmental and social risks as a corporate priority and, as such, many key Corporate Governance indicators may already be included in corporate disclosures. Nevertheless, the WEF continues,

> 'the G is foundational to the realization of both the E and S. Behind each breach of a company's environmental or social commitments lies ineffective corporate governance, be it inadequate anti-corruption practices, perverse incentive structures, contradictory lobbying activity, or ill-equipped leadership. Further, corporate governance affects the integrity of ESG disclosures, determining whether ESG indicators are ethically pursued and reported.'

To link supply chain to ESG, we can easily extend and transform our Triple Triangle as shown in Figure 1.17. If we bring the three triangles (profit, planet and people) together, replace planet and people with environmental and social, and then put governance at the heart, we get to the Quadruple ESG Triangle, with objectives in the profit, environmental and social dimension, and with the governance piece at the heart as the regulating mechanism.

Whether it is about the Triple Triangle shown in Figure 1.16, or the Quadruple ESG Triangle shown in Figure 1.17, the initial feedback from people is that this is complex. When you truly master a subject, you can explain a complex matter in a simple way. So this means I'm not yet there. At the same time, it feels to me that our new business and supply chain reality is complex, it is increasingly about balancing multiple objectives in parallel without having a good understanding on how they are connected.

Figure 1.17 Linking supply chain with ESG: The Quadruple ESG Triangle

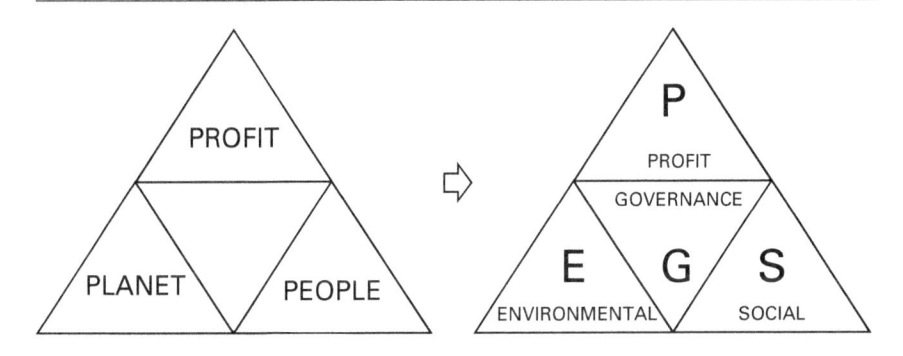

In any case, building models is a balancing act. Any model needs to be simple enough so that people can easily relate to it, but it also needs to be complex enough that it captures the key dynamics. I chose to include the models AS IS, for two reasons, to describe where I am in my thinking and my journey, and because I do believe the models are helpful. To illustrate so, I will use the Quadruple ESG Triangle to answer a long-standing question from my to-answer list 'How does the Supply Chain Triangle work for a non-profit like Médecins Sans Frontières (MSF)?'

Case Study: MSF – measuring output in the social triangle

Médecins Sans Frontières[19] (MSF), or Doctors Without Borders, is a non-governmental organization of French origin, which provides relief to populations in distress, to victims of natural and man-made disasters and to victims of armed conflict. In 2022, 7,823 health professionals, logistics specialists and administrative staff of all nationalities departed for assignments in medical programmes, to work with more than 40,000 locally hired staff in over 75 countries.[20]

MSF has an associative structure, where operational decisions are made, independently, by six operational centres: Amsterdam, Barcelona, Brussels, Geneva, Paris and West and Central Africa. In 2011, MSF International was registered in Switzerland and the first annual MSF International General Assembly (IGA) was held. The IGA comprises two representatives of each MSF association, two representatives elected by the individual members of MSF International and the International President. The IGA is the highest authority of MSF International and is responsible for safeguarding MSF's medical humanitarian mission and providing strategic orientation to all MSF entities.

Julio Victoria, logistics manager at MSF Supply in Brussels, comments that

> 'the supply chain of MSF is complex. The international catalogue of products counts around 20,000 references. MSF Supply, based in Brussels, and one of the three supply centres, next to Bordeaux in France and Amsterdam in the Netherlands, manages an inventory with around 3,000 SKUs on stock, with the other items purchased to order. Delivery lead times depend on the mission and/or product. Emergency responses to wars or natural disasters are obviously hard to plan and require a highly responsive supply chain. Programmes like HIV Antiretroviral (ARV) treatments can be planned and organized more efficiently. The speed of delivery depends on country specific policies and conditions in the field. One can imagine that delivering to war zones, take the Gaza strip in 2023, is an especially difficult and dangerous operation.'

When first drawing the Triple Triangle from Figure 1.16 or the Quadruple Triangle from Figure 1.17, I realized I could finally answer one of my long-standing questions: how does the Supply Chain Triangle work for a non-profit organization? If we limit ourselves to the traditional 'Financial' Supply Chain Triangle from Figure 1.11, we get stuck. MSF is not selling any services or products. That means there is no sales revenue, which means there is no EBIT and no ROCE as a balancing criterion, as shown in Figure 1.18.

Figure 1.18 The non-profit Supply Chain Triangle

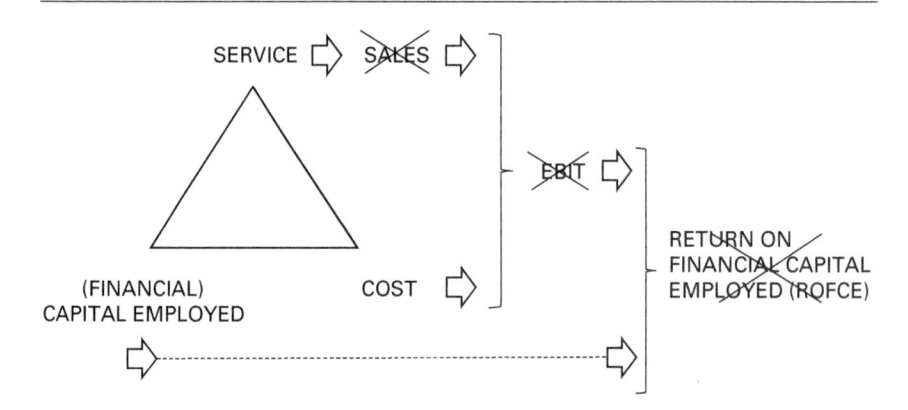

Figure 1.19 The Social Triangle leading for MSF

Médecins Sans Frontières provides assistance to populations in distress, to victims of natural or man-made disasters and to victims of armed conflict. They do so irrespective of race, religion, creed or political convictions. (www.msf.org)

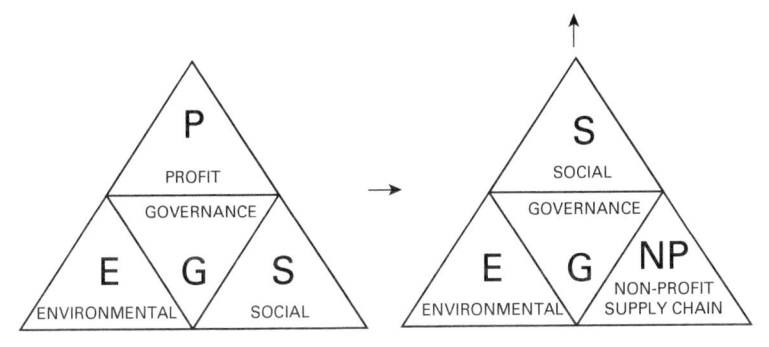

```
      P                              S
   PROFIT                         SOCIAL
  GOVERNANCE      →             GOVERNANCE
 E   G   S                    E   G   NP
ENVIRONMENTAL  SOCIAL      ENVIRONMENTAL  NON-PROFIT
                                          SUPPLY CHAIN
```

When zooming out and taking the Quadruple Triangle view, it becomes obvious that the objectives of MSF don't lie in the financial triangle. The objectives of MSF lie in the Social Triangle. The primary objective is to provide relief to people in distress. Given that the primary objectives lie in that social triangle, it is also more logical to put that triangle on top and put the 'Non-Profit Supply Chain Triangle' as a supporting triangle at the bottom, as I have done in Figure 1.19.

A non-profit such as Greenpeace has an environmental mission, in which case we could put the environmental triangle on top. In Chapter 5, I will introduce an 'impact company' like Tony's Chocolonely, that is striving for a world with only slave-free chocolate, and states that it is making a profit as a result. At Tony's, the financial success is a way to grow their impact. It allows to grow the company and pay a fair wage to a bigger share of the cocoa farmers in countries like Ghana and Côte d'Ivoire. So for Tony's, we could put the social triangle on top, but it will be supported by a for-profit supply chain, which is helping it to lift its impact in the social triangle. At a non-profit organization like MSF, the goal is to have a P&L at 0 as an average over the years, with the financial reserves allowing to swallow years with losses, without impacting the operations too much. In Figure 1.20 I have shown the example of Greenpeace and Tony's, you can imagine other examples or combinations, or even combinations where two triangles are leading on equal footing and one is following.

Figure 1.20 The environmental and social triangle leading for Greenpeace and Tony's Chocolonely

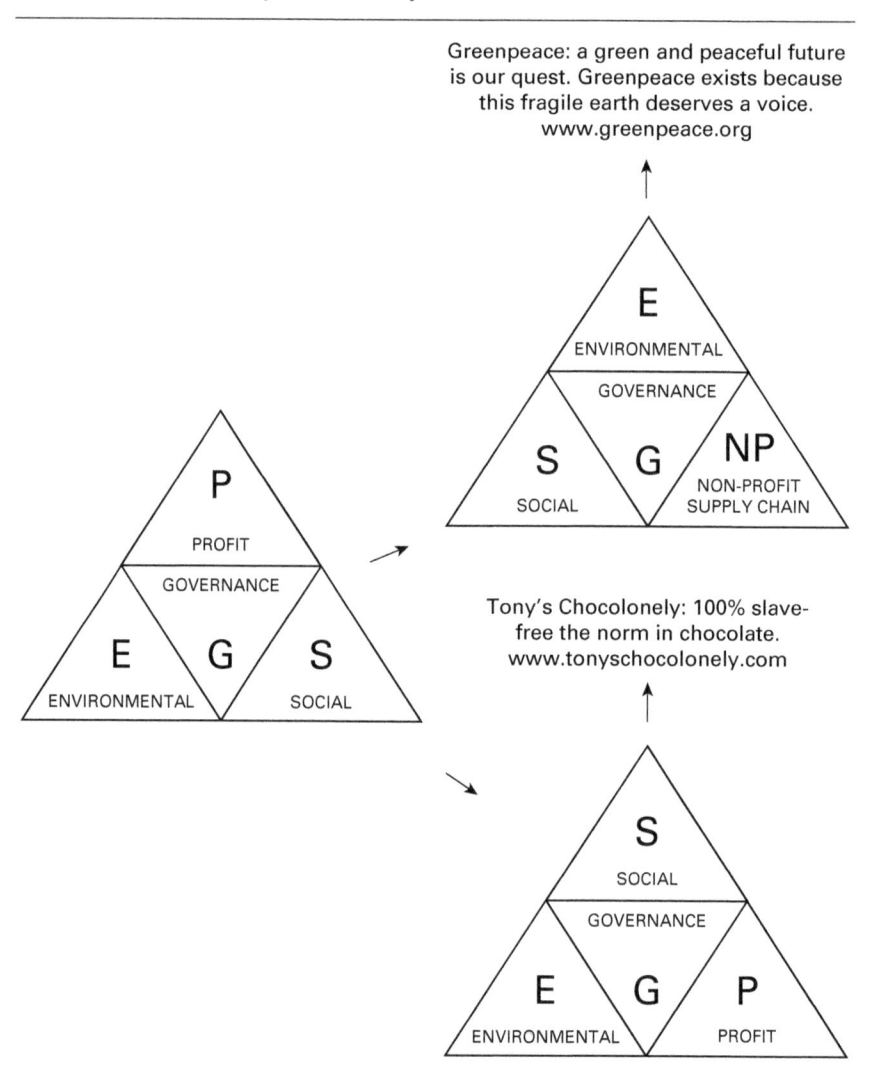

Greenpeace: a green and peaceful future is our quest. Greenpeace exists because this fragile earth deserves a voice. www.greenpeace.org

```
           E
      ENVIRONMENTAL
         GOVERNANCE
      S    G    NP
    SOCIAL     NON-PROFIT
               SUPPLY CHAIN
```

```
        P
       PROFIT
      GOVERNANCE
   E    G    S
ENVIRONMENTAL  SOCIAL
```

Tony's Chocolonely: 100% slave-free the norm in chocolate. www.tonyschocolonely.com

```
         S
       SOCIAL
      GOVERNANCE
   E    G    P
ENVIRONMENTAL  PROFIT
```

Also notice that there is a difference between ESG from a 'mission' and from a 'footprint' perspective. The mission of MSF can be in the social dimension, but it also has and manages its own social and environmental footprint. William Vannier, the supply chain director for MSF Belgium, comments that

> 'on the social dimension, MSF for instance has a very limited salary tension, which is the difference between the lowest and the highest salary. In Belgium the tension is a little above 3, meaning our lowest salaries are well paid and our highest salaries are lower compared to the market. We are also putting

effort into controlling our supplier base, ensuring there is no hidden form of child labour or slavery, and we are investing in becoming a real DEI (Diversity, Equity, Inclusion) and Anti-Racist Organization. On the environmental side we aim to reduce our carbon emissions by 50 per cent by 2030 compared to 2019. As MSF our mission is in the social dimension, but in the context of ESG, we also take our responsibility to manage our social and environmental footprint.'

Likewise, the mission of Greenpeace can be in the environmental dimension, but from an ESG perspective it will need to consider and manage its social and environmental footprint. In Chapters 5 and 6, I will include this type of trade-off into the heart of the strategy process of an organization. What is my mission or purpose, where do I want to make the difference, which dimension is leading, and which dimensions are following? As we have learned from John Elkington, in for-profit companies, the shareholder value and profit was for long the sole and most important objective without a lot of regard given to the social or the environmental dimension. Not only do these dimensions become more important, they become a potential source of differentiation, as we will explore in more detail in Chapters 5 and 6 using cases like Tony's Chocolonely, Patagonia, Interface or The Body Shop.

In Figure 1.21 I further analyse the 'Non-Profit Supply Chain Triangle'. As introduced, the MSF supply chain is a complex supply chain. It also means it is a costly and heavy-investment supply chain. The financing needs are the same as those of a for-profit supply chain. There are operational expenses that need to be covered (OPEX), there are investments in property, plant and equipment, think about tents, medical devices (CAPEX), and there may be swings in working capital (for instance increases in inventories of medical supplies) that need to be financed (WORKING CAPITAL). As MSF is not selling anything, the OPEX, the CAPEX and the changes in WORKING CAPITAL need to be financed from the FUNDING received. So, the objective in the non-profit Supply Chain Triangle becomes to maximize the 'service output' (e.g. availability of key materials, speed of response for new missions) within the limits of the funding (which should cover OPEX, CAPEX and changes in WORKING CAPITAL). Supply chain is challenged to optimize the output in the triangle while minimizing the inputs.

William Vannier comments that '25 per cent of the overall cost is cost of goods, with another 15 per cent cost of distribution of the goods (storage, transport and all associated costs until the place of delivery / dispensing), meaning that the supply chain easily accounts for 40–45 per cent of the operational expenditure'. He continues that:

> 97 per cent of the funding is fully private, which is a big difference with other NGOs, and MSF has built some financial reserves over the years. When we need to do a major CAPEX, we can draw upon those reserves to do so. Other NGOs may depend on institutional funds, which typically means they also need to go and ask for the funds and the CAPEX. Thanks to our private funding, MSF can fulfil its mission more autonomously.

In a for-profit supply chain, we can judge the service or service options by the margin they generate, and the capital employed needed to deliver them. Think about the expansion of the product portfolio, what is the impact on sales, on costs, so on EBIT, and what is the Capital Employed (working capital and/or fixed assets) needed to deliver that expansion. In a non-profit supply chain like the one of MSF, the service options should be judged by the contribution they bring to the objectives in the people triangle or the social triangle, in that of Greenpeace, they should be judged by the contribution they bring in the environmental triangle, in short, they should be judged by the contribution they bring to your purpose or mission.

Figure 1.21 Balancing the Non-Profit Supply Chain Triangle at MSF

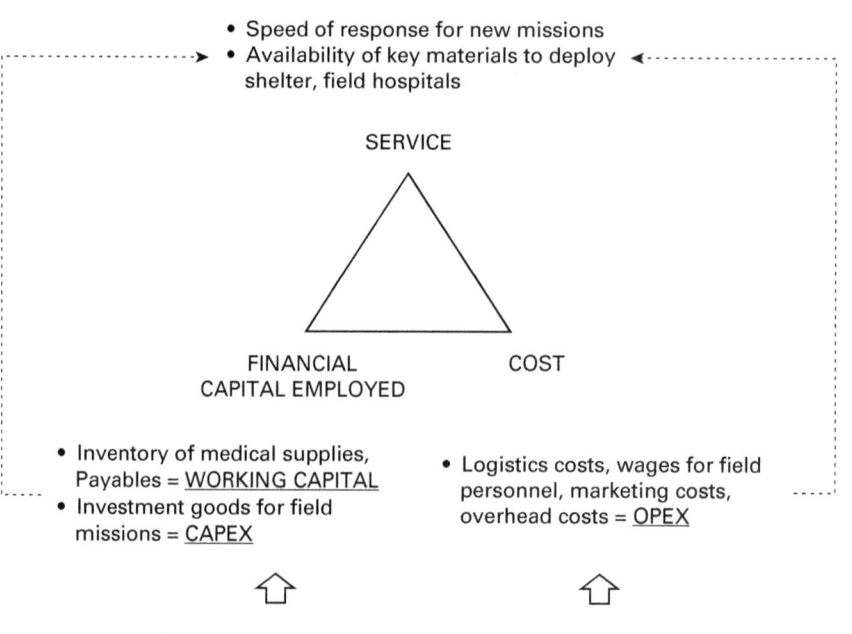

- Speed of response for new missions
- Availability of key materials to deploy shelter, field hospitals

SERVICE

FINANCIAL   COST
CAPITAL EMPLOYED

- Inventory of medical supplies, Payables = WORKING CAPITAL
- Investment goods for field missions = CAPEX

- Logistics costs, wages for field personnel, marketing costs, overhead costs = OPEX

FUNDING: 97% from individual private donors giving small amounts.

The sustainable triple triangle

The 'funding constraint' in the Non-Profit Supply Chain Triangle of Figure 1.21 seems hard, but in our experience the Free Cash Flow constraint can be equally hard in a for-profit supply chain. So, in our view, the difference is less in the cash flow aspects, they are the same, the true difference between for-profit and non-profit supply chains is in the way we measure the value of the services offered, and the way we (strategically) design the service side of the Supply Chain Triangle.

The case of MSF can also be used to illustrate the Governance aspects of the Quadruple Triangle. As shown in Figure 1.22, neutrality and impartiality are key principles for MSF, as is the ability for full and unhindered freedom in the exercise of its functions. As MSF is operating in conflict areas, having clear and strong governance principles is key. That same neutrality and impartiality requires independence in the funding, for which MSF states 97 per cent is coming from individual private donors giving small amounts.

'Our customers,' William Vannier comments, 'are the donors, not the beneficiaries in the strict sense of the term. Indeed, donors 'pay' for us to deliver a service, although they are not the direct recipient of the service. We are in a competitive environment.' As an example of that, he refers to the ICRC, the

Figure 1.22 Governance rules in the Quadruple Triangle of MSF (www.msf.org)

Médecins Sans Frontières provides assistance to populations in distress, to victims of natural or man-made disasters and to victims of armed conflict. They do so irrespective of race, religion, creed or political convictions. (www.msf.org)

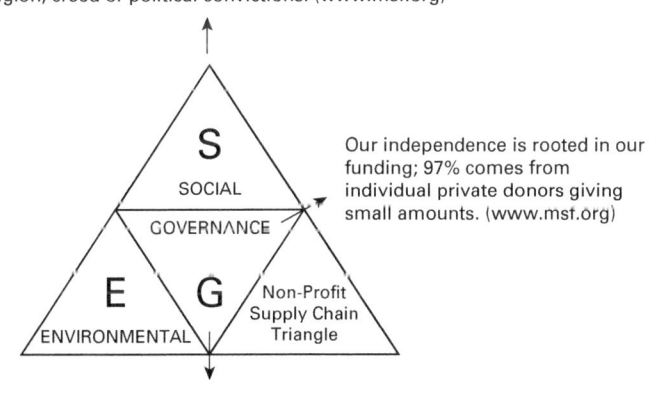

Our independence is rooted in our funding; 97% comes from individual private donors giving small amounts. (www.msf.org)

Médecins Sans Frontières observes neutrality and impartiality in the name of universal medical ethics and the right to humanitarian assistance and claims full and unhindered freedom in the exercise of its functions. (www.msf.org)

Members undertake to respect their professional code of ethics and maintain complete independence from all political, economic or religious powers. (www.msf.org)

International Committee of the Red Cross, that has announced to reduce 430 million CHF in global costs over 2023 and 2024.[21] It will impact the job of approximately 1,800 people worldwide and 26 out of their 350 locations around the world will close while others will be substantially reduced. Reasons mentioned are several end-of-year pledges in 2022 not coming through at the anticipated level, increased operating costs due to inflation and difficult global financial and economic trends making it increasingly challenging to raise unearmarked funds. William Vannier continues:

> If we have been supporting migrants in the Mediterranean, it had an impact on our donors. Some people did not like it, so we lost a lot of donors, while other people did like it, so we luckily also won a lot of donors. In our executive team, at MSF Belgium, we don't make choices in function of how it could impact our funding. We start from our mission and our governance principles, and we are confident that our private donors will keep following us based on that. With so many smaller independent donors, we are in a privileged position compared to other NGOs.

When I first thought this through, I was, and I still am, enthusiastic about how a case like MSF can be easily captured in the Quadruple Triangle. It feels like I have been able to connect two worlds, that of the for-profit and the non-profit supply chains. Connecting the two exposes the full continuum in between these two extremes. It more fully exposes the question how companies want to balance for-profit (financial) objectives with non-profit (non-financial) objectives and how we want to build a governance around that. So where the models may look complex at first, my feeling is they do capture some key dynamics that simpler models might not allow.

EXERCISE
Sustainability risk mapping

Gather your executive team, or a team of cross-functional experts. Ensure the different functions such as sales, marketing, R&D, operations, supply chain, procurement, finance, HR, IT are represented.
   Introduce the Triple Triangle shown in Figure 1.16.
   Hand out sticky notes and ask people to write down what they see as major disruptive risks. Ask them to take an extended view of the supply

chain, from the suppliers' supplier down to the customers' customer, and let them think about the broader ecosystem the company is embedded in, including governments, banks and shareholders, pressure groups.

Ask them to think through the three dimensions of the regular 'profit'-driven Supply Chain Triangle, the People and the Planet Triangle.

Corporate Governance is a lot about 'identifying and managing risks'. This exercise can be an integral part of your governance work.

EXERCISE
Sustainability materiality mapping

Another key topic in sustainability thinking is to investigate your materiality impact. As a steel or cement company, you may have a material impact on CO_2 within your Scope 1. As a supply chain consulting organization, you may have a material impact on the work-life balance of your consultants, when looking at CO_2, you may have a material impact on the CO_2 emitted by the customers you consult. When defining sustainability objectives, you first try to narrow down to those aspects where you have a material impact.

Gather your executive team, or a team of cross-functional experts. Ensure the different functions such as sales, marketing, R&D, operations, supply chain, procurement, finance, HR, IT are represented.

Introduce the Triple Triangle shown in Figure 1.16.

Hand out sticky notes and ask people to write down where they believe the company has a material impact. Ask them to take an extended view of the supply chain, from the suppliers' supplier down to the customers' customer, and let them think about the broader ecosystem the company is embedded in, including governments, banks and shareholders, pressure groups.

When looking for materiality, we may primarily be looking to relieve pressure from the People Triangle and the Planet Triangle. When doing this, we might try to understand what the options are to do so and how they could impact the Profit Triangle.

Conclusion

In this chapter I introduced two models to integrate sustainability thinking into our supply chain thinking and vice versa. A first is the Triple Triangle of people, planet and profit, in analogy to the triple bottom line. A second is the Quadruple Triangle, which links in ESG, Environmental, Social and Governance. I show how H&M uses the Supply Chain Triangle as the basis for designing, operating and controlling its supply chain. I show how a non-profit supply chain, like the one from MSF, can benefit from the concepts of the Triple and the Quadruple Triangle to better understand its supply chain design trade-offs. In the next chapter, I will explore extra models for incorporating sustainability into supply chain thinking and I will discuss the relevance of the different models introduced.

Endnotes

1. M Christopher (1992) *Logistics and Supply Chain Management. Strategies for reducing costs and improving service*, FT Prentice Hall, London
2. J Gattorna (1998) *Strategic Supply Chain Alignment: Best practice in supply chain management*, Routledge, London
3. I gave a more elaborate discussion of that in Chapter 8 of my first book, *Supply Chain Strategy and Financial Metrics*
4. B DeSmet (2018) *Supply Chain Strategy and Financial Metrics: The supply chain triangle of service, cost and cash*, Kogan Page, London
5. B DeSmet (2021) *The Strategy-Driven Supply Chain: Integrating strategy, finance and supply chain for a competitive edge*, Kogan Page, London
6. B DeSmet. Accounting Basics, 17 March 2024. www.bramdesmet.com/rethinkingsupplychain/ (archived at https://perma.cc/MJ8U-MZGR)
7. V Yee, J Glanz. How one of the world's biggest ships jammed the Suez canal, The New York Times, 17 July 2021. www.nytimes.com/2021/07/17/world/middleeast/suez-canal-stuck-ship-ever-given.html (archived at https://perma.cc/29HN-H3LQ)
8. Y Carrière-Swallow et al. How soaring shipping costs raise prices around the world, IMF blog, 28 March 2022. www.imf.org/en/Blogs/Articles/2022/03/28/how-soaring-shipping-costs-raise-prices-around-the-world (archived at https://perma.cc/B9JB-ER3C)
9. B DeSmet. FMCG Benchmark, 17 March 2024. www.bramdesmet.com/rethinkingsupplychain/ (archived at https://perma.cc/TCE7-NWYF)

10   H&M Group. Our brands and business ventures, 2023. hmgroup.com/about-us/ (archived at https://perma.cc/54YZ-TWZF)
11   J Elkington (1999) *Cannibals with Forks: The triple bottom line of 21st century business*, Capstone, Oxford
12   K Maher, J Keilmann. 3M Settles 'Forever chemicals' litigation for up to $12.5 billion, The Wall Street Journal, 22 June 2023. www.wsj.com/articles/3m-settles-forever-chemicals-litigation-for-up-to-12-5-billion-abbeba36 (archived at https://perma.cc/5YDM-WHFN)
13   ArcelorMittal. ArcelorMittal inaugurates flagship carbon capture and utilization project at its steel plant in Ghent, Belgium, 08 December 2022. corporate.arcelormittal.com/media/press-releases/arcelormittal-inaugurates-flagship-carbon-capture-and-utilisation-project-at-its-steel-plant-in-ghent-elgium (archived at https://perma.cc/F3TL-AR5M)
14   Council of the EU. Council reaches agreement on the nature restoration law, 20 June 2023. www.consilium.europa.eu/en/press/press-releases/2023/06/20/council-reaches-agreement-on-the-nature-restoration-law/ (archived at https://perma.cc/KSS9-H727)
15   E Weenk and H Rozanne (2021) *Mastering the Circular Economy: A practical approach to the circular business model transformation*, Kogan Page, London
16   J Badlam et al. The Inflation Reduction Act: Here's what's in it, McKinsey & Company Insights, 24 October 2022. www.mckinsey.com/industries/public-sector/our-insights/the-inflation-reduction-act-heres-whats-in-it (archived at https://perma.cc/LCE2-Q2S6)
17   S R Vejgaard et al. The effects of the US Inflation Reduction Act (IRA) on EU competitiveness, Copenhagen Economics Articles, March 2023. copenhageneconomics.com/publication/impact-of-the-inflation-reduction-act-on-eu-competitiveness/ (archived at https://perma.cc/2QYN-37HS)
18   World Economic Forum. Defining the 'G' in ESG: Governance Factors at the Heart of Sustainable Business, June 2022. www3.weforum.org/docs/WEF_Defining_the_G_in_ESG_2022.pdf (archived at https://perma.cc/H9EK-32SP)
19   Médecins Sans Frontières. https://www.msf.org/who-we-are (archived at https://perma.cc/TKD5-GDBW)
20   Médecins Sans Frontières. International Financial Report 2022, published 2023. www.msf.org/sites/default/files/2023-07/MSF_Financial_Report_2022.pdf (archived at https://perma.cc/9CUV-3QL2)
21   International Committee of the Red Cross. An update on ICRC's financial situation, ICRC article, 04 April 2023. www.icrc.org/en/document/update-icrc-financial-situation (archived at https://perma.cc/L9UA-NJUJ)

The sustainable supply chain 'zone': the social foundation and the environmental ceiling

02

Introduction

I start this chapter with a case on Schneider Electric, where sustainability has been integrated into the purpose and the mission of the company. It permeates the organization, the thinking and the decision-making processes.

Next, I introduce the Sustainable Supply Chain Zone, a third key model that allows integrating sustainability into supply chain thinking. It introduces the limits of a social foundation and an environmental ceiling within which we need to operate our core Supply Chain Triangle guided by the principles of 'Doughnut Economics'.

The case of Vandemoortele illustrates the concept of the social foundation and the environmental ceiling. As a European food company, Vandemoortele has defined clear sustainability objectives and is transparently reporting on its progress through its integrated report. The case of Danfoss shows how to use the '5D strategy-driven supply chain' model for defining the impact of supply chain and setting and following up key supply chain targets.

To close the chapter, I review the three key models introduced in Chapters 1 and 2: the Triple Triangle, the Quadruple Triangle and the Sustainable Supply Chain Zone and I provide guidance on when to use which model.

Case Study: Sustainability at Schneider Electric – integrating sustainability into the core, by Piao Jin, SVP Sere & Sustainability Global Supply Chain

Schneider Electric has turned itself into an impact company. In its 2022 integrated report[1], then-CEO Jean-Pascal Tricoire outlined how that year, with the combination of the climate crisis and an energy crisis, was an inflection point. The root cause of both crises is the same: an unsustainable energy model that relies heavily on carbon-dense energy sources like gas, coal and oil. Accelerating the energy transition has never made more sense. As a specialist in digitization and electrification, Schneider Electric has positioned itself to support that energy transition. Moreover, Schneider Electric has decided to do that by making a long-term positive impact across multiple dimensions on the planet and the societies around it. The logic behind it is simple: if you want to do well as a company, you must also do good and vice versa.

Piao Jin, SVP Global Supply Chain Sustainability, confirms that sustainability has been embedded into the core of the company. It starts at the top with the purpose and mission statement. The purpose of Schneider Electric is 'To empower all to make the most of our energy and resources bridging progress and sustainability for all.' Sustainability is not something separate, as it is in many companies, it is central to the company's purpose. The mission of Schneider Electric states 'Our mission is to be your digital partner for Sustainability and Efficiency'. Sustainability is therefore at the very core of the company's strategic intent, and from there it permeates every aspect of the company's operations.

The 2022 sustainability report[2] outlines six key long-term commitments and 11+1 targets from 2021 to 2025, called SSI targets (Schneider Sustainability Impact). The commitments range from Climate and Resources over Trust and Equality into Generations and Local initiatives by the global Schneider community. Schneider has also defined six long-term commitments in what it calls the Schneider Sustainability Essentials (SSE), with 25 (SSE) targets for 2021 to 2025 which Piao Jin comments need to be seen as enablers for the SSIs. Schneider reports on the SSI targets on a quarterly basis and on the SSE targets on a yearly basis.

When talking about the Supply Chain Triangle, Piao Jin commented that 10–20 years ago, the supply chain was indeed still heavily focused on the golden triangle of service, cost and cash with several KPIs including customer satisfaction, quality, productivity and cash linked to inventory control. Supply chain was judged by how well it was taking care of this triangle in the supply chain operations, supply chain strategy and supply chain transformation. Over the last 10 years, there has been an important shift to include sustainability metrics like CO_2 in the set of performance indicators, with ambitious targets like cutting the operational CO_2 by 80 per cent before the end of 2025.

Sustainability doesn't stop at the company boundaries, so Schneider has defined ambitious targets to reduce the upstream CO_2. It is doing this through the Zero Carbon Project, helping its top 1,000 suppliers that account for 70 per cent of the company's upstream carbon emissions to halve their Scope 1 and 2 emissions by the end of 2025. From this perspective, extending the traditional triangle with a sustainability dimension makes perfect sense.

When confronting her with the difficulties I see in many companies to balance the 'traditional' triangle of service, cost and cash, especially in the challenging markets circumstances of the Covid and the post-Covid world, how does she expect a company like Schneider Electric to be able to deal with that, and how can they align the struggles in the traditional triangle with the ambitious sustainability agenda and the desire to be an impact company? 'A first element, for sure, is that sustainability has been embedded in the heart of the business, in the purpose and the mission of the company,' said Piao Jin. 'Sustainability in that sense is not optional, it is a new reality. A second element is that the focus on sustainability, and any potential trade-offs with service, cost or cash, need to be embedded in the existing processes and the existing organization.' Piao Jin admits it is a transformation, and from her experience, any transformation will not be sustainable if it is not embedded in that way. As an example, she shared the business case or CAPEX approval process, where people may propose a separate process with more specific criteria and requirements. From her role, she pushes back on reinventing the wheel or bringing in new processes or tools. She turns it around and asks the question 'what do we have available and how does that need to be modified to include the sustainability perspective', like in the CAPEX approval process. She also talks about how sustainability is organized. She has a small team of experts reporting into her, on circularity or CO_2, for example, but for the execution she relies on the regional sustainability organizations, who report into the regional supply chain with a dotted line to her. She gives the example of a VP of procurement who is fully dedicated to sustainability. That person is reporting into the Chief Procurement Officer. The person is fully dedicated to sustainability, but she prefers the person to be in the procurement organization and be part of the management there. That is the only way to ensure the sustainability dimension is raised in any important management decision within the procurement domain.

As you read through the SSI and SSE targets, you feel that Schneider Electric is investing significant time, money and effort in driving the impact it is looking for. It invests in decarbonizing its operations, increasing green material content in its products, collaboration with key suppliers on decarbonization, education of people in energy management and so on. Not everything can be controlled through investments, however. So, I asked Piao Jin about one of the potential 'core conflicts' in our 'new sustainable Supply Chain Triangle', which is 'how to reduce CO_2 from transport in a globalized and over the last two years heavily disturbed supply chain'. Due to shortages, many companies have been putting goods on airfreight which they basically don't want to airfreight, neither from a cost or CO_2 perspective. How does Schneider Electric deal with that and how do they help their teams to deal with this type of setback?

She starts by confirming that the target for CO_2 efficiency in transportation has not been met yet. She also admits that this does frustrate people as they feel they have not met the expectations. 'I give people two minutes to share their frustrations but then we need to be positive and creative', she comments. 'Every crisis is an opportunity,' she continues, and 'supply chain people are used to working with conflicting priorities – that is in our DNA. If you are in supply chain, you have to be agile.'

Schneider Electric is increasing the regionalization ratio in their supply chains. Today it is organized into four big regions: China, International, Europe and North America. Take the example of North America, which includes Canada, the US and Mexico. When it is about balancing cost, lead time to customer, CO_2 reduction within that regional supply chain there is a lot of room to optimize everything. The strategy of more regional supply chains should help in driving the CO_2 efficiency in transportation, potentially not in the short term, but for sure in the mid-term.

Second, teams are asked to be creative. Despite the challenges, what can we have as a positive impact? We can continue to improve the load ratio, by improving the planning, or by improving the design of how we use the space by redesigning our packaging, or by making it lighter. She also witnesses how a crisis like Covid made the impossible happen. When the urgency is high, you see that qualification processes which before took months can now be done in weeks, for instance by doing some things in parallel. So, it will go both ways: on the one hand strategic elements like increasing the regionalization ratio in supply chain will help, but it will also come bottom-up. These may not have the short-term impact we want but they will have a mid-term impact for sure.

It is striking that the annual report and sustainability report talk about 'Digital and Electric: for a sustainable and resilient future', which brings us to the link with resilience. Piao Jin talks about the business continuity processes at Schneider Electric and how they were able to quickly adapt to the energy crisis in Europe. It was not reacting as the plans were already there, plans on how to react to a sudden energy crisis in any of the bigger countries in Europe and what were the options for instance in reducing the voltage. She continues with an example, how Schneider Electric started planning for a self-generated micro-grid, with energy generated by solar panels, storage capacity through batteries and the like. These are ways to increase the resilience of the supply chain and at the same time increase the sustainability. Sustainability in a direct way, as the energy from the solar panels may replace energy from fossil fuels, but also in times of crisis. More resilient supply chains are more sustainable, as absorbing unforeseen shocks typically not only comes at a financial expense but an environmental expense (extra CO_2) and social expense (stress on people) as well.

To conclude Piao Jin talks about how, indeed, it is a big challenge to keep all different dimensions addressed and balanced. One of the primary principles she uses to deal with this is consistency. When people get carried away by something fashionable, she lets them cool down. There is no easy or quick way to 'shine' in this matter. A lot of it is less-sexy-working-on-the-basics. People that work on those need to be encouraged, and it is important we show them the value that is being generated. Becoming more sustainable requires consistency, a positive mindset and some patience. If you can manage these, we will all shine in the end.

Doughnut economics

An alternative for the Triple Triangle or the Quadruple ESG Triangle, introduced in Chapter 1 in Figures 1.16 and 1.17, is the model of the Sustainable Supply Chain 'Zone', guided by the 'Doughnut' introduced in the book *Doughnut Economics*[3] by Kate Raworth.

In her book, Raworth talks about a 'revolution of economics', started by a 'generation of rebel students', about the need to 'bring economic theory and teaching in line with the needs of the 21st century', about students that are 'ready to chase the old goats out of power and reprogram the doomsday machine'.

Though Raworth agrees that extraordinary strides in human well-being have been made over the past 60 years, she lists that in the world, one person in nine does not have enough to eat, in 2015 six million children under the age of five died, more than half of those deaths due to easy-to-treat conditions like diarrhoea and malaria. She summarizes the unprecedented stress human activity is putting on Earth's life-giving systems, that global temperature has already risen 0.8 degrees Celsius and that we are on track for an increase of almost 4 degrees Celsius by 2100, threatening a scale and intensity of floods, droughts, storms and sea-level rise that humanity has never before witnessed. In a factual and engaging, rather than a populistic doomsday mode, she builds an argument that we cannot carry on our current way of operating our economies.

She builds up a critique that the economic thinking that is currently being practiced and taught is an outdated oversimplification, basically a caricature of reality, and that it needs to be replaced by updated and more nuanced thinking. She explains how the citizens of 2050 are being taught an economic mindset that is rooted in the textbooks of 1950, which in turn is rooted in the theories of 1850. One of the examples she gives is that of the 'rational economic man' or the 'Homo economicus', telling us that we, as humans, are self-interested, isolated, calculating, fixed in taste and dominant over nature. She describes how this 'infamous character' first appears in the works of Adam Smith, the 1759 book *Theory of Moral Sentiments* and the 1776 book *The Wealth of Nations*, and by subsequent generations and authors, like John Stuart Mill, was simplified. In the end, this understanding makes humans into a caricature of what a human being really is. Raworth does not just come with critique, what makes her work impressive is that she comes with alternative models, new economic principles and views, which as an example is the updated model of 'Social, Adaptable Humans', to replace the outdated 'Homo economicus'.

One of the other fundamentals she attacks is our 'addiction to GDP growth'. She describes how growth, falsely, has been seen as the cure to all problems, and how that blind pursuit of growth is putting our planet and our proper lives at severe danger. Her economic alternative for the blind pursuit of growth is the 'Doughnut'. The 'Doughnut' expresses that there are limitations to our economic activity and economic growth. There is a social foundation, a social minimum we should realize and respect, and there is an environmental ceiling we should stick to. In between the social foundation and the environmental ceiling, there is a safe and just space for humanity, for inclusive and sustainable economic development. Raworth defines topical areas on both the social foundation and the environmental ceiling, and provides statistics on where humanity is with regards to the limitations. It really takes a special combination of vision and guts to attack the fundaments of current economic thinking. For more information I kindly refer to her book, her personal website[4], and the website of the 'Doughnut Economics Action Lab[5]', which is 'making ideas, tools and resources freely available for change-makers to use to put the ideas of Doughnut Economics into practice'. In what follows, I will focus on the link with supply chain and the Supply Chain Triangle.

The Sustainable Supply Chain 'Zone'

When thinking through the concept of a 'social foundation' and an 'environmental ceiling' it resonated well with me. It seemed to capture the reality in the for-profit companies I work with and I talk to. We have defined a certain ceiling on our CO_2 emissions, and we have defined ambitions on how to bring the ceiling down within the safe and just space (which for many companies is net zero emissions). We have defined certain foundations in ethical labour practices for ourselves and our suppliers, so when we select suppliers and build our supply chains, we expect that as a minimum from suppliers to be able to do business. That minimum, or our social foundation, is non-negotiable.

It brought me to formulate the Sustainable Supply Chain 'Zone' model illustrated in Figure 2.1. We need to operate our supply chain, balance the Supply Chain Triangle or optimize the Profit Triangle, within the limits of a Social Foundation and an Environmental Ceiling.

Notice that I have incorporated the People triangle and the Planet triangle from our Triple Triangle introduced in Figure 1.16. Also notice that I have turned the triangles over 90 degrees so that the Gain versus Cost are now more on a vertical continuum. In the Supply Chain Triangle it is quite logical to put service on top and cost and cash as supporting. That's how companies operate in practice. That is probably different for the People and the Planet triangle, there the gain and costs are more plusses or minuses on the same continuum.

We're happy with the fact that the Supply Chain Triangle is put centrally. In practice, I see that 'sustainability follows resilience'. If we have delivery

Figure 2.1 The Sustainable Supply Chain 'Zone'

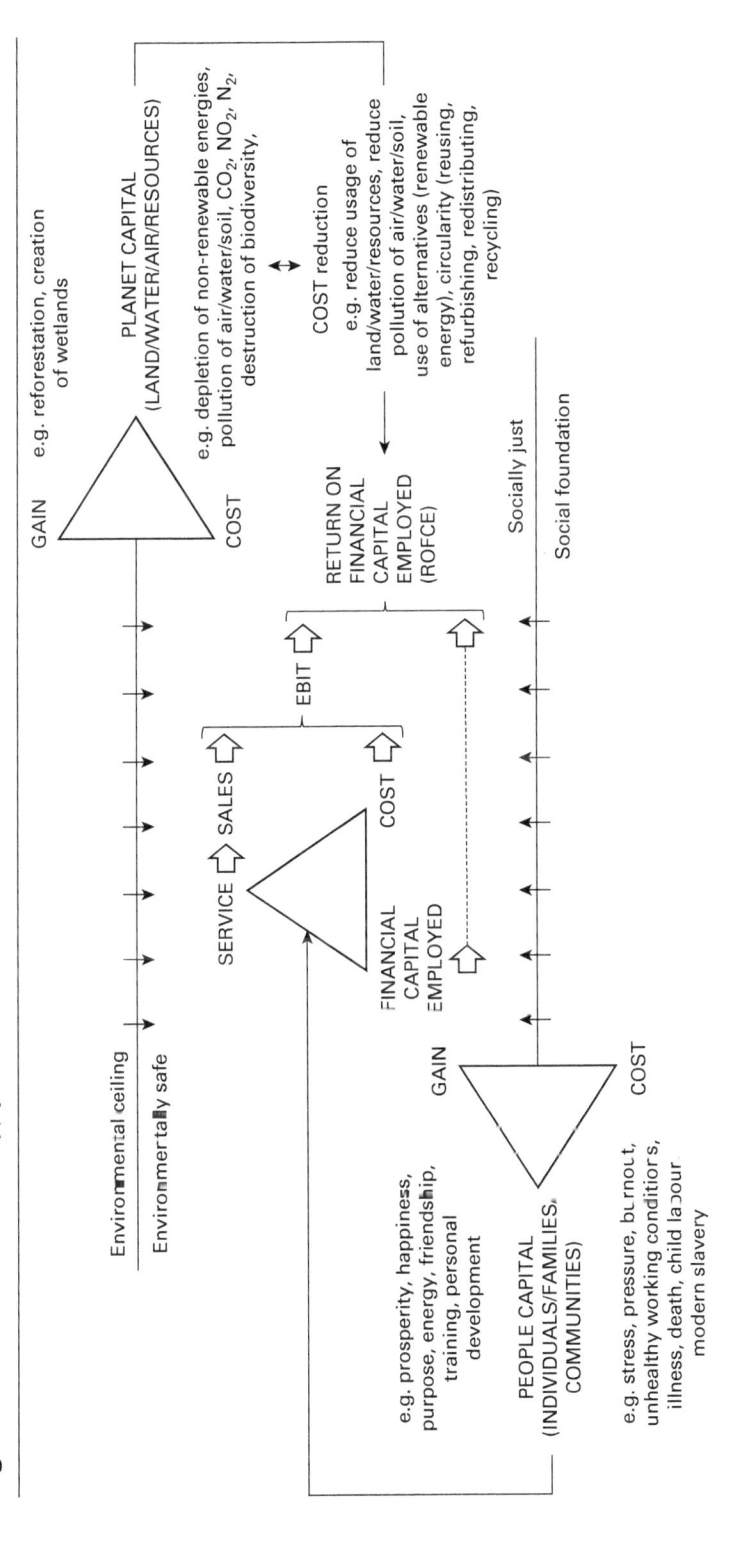

problems, like we had during the Covid pandemic, we will put goods on airfreight just to get them delivered. We're currently not delaying orders because we want to use a more environmentally friendly alternative. It means that in many organizations the traditional Supply Chain or Profit Triangle remains the central objective. That is nicely expressed in the Sustainable Supply Chain 'Zone'.

In Figure 2.2, I show some common metrics to be found on the social foundation and the ecological ceiling. I took them from workshops I did with executive teams and polls I did during conferences. Figure 2.2 also indicates that regulatory frameworks, such as CSRD, which is an evolution from the NFRD, will increasingly structure what we are expected to report upon as a company. We give a brief introduction on what the Corporate Sustainable Reporting Directive (CSRD) and the Non-Financial Reporting Directive (NFRD) are in the outline below. I will not go in more detail but rather focus on how to integrate them in a broader supply chain design and control model like the Sustainable Supply Chain 'Zone' shown in Figure 2.2.

CSRD – Corporate Sustainability Reporting Directive

On 5 January 2023, the European Union's Corporate Sustainability Reporting Directive (CSRD) came into force[6]. The CSRD modernizes and strengthens the rules concerning the social and environmental information that companies have to report. A broader set of large companies, as well as listed SMEs, will now be required to report on sustainability – approximately 50,000 companies in total across the EU.

The new rules will ensure that investors and other stakeholders have access to the information they need to assess investment risks arising from climate change and other sustainability issues. They will also create a culture of transparency about the impact of companies on people and the environment. Finally, reporting costs will be reduced from companies over the medium to longer term by harmonizing the information to be provided. The first companies will have to apply the new rules for the first time in the 2024 financial year, for reports published in 2025.

The rules introduced by the Non-Financial Reporting Directive (NFRD) remain in force until companies have to apply the new rules of the CSRD. The NFRD[7] was only applicable to approximately 11,600 companies with more than 500 employees and has been required since fiscal year 2018. The companies that started to report on non-financial information since the fiscal year of 2018 were allowed to choose between several reporting frameworks including: Global Reporting Initiative (GRI), Sustainability Accounting Standards Board (SASB), Climate Disclosure Standards Board (CDSB), Carbon Disclosure Project (CDP), Integrated Reporting (IR). CSRD streamlines the reporting requirements and options.

EXERCISE
Understanding your social foundation and ecological ceiling

Gather your executive team, or a team of cross-functional experts. Ensure different functions such as sales, marketing, R&D, operations, supply chain, procurement, finance, HR, IT are represented.

Give an introduction to the Sustainable Supply Chain 'Zone' shown in Figure 2.1.

Hand out sticky notes and ask people to write down what they see as key metrics on the social foundation and the ecological ceiling. As in the materiality exercise from Chapter 1, ask them to take an extended view of the supply chain, from the suppliers' supplier down to the customers' customer, and let them think about the broader ecosystem the company is embedded in, including governments, banks and shareholders, pressure groups. This can also be a follow-up exercise on the materiality exercise.

Ask people to think through how the social foundation and environmental ceiling interact with the core Supply Chain Triangle. How do we prioritize in case of conflicts? How do we balance the trade-offs in our budgeting process? Are we aware of the interactions? Are we revealing the trade-offs?

Case Study: Vandemoortele – Shaping a tasty future sustainably, by Roeland Rombaut, Operations & SC Director Plant and Jeroen Verstraeten, Supply Chain Manager, Plant Based Food Solutions

Vandemoortele was founded in 1899 as a Belgian family business, and has continued to grow and develop ever since. Over the last two decades, it became a European food company with leading positions in two business

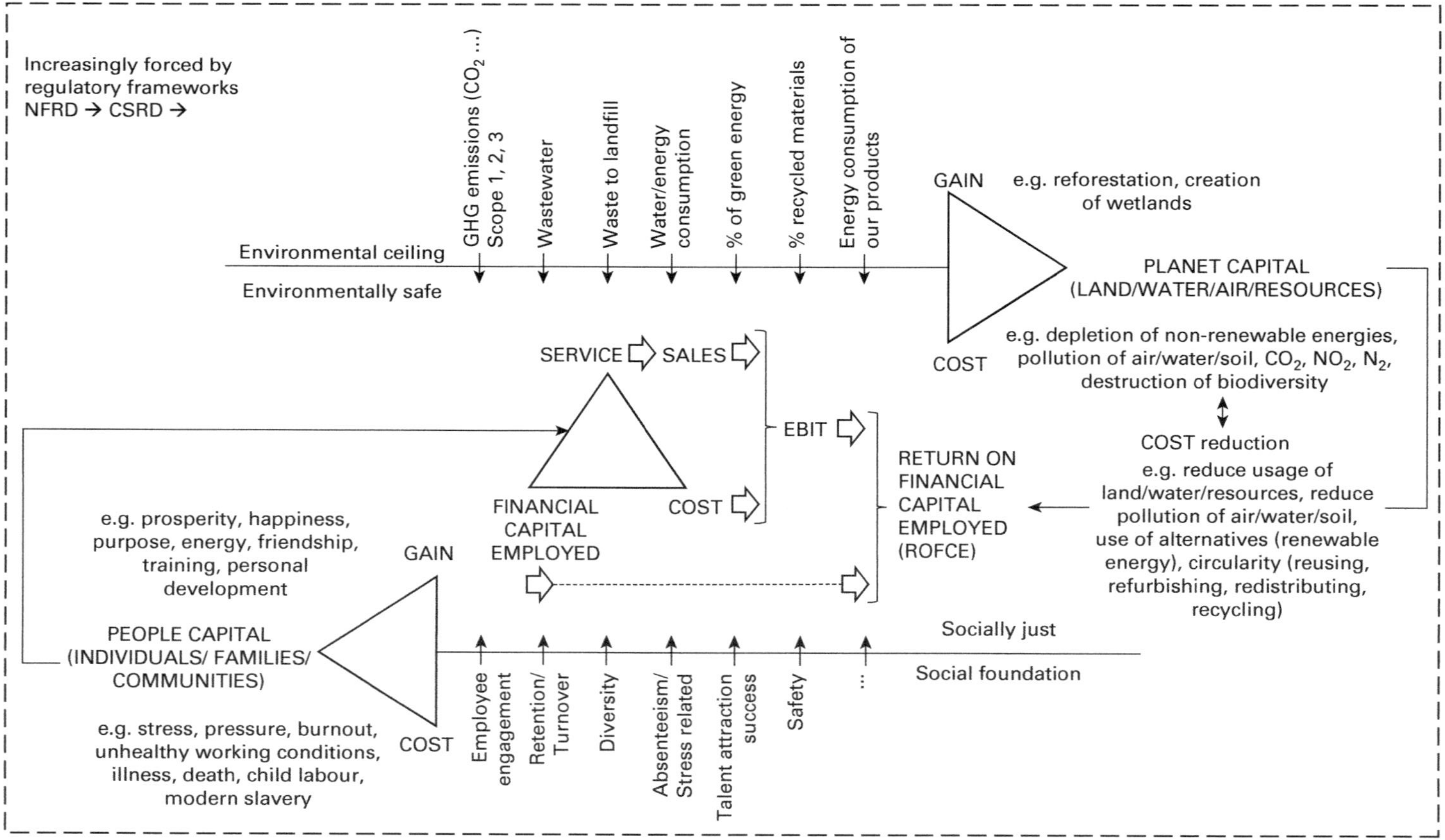

Figure 2.2 The Sustainable Supply Chain 'Zone': Example metrics and regulatory frameworks

lines: Bakery Products (BP) and Margarines, Culinary Oils and Fats (MCOF), the latter rebranded in September 2023 as 'Plant-Based Food Solutions' (PBFS)[8]. Vandemoortele is one of the European market leaders in its two business lines and is known for supplying innovative and high-quality products.

Bakery Products (BP) targets professional chefs and bakers with the Vandemoortele frozen bakery portfolio. The products are further crafted, baked or simply defrosted by these chefs and bakers, and sold to consumers as fresh bakery goods and snacks. They also supply their bakery products to retail customers. The Plant-Based Food Solutions (PBFS) targets industrial food producers who use margarines, culinary oils and fats. It also develops and manufactures private labels for retailers across Europe. Vandemoortele owns retail brands across Benelux and Germany, as well as dedicated professional brands for the food service and artisan bakery channels.

Let's analyse some of the financial and non-financial performance metrics for Vandemoortele NV. Everything I show and discuss is taken from the publicly available 2022 integrated report[9]. I start with some financial numbers in Table 2.1.

With an EBIT of 3.5 per cent and 5.6 per cent in 2021 and 2022 the margin seems low for a company that is supplying innovative and high-quality food products. As you can read from the food benchmark available on the website[10] of my book *The Strategy-Driven Supply Chain*, the EBIT or operating income from food companies like Danone, Mondelez or Nestlé is consistently above 10 per cent. Also in other sectors, I see that branders and product leaders typically report EBIT margins above 10 per cent. If we analyse the working capital, we see it is close to zero or even negative. The benchmarks on my website show this is common for the sector. The Net PPE turns (property, plant and equipment) are 3–4, which is also common in the sector. However, the fixed asset turns are 2–3, which is way above the sector average. It means that other food companies like Danone, Mondelez or Nestlé have a lot more intangibles on the balance sheet from historical acquisitions. Thanks to the relatively clean balance sheet, Vandemoortele is reaching a respectable ROCE of 15 per cent in 2022. However, if the company claims to be an innovator and premium quality player, its EBIT margin seems below par. Improving the EBIT would further boost the ROCE far above par in the industry.

Table 2.1 Key financials of Vandemoortele NV, as taken from the integrated report of 2022

Vandemoortele	2022	2021
Revenue	1,739	1,330
EBITDA	163	111
EBIT	98	46
EBIT%	5.64%	3.46%
Current assets	536	441
Current liabilities	506	476
Working capital	30	−35
Property, plant & equipment	372	398
PPE turns	4.7	3.3
Fixed assets	618	647
Fixed asset turns	2.81	2.06
Capital employed	648	612
ROCE	15.12%	7.52%

The Integrated Report of Vandemoortele also extensively reports on their non-financial, social and environmental impact. Through the type of products it produces and sells, it has an important impact on people's health. Through the type of ingredients it sources it has an important impact on farmers' lives, the resources used to grow the ingredients (water for instance) and the CO_2 emitted in growing or transporting them. Vandemoortele takes that responsibility seriously and won an award for its first integrated report over 2021, in the category of large companies, from the Belgian institute of company auditors[11]. One of the elements that struck me was that Vandemoortele has 12 pages reporting on their financial performance, versus 87 pages on their sustainability performance! This may be linked to the fact it doesn't have a public listing, but it may also reflect how it is trying to engage with its stakeholders, including the financial stakeholders that for instance buy the bonds that Vandemoortele as a private company is issuing.

In its 2022 integrated report, Vandemoortele structures its sustainability agenda under three pillars, with each pillar driven by four topical agendas:

- Balanced nutrition, with focus on:
  - improving the nutrition profile of their products;
  - offering clean label products (removing additives);
  - offering plant-based alternatives;
  - being a leader in food safety.
- Protecting nature, with focus on:
  - sourcing responsibly;
  - towards net zero carbon emissions;
  - minimizing food waste;
  - contributing to circular packaging.
- Enhancing lives, with focus on:
  - offering an engaging professional journey;
  - providing a diverse and inclusive workplace;
  - ensuring safety and fostering well-being;
  - working together to create a positive social impact.

The pillars were chosen after a study of the materiality of the Vandemoortele impact. What is impressive is that Vandemoortele, for each of the 12 topics above, has defined metrics and targets for 2025, and is reporting on the progress it is making. I have named the metrics and listed the 2025 targets:

- Balanced nutrition, with focus on:
  - Improving the nutrition profile of their products
    - A1: −15% salt reduction in bakery products compared to 2019 (volume %)
    - A2: −10% sugar reduction in pastry, sweet treats and patisserie compared to 2019 (volume %)
    - A3: +10% increase in bread products with health or nutrition claims compared to 2019 (number %)
    - A4: +7% increase in products with claim high in UFA + other claim in spreading and cooking compared to 2019 (number %)
    - A5: +7% shift to an improved Nutri-Score in spreading and cooking compared to 2019 (number %)

- Offering clean label products (removing additives)
  - B1. 80% clean label for bakery products in 2025
- Offering plant-based alternatives
  - Vandemoortele reports that their goal is 'to achieve a good balance in their assortment, so that we can offer tasty solutions to everybody's liking' and that they 'do not aim for a 100% plant-based product assortment'. They however report on the following metrics.
  - C1. % of MCOF products plant-based
  - C2. volume of MCOF products plant-based
  - C3. % of bakery products plant-based
  - C4. volume of bakery products plant-based
- Being a leader in food safety
  - D1. 100% unannounced GSFI (Global Food Safety Initiative[12]) certification of our production sites
  - D2. 98% compliance with GFSI principles of suppliers, traders and logistic partners
  - D3. −63% reduction of food safety complaints compared to 2016
  - D4. 0 incidents of food defence and food fraud

- Protecting nature, with focus on:
  - Sourcing responsibly
    - E1. 100% physically sustainable certified palm
    - E2. 100% palm traceable to mill
    - E3. 75% palm traceable to plantation (supplier score)
    - E4. 100% key palm oil suppliers have an NDPE (No Deforestation, No Peat and No Exploitation[13]) policy
    - E5. 100% verified palm grievances have an action plan
    - E6. 100% RTRS-certified (Round Table on Responsible Soy[14]) soy - consumer and professional brands
    - E7. 100% RTRS-certified soy – all products
    - E8. 100% physically sustainable certified cocoa (consumer and professional brands)
    - E9. 100% barn eggs

- Towards net zero carbon emissions
  - F1. 100% green electricity
  - F2. 15% 'on site' green electricity generation
  - F3. −70% CO_2-intensity reduction in production compared to 2015
  - F4. −15% CO_2-intensity reduction in transport and mobility compared to 2020
  - F5. −10% reduction in energy intensity compared to 2020 – group
  - F6. −10% reduction in energy intensity compared to 2020 – bakery
  - F7. −10% reduction in energy intensity compared to 2020 – MCOF
- Minimizing food waste
  - G1. −30% reduction of scrap in bakery products compared to 2020
  - G2. −10% reduction of scrap in MCOF compared to 2020
- Contributing to circular packaging
  - H1. 25% r-PET in our packaging
  - H2. 100% recyclable, reusable or compostable packaging
  - H3. 100% sustainable certified FSC (Forest Stewardship Council[15])/PEFC (Programme for the Endorsement of Forest Certification[16]) paper and cardboard
  - H4. −5% reduction water usage (excluding water ingredient) vs 2020
- Enhancing lives, with focus on:
  - Offering an engaging professional journey
    - I1. 63 points on the AES (Associate Engagement Survey) on Training and Development
    - I2. 78 points on the AES on Sustainable Engagement
    - I3. 82 points on the AES on Sustainability
    - I4. 40 hours on average training, for each associate category
    - I5. 95% associates that followed at least one training
    - I6. 95% associates who adhere to P&DMP (Performance & Development Management Process)
  - Providing a diverse and inclusive workplace
    - J1. 40% representation of women in senior leadership (B+ level)
    - J2. Equal average training hours per associate per gender category

- J3. Equal % of associated per gender category that followed a minimum of one training
    - J4. Equal % of associates per gender category who adhere to P&DMP
    - J5. 70% female successors in C+ jobs with a successor
    - J6. 83 points on the AES on inclusive workplace
    - J7. Zero pay gap
  ○ Ensuring safety and fostering well-being
    - K1. Zero accidents leading to permanent disability
    - K2. 15 frequency rate of lost workday cases
    - K3. 0.5 severity rate of lost workday cases
    - K4. 76 points on the AES on well-being
  ○ Working together to create a positive social impact
    - L1. 100% of direct key suppliers accepted/signed our supplier code of conduct
    - L2. 100% critical suppliers verified according to our sustainability criteria - palm
    - L3. 100% of key commodities are participating in a project on the ground

Figures 2.3 and 2.4 show the actual performance in 2022 versus the 2025 targets. I have split them in those metrics that are part of the environmental ceiling versus those that are part of the social foundation. Both are repeated as such in Figure 2.5. It is striking that there are many more metrics on the social foundation versus the environmental ceiling. You can also see that not all metrics move in the right direction, for example food waste. Vandemoortele reports that for bakery products, as a result of the energy crisis, consumers started buying more consciously, which had an impact on demand. In addition, there was a significant setback when the freezer warehouse in Eeklo (Belgium) collapsed and they had to destroy more than 3,000 pallets with spoiled, defrosted food, leading to a food waste increase of 10.9 per cent compared to 2020. For the PBFS division they report a production issue at their manufacturing site in Zeewolde, which caused a fair amount of food loss. Next to that, they report that the forecasting efficiency in PBFS was sometimes affected by last-minute orders, which resulted in planning changes and extra production line changeovers. Smaller production volumes (a result of the aftermath of Covid) and more complex customer demands

Figure 2.3   The environmental ceiling at Vandemoortele

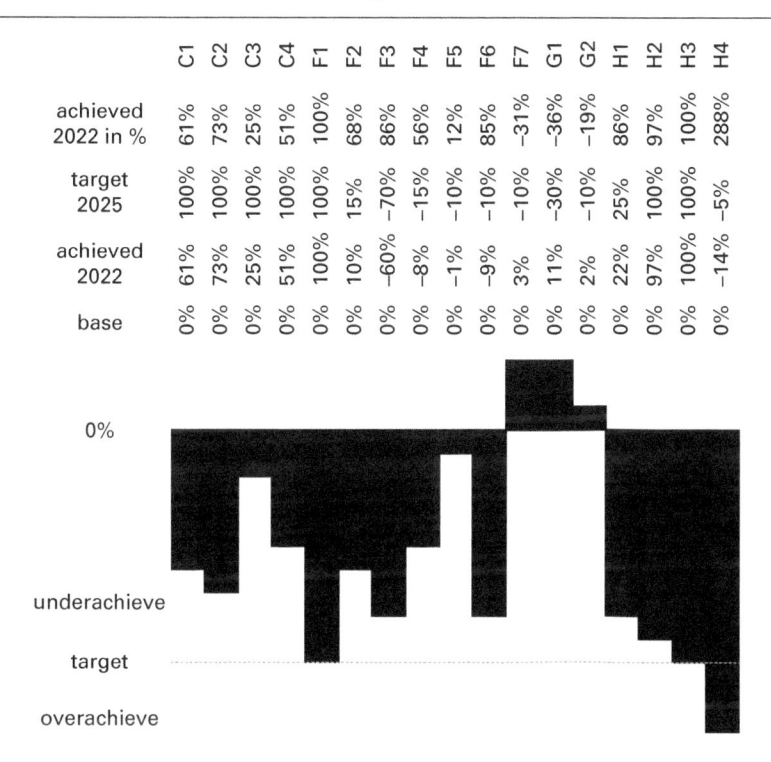

	C1	C2	C3	C4	F1	F2	F3	F4	F5	F6	F7	G1	G2	H1	H2	H3	H4
achieved 2022 in %	61%	73%	25%	51%	100%	68%	86%	56%	12%	85%	−31%	−36%	−19%	86%	97%	100%	288%
target 2025	100%	100%	100%	100%	100%	15%	−70%	−15%	−10%	−10%	−10%	−30%	−10%	25%	100%	100%	−5%
achieved 2022	61%	73%	25%	51%	100%	10%	−60%	−8%	−1%	−9%	3%	11%	2%	22%	97%	100%	−14%
base	0%	0%	0%	0%	0%	0%	0%	0%	0%	0%	0%	0%	0%	0%	0%	0%	0%

0%

underachieve

target

overachieve

led to a larger number of changeovers, making it harder to further decrease the food losses. These are examples where the metrics in the base Supply Chain Triangle are affecting metrics on the environmental ceiling.

Extra examples on how the environmental ceiling and the social foundation interact with the financial triangle are, for instance, that reducing salt and sugar affects the taste of the products and may conflict with the 'product quality' in the service dimension of the triangle. As Vandemoortele reports to differentiate on high quality products that is obviously an important conflict. They report to change ingredients at a gradual pace so consumers can get used to the new taste when changing recipes. Another example is the reduction of CO_2 in transport. They report that a breakthrough may come from hydrogen trucks but that in the short term it will be difficult to achieve CO_2 reductions through hydrogen and electrified transport due to current technological limitations. More can only be deployed once electrified and hydrogen transport vehicles are available on the market and once the ecosystem including charging stations has matured sufficiently. In the meantime they continue working on other strategies such as optimizing routes

Figure 2.4 The social foundation at Vandemoortele (to be rotated left)

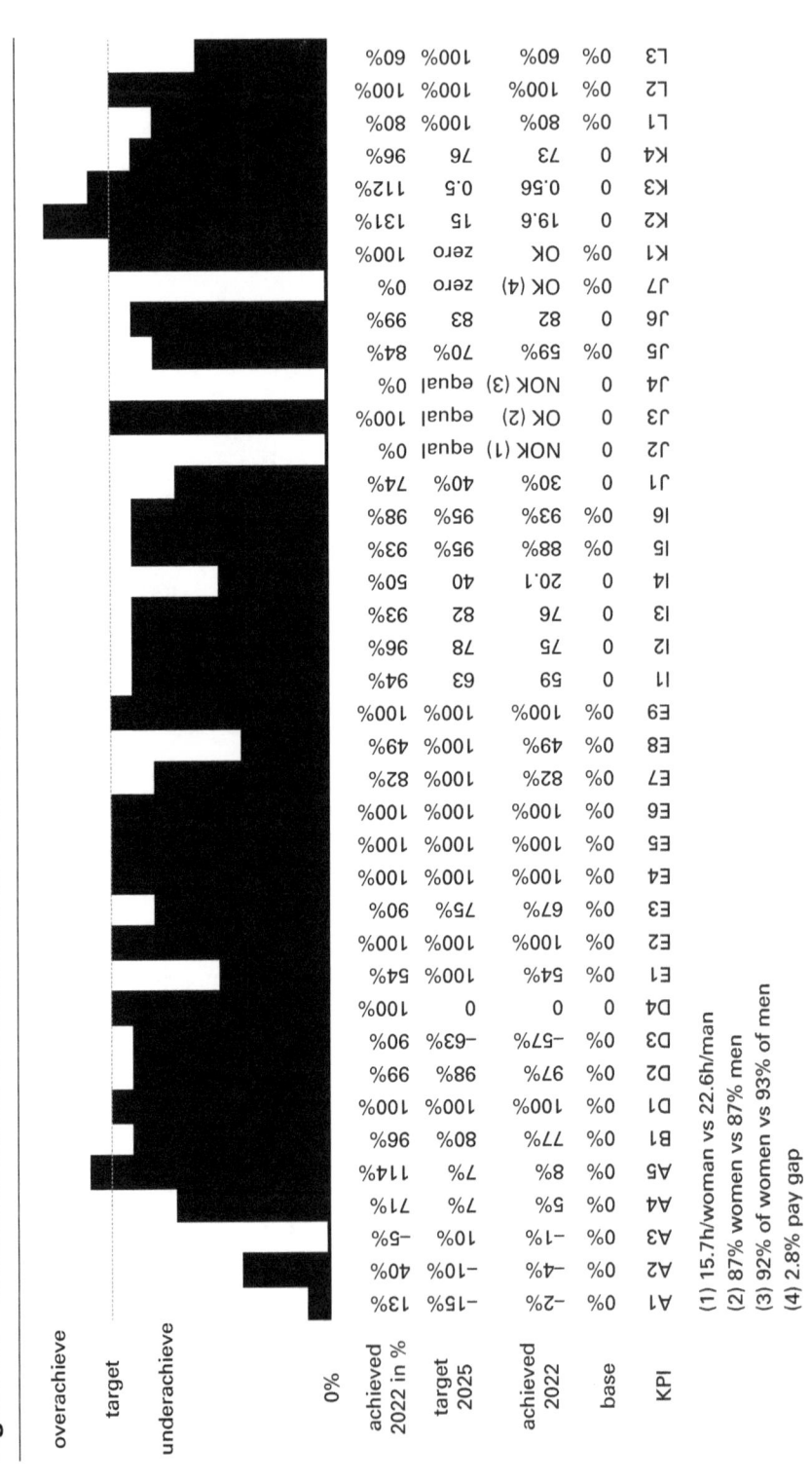

KPI	base	achieved 2022	target 2025	achieved 2022 in %
A1	0%	-2%	-15%	13%
A2	0%	-4%	-10%	40%
A3	0%	-1%	10%	-5%
A4	0%	5%	7%	71%
A5	0%	8%	7%	114%
B1	0%	77%	80%	96%
D1	0%	100%	100%	100%
D2	0%	97%	98%	99%
D3	0%	-57%	-63%	90%
D4	0	0	0	100%
E1	0%	54%	100%	54%
E2	0%	100%	100%	100%
E3	0%	67%	75%	90%
E4	0%	100%	100%	100%
E5	0%	100%	100%	100%
E6	0%	100%	100%	100%
E7	0%	82%	100%	82%
E8	0%	49%	100%	49%
E9	0%	100%	100%	100%
I1	0	59	63	94%
I2	0	75	78	96%
I3	0	76	82	93%
I4	0	20.1	40	50%
I5	0%	88%	95%	93%
I6	0%	93%	95%	98%
J1	0	30%	40%	74%
J2	0	NOK (1)	equal	0%
J3	0	OK (2)	equal	100%
J4	0	NOK (3)	equal	0%
J5	0%	59%	70%	84%
J6	0	82	83	99%
J7	0%	OK (4)	zero	0%
K1	0%	OK	zero	100%
K2	0	19.6	15	131%
K3	0	0.56	0.5	112%
K4	0	73	76	96%
L1	0%	80%	100%	80%
L2	0%	100%	100%	100%
L3	0%	60%	100%	60%

(1) 15.7h/woman vs 22.6h/man
(2) 87% women vs 87% men
(3) 92% of women vs 93% of men
(4) 2.8% pay gap

overachieve / target / underachieve / 0%

and multi-modal transport, but they report that will only lead to slight reductions in their transport emissions. Some of the defined priorities are driven by government regulations. As an example, by 2030, the EU aims for European companies to use at least 30 per cent recycled PET or so-called r-PET in their packaging. In anticipation of that target, Vandemoortele is moving in that direction. H1 specifies a 25 per cent r-PET target by 2025. The 'combined' result of the financial triangle, embedded within the social foundation and the ecological ceiling, is shown in Figure 2.5.

When talking to Roeland Rombaut and Jeroen Verstraeten on how they experience the challenges in the Supply Chain Triangle and how it interacts with the social foundation and ecological ceiling, they comment that

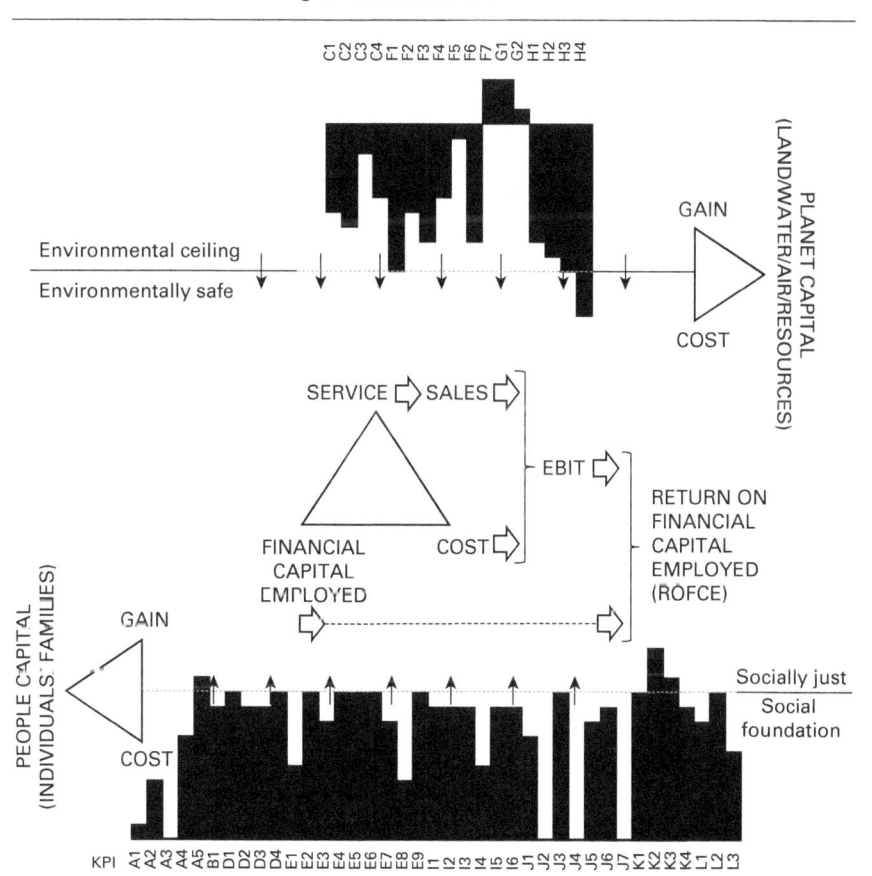

Figure 2.5 The Supply Chain Triangle within its social foundation and environmental ceiling at Vandemoortele

'they experienced the biggest volatility during the Covid pandemic and the start of the war in Ukraine. A lot of that has gone back to normal, though we still have lead times on packaging, ingredients and capex related goods that are substantially longer than before. Also the commodity pricing of our key raw materials remains more volatile. We for instance have more harvest warnings which can be linked to the impact of climate change and which impacts our contracting periods.'

They continue that 'it requires a lot of agility within supply chain and operations to accommodate the continued volatility.'

As a big impact from the reporting side, Roeland comments that:

'so far it was about reporting numbers, but as of 2025 these numbers will be audited. Auditors will not question your targets, but they will validate the data integrity. Take for instance numbers of food loss… different systems may have a slightly different interpretation. Setting up the systems and harmonizing the data will be key. And then you have scope three emissions, you can demand your suppliers to give insights, but how auditable are those numbers?'

When asking about how conflicting the sustainability targets are, or are not, with the Supply Chain Triangle, Roeland comments that:

'for now, they are not really conflicting. If we continue to improve forecasts, food loss can be reduced, or there is a reduction in costs. When we do investments in energy efficiency, the CAPEX is still relatively easy to defend. A question is how the trade-offs will look like once these investments have all been done. By how far do you invest in more sustainable raw materials, local sourcing versus global sourcing,… in the assumption that you have an actual choice.'

Jeroen continues:

'Maybe it could go to dual pricing if you are talking to customers, you may provide product variants, which are sustainably sourced or produced, or you may offer greener transport options…'

Roeland comments that

'as a European player, we, Vandemoortele, will go more sustainable. Consumers, legislation, financing,… will require it. But what about global players? There may be some kind of arbitrage where they fill part of the market with less sustainable imports.'

The conclusion for both Roeland and Jeroen is that:

'the trend is to become more sustainable, and as all players increase their sustainability, the question, at least in a low margin sector like food retail, will be at what cost you are able to deliver it. A lot of things still have to take shape and form. Think about the legislation, or data about CO_2 which today is manually collected. All of that will gradually be automated. In that sense, we, as Vandemoortele, should be proud and happy we have a board that takes a leading role in the sustainability agenda. It puts the questions and trade-offs on our table at a moment we can still consider and explore the options. It will make us better prepared for a more sustainable future.'

The supply chain diamond, square, pyramid? Costing for externalities?

As I mentioned at the start of this chapter, ever since I first presented the base Supply Chain Triangle, people have been asking me how to incorporate sustainability, and they have been proposing alternatives, like the ones shown in Figure 2.6. Many like to show it as a diamond or a square, to indicate sustainability as a fourth dimension. The square, as opposed to the diamond, allows us to put service and sustainability on top. In the square we might picture that we occur costs and commit capital not just for service or profit related metrics and objectives but for sustainability related metrics as well. Or as shown in the bottom of Figure 2.6, we could show it as a pyramid, to protect the original service-cost-cash triangle and add sustainability as a truly separate dimension.

While each of the models shown in Figure 2.6 helps in clarifying that sustainability is something different, I have not retained them as the 'base' models for two reasons. A first is that I didn't want to touch upon the base triangle and its link to financial metrics. That base triangle has proven very valuable to capture and structure the base struggles in supply chains. It didn't feel right to just throw that away. The models I have introduced so far, the Triple Triangle of Figure 1.16, the Quadruple ESG Triangle of Figure 1.17 and the Sustainable Supply Chain 'Zone' of Figure 2.1, all leave the base triangle intact. A second reason is that I want to be able to bring sufficient nuance in the debate. As far as I understand the environmental and the social dimension are two essential but at the same time very different dimensions of sustainability. The social dimension, for example, seems to be much harder to quantify and capture in metrics. The models I have presented allow bringing that nuance.

Instead of creating an 'extra dimension', another common approach is trying to monetize all parameters and squeeze everything into a single financial profit or return metric. This is linked to the observation that so-called 'externalities' are not showing up on the company P&L, so if we can put a cost on a ton of CO_2, we can account for the CO_2 emissions in the P&L. Though I understand it is tempting and it would allow for

Figure 2.6 The Supply Chain diamond, square or pyramid

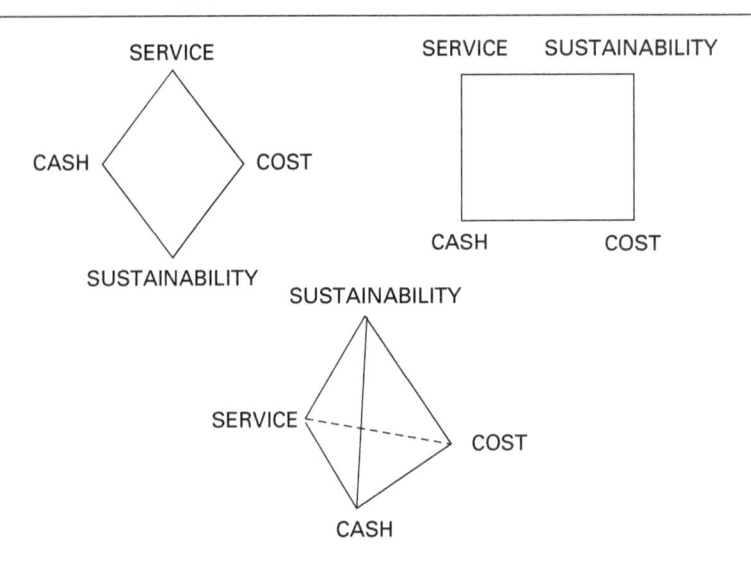

easy comparison of alternative scenarios or even companies, this 'costing of externalities' approach never felt right to me. On the one hand because some things will be hard to monetize, on the other hand because it feels like we have difficulties to let go of the financial dimension as the single decision criterion. It felt and still feels as a too narrow-minded solution potentially locking us into a too narrow system. When I was attending a keynote speech from Robert Kaplan on 'e-liability accounting'[17] he also strongly voiced against it. He compared it to attempts in the 1980s to valorise human capital as an asset on the balance sheet. We discussed it for 20 years but could never agree on an appropriate way to do so. That Robert Kaplan as an accounting and broader management guru didn't support this as the way to go strengthened my personal belief to stay out of this approach.

On Scope 1, 2, 3 and e-liability accounting

When reporting on CO_2 or Green House Gas (GHG) emissions in general, the regulatory standards refer to Scope 1, 2 and 3 emissions. Scope 1 is what we directly emit, Scope 2 are the emissions from the energy we buy, and Scope 3 is what is emitted by suppliers and customers.

In his recent research from 2021 and 2022, Robert Kaplan[18, 19, 20] attacks the Scope 1-2-3 as a flawed system. Two major critiques are that it is hard or impossible to estimate Scope 3 emissions. As you may not exactly know the GHG emissions of all your suppliers, you are allowed to use and report based on industry averages. According to Kaplan, that leaves the reporting vulnerable to greenwashing. You can imagine companies selling a highly polluting activity and then buying the resulting products while reporting them at an industry average instead of the actual numbers. Kaplan also questions the relevance of Scope 2 versus Scope 3, stating that the only reason we separated Scope 2 from Scope 3 was that Scope 2 was relatively easy to measure, not really a structural fix to the problem. I sympathize with his argument and I also sympathize with what he proposes as an alternative.

Kaplan makes clear that the only CO_2 we really emit is Scope 1. So what we need is an accounting system for e-liabilities like CO_2, in a comparable way we have built accounting systems for financial costs. He gives the example on how through these cost accounting systems, companies like Airbus and Boeing, where millions of parts go into a finished product, are able to track the total cost of the assembled product. If in a comparable way, when we buy components or raw materials from suppliers, we'd not only account for the cost, but also for the embedded CO_2, and when next, in our BOMs and routings we'd define how much CO_2 we add, just like we add financial costs. Then we'd be able to roll up the total CO_2 in a finished product and pass that information to the customer when our products are sold. If everybody did proper accounting of its Scope 1 emissions and passed on that information, then the whole Scope 2 or 3 problem would be gone. A structural fix to a structural problem.

Case Study: Danfoss – driving sustainable value through a 5D Strategy-Driven Supply Chain, by Frank Vorrath, VP Supply Chain Services, Danfoss Climate Solutions

Danfoss is a global multinational with revenues exceeding €10 billion, employing more than 40,000 people. Its operations span across more than 100 countries and around 100 factories in over 20 countries. In its DNA, it is an engineering company, an innovator, a true product leader, as witnessed by its customer promise[21] to 'deliver value through leading application know how, sustainable innovation and by taking leading positions in its markets'. The key focus has become to 'decarbonize the world', as illustrated by the company purpose, which states 'decarbonizing with our customers and long-term value creation'. The 2022 annual report explains 'the company is foundation- and family-owned, with focus on the longer view, courage, and sustainability. It targets over-proportional growth through investment-driven value creation. The profitable growth and strong free cash flow, allow it to invest significantly in the future.' And it talks about continued bold investments in the 'green growth strategy'. One could state that Danfoss is a product leader that is unleashing all its expertise and competences on solutions for driving the green transition, through energy efficiency, machine productivity, lower emissions and electrification.

Danfoss currently has three business segments: Danfoss Power Solutions, Danfoss Climate Solutions and Danfoss Power Electronics and Drives. Frank Vorrath is Vice President of Supply Chain Services at Danfoss Climate Solutions. Climate Solutions itself is driven by five divisions and 28 underlying product lines, ranging from compressors for refrigeration, air-conditioning, and heating, to the heating and cooling valves, which you may find in your house in your heating and cooling system.

Frank states that a first element of the supply chain strategy for Climate Solutions is to 'create more regional and more tailored value streams for customers. We have different types of customers,' he comments, 'OEMs like Daikin, Trane, Carrier or Johnson Controls, Wholesalers, and project-based businesses that go through Project Installers. Each of these have very different requirements and these may differ per region. So, one key element of our strategy is to organize more regional and more tailored supply chains meeting the specific needs of the various customer segments.' For this, Frank relies on the supply chain segmentation approach from John Gattorna which has been used successfully in other industrial companies[22]. That approach brings clarity to the organization on what are the options from a supply chain perspective and which type of supply chain to configure to which type of customer. It is all about customer and product segmentation linked to an appropriate supply chain response and configuration on a regional or country specific level.

'A second key element in our strategy,' he continues, 'is to de-risk our supply chain. This is based on the disruptions we are experiencing, of which the frequency and the magnitude of the impact has increased dramatically in the last few years. So, we need to be more resilient and responsive.' As a third and fourth element he adds the need to be 'more connected and intelligent. We need better sensing capabilities and turn that into more business intelligence driving our high-quality decision making. In today's volatile and dynamic markets, we also need to be faster, more agile, and more effective in our supply chain response which must become more tailored and configured in line with the different needs of our customers in the regions we serve them.'

'To be effective and sustainable to create long-term value through our strategic supply chain management, it is essential for us to perform and transform at the same time with speed and balance as a key strategic enabler', Frank continues. 'You need to run the day-to-day operations while building new future capabilities in parallel in the right balance combined with the right clockspeed to stay competitive in the long-term. Balancing the two and to find the right speed is a key challenge to any supply chain professional.' The methodology used to define priorities and roadmaps is the Hoshin Kanri method. It comes from the area of lean manufacturing, a philosophy and practice that aims to set focus, eliminate waste, improve quality and increase efficiency which has been used by Japanese companies like Bridgestone and Toyota. 'It helps in prioritizing and creating focus combined with the right speed of the execution for the organization,' Frank comments. 'It helps in defining key priorities and breakthrough objectives, key initiatives and key success indicators linked to breakthrough goals. By integrating the improvements in our day-to-day processes and capabilities, we gradually improve our performance level and capabilities over the years in a focused manner and on a sustainable basis.'

'To make things tangible, we use the Supply Chain Triangle and link it to service, cost and cash,' Frank continues. 'Everything we do in our supply chain strategy is linked to that and we are becoming better in our under-

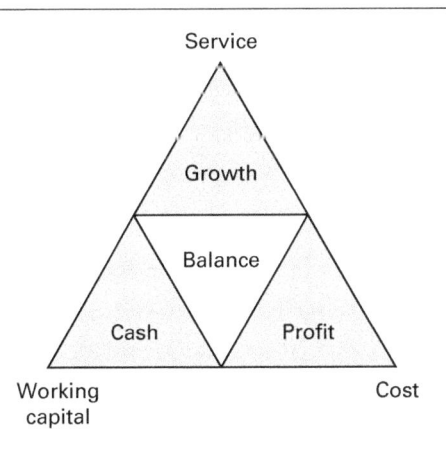

Figure 2.7 The Danfoss Supply Chain Triangle and how it supports the business objectives of profitable growth while driving a strong cash flow

standing of the required trade-off decisions to make.' Figure 2.7 shows how the triangle supports the company objectives and the company track record of delivering profitable growth while driving strong cash flows, which as introduced above, is needed to drive the 'green growth strategy'.

'To make it stick and easier to understand in the organization, our strategic program for 2023 was Save 35, Cash in 50 and Serve 90,' Frank continues. It is illustrated in Figure 2.8.

> When you go into our offices and distribution centres, you will see posters of the Save 35, Cash in 50 and Serve 90. We committed ourselves to save 35 million through cost downs, productivity improvements, and reducing direct material costs as well as freight and transportation cost. By the year end, we will exceed that target through focusing on a lot of basics and fundamentals. But don't be mistaken, there is nothing basic about getting the basics right. For the Cash in 50, we focused on things like our replenishment lead time management, better supply chain planning competencies and a better use of our existing advanced planning technology.
>
> During the Covid period and afterwards, replenishment lead time parameters were not updated at an accurate level and sufficiently within a high frequency which created a lot of challenges. If you plan and fulfil based on the wrong parameters in the system, your Supply Chain Triangle will be heavily disturbed, and customers and your business will be negatively impacted. We have been very firm together as a team on getting that basic right as a key foundational layer. We also improved our ABC/XYZ product segmentation in our system setting and questioned the added value of keeping inventory for C-items, especially CY and CZ. We also aligned our SIOP processes, competencies, and organizational structure to be more value adding to our five business divisions and product lines within Danfoss Climate Solutions.
>
> We now have more dedicated teams with higher competencies that understand the unique and specifics needs of our businesses. 2023 was a challenging year for many companies including Danfoss Climate Solutions from a sales perspective because of some of the de-stocking strategies of our customers combined with the impact of changing monetary policies slowing down investment in some regions. With more than 76,000 SKUs in our product portfolio and our sometimes very long supply chains of up to three to six months, planning and fulfilment cycles, we always run a risk of being either too high on our days on inventory on hand with a lot of excess inventory as a result or a negative impact on our service reliability towards our customers. Through our improved SIOP processes and competencies as well as by using our digital advanced planning technology, we have been better in control of this situation

Figure 2.8 The 2023 strategic objectives for the Danfoss Supply Chain

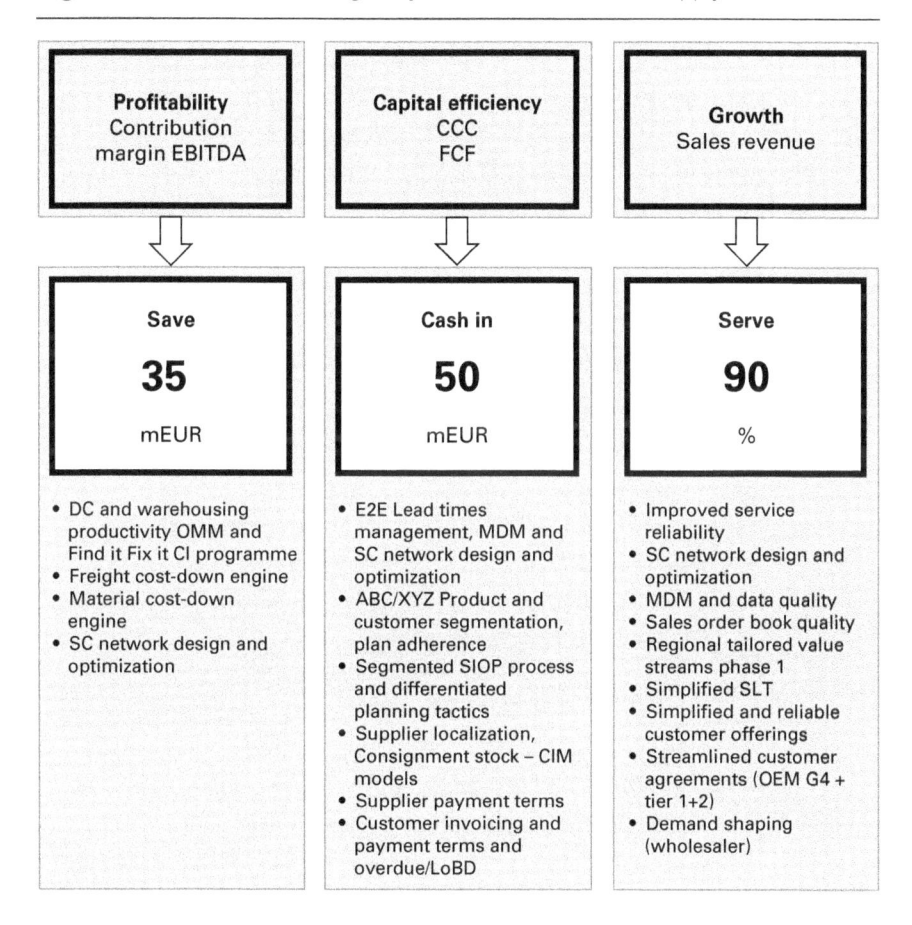

Profitability Contribution margin EBITDA	Capital efficiency CCC FCF	Growth Sales revenue
⇩	⇩	⇩
Save **35** mEUR	**Cash in** **50** mEUR	**Serve** **90** %
• DC and warehousing productivity OMM and Find it Fix it CI programme • Freight cost-down engine • Material cost-down engine • SC network design and optimization	• E2E Lead times management, MDM and SC network design and optimization • ABC/XYZ Product and customer segmentation, plan adherence • Segmented SIOP process and differentiated planning tactics • Supplier localization, Consignment stock – CIM models • Supplier payment terms • Customer invoicing and payment terms and overdue/LoBD	• Improved service reliability • SC network design and optimization • MDM and data quality • Sales order book quality • Regional tailored value streams phase 1 • Simplified SLT • Simplified and reliable customer offerings • Streamlined customer agreements (OEM G4 + tier 1+2) • Demand shaping (wholesaler)

and will be able to deliver on our promise to Cash in 50. On Serve 90, we will get close to the 90 per cent target, coming from a level of 76 per cent last year. That is a very big improvement which was again based on getting some of the basics right, like revising our concept of replenishment lead times, better order book quality, improved master data quality and higher competencies enabled by making better use of our digital technology across planning, sourcing, and fulfilment. Streamlining your service promise is a key element in reliably delivering upon it.

Frank continues that they:

> also worked a lot on people and team recognition. We created a dedicated virtual environment on Viva Engage which is our internal communication platform where people and teams can share knowledge and success stories with a broader audience. They can also nominate their teams for their contribution to our strategic objectives and the desired Danfoss behaviours. On a quarterly

basis we will celebrate teams by awarding certificates and trophies which are linked to their great accomplishments which is part of our people strategy. One of the categories in our team recognition program is getting the basics right. It is a way to make our strategic program of Save 35, Cash in 50 and Serve 90 very tangible to everyone in our global supply chain community. Another thing to bring the triangle alive is our End-to-End digital dashboard.

Our End-to-End Supply Chain Cockpit is built around our four strategic objectives of Service, Cost, Cash and ESG and allows us to track our key priorities and key initiatives, our success indicators where we are according to our targets and to drill down into the Service, Cost, Cash, and ESG aspects which brings the triangle and in future our supply chain diamond alive.

On where we move from here, Frank comments that:

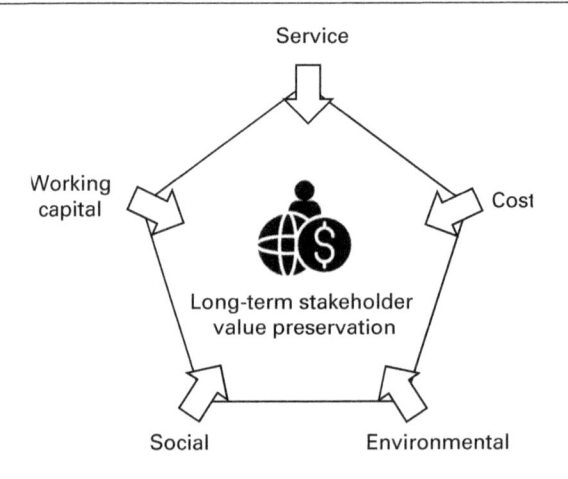

from 2024 moving forward, we will expand to a 5D strategy-driven supply chain model and will launch our 2024 strategic program, "The Power of 4 in 2024". Next to Service, Cost and Cash, we will add the environmental and the social dimension combined in our ESG efforts by transitioning from our focus on our Supply Chain Triangle into our supply chain diamond, with as the overarching goal to drive long-term stakeholder value preservation.

This is illustrated in Figure 2.9.

Frank explains:

Our targets for 2024 will most likely be to save another 35 million, which over two years may accumulate into more than 70 million, to cash in 50 million, where we will need to work even harder, and where we may need to make more strategic trade-off decisions and deliberate choices by business divisions and

Figure 2.9 The 5D strategy-driven supply chain at Danfoss Climate Solutions

Figure 2.10 The 2024 strategic objectives based on the 5D strategy-driven supply chain model

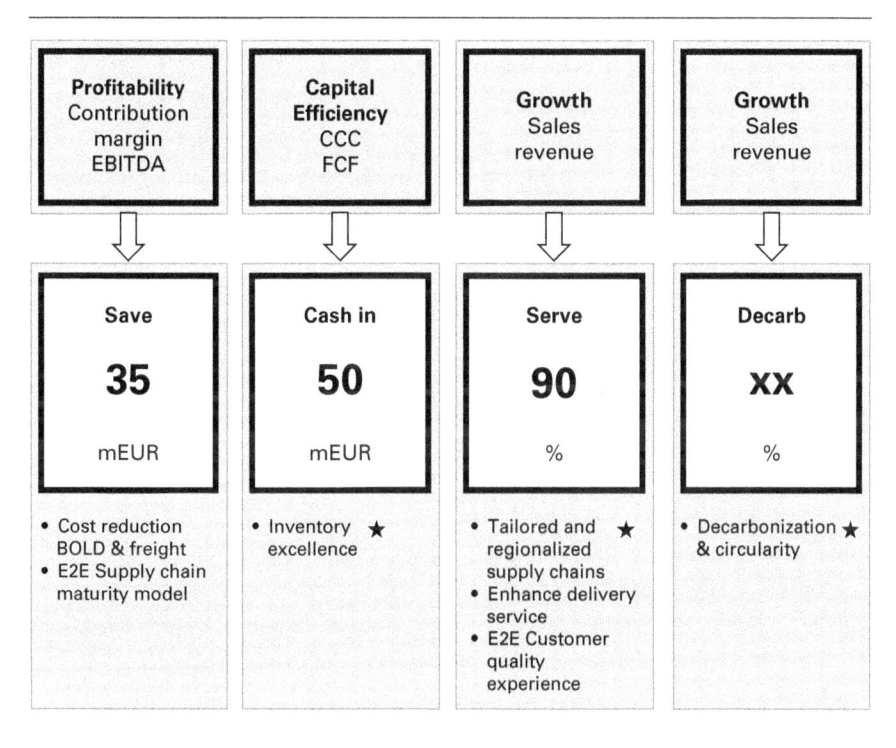

Profitability Contribution margin EBITDA	Capital Efficiency CCC FCF	Growth Sales revenue	Growth Sales revenue
⇩	⇩	⇩	⇩
Save **35** mEUR	Cash in **50** mEUR	Serve **90** %	Decarb **XX** %
• Cost reduction BOLD & freight • E2E Supply chain maturity model	• Inventory ★ excellence	• Tailored and ★ regionalized supply chains • Enhance delivery service • E2E Customer quality experience	• Decarbonization ★ & circularity

product lines linked to their strategic value proposition, and to serve 93 per cent, which over two years would be a 17 per cent improvement, and where the target is to be at 97 per cent by 2025 as defined by the Danfoss Group Executive Team. In 2024, we will expand that with a target on decarbonization as well as a strong focus on the social aspect of our strategic End-to-End Supply Chain Management (as illustrated in Figure 2.10). Next, we have defined some key strategic priorities for 2024 and beyond such as tailored and regionalized supply chains by further optimizing our End-to-End supply chains and footprint on a regional level, working on inventory excellence by working with our key customers as well as our customer service, factory order fulfilment teams and on decarbonization and circularity. As in 2023, there is again a lot of basic work to be done around perform as well as around transform. We will also even more be aligning our planning and fulfilment tactics to the go-to-market strategies from the businesses divisions and products lines on a regional level. Starting from an outside-in view, for our customers and how we will serve them. We will turn this into an annual process. Historically and prior to Covid, we set things up, but we never really changed it afterwards because in the past we had very stable markets and global supply chains. Today's markets are very volatile and extremely dynamic. Suddenly, we may be faced with even higher volatility, more geopolitical challenges, changing regulations enforced at a high speed, more competitor and price pressure as more capacity has been added to the market, or we may be faced with substitutes or even more supply chain disruptions. If you don't have an ongoing strategic process on an annual basis for reviewing your strategy per business division and product line, it will be almost impossible in the future to deal with the volatility and the changing market conditions as well as to align an effective supply chain response with it to create long-term stakeholder value. To deal with volatility and changing market conditions more effectively, I see one of the biggest opportunities for us to put a more robust strategic outside-in process on annual basis in place

'The approach we follow for 2024 is comparable to the one of 2023,' Frank continues.

We start from our strategy compass and strategic house, our Hoshin Kanri deployment model, where every year we have a cycle on defining our strategic priorities and key initiatives which are aligned with our business divisions. This one started in summer 2023 for 2024 priorities already. We go through the whole cycle of defining breakthrough goals and narrowing down the list of our key priorities and key initiatives and projects to create focus. By the end of December everything gets locked in, and we allocate our available resources accordingly. We have monthly Hoshin reviews, supported by our digital End-to-End Supply Chain Cockpit, where we are seeing whether we move in the right direction. We have defined our must-win battles and priorities per department visible in our digital End-to-End Supply Chain Cockpit and through colour coding green-yellow-red linked to our 8D digital corrective action reporting, we can follow up where we are at any given point of time which brings our Supply Chain Triangle and in the future our Supply Chain Diamond alive. To bring it even more alive and to make it very sustainable in the long-term, we implemented a recognition program. By nominating teams for concrete accomplishments contributing to our strategic objectives, by celebrating winners and our teams through awarding certificates and trophies, we engage our global supply chain community in driving the improvements and our transformation on a global and scalable level.

We believe that the Danfoss Climate Solutions approach, the work of Frank and his team, serves as an excellent illustration on how to bring the triangle alive as a balanced way of setting breakthrough goals and targets, powered through a strategy deployment model like Hoshin Kanri. With this we have a basis for a balanced dashboard that allows tracking progress, as a basis for communication towards a broader stakeholder community, and as a basis for celebrating successes as teams release their creative energy into improving supply chain performance, and driving more financial, environmental and social value for the broader stakeholder community.

> **EXERCISE**
> Understanding your key targets and business contributions for supply chain
>
> Consider the 5D supply chain model used by Danfoss and shown in Figure 2.9. Can you define what are your key targets and contributions from a supply chain perspective? Service improvement? Cost reduction? Cash generation? CO_2 reduction?
> And what needs to be done to deliver that AND-AND? Do you have low hanging fruit? Fixing the basics? Will it be driven by simplification of the service promise and the product portfolio?
> Is your executive team aligned with the targets for supply chain? Are there any conflicts of interest? Can those be debated? Can they be addressed?
> Are we clear on how individual improvement projects will contribute to our key targets and contributions? Are we driven by trends and hypes or are we driven by output?

Three models to describe the fourth generation 5D supply chain

In Chapters 1 and 2, I introduced three main models to better understand the fourth generation 5D supply chain. We have the Triple Triangle shown in Figure 1.16, the Quadruple ESG Triangle shown in Figure 1.17 and the Sustainable Supply Chain 'Zone' shown in Figure 2.1. And next to these you could think about the diamond, the square or the pyramid introduced in Figure 2.6. Do we need as many? And which one to use?

My feeling is that the Triple Triangle and the Quadruple ESG Triangle are the most universal models that will survive over the longer term. They are the most complex as they require an understanding of the individual triangles and how they interact. We are still in the early stages of that understanding. The case of MSF, discussed in Chapter 1, is a proof for me of the robustness of these models. It shows that the models allow capturing different ends of the spectrum, for-profit and non-profit supply chains, and provides the perspective that, going forward, companies will need to position themselves somewhere on the continuum between them. As a purpose-driven company, how do we trade-off financial and non-financial metrics? We believe that will become part of the strategic trade-offs companies have to make. I will further elaborate upon those strategic trade-offs in Chapters 5 and 6.

I believe the Sustainable Supply Chain 'Zone' is a bit simpler, and closer to where for-profit supply chains are today. Instead of optimizing across triangles, the social foundation and the environmental ceiling function as extra constraints on the basic Supply Chain Triangle. We need to drive profitable growth while reducing our CO_2 by x per cent, and while guaranteeing ethical labour practices at our suppliers. Discussing which KPIs are on the foundation and which ones are on the ceiling is practical, relevant and helpful to supply chain professionals today. As the discussion moves from constraints to optimizing across the different dimensions, the 'Zone' model may be replaced by the Triple Triangle or the Quadruple ESG Triangle.

All models, including the diamond, the square or the pyramid, indicate and confirm that we are gradually moving on from a 3D towards a 5D, or from a third generation to a fourth generation supply chain. We need to understand the impact of our decisions on the environmental (fourth dimension) and social (fifth dimension) metrics and objectives we have put forward. Understanding that broader impact requires a further broadening of the interest, knowledge, skillset and involvement of the supply chain professional. The move from the second generation (2D) to the third generation (3D) supply chain introduced the need for strategic trade-offs, the OR-OR as opposed to the AND-AND. It also required supply chain to be an integral part of those strategic trade-offs as opposed to the tactical-operational role it was stuck in for 20–30 years. Moving to the fourth generation 5D supply chain will only confirm that need and role evolution. I will further elaborate on the strategic trade-offs and their impact on the supply chain in Chapters 5 and 6.

Conclusion

In this chapter I introduced a third model for integrating sustainability into supply chain thinking: the Sustainable Supply Chain Zone. In purpose-driven companies, where profit is not the goal but a by-product, the Triple and the Quadruple Triangle may be more helpful, as it puts the three triangles on an equal footing. Operating the base Profit Triangle, while respecting extra social and environmental constraints, may be close to reality for many 'for-profit' companies today. As the boundaries between the two will fade, it is better to have the different models at our disposal.

In the next two chapters, I will explore a second important challenge to supply chains today. I will analyse increased volatility, what are the drivers for that volatility and what can be done to become more resilient. Together with sustainability, I defined that as a second key characteristic of the fourth generation supply chain.

Endnotes

1. Schneider Electric. Integrated Report 2022, Digital and Electric: for a sustainable and resilient future, published 2023. www.se.com/ww/en/assets/564/document/398634/integrated-report-2022.pdf (archived at https://perma.cc/H92R-8633)
2. Schneider Electric. 2022 Sustainable Development Report, Digital and Electric: for a sustainable and resilient future, published 2023, https://www.se.com/ww/en/assets/564/document/396659/2022-sustainability-report.pdf (archived at https://perma.cc/Z2AZ-93U3)
3. K Raworth (2017) *Doughnut Economics. Seven ways to think like a 21st-century economist,* Penguin Books, London
4. K Raworth. Exploring doughnut economics, 2013–24. www.kateraworth.com (archived at https://perma.cc/5YKX-MCEF)
5. Doughnut Economics Action Lab, 2024. doughnuteconomics.org (archived at https://perma.cc/27RJ-FH4K)
6. European Commission. Corporate sustainability reporting, 2024. finance.ec.europa.eu/capital-markets-union-and-financial-markets/company-reporting-and-auditing/company-reporting/corporate-sustainability-reporting_en (archived at https://perma.cc/4CP2-NJER)
7. R de Roo van Alderwerelt. Non-Financial Reporting Directive (NFRD) vs Corporate Sustainability Reporting Directive (CSRD), cpmview news & blogs, 22 April 2022. www.cpmview.com/news/csrd/nfrd-vs-csrd/ (archived at https://perma.cc/R8HX-4LXS)

8   Vandemoortele. About Vandemoortele, 2024. vandemoortele.com/en/contact-us (archived at https://perma.cc/6U5T-967H)
9   Vandemoortele. Annual Integrated Report 2022: Shaping a tasty future sustainably, 20 March 2023. vandemoortele.com/en/tags/investor-news/financials (archived at https://perma.cc/M2RZ-54LM)
10 Strategy-driven Supply Chain. Benchmark report – Food & Tobacco, 2024. www.strategydrivensupplychain.com/resources/benchmarkreport/food-tobacco/ (archived at https://perma.cc/5GBL-PPT9)
11 Awards for best Belgian Sustainability Reports. Winners 2022. 2024, www.sustainabilityreports.be/previous/winners/2022 (archived at https://perma.cc/PUH6-D8L6)
12 Global Food Safety Initiative. The Coalition of Action on Food Safety, 2024. www.mygfsi.com (archived at https://perma.cc/N2WQ-LTHM)
13 The Sustainable Palm Oil Choice, 2024. www.sustainablepalmoilchoice.eu (archived at https://perma.cc/28WD-K8LU)
14 Round Table on Responsible Soy, 2024. www.responsiblesoy.org (archived at https://perma.cc/9SYP-HG9N)
15 Forest Stewardship Council. The future of forests is in our hands, 2024. www.fsc.org (archived at https://perma.cc/6GNW-87P4)
16 Programme for the Endorsement of Forest Certification. Responsible Packaging. How can retailers and brand owners adopt responsible packaging, 2024. https://pefc.org/what-we-do/our-collective-impact/our-campaigns/responsible-packaging-a-new-forest-centric-way-to-look-at-sustainable-packaging (archived at https://perma.cc/42H2-AG8P)
17 R S Kaplan and R Karthik. Accounting for climate change, *Harvard Business Review*, 2021, 99(6), 120–31
18 R S Kaplan and R Karthik. Accounting for climate change, *Harvard Business Review*, 2021, 99(6), 120–31
19 R S Kaplan and D McMillan. Reimagining the balanced scorecard for the ESG era, *Harvard Business Review Digital Articles*, 2021
20 R S Kaplan and R Karthik. We need better carbon accounting. Here's how to get there, *Harvard Business Review Digital Articles*, 2022
21 Danfoss. Annual Report 2022: Investing to build a better future, 1 March 2023. files.danfoss.com/download/CorporateCommunication/Financial/Annual-Report-2022.pdf (archived at https://perma.cc/9S3E-X653)
22 J Gattorna and D Ellis (2019) *Transforming Supply Chains*, Pearson, London

The resilient supply chain 03

Introduction

In this chapter, I introduce drivers for volatility and ways to measure and visualize them. In this and the next few chapters, I will ask you to do a number of exercises with your executive team or a cross-functional group. I will show you the result of comparable exercises that I did with my 'book council'. In the preparation of the book, I gathered 20–30 senior supply chain and finance professionals from around 20 companies in five sessions of two hours to validate some of the key concepts of this book. I will use the result of their exercises as a foundation for improving our understanding here. I will talk about external drivers, that are out of our direct control, versus internal drivers, on which we have a more direct control, and how to address both to become more resilient.

I will argue that our supply chains have not been designed for resilience but for lowest cost. A first case study describes the supply chain of a fashion company, and how it has been setup to control costs and inventory risks. I show an alternative setup, that is more agile, has a higher cost, leads to a comparable profit, but provides a better fit with the needs of a fashion company. It allows to deliver upon the booming sales of iconic blockbuster products building the brand, while managing the inventory risk of unsuccessful products. A second case study of a high-tech company describes how the supply chain for new product introductions is designed for cost and time-to-market. I again show an alternative setup, which is more agile but has a higher cost. I show how in this case it improves the financial performance, and above all, how it provides a better fit with the needs of a high-tech product leader, which is to 'scale fast or fail fast'.

EXERCISE
Assessing drivers for supply chain improvement

Gather your executive team, or a cross-functional team, for a three-hour workshop. It is important that you gather the different key functions in the company: sales, operations, marketing/product management/R&D, supply chain, finance.

Ask your team to read the vision paper on the Supply Chain Triangle that can be downloaded from my website[1]. Hand out sticky notes (or use a virtual alternative like Miro). Ask people to write down 'What have been our key issues in the triangle over the last 18 months?' Take a flipchart or stick brown paper on the wall, draw a triangle and on the triangle starting at the top write service, cost, cash in a clockwise order (the order in the triangle is important). Ask people to stand up, and one by one, add their sticky notes to one of the three corners: service-related issues, cost, cash or CAPEX related issues. Some issues might affect all three corners, like a lack of visibility or a lack of integration between different planning systems. Take time for the discussion. Ask for clarifications ('What do you mean by that?').

When all sticky notes are on the triangle, ask the question 'Is this a problem?' People may look strange but repeat the question 'Is this a problem?' Feel free to provoke the group and state 'we are X, we have ambitious plans, we grow by hitting the gas, some of this may just be collateral damage'. What you want people to confirm is 'yes, we agree, this is a problem'. Only if the executive team or the cross-functional group agrees that 'yes, this is a problem', is there a platform to change our current approach, the processes, the systems, the people capabilities or the data. Supply chain people like to turn this around and say 'we want an advanced planning system' or 'we need to improve our S&OP'. My advice is 'if you want to improve S&OP, don't talk about S&OP'. S&OP is not a goal in itself, it is only a means to an end, so it is crucial to start with the triangle and see how S&OP, more flexibility in the plants (potentially requiring CAPEX), supply chain training for non-supply chain executives, can help to tackle the challenges we have identified in the triangle.

Turn the search for solutions into the second part of the workshop. 'What can we do about it? Where are the possible improvements?' You can classify them over processes, systems, people and data. Or you can classify them in effort versus expected impact.

The Covid paradox

When starting my third book, I was primarily confused. Confused by the following. I was doing exercises with executive teams like the one described above. Next to the questions listed above, I was adding the question 'Has the volatility increased?', to which people answered 'yes, it has, no doubt about that'. Then I continued with the question 'Should we prepare for continued disruptions, or will it be back to normal?' To which people, after some hesitation or debate would answer 'no, it will not be back to normal, we need to prepare for continued disruptions'. Which created an expectation on my side, that executive teams would start working on the listed improvements, more regional sourcing and production, more flexible assets, scenario capabilities in the planning processes, supply chain education to improve supply chain understanding, but that didn't happen. The day after the executive teams returned to their desks and de-prioritized the supply chain improvements for which we had so carefully identified the need. So, there was a disconnect. I got executive teams to intellectually agree that something has to change, but I didn't get the executive teams to turn that into action. That got me puzzled and confused.

It is what I would call the Covid paradox. On the one hand, the disruptions caused by Covid, as discussed in Chapter 1 and illustrated in Figure 1.3, showed how vulnerable our supply chains were. I often say that the supply chains we have built pre-Covid obviously have not been able to deal with the Covid volatility. So, if we assume that volatility is here to stay, something needs to be done. And that's where the paradox comes in. Instead of acting, we either do nothing, or we move very cautiously.

In this chapter we will explore the drivers of volatility, what a lack of resilience brings as a result, and what we can do to make our supply chains more resilient. I believe that resilience, next to sustainability, is a key requirement for the fourth generation supply chain thinking and capabilities. Let's explore how resilience can be integrated, next to sustainability.

Book council
In the preparation of this book, I decided to organize five working sessions with what I called my 'book council'. Around 50 people from around 20

companies confirmed interest. Around 30 people joined in the first session and around 20 stayed until session five. Different sectors were represented including chemicals, pharma, FMCG, discrete manufacturing, high tech. All participants were senior supply chain leaders, in regional or global roles with important operational responsibilities or important strategic or transformation responsibilities. Some participants such as Danfoss, Reckitt, Ricoh and Siemens volunteered to share their stories via case studies throughout this book.

Each working session consisted of two hours, where I was briefly presenting a key concept I planned to include in the book, followed by a break-out session of 20–30 minutes, in smaller industry groups of five to six people, followed by a joined debrief. As an example, I could have presented the Sustainable Supply Chain Zone and asked what type of KPIs the companies had on their social foundation and ecological ceiling, and whether they were experiencing any conflicts with the core Supply Chain Triangle.

In this chapter, I will give a couple of exercises you can do with your executive team, which I have done with the book council, and on which I will share their results. I am grateful for the time and energy the book council has put in. It has validated the relevance of the thinking and the models and has provided real-life illustrations from the supply chain cockpit of leading supply chain companies.

Volatility: external drivers

EXERCISE
Assessing drivers of volatility

Gather your executive team, or a cross-functional team, for a 1.5 hour workshop. It is important that you gather the different key functions in the company: sales, operations, marketing/product management/R&D, supply chain, finance. Ideally you have a somewhat larger group of around 16–20 people.

Divide the group into four or five groups of four or five people, don't make them any larger. Hand out an empty fishbone template in PowerPoint and ask them to come up with ideas for 'what they think is driving volatility'. I made a template fishbone available on my website[2]. Try to give as little information as possible, you want to pick people's untouched brains. Give people 30–40 minutes to come up with ideas in the smaller teams, then bring them back together and have the team debrief their fishbone one by one.

As a follow-up to the workshop, consolidate the different fishbones into one, and add some general notes and observations.

I did exactly this exercise with my book council. The result is shown in Figure 3.1. I identified two big clusters of volatility drivers, one which I called the 'external' drivers, as they are out of our direct control, and which I tried to capture under the typical PESTELE drivers that are also used in strategic analysis. The second big cluster, which I called the 'internal' drivers, as we have a more direct impact, I tried to capture under the different processes of the SCOR model.

PESTELE stands for political, economic, societal, technological, environmental, legal and ethical drivers. For each of the drivers, I have listed a couple of examples gathered from the exercise with the book council in Figure 3.1.

On the political side, we might give examples of tariffs and duties, like the trade war Donald Trump started with China, imposing tariffs on $200billion of Chinese goods in 2018[3], and another $300billion of Chinese goods in 2019[4]. Or we can think about the war between Russia and Ukraine, which led to skyrocketing energy prices and was shutting down Europe's most energy-intensive companies in the second half of 2022[5]. Political drivers typically spill over into economic impact and drivers.

On the economic side, we can think about what Ray Dalio[6] calls the 'short-term debt cycles'. When economic growth slows down, central banks will stimulate the economy by lowering interest rates and providing extra credit (printing money). When money is cheap, that tends to create bubbles, where all kinds of asset prices get inflated. When inflation rises, the central banks will try to cool down the economy by raising interest rates. As interest rates rise, economic growth will slow down, which starts the cycle again. There is a wealth of publicly available data on this. A recommended source is the Federal Reserve Economic Data from the St Louis FED[7].

Figures 3.2 and 3.3 show the year-on-year change in the Consumer Price Index (CPI), which we can consider as a proxy for inflation, and the Federal

Figure 3.1 External and internal drivers of volatility

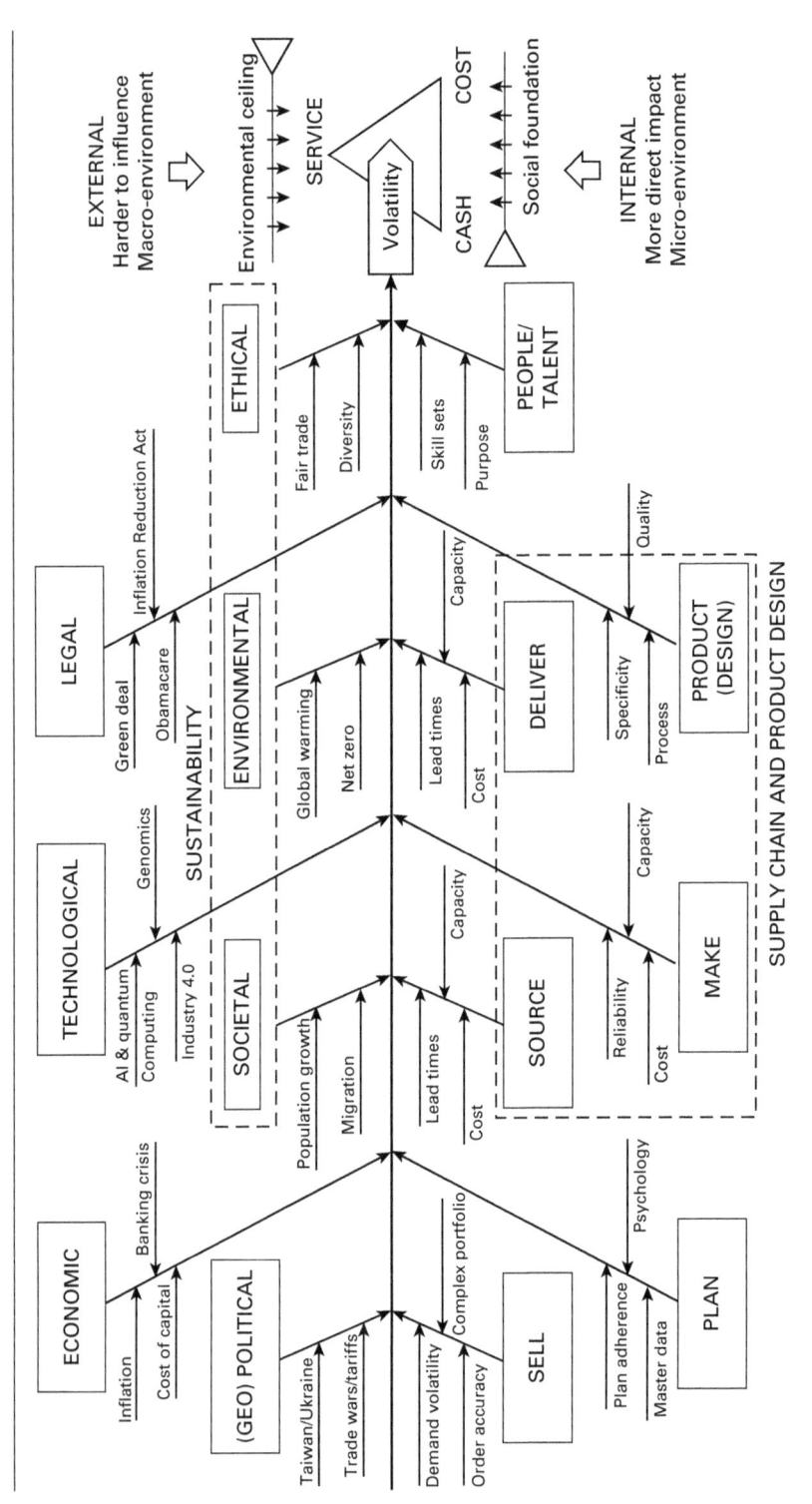

Figure 3.2 Consumer Price Index (CPI), per cent change from year ago, for 2010–2023

Consumer Price Index for all urban consumers

All items in US city average, per cent change from year ago, monthly, seasonally adjusted

Figure 3.3 Federal funds effective rate, in per cent, for 2010–2023

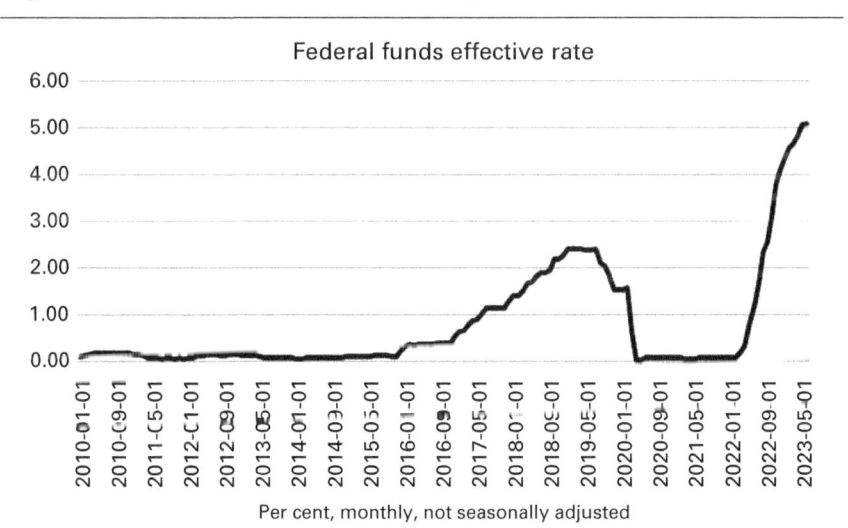

Federal funds effective rate

Per cent, monthly, not seasonally adjusted

funds effective rate, which is the interest rate at which depository institutions trade federal funds and which is driving other interest rates in the market. What one can derive from these graphs is that the decade 2010–2019 has

Figure 3.4 Consumer Price Index (CPI), per cent change from year ago, for 1948–2023

Consumer Price Index for all urban consumers

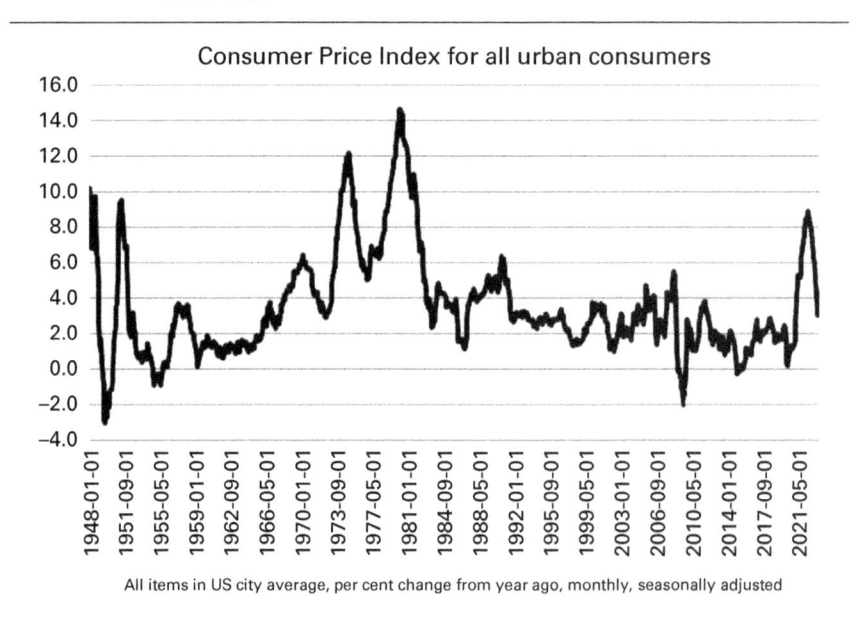

All items in US city average, per cent change from year ago, monthly, seasonally adjusted

Figure 3.5 Federal funds effective rate, in per cent, for 1954–2023

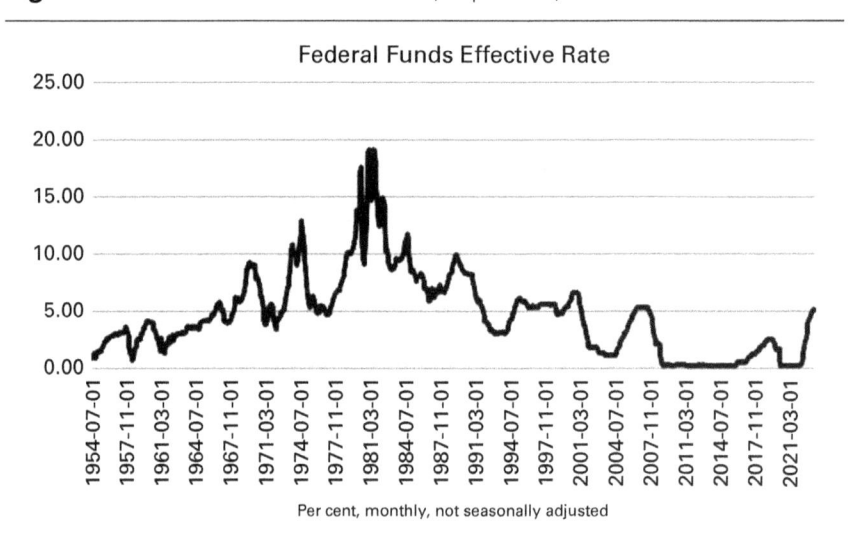

Federal Funds Effective Rate

Per cent, monthly, not seasonally adjusted

seen a high relative stability, with inflation relatively stable around two per cent, interest rates close to zero in the first half of the decade, followed by a slow and gradual increase to around two per cent in the second half of the decade. The outbreak of Covid made an abrupt end to this. Central banks lowered interest rates back to zero to stimulate the economy. The war between Russia and Ukraine fuelled a huge increase in energy prices, which fuelled inflation to a level of 8 per cent in the US and 10–12 per cent in Europe. That important inflation led to a fast and steep increase in interest rates by the central banks in an attempt to cool down the economy, which pushed the Eurozone into a recession in the first quarter of 2023[8]. What we can learn from this is that the speed at which we had to accelerate and decelerate our supply chains in the period 2020–2023 is of a completely different order of magnitude than that of the previous decade 2010–2019.

The key question remains whether it will be 'back to normal' or whether we should prepare for continued volatility? Figures 3.4 and 3.5 show the same data, but over a longer period, since 1948 and 1954 respectively. When taking a longer-term perspective, we see that inflation at eight per cent is high, but we have seen worse, in the 1970s as a result of the oil crisis in 1973 and 1979, both the result of political events[9]. The first an embargo by the Arab members of OPEC, as a retaliation for Western support of Israel against Egypt and Syria during the Yom Kippur War. The second, a result of the Iranian Revolution followed by the war between Iran and Iraq. There is an even more nuanced story for the interest rates. Five per cent is high in the timeframe 2010–2023, but it has basically been higher or even much higher, for a lot of the period 1970–2000.

So basically, what the analysis of this economic data tells us is that what we have seen in the period 2020–2023 is not extreme from a longer-term perspective. We may turn that argument around and say that the period 2010–2019 seems to have been more extreme, from the perspective of relative stability.

As I will continue to argue, the supply chains that we have built pre-Covid, in the period 2010–2019, the period of high relative stability, have not been able to deal with the Covid and the post-Covid volatility. Given the volatility of that period 2020–2023 is not extreme, if we have a longer-term perspective, it is the safer bet that things will not just go back to the 'normal' of the 2010–2019 stability. As a result, we need to upgrade our supply chain capabilities which I will develop further in this chapter and the following chapters.

But let us first continue our exploration of volatility drivers in Figure 3.1 and talk about technological drivers next. A combination of AI and quantum computing could disrupt many industries. Advances in genomics could disrupt pharma and healthcare. From the legal perspective the European Green

Deal and the Inflation Reduction Act in the US will quickly change the regulatory environment for companies and force them to be more transparent about their environmental and social risks and as such push them to become more sustainable.

I clustered the social, environmental and ethical drivers under a Sustainability umbrella. As public awareness increases, pressure on companies in these areas is increasing. In each of these areas, what used to be normal and accepted can turn into the opposite overnight. A recent example is the public discussion about PFAS[10], also dubbed 'forever chemicals', as they do not easily break down in the human body nor the environment. PFAS are used in a wide range of products, from non-stick cookware to cosmetics, and have been linked to cancer, hormonal dysfunction and environmental damage. The chemical manufacturer 3M reached a $10.3billion settlement with a host of US public water systems, to resolve water pollution claims, in just one of the more than 4,000 lawsuits filed against 3M and other chemical companies. 3M has set a 2025 deadline to stop producing PFAS. Continuing that same case from an ethical perspective, the chemical industry is said to have used 'big tobacco's tactics to conceal evidence of PFAS risks'. According to the Guardian[11], DuPont scientists found PFAS enlarged lab rat's livers and likely caused birth defects in workers, but still the company told its employees the cancer-linked compounds were 'about as toxic as table salt' and, like the tobacco industry before it, the chemical industry managed to keep PFAS's health risks hidden from the public for decades. It illustrates how events at all of the external drivers can have a huge impact, and potentially knock a company off its feet.

Volatility: internal drivers

Next to the 'external' PESTELE drivers, I classified a second part as 'internal' drivers along some of the classic SCOR processes: Plan, Source, Make, Deliver to which we added Sell, Product (Design) and People/Talent (Management).

When starting with the sales side of the supply chain, companies struggle with the volatility and the predictability of the demand. In Figure 1.3 I discussed how shortages of key raw materials inflated demand during the Covid period, and how after the Covid period, there was a demand correction, with customers depleting some of the expensive inventories they had built up. As companies were looking for alternative sourcing and dual sourcing, new customers all of a sudden popped up, and the volumes of existing customers all of a sudden could change, all adding to the demand volatility.

A general driver for volatility is complexity, when things are more complex, more things can go wrong. As I indicated above, the period 2010–2019 was one of relative stability, though I don't have good data points about that, my expectation is that companies during that period increased their complexity in pursuit of growth. More complex product portfolios, more complex products, more complex global supply chains, more complex production processes, all of which adds to the volatility within our supply chains.

When it is about our supply chain design, and the corresponding product design, I have discussed in the previous chapter how the access to low-cost labour and the reduction of shipping costs has led to massive offshoring and a greater dependency on cross-regional flows. It has exposed us to the shortage of shipping capacity and the corresponding dramatic rise in shipping prices. It also has exposed us to longer lead times in our supply chain, further strengthening the bull-whip effect, as the effect of our decisions comes with a delay, which potentially can double their impact.

On the 'planning' side we add volatility by inaccuracy of our data. Take the example of the increase in lead times, and the corresponding decrease in lead times afterwards. How many companies do you think were reviewing and adjusting lead times and other planning parameters on a frequent basis? I haven't seen any. Combine that with less accurate forecasts or order information, and the resulting planning information becomes unreliable. I have seen companies bypass the planning system and start planning in Excel based on well, indeed, based on what? When things get rough, planners go on manual planning and as humans we are prone to overreact and further aggravate the bull whip, further adding to the volatility.

And people have been a source of volatility as well. During Covid we lacked skilled labour and lacked base capacity like truck drivers to bring our goods to market. In the post-Covid world, as we need to upgrade our supply chain capabilities, having access to the right skilled people may be a challenge and a source of volatility as well.

The 'internal' drivers shown in Figure 3.1 match closely to the supply chain, which is to be expected if you do the exercise with a supply chain audience. I recommend you map your own volatility drivers and do it with a cross-functional team. Recent examples I came across is volatility from M&A activity, which could be important to you as a company. Or volatility because of a failure at the logistics provider upon the implementation of a

Figure 3.6 Major hurricanes in the North Atlantic, for 1960–2022

Figure 3.7 Major hurricanes in the North Atlantic, for 1851–2022

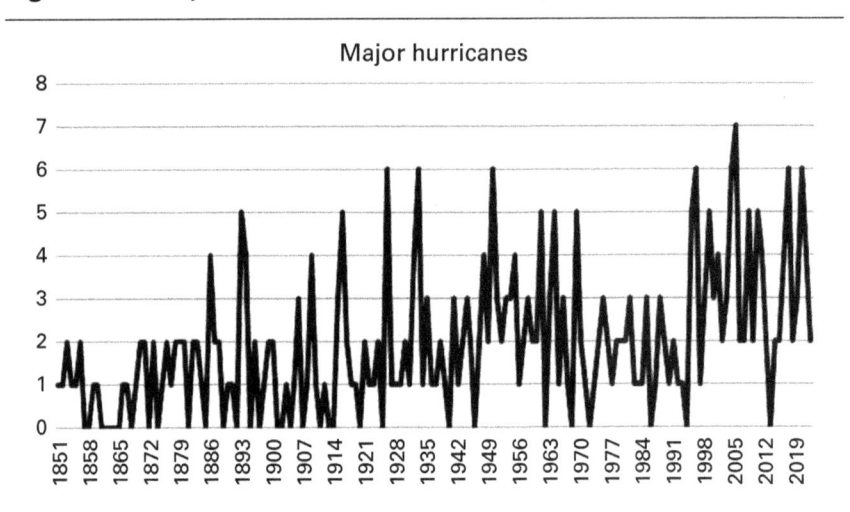

new WMS, which would fit under the delivery umbrella. Or volatility because of a dependency on Russia, as the divide between Russia and western countries was increasing, which would fit under the political umbrella.

And after defining your volatility drivers, try to substantiate it with data. Can we find data points that show an increase in volatility? Next to the economic indicators shown in Figure 3.4 and 3.5, we can for instance look at weather or climate indicators. Here the Tropical Weather and Climate Research from Colorado State University[12] (CSU) and the National Centres for Environmental Information (NCEI) from the National Oceanic and Atmospheric Administration[13] (NOAA) provide a lot of data. Figure 3.6 shows the number of major hurricanes, per year, in the North Atlantic since the 1960s. I have added a 10-year moving average to see the evolution. Since the mid of the 1990s, until 2010, we see a steep increase in major hurricane activity, from an average of two to an average of four, that is double. Since 2010 the average seems to have dropped back to an average of around three. Figure 3.7 shows the longer-term data, since 1851. The increasing trend is even more easily visible there. We can fairly assume this is an effect of global warming and this will continue causing volatility in global supply chains. The NOAA reports a total cost of damages in the US of $623 billion over 2018 to 2022, caused by 90 weather and climate disasters[14]. Since the 1980s, the number of disasters and the average cost is rising. So, all of this is very real.

If we want to better understand and manage our supply chains, we'll need to start by mapping our sources of volatility and understanding how they evolve. Seeing is believing, only when we see the increased volatility do we truly understand we really need to upgrade our supply chain capabilities.

EXERCISE
Assessing drivers of volatility – continued

When mapping the drivers for volatility, end your workshop with the questions 'Has volatility increased over the last five years?', 'Is it here to stay or will it reduce?' There may be hesitation. Don't push any conclusion. If people don't see it as a problem, it will never be a driver for supply chain improvement. So, ask questions, look for clarification 'Why are you saying that? Do you think it will be different region per region?' And look to gather data, can we analyse our order profiles? Has their volatility gone up? Can we analyse our portfolio? Has the number of SKUs gone up? Can we analyse the number of touchpoints to come to a finished product? Has the number gone up? Move away from the gut feeling. Only when we see the data we will truly believe that volatility has gone up. Take that data with you into your next workshop where you will explore resilience.

Case Study: Solvay – leading indicator forecasting at specialty polymers, by Christian Backaert, Global Supply Chain Excellence Manager

Solvay is a Belgian multinational chemical company established in 1863, with its headquarters located in Neder-Over-Heembeek, in Brussels, Belgium[15]. At the end of 2023 the company completed a partial demerger of the specialty activities[16]. These activities are now under Syensqo, a pure play specialty leader. Solvay continues as the 'EssentialCo' (as opposed to the 'SpecialtyCo') with businesses as Soda Ash, Peroxides, Silica and Coatis. As a global and diversified chemical company, Solvay also faces a lot of volatility in both demand and supply markets. In this case I want to illustrate how Solvay has leveraged external data, in the form of leading indicators, to enhance its visibility on where some of its demand markets are going.

Traditional extrapolation techniques, like Holt-Winters or ETS, or the 'sales force composite' method, where you ask salespeople for their input and then consolidate that, are known to be lagging behind and to be biased, meaning we're either too optimistic or too pessimistic. The lagging and the bias are illustrated in Figure 3.8. I have seen many examples of this during the Covid and the post-Covid shortages and the subsequent market corrections.

As illustrated in Figure 3.9, the continued disruptions from Covid, the Russia-Ukraine war, the war in Gaza, means that sales history itself has become a poor predictor of future sales. People are increasingly puzzled on where the market is and where it is going. They are in need of better techniques and better answers.

Figure 3.8 Lagging and bias in traditional forecasting methods

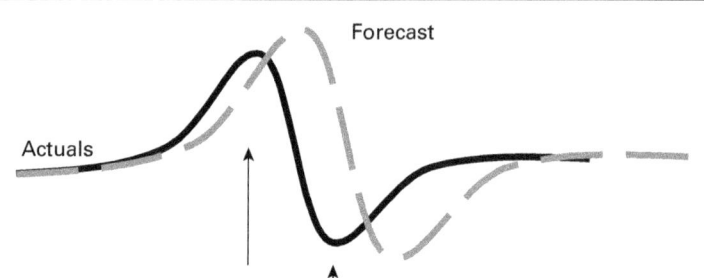

Forecast

Actuals

A lot of uncertainty. What is 'true demand/consumption'.
What is 'hoarding' by customers due to shortages or due to price increases?

A lot of uncertainty. What is 'true demand/consumption'.
What is stock build-off triggered by working capital reduction?

Figure 3.9 Repeated disruptions leading to actual sales as a poor predictor of future sales

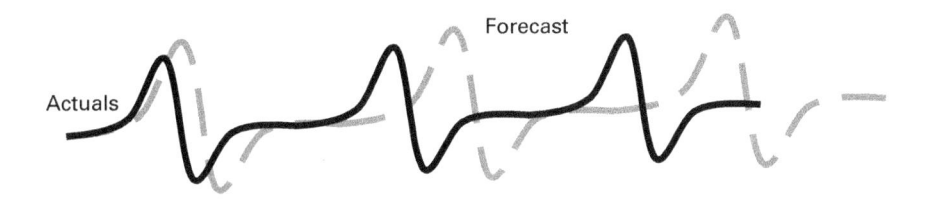

Figure 3.10 Leading indicators as a way to understand what is driving the actual sales

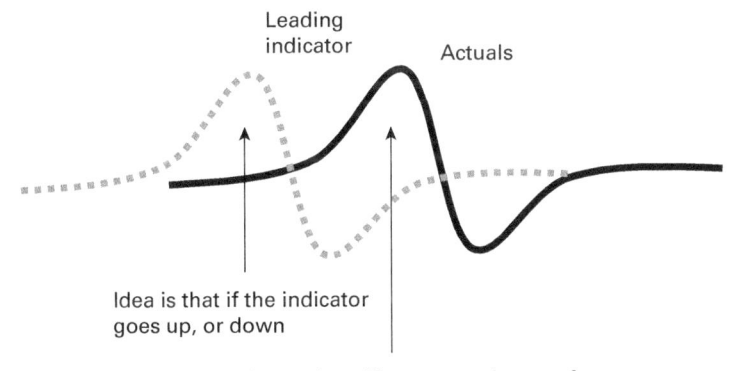

At Solventure, we have done PhD research that is focused on finding causal leading indicators. We have also built a software product[17] around it that is called Solventure 'LIFe' which stands for 'Leading Indicator Forecasting engine'. As an example, let's assume that your sales are linked to the construction market. You may not be a first-tier supplier, such as a manufacturer of bricks or roofing, but you may be somewhere in the second or the third tier, for instance producing some of the basic chemicals being used in the downstream manufacturing processes.

To understand where the demand in the end-market is going, you may look into indicators on the housing market, for instance the number of new housing permits, or into retail figures of the DIY sector to have an idea of the renovation activity. As illustrated in Figure 3.10, an indicator is said to be leading, if your sales will go up or down, a number of months after the indicator is going up or down.

To get a full understanding of your sales, you may need a collection of indicators. As discussed, new housing permits may be a good indicator for the new constructions, but you may need a different indicator to understand the demand driven by renovations. Remember that renovations went significantly up during the Covid pandemic[18]. And there may be other factors at play, like the inventories of raw materials, semi-finished and finished products at the intermediate steps in the value chain. When markets are up, and especially when shortages are popping up, companies have the tendency to start ordering extra and to start hoarding surplus inventory. When markets start going down, those inventories are flushed, which will further reduce upstream demands. The two together form the famous and well-studied bull-whip effect[19]. Price increases and decreases have a comparable effect so can also be relevant inputs.

In 2021, Solvay started a project with Solventure to improve the accuracy and the maturity of the forecasting process. Two explicit goals were to detect potential sales turning points, and to identify and include leading macro-economic indicators in the forecasting processes. The timeline of the project is shown in Figure 3.11. A first step in the project was building a leading indicator forecasting model for two business units: Automotive Resin, and Healthcare pvdc. In what follows, I will show some results for Automotive Resin in the Americas, as those easily illustrate the value external data can bring.

Figure 3.12 shows the historical sales for the Automotive Resin in the Americas. You see the obvious sharp drop in sales in 2020, due to the start of the Covid pandemic, and the quick recovery afterwards. But you also see that sales were already declining since the beginning of 2018, so this market wasn't necessarily in a good shape before. As I will come back to later, that is important from a psychological perspective.

Figure 3.11   Project timeline for leading indicator forecasting at Solvay

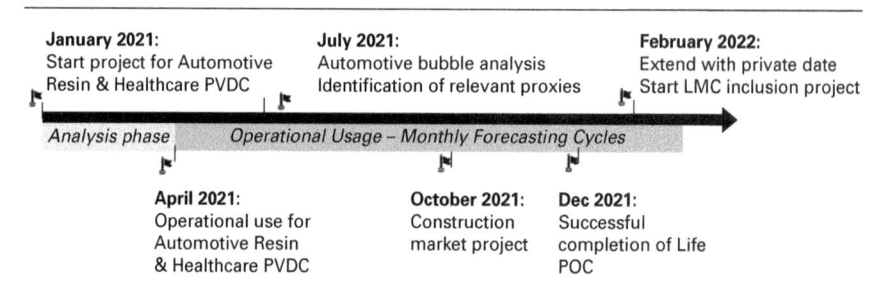

January 2021:
Start project for Automotive Resin & Healthcare PVDC

July 2021:
Automotive bubble analysis
Identification of relevant proxies

February 2022:
Extend with private date
Start LMC inclusion project

Analysis phase   *Operational Usage – Monthly Forecasting Cycles*

April 2021:
Operational use for Automotive Resin & Healthcare PVDC

October 2021:
Construction market project

Dec 2021:
Successful completion of Life POC

Figure 3.12 Historical sales and turning points in the Automotive Resin sales for the Americas

Automotive Resin – Americas

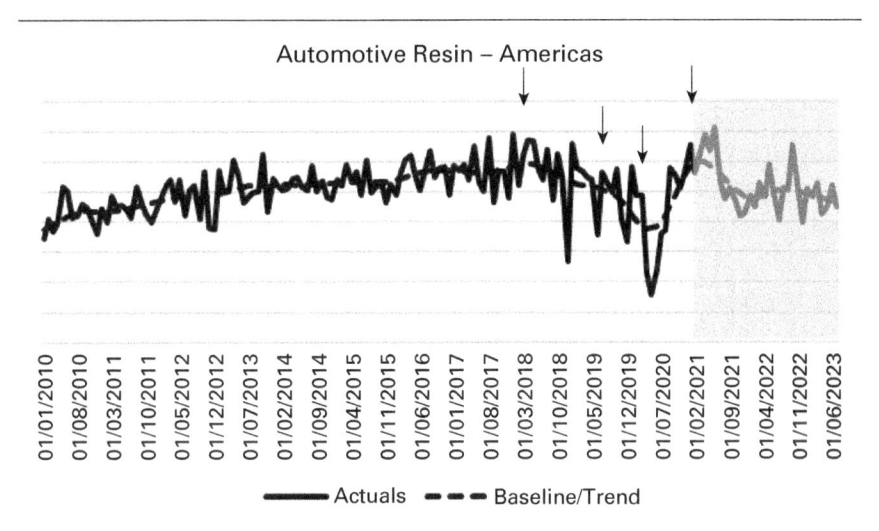

― Actuals ― ― Baseline/Trend

Figure 3.13 Leading indicator forecast versus sales rep forecast for Automotive Resin for the Americas

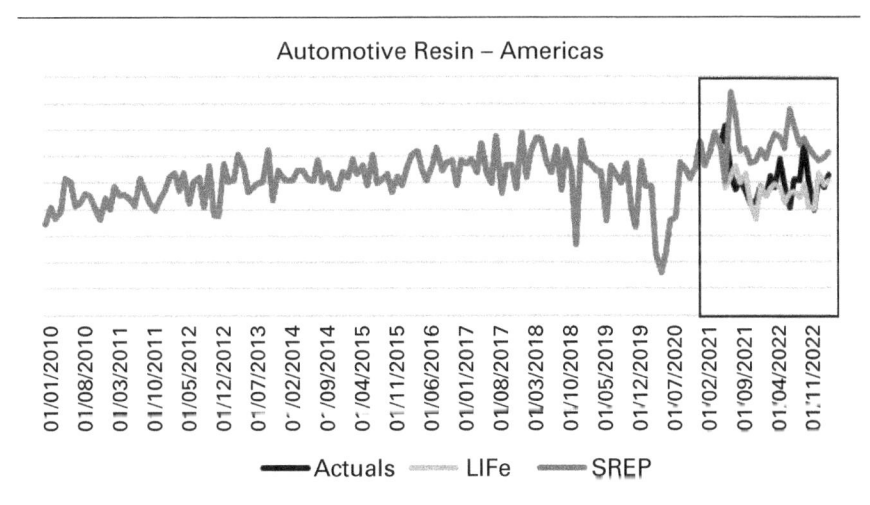

Automotive Resin – Americas

― Actuals ― LIFe ― SREP

The arrows indicate historical turning points. Turning points are where the trend, shown in the dashed curve, changes. These turning points are essential in the modelling. We basically want indicators that help us to predict trend changes. These are the 'moments of truth'.

As shown in the timeline in Figure 3.11, the models for the Automotive Resin were constructed in January to March and they went live in April

2021. As you can see from Figure 3.12, in the greyed out area, the sales of the Auto-Resin in the Americas was about to hit another important turning point in August 2021. An ideal case to test the added value of using external data.

Figure 3.13 shows the three-month ahead leading indicator forecast versus the three-month ahead sales rep forecast. Three-months ahead means that for August 2021, we show the forecast made at the end of May, or for September 2021, we show the forecast made at the end of June. Figure 3.14 shows the underlying trend of the leading indicator forecast, the sales rep forecast and the actual sales.

The result speaks for itself. Coming back to the psychological aspect, if you go back to Figure 3.12 and you put yourself in the shoes of a sales rep in March 2021. After three difficult years, 2018–2020, you see the sales dramatically picking up. That trend is basically confirmed in the second quarter, April–June 2021. Without appropriate (external) data, there is no way you will predict the market is going into a decline in Q3 and Q4. As humans we are also prone to 'confirmation bias'. As a sales rep, I will look for arguments that support my conviction that sales will remain strong. The result is shown in Figure 3.13, and it is even more obvious from the trend graph in Figure 3.14. We are significantly over-forecasting, and are slow, almost resistant to adjust our numbers.

I will avoid technical discussions on how to calculate forecast accuracy, but in short, over the period from June 2021–May 2022, the bias on the sales rep forecast was more than 30 per cent, so on average 30 per cent too

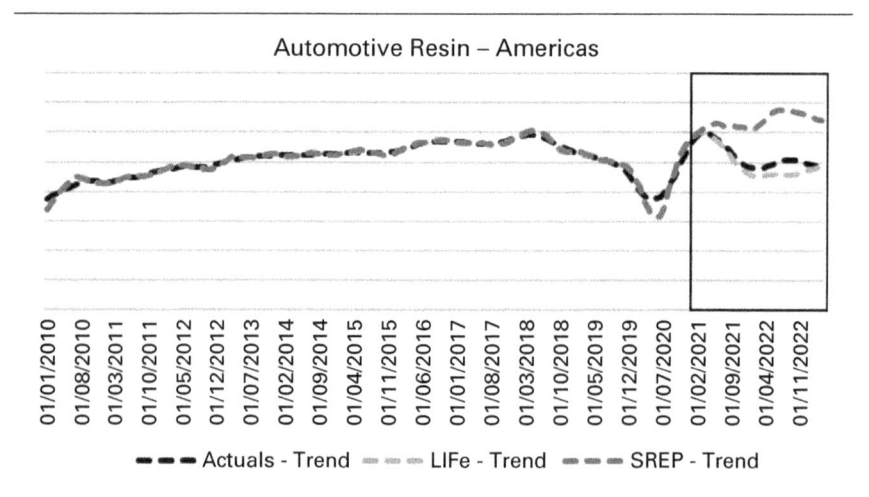

Figure 3.14 Underlying trend in the leading indicator forecast versus sales rep forecast for Automotive Resin for the Americas

high, putting a huge inventory burden on the Solvay supply chain. The bias of the leading indicator forecast over that same period was -4 per cent meaning the leading indicator forecast on average was 4 per cent too low. I consider +/- 5 per cent to be a target range for the bias. The forecast accuracy, indicating how accurately can we predict the sales of a given month, was 66 per cent for the sales rep forecast, and 90 per cent for the leading indicator forecast, or a staggering 24 per cent absolute improvement. The forecast accuracy is directly linked to the amount of safety stock we need to carry in the supply chain. Improving the accuracy allows us to reduce the safety stock. The value impact is obvious in this case.

As is shown in the timeline in Figure 3.11, another part of the project was better understanding the end-to-end value chain, the so-called 'bubble analysis'. As is shown in Figure 3.15, Solvay, for the Automotive Resin, is delivering into moulders. The moulders deliver to first tier automotive suppliers, who would deliver their products such as thermostat housings, clutch cylinders, charge air coolers or the like to the OEMs. The OEMs deliver to the dealers. In the US, dealers carry a lot of finished car inventories and typically deliver to the end consumers from stock.

The visibility for Solvay in that chain was, so far, limited to their relationship with the moulders. There was little to no visibility on the downstream value chain. In the so-called 'bubble analysis', we started identifying indicators that tell something about the level of production output in each of the downstream steps. We also collected information on the inventories throughout the chain, such as domestic auto inventories, inventories at manufacturers of motor vehicles and parts, inventories at suppliers of motor vehicle parts, and auto parts. Better understanding the level of production output and inventories in every step of the value chain is essential in better understanding

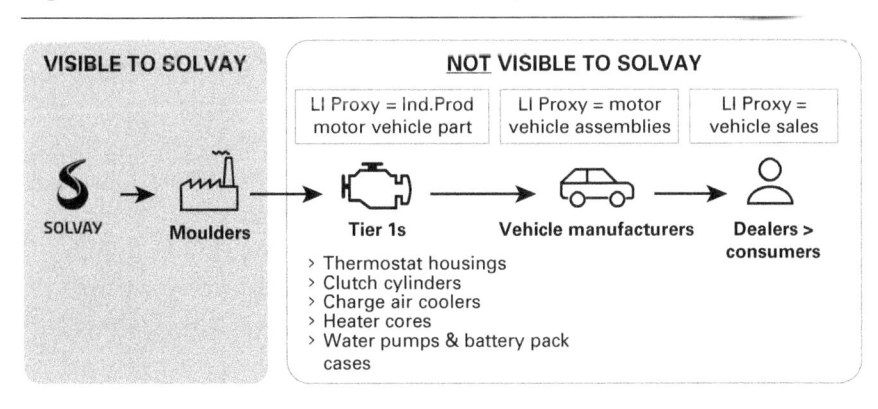

Figure 3.15 The value chain or 'bubble' analysis for Automotive Resin

what is ultimately driving your demand, and better understanding and anticipating the bull-whip effect.

When asked for what the organization names as the biggest benefits, Christian Backaert, the global supply chain excellence manager at Solvay, mentions:

> There are many aspects. Leading indicator forecasting moves the focus from this and next month to the next six months. It gives a further and deeper visibility. It also changes the dynamics of the demand review meetings. The biggest question becomes, do we understand why the sales rep forecast is different? The comparison of the bottom-up sales rep forecast and the leading indicator forecast, and collecting arguments for one or the other, enriches the forecast insights and helps us better anticipate turning points.
>
> As part of our supply chain excellence, I am a big believer that using external data is an enabler for forecast improvement, by challenging the sales teams on their forecast assumptions, and allowing them to reconsider their view of the future. As the forecast is the starting point for the supply chain planning, improving the forecast has been a key area for our supply chain excellence team.

Resilience: service, product, supply chain and organization design

> **EXERCISE**
> Assessing drivers for resilience
>
> Gather the same group you gathered for mapping the volatility drivers. Your executive team or another cross functional group involving sales, operations, marketing/product management/R&D, supply chain, finance. Preferably a group of 16–20 people so you can split them in smaller groups of four to five people. Never put more than five people in one group.
>
> As with the volatility exercise, give each group an empty fishbone diagram, and give them 30–40 minutes on 'how we think we can build resilience' into our supply chains. I have made a fishbone template available on my website[20]. Try to give as limited upfront information as possible. You want to pick people's pristine brain to get the broadest possible input. You may start with a recap of the volatility workshop and the resulting fishbone and any supporting data you collected in the meantime. We are trying to find solutions on how to better respond to the challenges and disruptions identified there.

I did the same exercise with my book council, which I introduced earlier in this chapter. The result is summarized in Figure 3.16. At the bottom of the fishbone, I have used the same process blocks to cluster the ideas generated by the book council. In general, to become more resilient, we need to better think through the design of our supply chains and each of these processes. I will give some real-life examples here and will continue with supply chain design and how to better incorporate sustainability and resilience considerations in Chapters 5 and 6. In Chapters 7 and 8 I will do the same for integrated planning processes.

Let us start in the 'selling' process and focus on portfolio complexity and the service promises we make to our customers. I meet companies that promise a different lead time to different customers on a portfolio of over 50,000 SKUs. There is no way, not even with the best processes or systems you will ever be able to reliably deliver that. This level of complexity kills your resilience. In many companies the customer order lead times are considered a decision of sales, as sales manages the relationship with the customer. This is a mistake as sales cannot judge the impact of lead times on the supply chain. For instance, it doesn't really help to promise a two-week lead time to the customer if the production lead time is four weeks. To keep things simple, stupid (KISS), you want to stick to Make-To-Stock (MTS, available from stock) or Make-To-Order (MTO, we start production/assembly once we receive the order). If four weeks seems a lot, we should sit down with production and R&D to understand what can be done to reduce the production lead time, for instance by having intermediates and subassemblies which are then finished to order. In a sense, it is simple, the customer order lead times and the whole 'service design' should be the responsibility of a cross-functional team, a 'service design committee'. It should not be the decision of a single department, and an important criteria should be the resilience and the robustness of the designed solution. Will we be able to reliably deliver upon our promise, also when facing important volatility?

If we continue at the bottom of the fishbone, with the 'source', 'make', 'deliver' or 'product design', I believe many companies optimize their products and supply chains for cost rather than flexibility. I refer to the two example cases below, one from the fashion industry, one from the high-tech industry. I discuss how the cost and inventory focus is a drag on the success of the fashion company, and how a more costly but more responsive supply chain makes a positive difference. For the high-tech company, I give a comparable analysis of New Product Introductions (NPIs). I show how a more costly but more responsive supply chain looks worse from the perspective of an individual NPI,

Figure 3.16 Drivers for resilience

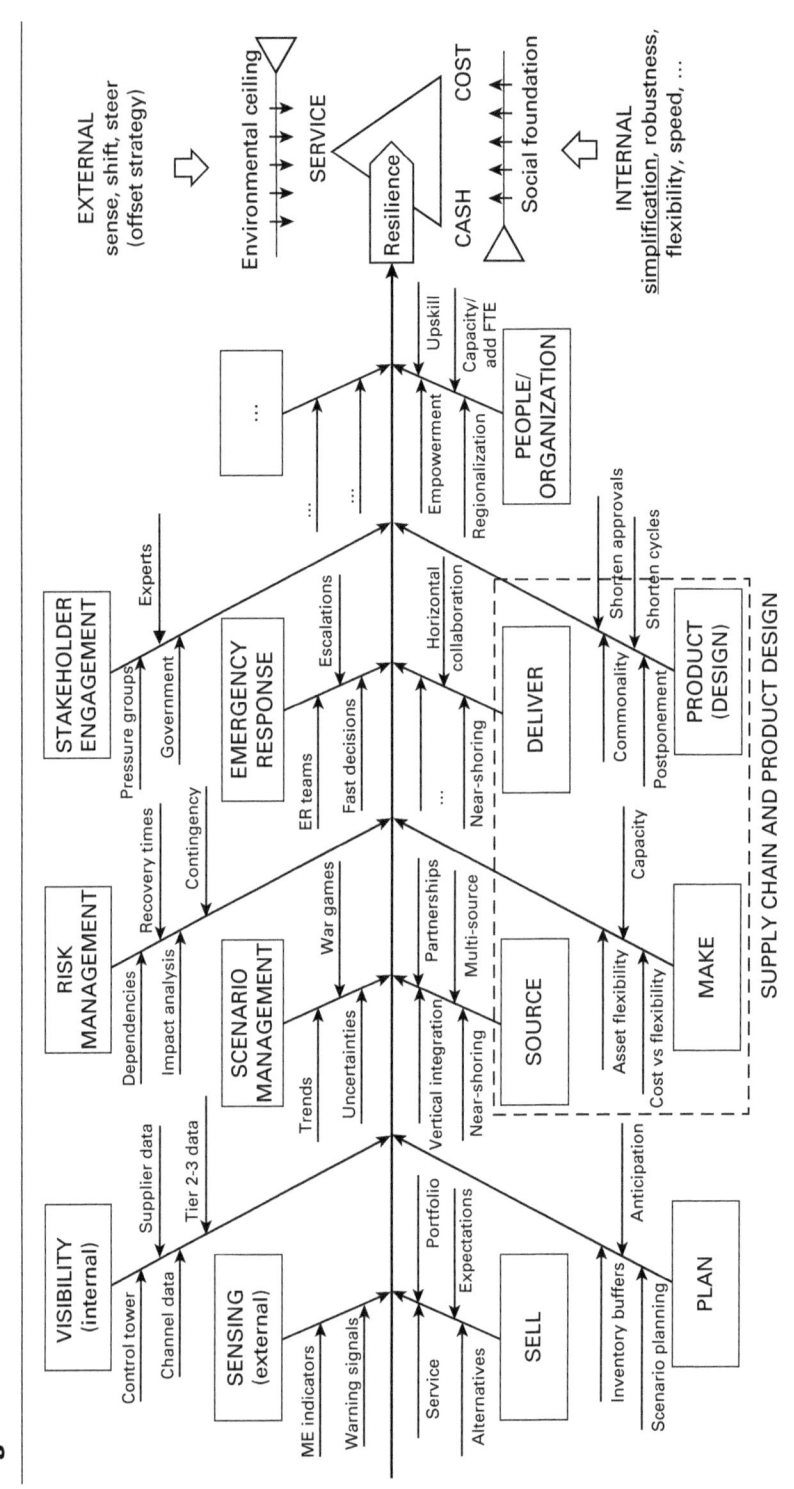

but is a more reliable estimate of the actual performance and leads to a better outcome on a portfolio level.

The main problem with bringing more flexibility and resilience in the design of products and supply chains is that it increases the cost and the capital employed and it is often hard to calculate the return. Looking at the case studies from the fashion and the high-tech industry, you could say the gains come from the unexpected, what if we'd sell only five instead of 100, or what if we'd be able to sell 400 instead of the expected 100. If we make the business case on the 'expected' numbers, flexibility will simply cost more, so we tend to ignore it, as people will ask questions, and we don't know how to defend it. If we want to see the value of flexibility, we need to run what-if scenarios, take a so-called 'stochastic' view of the world, prepare for the unpredictable. The two cases I describe give an idea on how that can be done.

Instead of trying to quantify the potential value of a second source, or a second plant, what I have seen working well is to define 'design principles' or you can call it 'design axioms' as you merely assume them, you don't try to question them. 3M is known to have 'each technology in at least three plants' and 'at least three technologies in each plant', and to 'have at least 80 per cent of the regional demand produced and sourced locally'. You know that is not going to be the lowest cost or capex solution, but you equally know this will deliver a robust and highly resilient supply chain. Product leaders like 3M, which are driven by innovation, understand that the demand for new or niche products is difficult to predict and suddenly can explode. Examples are a surge in demand for reflective coatings, when Europe introduced new seven-digit license plates, or think about the surge in demand for facemasks during the Covid period. More flexibility in the network allows you to better react. If the demand surges, you can typically sell at a higher price point. The inverse happens as well. Product leaders know they will have to step in and step out of application markets on a frequent basis. With each plant having at least three technologies, stopping a technology like PFAS[21] doesn't imply shutting down plants, which would further increase the cost and leaks a lot of knowledge as people are leaving the company. As in the fashion and the high-tech case, flexibility doesn't pay off for the averages, it pays off in the extremes. If the volatility is high, you should organize for the extremes if you want to be more resilient.

A final comment about the design of our service offering, our products and our supply chains: we have the tendency to overengineer them. Think about the example of offering different lead times to different customers on a portfolio of 50,000 SKUs. If you are doing that, I'm sure you have the perfect explanation why it really needs to be that way. Please, kill it. We have the tendency to engineer our supply chains to satisfy 100 per cent of the customers. That's beyond optimal. Design your supply chain to satisfy 80 per cent of the customers (if your strategy is operational excellence, with 20 per cent of the complexity), or to satisfy 90 per cent of the customers (if your strategy is customer intimacy, with 50 per cent of the complexity), but never design it to satisfy 100 per cent of the customers (with 100 per cent of the complexity). Complexity drives volatility and makes resilience harder. Simplicity will reduce volatility and makes resilience easier. In volatile times, it is preferable to be robust and resilient for 80 to 90 per cent of the customers, as opposed to being unreliable for 100 per cent of your customers. I will continue our discussion of how to include sustainability and resilience into our strategic trade-offs and supply chain design in Chapters 5 and 6.

Let's continue our discussion of the fishbone with the impact of 'planning' on resilience. In planning, we should think more in scenarios and think through how much buffer we need, which type of buffer we need (inventory, capacity or lead time) and where to position that buffer (for instance inventory in raw materials/components, semi-finished or finished). We have become addicted to Just In Time (JIT) supply chains, where all the intermediate buffers are gone. What people forget is that JIT supply chains require a stable demand. Lean manufacturing[22] has a principle called 'heijunka' or 'levelling'. We mix different types of cars on the assembly line to create a smooth flow of components towards suppliers. If the demand gets disrupted no buffers will mean a longer lead time. Think about the lead times of more than one year to get an electric car in Europe in the period 2021–2022. If the volatility is here to stay, we need to think through our buffers and how to use them. I will continue our discussion of the importance of more mature and better integrated planning processes in Chapters 7 and 8.

The final block at the bottom of our fishbone in Figure 3.16 is people and organization. There are different dimensions to the people aspect. If there is a lot of volatility and we don't have the appropriate supply chain design and processes, there is a lot of pressure on people and there is simply more work to be done. So sometimes improving resilience is as basic as foreseeing sufficient capacity of skilled people. If we want to evolve in our supply chain maturity, we will also need to train people in what that means, for instance how to properly design supply chains (as introduced above and further explained in Chapters 5 and 6) or how to run more mature and better integrated planning processes (as introduced above and explained in Chapters 7 and 8).

In the book council there was also a lot of discussion on whether we should organize differently, for instance more on a regional level, and how we could empower people or teams. Our traditional hierarchical organizations are focused on 'standardization and control'. Organizational management guru Henry Mintzberg called these 'machine bureaucracies'[23]. These work well in stable and predictable environments. Giving more authority to regional and/or product teams, and making more decisions in cross-functional committees, to ensure we have a 360° understanding, will help in making better decisions faster. Mintzberg would call these 'adhocracies'. If we want to be more resilient, we will need to change the way we make decisions in our companies.

Case Study: Fashion company

Many fashion companies have a supply chain for which the complexity is above average. Some of the characteristics are that fabrics often need to be ordered six to nine months before the start of the season, stitching is often offshored to countries in North Africa like Tunesia or to countries in the Far East like Bangladesh or Myanmar, often again with a 10-to-12-week lead time. If you have a high-fashion product with four seasons a year, that implies that you can often not react during the season. That puts a lot of pressure on the so-called 'blind' forecast where we have no information on the actual sell out in the market. The blind forecast is typically the result of an internal judgemental forecasting process. In this situation, a wrong forecast directly impacts the top-line and the bottom-line. If we don't forecast enough, we will have lost sales (which gives an incentive to increase the forecast). If we forecast too much, the bad news comes at the end of the season, when we need to write off our unsold products. Especially for luxury goods we may want to avoid outlet type of sales to protect our premium brand. To make things worse, fashion comes with different sizes, and if it is lingerie or swimwear with tops and with bottoms, which further increases the gamble we have to make with the blind forecast, and which further increases the top line (lost sales) and bottom-line (write-off) risk.

Table 3.1 illustrates the situation of one of the fashion companies I worked with. Say we launch 10 new product families, basically every season. Let's assume the blind forecast for each of them is 100 (in practice they will differ but let's focus on the uncertainty on that forecast and how we deal with balancing the top-line and the inventory risks). We may never know the true demand or the true sales because, as we will see, our supply chain is not flexible enough to deliver it, but let's assume the true demand is shown in the second column. Half of the products are over-forecasted in the

Table 3.1 Base supply chain for fashion company – output in units

	Blind forecast	Demand	Prod1	Prod2	Prod3	Sum Prod	Sales	Missed sales	Write offs
Fam 1	100	400	60	60	60	180	180	220	0
Fam 2	100	150	60	60	30	150	150	0	0
Fam 3	100	150	60	60	30	150	150	0	0
Fam 4	100	100	60	40		100	100	0	0
Fam 5	100	100	60	40		100	100	0	0
Fam 6	100	50	60			60	50	0	10
Fam 7	100	20	60			60	20	0	40
Fam 8	100	20	60			60	20	0	40
Fam 9	100	5	60			60	5	0	55
Fam 10	100	5	60			60	5	0	55
Total	**1,000**	**1,000**	**600**	**260**	**120**	**980**	**780**	**220**	**200**

blind forecast. Half of the products are under-forecasted. On a company level, the forecast is quite accurate, we think we will sell 1,000, the true market demand is also 1,000. How difficult could it be, right? One of the families will be the absolute darling and top product. Where the forecast is 100, the true demand for the product is assumed to be 400. The supply chain has been designed as such that we have three production runs, one before the seasons starts, which is needed to fill the channels with product. We have a second and a third production run of which the products arrive during and near the end of the season.

To limit our inventory risk, historically, we haven't loaded the full blind forecast into the initial production run, we load only 60 per cent. We may be right to do so as Table 3.1 shows that for families 6–10 this is leading to 200 of unsold inventories already. As the season progresses, we see that some families are doing better than the others, so we will launch extra production, but as we remain cautious for the inventory risk, we keep limiting the production, we don't go all the way, which in Table 3.1 is shown as that we limit the extra production runs to the same 60 units. Table 3.1 shows that in the end we produce 980 units, of which we sell 780, so we have 200 unsold units (or 20 per cent of our production) which at the end of the season we will write off. We also see that we sold 780 of the total demand of 1,000, where the missed sales of 220 is completely in the Family 1.

If we add financials to it, shown in Table 3.2, assuming for instance a sales price of €1 and a cost price of €0.50, or a theoretical gross margin of 50 per cent (which for a fashion product should be more than realistic), we can also calculate the financial output, as shown in Table 3.3. What we see is that the theoretical gross margin of 50 per cent, after accounting for the write-offs, becomes 37 per cent, we will call that net margin in this example.

When discussing the supply chain with the fashion company, it didn't feel right to me. I compared it to stepping on the gas with the handbrake on. It is bad for the engine and it gets very smelly. Taking two steps back I challenged them that maybe their gross margin was not high enough as their price point was not high enough. If you want to be a leading fashion brand, maybe you should be happy if you sell 70 per cent of what you produce and you should ensure you can drive the right price so you can (at least finan-

Table 3.2 Base supply chain for fashion company – sales and cost price

Sales price	€ 1.00
Cost price	€ 0.50
Gross margin	50%

Table 3.3 Base supply chain for fashion company – output in Euros

Total sales	€ 780
Cogs	€ 390
Gross profit	€ 390
Gross margin	50%
Write-offs	€ 100
Net profit	€ 290
Net margin	37%

cially) afford the write-offs. I challenged them that maybe this wasn't a supply chain challenge or problem but that it was a business and marketing problem. I was worried by the idea that for their really top products, the products that build the brand, create the brand loyalty, and make the brand grow, the very supply chain setup was limiting the upside. As shown in Table 3.1, we realized only 180 on a potential of 400. Nobody knew the real demand or the 400 so the argument in practice was hard to make.

I simulated exactly that in Tables 3.4, 3.5 and 3.6. Suppose we could increase our sales price to €1.25, yes, that's a 25 per cent increase. That would allow us to take more inventory risk as shown in the committed 100 in production run 1 in Table 3.4 and the continued commitment of 100 in production run 2 and 3. Yes, on the downside, that would increase our write-offs it would basically double them. But the good news is that we now capture 330 of the true demand of 400. Imagine how that will drive future growth and brand loyalty. People want to be in love with their brand, and brands are built by iconic products, products that everybody wants.

Table 3.6 compares the financials of the base and the higher price scenario. Assuming all things equal, we see we unlock 44 per cent growth, of

Table 3.4 Higher margin supply chain for fashion company – output in units

	Blind forecast	Demand	Prod1	Prod2	Prod3	Sum prod	Sales	Missed sales	Write offs
Fam 1	100	400	100	100	100	300	300	100	0
Fam 2	100	150	100	50		150	150	0	0
Fam 3	100	150	100	50		150	150	0	0
Fam 4	100	100	100			100	100	0	0
Fam 5	100	100	100			100	100	0	0
Fam 6	100	50	100			100	50	0	50
Fam 7	100	20	100			100	20	0	80
Fam 8	100	20	100			100	20	0	80
Fam 9	100	5	100			100	5	0	95
Fam 10	100	5	100			100	5	0	95
Total	1,000	1,000	1,000	200	100	1,300	900	100	400

Table 3.5 Higher margin supply chain for fashion company – sales and cost price

Sales price	€ 1.25
Cost price	€ 0.50
Gross margin	60%

Table 3.6 Higher margin supply chain for fashion company – output in Euros

	Higher Price	Base	Growth
Total sales	€ 1,125	€ 780	1.44
Cogs	€ 450	€ 390	
Gross profit	€ 675	€ 390	1.73
Gross margin	60%	50%	
Write-offs	€ 200	€ 100	2.00
Net profit	€ 475	€ 290	1.64
Net margin	42%	37%	1.14

which 25 per cent is driven by the price increase, and 15 per cent by the extra sales in units (from 780 to 900). Yes, we double the write-offs, but this is compensated by the higher gross margin. Including write-offs, we get to a 42 per cent net margin which is higher than the 37 per cent in the base scenario, and the 42 per cent counts on higher sales so our net profit in euros is going up by 64 per cent! People will say 'Bram, this is fake, if you increase prices by 25 per cent you will lose customers'. My answer is yes, as you lose loyal customers today, because your supply chain is unable to scale, and those customers will be less price sensitive than some of the customers you currently serve. So, where it is hard to predict where this will really land, pushing prices to create space to absorb more risk seems like a logical thing to do in a fashion supply chain. If you don't create space to take risk, you will be limiting the growth of your fashion company.

An alternative approach could be to increase the flexibility of our supply chain, which is simulated in Tables 3.7, 3.8 and 3.9. Let's assume our sales price is back at €1, and we are 'doubling' the flexibility for a 30 per cent higher cost (€0.65 instead of €0.50) or 15 per cent less gross margin (35 per cent instead of 50 per cent). These are significant cost and gross margin differences. The 'double' flexibility is shown in Table 3.7, as that we have six production moments instead of three and that we are able to reduce the first batch from 60 to 30 to acknowledge and manage the (demand) uncertainty on the first batch. In practice the flexibility could be created by having a local, more expensive workshop, where part of the flexible production can be done.

From a unit's perspective there is only good news. We can scale up to sales of 330 for the top product and push the sales in units to 930, while reducing the write-offs to 70. Table 3.9 shows the financial impact. The gross margin drops to 35 per cent (as we could expect) but the net profit, accounting for the write-offs, is at €280, comparable to the €290 for the 'inflexible' supply chain. It looks worse from a percentage perspective as the net margin drops to 30 per cent instead of 37 per cent, but that is compensated by a top-line growth of 19 per cent. Investors may look at the combination of growth and profit, and after a period of stagnation, be delighted to see the growth perspectives.

Next to the financials, I believe the flexible supply chain provides a much better strategic fit. We tend to focus on the write-offs, but a fashion company should focus on the missed sales. As mentioned above, building a brand happens through the iconic top products that everybody wants. If your supply chain is structurally incapable, you stay stuck in the middle.

If you're still not convinced, let's also include an important sustainability aspect. The 'Fast Fashion' world has been under increasing pressure to reduce the amount of waste. Bloomberg[24] reported in 2022 that less than one per cent of used clothing gets recycled into new garments, overwhelming countries like Ghana with discards. From the two options above: ensure we make more margin so we can allow more write-offs or make our supply chains more agile so we can capture more growth and reduce our waste, the second is obviously preferable. As I will continue exploring in this and next chapters, improved agility, responsiveness or resilience, however you want to call it, helps, not just in facing the increased complexity and volatility, but in facing our sustainability challenges as well.

Table 3.7 Flexible supply chain for fashion company – output in units

	Blind forecast	Demand	Prod1	Prod2	Prod3	Prod4	Prod5	Prod6	Sum prod	Sales	Missed sales	Write offs
Fam 1	100	400	30	60	60	60	60	60	330	330	70	0
Fam 2	100	150	30	60	60				150	150	0	0
Fam 3	100	150	30	60	60				150	150	0	0
Fam 4	100	100	30	60	10				100	100	0	0
Fam 5	100	100	30	60	10				100	100	0	0
Fam 6	100	50	30	20					50	50	0	0
Fam 7	100	20	30						30	20	0	10
Fam 8	100	20	30						30	20	0	10
Fam 9	100	5	30						30	5	0	25
Fam 10	100	5	30						30	5	0	25
Total	**1,000**	**1,000**	**300**	**320**	**200**				**1,000**	**930**	**70**	**70**

Table 3.8 Flexible supply chain for fashion company – sales and cost price

Sales price	€ 1.00
Cost price	€ 0.65
Gross margin	35%

Table 3.9 Flexible supply chain for fashion company – output in Euros

	Flexible	Non-flexible	Growth
Total sales	€ 930	€ 780	19%
Cogs	€ 604.50	€ 390	
Gross profit	€ 325.50	€ 390	−17%
Gross margin	35%	50%	
Write-offs	€ 45.50	€ 100	−55%
Net profit	€ 280	€ 290	−3%
Net margin	30%	37%	

Case Study: High-tech company

I used the fashion example in a recent discussion with a high-tech company. The company can be qualified as a product leader in visualization solutions for different types of markets and it was looking to make its new product introduction (NPI) process more resilient. Their line of thinking was to extend the existing NPI checklist, and next to criteria on expected volumes, costs and gross margins, add criteria like whether there is a second source for key components, or whether there is an option to (re)negotiate minimum order quantities (MOQs).

I pushed back on any of these as I thought their base assumptions for the NPI process were flawed. As I understood, there was a high pressure on cost in the initial design. When I was suggesting that they shouldn't accept a design if there was no approved second source for key components, the pushback was that R&D would never foresee time for this, as they were also under pressure to reduce time-to-market. It quickly led me to the conclusion that if cost and time-to-market are the two primary KPIs in the NPI process, no 'checklist' would ever succeed in building the necessary flexibility or resilience.

So, I used a comparable example as shown for the fashion company. If you launch 10 new products, you know half of them will fail, two or three will be so-so, one or two will be successful and one will have the potential to be your next blockbuster. If there is so much uncertainty on 'how much you're going to sell', it doesn't even make sense to make the business case on an individual NPI, so forget about the checklist anyway. Any assumptions you make on cost and margin are inherently flawed as the error on the demand is so big.

The supply chain person who was part of the discussion told me they wanted to have different supply chain options to choose from after the launch, which made me deeply puzzled. For me, for a product leader there is only one possible supply chain for an NPI and that is a flexible supply chain. The supply chain must be able to scale fast or fail fast. I explained that the cost should not be considered as an important parameter at the start and that it could still be optimized later. This makes people very uncomfortable. If cost is not important then what is important? It feels like we're completely letting go of the situation.

To further explore this argument, let's continue building a simulation as we've done for the fashion supply chain. Table 3.10 shows the typical business case table. We have 10 NPIs, each of them has a forecast of 100 (in practice that may be different but let's again focus on the uncertainty on the 100 as we did for the fashion example). We have designed our supply chain for minimum cost (given the cost pressure) and have not been able to make it very resilient (given the time pressure). However, the individual business cases look OK. The R&D costs of 50k per NPI can be recovered by the gross margin generated in the initial period, which could be a year or a quarter, whichever would be the norm in your company.

The problem, as with the fashion company, is that reality turns out to be different. Let's assume that the demand for NPI 1–10 is the 400 down to the five units (and euros) we've also used in the fashion case (as introduced in Table 3.1). And as our supply chain has been designed for minimum cost, it may not have the flexibility to quickly adjust because of long lead times, minimum order quantities, a limitation on the allowed deviations from the forecast one, two, three months out. So, let's assume that the supply of our 'base supply chain' here is comparable to the supply of the 'base supply chain' from the fashion case (the 180 down to the 60 introduced in Table 3.1).

Table 3.10 Business case and theoretical payback with base supply chain

	Business case forecast	Cost of goods	Fixed cost (75%)	Variable cost (25%)	Variable cost/ Unit	Gross profit	R&D cost	Pay back
NPI 1	100	50	37.50	12.50	0.13	50	50	1.00
NPI 2	100	50	37.50	12.50	0.13	50	50	1.00
NPI 3	100	50	37.50	12.50	0.13	50	50	1.00
NPI 4	100	50	37.50	12.50	0.13	50	50	1.00
NPI 5	100	50	37.50	12.50	0.13	50	50	1.00
NPI 6	100	50	37.50	12.50	0.13	50	50	1.00
NPI 7	100	50	37.50	12.50	0.13	50	50	1.00
NPI 8	100	50	37.50	12.50	0.13	50	50	1.00
NPI 9	100	50	37.50	12.50	0.13	50	50	1.00
NPI 10	100	50	37.50	12.50	0.13	50	50	1.00
Total	**1,000**	**500**	**375.00**	**125.00**	**0.13**	**500**	**500**	**1.00**

Table 3.11 shows what that leads to. For our star product we have difficulties to scale, so where the demand is 400, we can supply and hence sell only 180. For NPI 6 to 7 we have basically over-ordered or over-produced leading to an excess inventory of 200. Table 3.11 also translates this into cost. We make the assumption here of a relatively high fixed cost and a relatively low variable cost. In a minute we will look at an alternative where we try to 'buy flexibility', we pay more per unit, but the ratio of fixed versus variable costs is inverse. The high ratio of fixed versus variable costs could have to do with the fact that suppliers need to buy a certain mould or other specific equipment. Alternatives like 3D printing could be more flexible but more expensive, which is comparable to the examples the supply chain manager was giving.

Table 3.11 summarizes that the overall gross profit is 384 on sales of 780 which is 49 per cent so on average relatively good. That obviously conceals some of the dramas on the individual NPI level. The gross profit for NPIs 6 to 10 drops from 12.5 to 1.25, which to recover the R&D cost of 50 on the individual NPI, leads to paybacks of a factor 4 to 40. It gets truly dramatic if we include the write-offs. Let's assume that products 6 to 10 will be discontinued, and we have to write-off the inventory. NPI 7 to 10 now have a negative contribution of −25 to −40. Accounting for the write-offs of the unsold inventory, our net profit drops to 234, which on sales of 780 is a meagre 30 per cent, which is way below the 50 per cent we saw in the individual business cases. If the net profit is 234k, that will be the ultimate cash effect, so the net payback on our total R&D investment of 500 becomes a factor two instead of the anticipated factor one!

As we did for the fashion supply chain, let's look at an alternative, where we double the flexibility (more production moments, flexibility to reduce the first order). Flexibility comes at a cost, so as for the fashion supply chain, let's assume we allow a 30 per cent increase in cost (from 0.5 to 0.65 per unit) or 15 per cent drop in gross margin, from 50 per cent to 35 per cent.

Table 3.11 Actual payback with base supply chain

	Business case forecast	Demand	Produced/ bought	Sales	Inventory	Fixed cost (75%)	Variable cost (25%)	Fixed + variable cost	Cost/ unit
NPI 1	100	400	180	180	0	37.50	22.50	60.00	0.33
NPI 2	100	150	150	150	0	37.50	18.75	56.25	0.38
NPI 3	100	150	150	150	0	37.50	18.75	56.25	0.38
NPI 4	100	100	100	100	0	37.50	12.50	50.00	0.50
NPI 5	100	100	100	100	0	37.50	12.50	50.00	0.50
NPI 6	100	50	60	50	10	37.50	7.50	45.00	0.75
NPI 7	100	20	60	20	40	37.50	7.50	45.00	0.75
NPI 8	100	20	60	20	40	37.50	7.50	45.00	0.75
NPI 9	100	5	60	5	55	37.50	7.50	45.00	0.75
NPI 10	100	5	60	5	55	37.50	7.50	45.00	0.75
Total	1,000	1,000	980	780	200	375.00	122.50	497.50	0.51

(*continued*)

Table 3.11 (Continued)

	Cost of goods	Gross profit	R&D cost	Payback	Inventory in EUR	Net profit	R&D cost	Payback on net profit
NPI 1	60.00	120.00	50	0.42	–	120.00	50	0.42
NPI 2	56.25	93.75	50	0.53	–	93.75	50	0.53
NPI 3	56.25	93.75	50	0.53	–	93.75	50	0.53
NPI 4	50.00	50.00	50	1.00	–	50.00	50	1.00
NPI 5	50.00	50.00	50	1.00	–	50.00	50	1.00
NPI 6	37.50	12.50	50	4.00	7.50	5.00	50	10.00
NPI 7	15.00	5.00	50	10.00	30.00	– 25.00	50	– 2.00
NPI 8	15.00	5.00	50	10.00	30.00	– 25.00	50	– 2.00
NPI 9	3.75	1.25	50	40.00	41.25	– 40.00	50	– 1.25
NPI 10	3.75	1.25	50	40.00	41.25	– 40.00	50	– 1.25
Total	**395.97**	**384.03**	**500**	**1.30**	**150.00**	**234.03**	**500**	**2.14**

The individual business cases are now shown in Table 3.12. This is where people get cold feet. With a gross profit of only 35, the payback increases with 43 per cent to 1.43. And how will we explain the flexibility when we get questions? Do we dare to admit that instead of 100 we're maybe only going to sell five? There's little incentive for individuals to be open about their doubts.

A 30 per cent higher cost or a 15 per cent lower gross margin should allow us to create a lot more flexibility. So, as in our fashion supply chain example, let's assume that our supply now ranges from 330 for NPI 1 down to 30 for NPI 7–10 (comparable to Table 3.7). Table 3.13 shows the result. For NPI 1 we are able to scale faster and realize more of the demand (330 out of 400). For NPI 7 to 10 we have less unsold inventory as we reduced the initial batches or commitments.

Table 3.13 also translates this into financials. As introduced above the cost per unit is higher, and we assume a different split of fixed (25 per cent) versus variable (75 per cent) costs (for instance through using more 3D

Table 3.12 Business case and theoretical payback with flexible supply chain

	Business case forecast	Cost of goods	Fixed cost (25%)	Variable cost (75%)	Variable cost/unit	Gross profit	R&D cost	Pay back
NPI 1	100	65	16.25	48.75	0.49	35	50	1.43
NPI 2	100	65	16.25	48.75	0.49	35	50	1.43
NPI 3	100	65	16.25	48.75	0.49	35	50	1.43
NPI 4	100	65	16.25	48.75	0.49	35	50	1.43
NPI 5	100	65	16.25	48.75	0.49	35	50	1.43
NPI 6	100	65	16.25	48.75	0.49	35	50	1.43
NPI 7	100	65	16.25	48.75	0.49	35	50	1.43
NPI 8	100	65	16.25	48.75	0.49	35	50	1.43
NPI 9	100	65	16.25	48.75	0.49	35	50	1.43
NPI 10	100	65	16.25	48.75	0.49	35	50	1.43
Total	1,000	650	162.50	487.50	0.49	350	500	1.43

printing as opposed to making moulds and using injection moulding). Our gross profit of 325 on a total sales of 930 is around 35 per cent, in line with the business case. The underlying dramas remain. The gross profit for NPI 7–10 is now even negative as the cost per unit is higher, and there is less produced inventory over which the fixed costs can be spread. The payback on the gross profit is a factor 1.5 which is a bit worse than the planned 1.43, but still in the same order of magnitude. As there is less inventory to write-off, the numbers take a less steep dive when we account for those write-offs in the net profit. That net profit is 253, which is higher than the net profit of our base supply chain. The payback on the net profit is 1.97, which is better than the 2.14 of the base supply chain, and closer to the business case return of 1.43 (which was 1 for the base supply chain). In conclusion: a better performance with less surprises, while starting from a higher cost supply chain. Table 3.14 shows another summary and comparison. With a more flexible supply chain, even if that has a 30 per cent higher cost or a theoretically 15 per cent lower gross margin, we capture an extra 19 per cent growth and

Table 3.13 Actual payback with flexible supply chain

	Business case forecast	Demand	Produced/ bought	Sales	Inventory	Fixed cost (25%)	Variable cost (75%)	Fixed + variable cost	Cost/ unit
NPI 1	100	400	330	330	0	16.25	160.88	177.13	0.54
NPI 2	100	150	150	150	0	16.25	73.13	89.38	0.60
NPI 3	100	150	150	150	0	16.25	73.13	89.38	0.60
NPI 4	100	100	100	100	0	16.25	48.75	65.00	0.65
NPI 5	100	100	100	100	0	16.25	48.75	65.00	0.65
NPI 6	100	50	50	50	0	16.25	24.38	40.63	0.81
NPI 7	100	20	30	20	10	16.25	14.63	30.88	1.03
NPI 8	100	20	30	20	10	16.25	14.63	30.88	1.03
NPI 9	100	5	30	5	25	16.25	14.63	30.88	1.03
NPI 10	100	5	30	5	25	16.25	14.63	30.88	1.03
Total	1,000	1,000	1,000	930	70	162.50	487.50	650.00	0.65

	Cost of goods	Gross profit	R&D cost	Payback	Inventory in EUR	Net profit	R&D cost	Payback on net profit
NPI 1	177.13	152.88	50	0.33	-	152.88	50	0.33
NPI 2	89.38	60.63	50	0.82	-	60.63	50	0.82
NPI 3	89.38	60.63	50	0.82	-	60.63	50	0.82
NPI 4	65.00	35.00	50	1.43	-	35.00	50	1.43
NPI 5	65.00	35.00	50	1.43	-	35.00	50	1.43
NPI 6	40.63	9.38	50	5.33	-	9.38	50	5.33
NPI 7	20.58	-0.58	50	-85.71	10.29	-10.88	50	-4.60
NPI 8	20.58	-0.58	50	-85.71	10.29	-10.88	50	-4.60
NPI 9	5.15	-0.15	50	-342.86	25.73	-25.88	50	-1.93
NPI 10	5.15	-0.15	50	-342.86	25.73	-25.88	50	-1.93
Total	604.50	325.50	500	1.54	72.04	253.46	500	1.97

Table 3.14 Comparison of theoretical payback with actual payback in base and with flexible supply chain

Comparison	Business case	Base supply chain	Flexible supply chain	Growth
Blind Forecast in units/EUR	1,000.00	1,000.00	1,000.00	
Demand in units/EUR		1,000.00	1,000.00	
Sales in units/EUR		780.00	930.00	0.19
Produced in units		980.00	1,000.00	
Inventory in units		200.00	70.00	−0.65
Cost of Goods in EUR	500.00	395.97	604.50	
Gross Profit in EUR	500.00	384.03	325.50	−0.15
Gross Margin		49.23%	35.00%	
R&D cost	500.00	500.00	500.00	
Payback in years	1.00	1.30	1.54	
Inventory in EUR		150.00	72.04	
Write-off in EUR		150.00	72.04	
Net profit		234.03	253.46	0.08
Net margin		30.00%	27.25%	
R&D cost		500.00	500.00	
Payback in years		2.14	1.97	

grow our net profit with eight per cent. It also provides a better strategic fit. Product leaders live for the blockbusters and the top products they are able to launch every two to three years. Instead of overly focusing on cost and a flawed business case on an individual new product, companies should much more look at it from a portfolio perspective. If we invest 500 in R&D, what we want is to test new products, find out which are the ones we really want to scale and find easy criteria to kill the ones which don't, while limiting the working capital impact. We know that the business cases of individual NPIs are flawed because of the big uncertainty on the demand. If we have the courage to design the supply chain for flexibility instead of cost, we will win back the extra costs by the extra sales we are able to drive on the top products, and the reduced write-offs we have on those products that flop. It will help us build our reputation as a product leader and start a self-reinforcing cycle. As we have less waste in the supply chain it will also help our sustainability objectives.

Resilience: sensing, shifting, steering

After some considerations on how to more intelligently design the service or sales side, our products, our supply chains and our organizations, let's continue exploring our resilience fishbone shown in Figure 3.16. The top side of the fishbone contains elements to respond to the 'external' volatility drivers, shown at the top side of our volatility fishbone from Figure 3.1. At the London 2022 European Supply Chain Conference, Gartner introduced the idea of 'sense, shift and steer', or what it called the 'offset strategy'[25]. With the Covid disruptions fresh in our minds, supply chain people were looking for answers on how to deal with that new volatility. We have added the 'sense, shift steer' as the overall umbrella in Figure 3.16. By reviewing the individual blocks in the fishbone, let's try to further refine what an 'offset strategy' could practically mean.

A first step is building sensing capabilities. In his book[26] *The Changing World Order: Why Nations Succeed and Fail*, Ray Dalio builds a convincing case, that first of all, there's a cycle as nations rise and subsequently fall. Secondly, he builds the case that based on 18 indicators, he can predict where in their cycle the current big nations are and what is expected as their rise or fall in the next two to three decades. Out of those 18 indicators, five had the biggest impact in the past: innovation, the debt/money/capital market cycle, the internal order and disorder cycle, the external order and disorder cycle and acts of nature.

So how can we model our end-to-end value chain? How do we understand the behaviour of our markets? How do we collect data around them? What are our leading indicators that tell us where our markets are going? People will tell me not everything can be predicted. That may be true, but let's at least predict what can be predicted. After all we're living in the age of big data! Think about the case of Solvay specialty chemicals, introduced earlier in this chapter. By increasing visibility on the activity of the individual tiers in their end-to-end value chain, the inventories building up, Solvay could much better predict turning points. The data and the data science are available to realize this type of solution, so you could do the same. And for sure, more resilient supply chains have better sensing capabilities.

A related capability, and second block at the top of our resilience fishbone, is creating visibility. Visibility internally within the company, and visibility across the extended supply chain, into customers and the customers' customers (like in the Solvay example), into suppliers and our suppliers' suppliers (take the example of the Covid period, to understand where are our key bottlenecks). That need for visibility and transparency is reinforced by the pressure for more sustainability. Next to capacities, inventories, planned production or consumption, we also need visibility on the CO_2 emissions, the energy consumption and the labour conditions.

To create that visibility, connecting our otherwise disconnected systems comes at a significant cost. We will also need people to process that information, and manage the upstream and downstream relationships, that may also come at an extra cost. A bit as with the Fashion and High-Tech cases discussed above, these extra costs may only payoff beyond the average, in the extremes, which makes it hard to understand, to quantify and to defend. We know that we ought to do it, but there seem to be many hurdles to actually get it done.

So, as introduced above, it may again be helpful to introduce 'design axioms', and for instance state: we want visibility on inventories and planned consumptions for the top 20 per cent customers delivering 80 per cent of the volume. From those customers, we want visibility on the inventories and planned consumptions of their 20 per cent top customers, delivering 80 per cent of their related volumes, which translates into a two-tier visibility for 64 per cent of our volume. And likewise on the supplier side. Visibility on inventories and planned production for the 20 per cent suppliers delivering 80 per cent of the critical supplies, and visibility on the inventories and production plans of their 20 per cent key suppliers, delivering 80 per cent of their key supplies, extending in a two-tier visibility for 64 per cent of key supplies. Collaboration models like CPFR[27] have been around since the late 1990s[28] but their adoption has been slow potentially for the same reason explained above, that the benefits are to be sought in the extreme cases, which we are not used to look for. Maybe the combination of resilience and sustainability, captured in 'design axioms' is a way to drive more courageous and intelligent supply chain design, including the creation of better upstream and downstream visibility.

As we continue at the top of our resilience fishbone shown in Figure 3.16, better visibility and better sensing capabilities should allow us to become more pro-active and more actively do scenario management. If we see downstream stocks building up in our automotive supply chain and our leading indicators show an inflection point, what are the options? What if demand drops 20 per cent next quarter? What if next quarter is still stable but the quarter after drops 40 per cent as customers are depleting their inventories? How low do we go with our inventory to anticipate? What is the service and sales risk we are willing to take? While these are logical, even obvious, questions, we don't run these scenarios nor do we discuss them in our executive teams.

For things that cannot be foreseen, we'll need to think about deploying Emergency Response teams. Think about a ship blocking the Suez Canal. Have a dedicated team analysing the potential impact, the possible alternatives, the service, cost, cash and sustainability impact and having fast decision cycles and short loops to key decision makers. Extraordinary situations require extraordinary measures.

And we might try to prepare for the unforeseeable, by doing proper risk management and stakeholder engagement. If we understand our risks, our exposures to supply, to environmental or to social risks, we might be better prepared when the unforeseen happens. And we might pro-actively engage with stakeholders, pressure groups, the government, to understand their point of view, their concerns, and anticipate potential actions before they hit us. An example of 2022 is where Solvay[29] came under pressure from environmentalists and activist Bluebell Capital Partners to reduce the release of limestone residue into the sea at its facility in Rosignano, Italy. Solvay had initially pushed back on concerns that the waste may have been harmful, but now plans to invest around 15 million euros to cut the release by 20 per cent compared to what regulators currently allow. Sensing and visibility is not just about the goods that flow through our supply chain, it is also about the broader stakeholders around us, what are their concerns, from an environmental and social perspective, and how that could potentially impact us as a company. A resilient supply chain is pro-active in these aspects as well.

Conclusion

In this chapter, I have introduced drivers for volatility, some of them external, or outside of our direct control, some of them internal, and more directly within our control. I have defined how to respond to that volatility, how to be more resilient, how to better organize for the external drivers, how to better organize for the internal drivers. I have encouraged you to define your drivers and your responses. I have shown the result of my book council as a starting point for improving our understanding.

Using two case studies I have shown how our supply chains are often designed for cost instead of agility or resilience. More agile supply chains can have a higher cost, but I have shown that it pays off and that it can lead to supply chains that are better supporting the strategic positioning of the company.

In the next chapter I will continue exploring the mismatch between our current capabilities, which are mostly reflected by the second generation supply chain thinking, and our true needs, which are reflected by the fourth generation supply chain thinking. My intent is that further detailing the mismatch and its impact will help increase the sense of urgency with supply chain and non-supply chain professionals.

Endnotes

1 B DeSmet. The Supply Chain Triangle concept – the essentials, 13 December 2017. www.bramdesmet.com/2017/12/13/the-supply-chain-triangle-concept-essentials/ (archived at https://perma.cc/8H5J-9X5V)
2 B DeSmet. Fishbone template, 2024. www.bramdesmet.com/rethinkingsupplychain/ (archived at https://perma.cc/B6H5-39KQ)
3 J Politi, D Sevastopulo. Donald Trump imposes tariffs on $200bn of Chinese goods, Financial Times, 18 September 2018. www.ft.com/content/a88cec7e-babf-11e8-94b2-17176fbf93f5 (archived at https://perma.cc/Y94Y-SNEX)
4 S Shrikanth. China stocks slide as Trump expands tariffs on $300bn in exports, Financial Times, 2 August 2019. www.ft.com/content/813f59f6-b4c2-11e9-8cb2-799a3a8cf37b (archived at https://perma.cc/3N24-BPL6)
5 G Chazan. German companies halt production to cope with rising energy prices, Financial Times, 31 August 2022. www.ft.com/content/d0d46712-6234-4d24-bbed-924a00dd0ca9 (archived at https://perma.cc/H2BT-ZFZR)
6 R Dalio (2021) *Principles for Dealing with the Changing World Order: Why nations succeed or fail,* Simon and Schuster, London
7 Federal Reserve Bank of St. Louis. Federal Reserve Economic Data, 2024. fred.stlouisfed.org (archived at https://perma.cc/GX37-R8AY)
8 R Partington. Eurozone sinks into recession as cost of living crisis takes toll, The Guardian, 8 June 2023. www.theguardian.com/business/2023/jun/08/eurozone-sinks-into-recession-as-cost-of-living-crisis-takes-toll (archived at https://perma.cc/B5GG-VBGH)
9 S Kettel. Oil crisis, Britannica Money, 20 February 2024. www.britannica.com/money/oil-crisis (archived at https://perma.cc/BA6L-BGDY)

10. Reuters. 3M pays $10.3bn to settle water pollution suit over 'forever chemicals', The Guardian, 22 June 2023. www.theguardian.com/environment/2023/jun/22/3m-settlement-municipal-water-systems-pfas-contamination (archived at https://perma.cc/SC4U-DLKN)
11. T Perkins. Chemical industry used big tobacco's tactics to conceal evidence of PFAS risks, The Guardian, 7 June 2023. www.theguardian.com/environment/2023/jun/07/pfas-3m-dupont-chemical-industry-health-toxic-study (archived at https://perma.cc/A4PV-SZUD)
12. Colorado State University Tropical Weather & Climate Research, 2024. tropical.colostate.edu (archived at https://perma.cc/Z47N-ZMB6)
13. National Centers for Environmental Information, NCEI, 2024. www.ncei.noaa.gov (archived at https://perma.cc/ZPD7-TZUY)
14. National Centers for Environmental Information, NCEI, U.S. Billion-Dollar Weather and Climate Disasters, 2024. www.ncei.noaa.gov/access/billions/ (archived at https://perma.cc/3VLW-QMMB)
15. Solvay S.A. https://www.solvay.com/en/our-company (archived at https://perma.cc/67Q7-DHTA)
16. Solvay. Solvay marks new era after successful Syensqo spin-off, 11 Dec 2023. www.solvay.com/en/press-release/solvay-marks-new-era-after-syensqo-spinoff (archived at https://perma.cc/G6RY-CH5M)
17. Solventure. Anticipating on business turning points, Solventure LIFe, 2024. www.leadingindicatorforecasting.com (archived at https://perma.cc/TD27-3L9X)
18. K Baker. Despite devastating effects on the broader economy, the pandemic has been a boon for US home improvement, Joint Center for Housing Studies, 25 March 2021. www.jchs.harvard.edu/blog/despite-devastating-effects-broader-economy-pandemic-has-been-boon-us-home-improvement (archived at https://perma.cc/9T6R-P39J)
19. H Lee, P Venkata and S Whang. Information distortion in a supply chain: The bullwhip effect. *Management Science*, 1997, 43 (4), 546–58
20. B DeSmet. Fishbone template, 2024. www.bramdesmet.com/rethinkingsupplychain/ (archived at https://perma.cc/B6H5-39KQ)
21. 3M. 3M to Exit PFAS manufacturing by the end of 2025, 3M News Center, 20 Dec 2022. news.3m.com/2022-12-20-3M-to-Exit-PFAS-Manufacturing-by-the-End-of-2025 (archived at https://perma.cc/C2GZ-CKBZ)
22. J P Womack, D T Jones (2003) *Lean Thinking: Banish waste and create wealth in your corporation*, Free Press, New York
23. H Mintzberg (1979) *The Structuring of Organizations*, Prentice Hall, London
24. N O Pearson, E Dontoh, D Pandya. Fast-fashion waste is choking developing countries with mountains of trash, Bloomberg UK, 2 Nov 2022. www.bloomberg.com/news/features/2022-11-02/h-m-zara-fast-fashion-waste-leaves-environmental-impact (archived at https://perma.cc/U5HC-6XQ7)
25. Gartner, Inc. Gartner Supply Chain Symposium/Xpo 2022 London: Day 1 Highlights, Gartner, 27 Sep 2022. www.gartner.com/en/newsroom/press-releases/2022-09-27-gartner-supply-chain-symposium-xpo-london-day-1-highlights (archived at https://perma.cc/9L95-ZHLW)

26 R Dalio (2020) *The Changing World Order: Why nations succeed and fail*, Avid Reader Press, London

27 ECR Europe. A guide to CPFR implementation, April 2001. www.ecr.digital/whitepaper/a-guide-to-cpfr-implementation-2001/ (archived at https://perma.cc/JQ8K-M736)

28 ECR Europe. A guide to CPFR implementation, April 2001. www.ecr.digital/whitepaper/a-guide-to-cpfr-implementation-2001/ (archived at https://perma.cc/7FNA-2WMW)

29 B H Meijer, E Martinuzzi, S Jessop. Solvay to cut waste discharged off Italy, ending tussle with activist, Reuters, 6 Sep 2022. www.reuters.com/business/sustainable-business/solvay-ends-dispute-with-activist-bluebell-over-italy-sea-waste-2022-09-06/ (archived at https://perma.cc/4AEN-VEWS)

The need for a sustainable and resilient fourth generation supply chain

04

Introduction

In this chapter I will visualize the impact of a lack of resilience through what I will call an 'inverse fishbone' diagram. You will do an exercise around that with your executive team and I will show the result from a comparable exercise with my book council to improve our understanding of that impact.

To make the required capabilities more concrete, I will detail what I see in companies today, typical second generation supply chain capabilities, and contrast that with what I believe we need, the so-called fourth generation capabilities. I will analyse that on the level of strategic planning and supply chain design. I will do so on the level of tactical planning and supply chain steering. I will provide exercises that help you in mapping where you are in your second versus fourth generation strategic and tactical supply chain capabilities.

Managing a fourth generation supply chain with second generation supply chain capabilities leads to all the negative impacts I will show in the inverse fishbone. This is illustrated by the case studies from the fashion and high-tech companies in the previous chapter. In this chapter we will study the lack of visibility and control in the typical supply chain in the bike industry. While that was working relatively well in stable markets with no supply issues and predictable market growth, the industry ran out of control during and after the Covid pandemic. I will introduce an alternative supply chain setup, still primarily outsourced for its manufacturing, but with better visibility and better control. I will introduce how this supply chain enables a breakthrough business model, for bike riders, for bike companies, for dealers, providing a personalized 'configure-to-order' platform. It illustrates the power of fourth generation supply chain design and planning.

> **EXERCISE**
> Assessing the impact of a lack of resilience
>
> Let's continue our series of workshops with our executive team or our cross-functional team representing sales, operations, product management/marketing/R&D, supply chain, finance. Just like before, try to assemble a somewhat larger group, preferably 16–20 people so you can break up in smaller teams of four to five people.
>   Hand out blank what I would call 'inverse fishbone' and ask the question 'What do the teams see as the impact of a lack of resilience within the supply chain?'. I have made such a reverse fishbone template available on my website[1]. As before, limit the amount of explanation so you can pick people's fresh brains and multiply the insights. You might debrief the previous fishbone on what is driving resilience. In the end it is about understanding what a lack of resilience causes as an impact.

The impact of a lack of resilience

As with the other exercises, I did exactly this exercise with my book council, which I introduced in Chapter 3. The result is shown in Figure 4.1. As I was processing the results of the individual groups, I noticed I could easily cluster them around the 5Ps from the Sustainable Development Goals or SDGs developed by the United Nations[2]: Prosperity (which links to Profit), People (which links to Social), Planet (which links to Environmental), Partnerships (which is a less explicit focus in ESG) and Peace (likewise).

It starts with the prosperity or profit impact. Think about our fashion or high-tech example from Chapter 3. A lack of resilience leads to an important financial impact. As we are hurting service, we are also hurting the topline. What I didn't discuss but what happens in practice is that when service is under pressure we get inefficiencies and firefighting that is raising costs

Figure 4.1 The impact of a lack of resilience

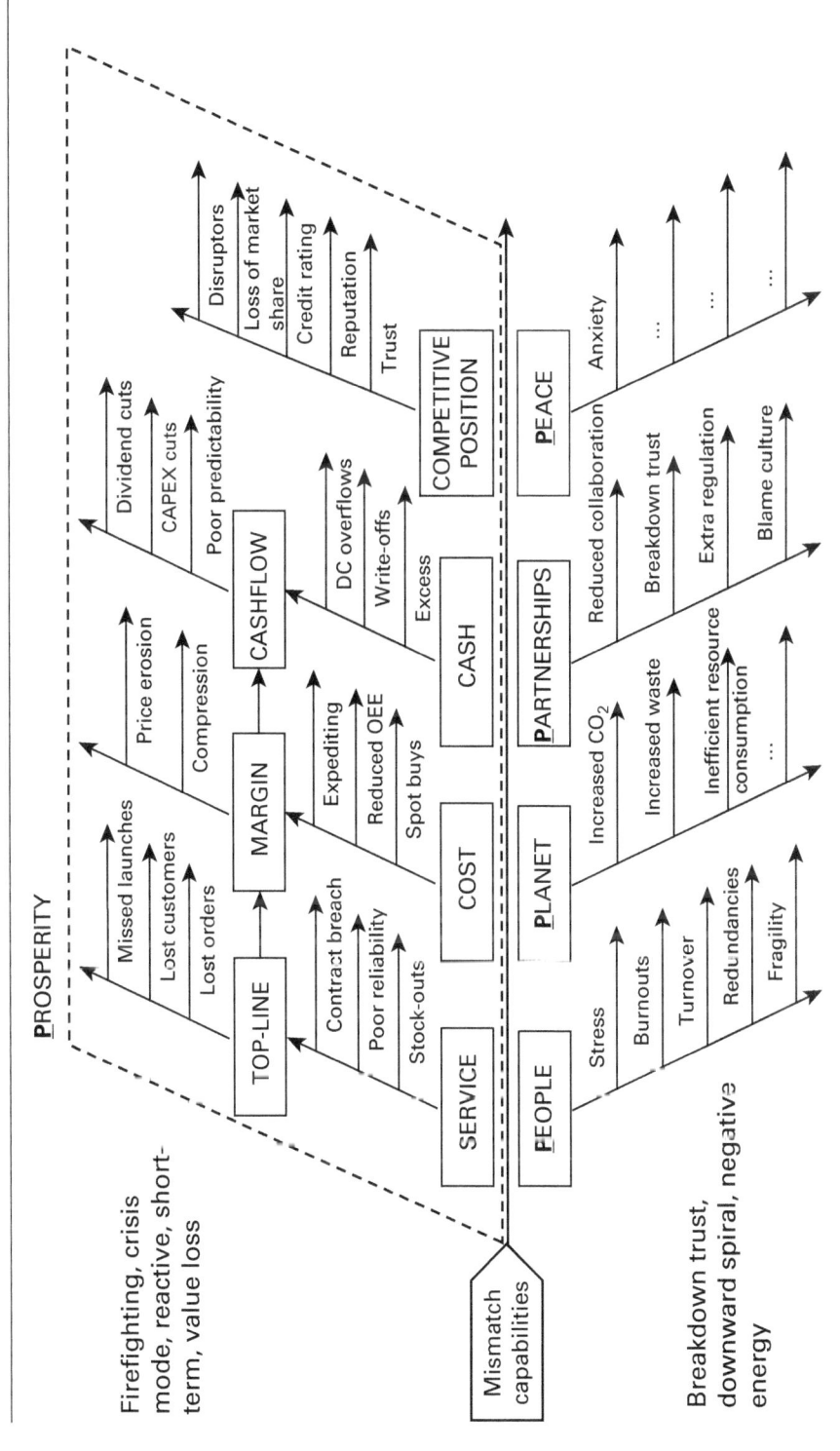

PROSPERITY

Firefighting, crisis mode, reactive, short-term, value loss

Breakdown trust, downward spiral, negative energy

Mismatch capabilities

TOP-LINE: Missed launches, Lost customers, Lost orders
MARGIN: Price erosion, Compression
CASHFLOW: Dividend cuts, CAPEX cuts, Poor predictability
COMPETITIVE POSITION: Disruptors, Loss of market share, Credit rating, Reputation, Trust

SERVICE: Contract breach, Poor reliability, Stock-outs
COST: Expediting, Reduced OEE, Spot buys
CASH: DC overflows, Write-offs, Excess

PEOPLE: Stress, Burnouts, Turnover, Redundancies, Fragility
PLANET: Increased CO_2, Increased waste, Inefficient resource consumption
PARTNERSHIPS: Reduced collaboration, Breakdown trust, Extra regulation, Blame culture
PEACE: Anxiety

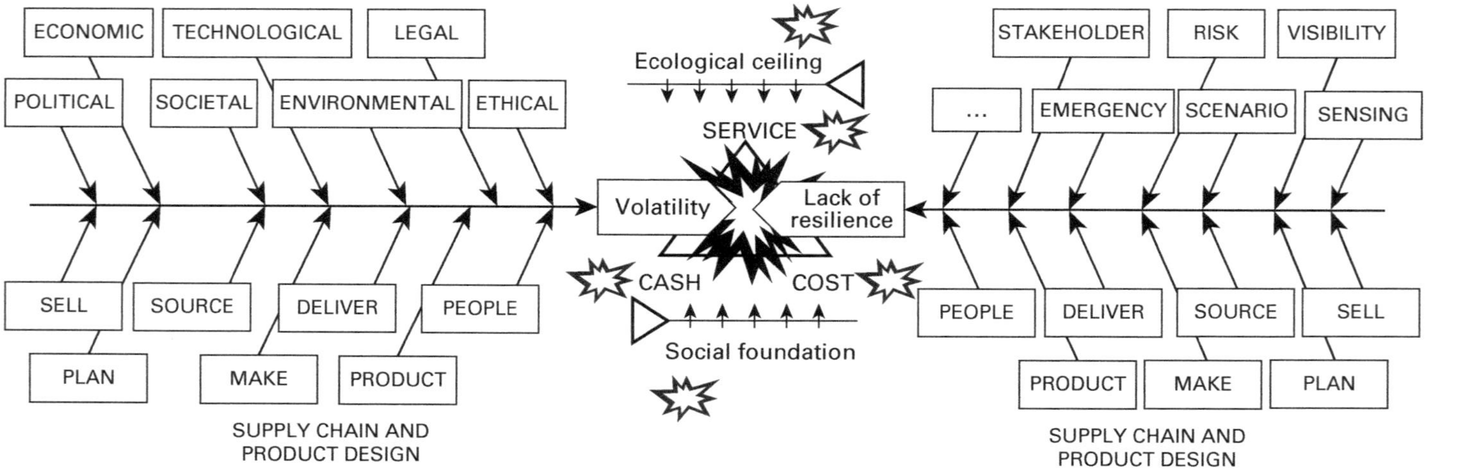

Figure 4.2 Volatility and a lack of resilience clashing at the heart of the triangle

and negatively impacting margins. Our gross margins of the previous chapter are in that sense overstated. Those cases show we put down the wrong inventories which is impacting cashflow. What I didn't discuss but what happens in practice is that too many failures may lead to CAPEX cuts compromising our strategic roadmap. If we get into this negative spiral, our competitive position erodes as we lose market share, trust and reputation, which potentially leads to a degraded credit rating which all together makes us prone to disruptors.

Next to the financial or 'Profit' or 'Prosperity' impact, there is a broader sustainability impact. On the 'People' or 'Social' side, the reactive firefighting puts a lot of stress on people. When that stress is sustained over a longer period, it leads to burnouts and employee turnover. If our business degrades we may need to lay off people, which makes us lose a lot of human capital and which invigorates employee turnover. The good ones may leave while the bad ones choose to stay.

On the 'Planet' or 'Environmental' impact, resilience beats sustainability I learned from the book council. If the top-line is at risk and our service is under pressure, we use airfreight and expediting to close the service gap. That negatively affects our CO_2 emissions. Likewise, last minute changes and surprises will lead to inefficiencies, inefficient resource consumption (energy, water, raw materials) and increased waste (for instance more wastewaters from cleaning or more off-grade product).

In the 5Ps from the SDGs there is one for 'Partnerships'. A lack of resilience puts our partnerships under pressure. We see a breakdown of trust, a growing blame culture, and reduced collaboration. And if this is an economy wide phenomenon, which was the case during Covid-19, it could feed anxiety with people, which fits under the last P of 'Peace'.

The reason for using the inverse fishbone is because it illustrates that a lack of resilience causes problems all over the place. An alternative illustration is shown in Figure 4.2. When volatility and a lack of resilience clash, they clash at the heart of the Supply Chain Triangle, causing damage across the triangle, the social foundation and the ecological ceiling, which is shown in Figure 4.2.

From second to fourth generation supply chain capabilities

When looking at Figure 4.2, one can ask the question 'How bad is it? How mature or immature are our supply chain processes and capabilities? How

Figure 4.3   Fourth generation supply chain

1970s–1980s 1st generation	1990s–2000s 2nd generation	2010s–2020s 3rd generation	2020+ 4th generation
1D SC Service-driven	2D SC Service & cost-driven	3D SC Service, cost & cash-driven	5D SC Sustainable & resilient supply chains
Just deliver what the customer wants	Improve service while reducing cost	Improve return on capital employed	Balance service, cost and cash with ESG in a VUCA world

well do they match with the complexity, the volatility and the needs of the world around us?' My answer is that the situation is pretty bad. I believe the supply chain patient is critical.

Continuing the discussion from Chapter 1, I believe we are trying to manage the needs of a fourth generation supply chain, with the recipes and capabilities of a second generation supply chain. The world has moved on, but our supply chain capabilities have not. That causes continuous friction in all of the dimensions of Figure 4.1.

As a reminder, the second generation supply chain is the one where we expect supply chain to deliver more service while reducing cost. Our supply chain is not involved in strategic considerations rather it is basically expected to execute what has been decided by the business. The third generation supply chain considers not just service and cost, but working capital and fixed asset impact. It also introduces the need for strategic trade-offs, the OR-OR next to the AND-AND. I can't have the service of a traditional supermarket at the inventory and cost levels of a hard discounter. The fourth generation supply chain expands the trade-offs to include the environmental and social aspects. It is 5D instead of 3D.

Based on the discussion in Chapter 3, we can now also include the needs and trade-offs linked to resilience. Instead of being reactive and being continuously caught by surprise, a fourth generation supply chain has thought through how to deal with resilience, how to organize for it, and how a lack of resilience impacts financial, environmental and social metrics. So the fourth generation supply chain is Sustainable and Resilient, and balances Service, Cost, Cash and ESG in a volatile world. In Figure 4.3 we have now included the resilience aspect of the fourth generation supply chain.

In Chapters 5 and 6 we will include both sustainability and resilience in our strategic trade-offs and into our strategy-driven supply chain design. In Chapters 7 and 8 we will do the same for (tactical) integrated planning. In this chapter we will try to illustrate the gap between second and fourth generation supply chain capabilities, and the impact of managing the needs of a fourth generation supply chain with second generation capabilities. We will start with strategic planning and supply chain design capabilities and then dive into tactical business planning capabilities. We will give examples and elaborate cases to increase the understanding and awareness of the gap.

From second to fourth generation capabilities: strategic planning and design perspective

Many of the supply chains I encounter have been designed for minimum cost. Think about the fashion example in Chapter 3. We will see the same in the example from the bike industry later in this chapter. Part of the problem, as we explained in Chapter 3, is that flexibility only pays off in the extremes (the true demand is 400 instead of the expected 100, or it is only 5), and we design our supply chain for the averages, not for the extremes, nor do we

Table 4.1 Strategic planning and design capabilities in a second versus fourth generation supply chain

Second generation supply chain	Fourth generation supply chain
Designed for minimum cost	Designed for competitive advantage
Waterfall: first business, then supply chain	Integrated: strategic value proposition & corresponding supply chain
Disconnected from product design	Integrated product & supply chain design
Focus on distribution network	Focus on extended supply chain
Poorly designed service promise	Smartly designed service promise
One-size-fits-all	Supply chain segmentation
Separate sustainability plans & metrics	Integrated sustainability plans & metrics
Unclear trade-offs of sustainability vs financial metrics	Integrated design of sustainability & financial metrics

dare to defend those extremes. In general we don't design our supply chains for a competitive edge, to truly support our strategic positioning in the market. Another illustration of that links to sustainability.

In a bid to reduce CO_2, I've seen supply chain managers considering putting goods on ocean transport instead of airfreight. A good idea in itself, if it weren't that the company was a product leader. By putting products on the boat we're increasing the time-to-market by at least four weeks. If we have frequent engineering changes, which we could expect, we are basically constantly shipping old products to the market. There is an inherent conflict with the strategic positioning of the company. The tougher but better choice would be to consider regional sourcing and regional manufacturing. Supply chain managers don't want to propose that as it would be increasing costs and CAPEX. Regional sourcing and production would also reduce the CO_2 emissions, and it could potentially sharpen the competitive edge. By producing in local markets we could provide local variants, which could potentially boost sales. That more integrated design, across CO_2, cost, sales potential, is what a fourth generation supply chain needs. In Chapters 5 and 6 we will talk in more detail about 'Strategy-Driven, Sustainable and Resilient Supply Chain Design'.

A second common pitfall is the 'waterfall approach'. The business conceives a new business idea, in isolation of supply chain, and once that business idea or the 'business strategy' is ready, we transfer it to supply chain who has to translate it into a 'supply chain strategy'. It fits in the mental model that supply chain is an operational or tactical-operational function that is there to execute and hence should not be involved in the more strategic business discussions. It is a failed process. Let me try to illustrate with an example. I had a call with a finance director. That person had been filling out the triangle[3] and the strategy[4] surveys from the previous book via the website. When I asked her what was the reason, she said she felt the strategic choices in the business unit were not 100 per cent clear. She continued that the business, in the pursuit of growth, wanted to offer a high performance piece of technology, for a desalination application in the Middle East. The only problem was that something had to be done about the cost, as that market was more price sensitive, and performance was less of a differentiator. Plus we were going to need regional stocks, for service parts, and we were going to set up a service division in the Middle East. I apologized for the bad news, but I told the finance director that my gut feeling was this was never going to add up. To which she reacted surprised. Which made me surprised. I explained that I got to know the company as a true product leader, where engineers focus on making the best. You were now going to ask those same engineers to modify that existing technology and come up with something which was good enough. Plus you were going to add regional stocks of service parts which we know are inherently slow moving. I felt a lot of margin pressure, so margins were going to go down, and we were going to make a lot of extra investments in fixed assets and working capital. This was going to be bad from a bang-for-the-buck perspective. And it was outside of the strategic fit for this type of product leader organization. Yes, but it has already been decided. 'Eeuhm, I'm sorry?' Typical example of a waterfall approach. There is no strategy as long as there is no supply chain. Without the supply chain we don't understand the cost or the capital employed so we don't understand how we will drive return. Set aside that in this type of waterfall approach we can make reasonable considerations about sustainability or resilience. For the fourth generation supply chain, we need to professionalize our approach towards integrated business and supply chain design, which we will further explore in Chapters 5 and 6.

A third common disconnect is the one between product design and supply chain design. Our case of the bike industry below illustrates in an excellent way how closely the two are intertwined or should be intertwined. We start by analysing the archaic outsourced supply chain setup, explain how not just the bike company, but basically the whole bike industry, ran out of control during and after the Covid crisis. We explain what would be needed to set up an ATO supply chain, where bike riders can configure their bike from a portal and have it assembled at one of the dealers. And we discuss how a comparable supply chain setup could be a more flexible and resilient alternative to the current antiquated supply chain setup. We also discuss how R&D and product management are needed to define the configuration options, how as a result products may need to be redesigned, how to implement that in the supply chain and how the supply chain can provide a feedback loop on which there are configurations and options to reconsider.

Sustainability is also an important driver for a more integrated product and supply chain design. In his book *Sustainable Logistics and Supply Chain Management*[5], David Grant states that 80 per cent of the environmental impact of a product is determined at the design stage. If we want to understand the CO_2 footprint of our products, we need to understand the embedded CO_2 of the raw materials and the components that go into the product (Scope 3), we need to understand the CO_2 that will be emitted during the use of the product (for instance the energy consumption, also Scope 3) and we need to understand the supply chain that brings in the raw materials and components, transforms them into finished products, brings them to customers, and re-uses, repairs or recycles them (Scope 1 and Scope 2). If we want to optimize the CO_2 (Scope 1, 2 and 3), we will need to concurrently design the product and the supply chain.

The idea of 'concurrent engineering' was already proposed long before sustainability was as dominant, in 1998, by Charles Fine[6], in his book *Clockspeed*. He introduced the idea of 3DCE, 3D Concurrent Engineering, where he talks about concurrent engineering of the Product (performance specifications and functions), the Process (technology and equipment used for production) and the Supply Chain (the set of organizations involved and the allocation of tasks). In our mind, the production is part of the broader supply chain setup, hence we'd rather see it as 2DCE or 2D Concurrent Engineering. The primary driver for Charles Fine to integrate product and supply chain engineering is to increase the clockspeed, to reduce the time-to-market with new ideas, in the age of 'temporary advantage'. Disconnects are common though, think about the case of the high-tech company in the previous Chapter. R&D didn't have time to qualify a second source as they were under pressure for time-to-market, leading to a lack of resilience in the supply chain. Likewise we see that products may be designed for functionality and direct costs (the materials going in), but they may not be designed for manufacturability or serviceability. In the fourth generation supply chain, product and supply chain design are integrated, to ensure resilience, sustainability and clockspeed in the world of temporary advantage.

A fourth element I see in companies is that supplier selection, optimization of manufacturing footprints and optimization of distribution footprints are disconnected exercises, run by different departments, procurement, manufacturing and logistics. The literature is heavily biased towards 'distribution network design', where we use mathematical programming techniques (linear programming or integer programming) to find the network that is minimizing the warehousing and transportation cost, based on simplified service assumptions such as 'what is the per cent of customers that can be reached within 24/48/72 hours'. When we optimize the distribution network, the manufacturing is typically out of scope, when we optimize the manufacturing, the suppliers are out of scope. One of the aspects that, as an example, cannot be covered appropriately in this fragmented approach is upward or downward volume flexibility. Let's say doubling or tripling sales volumes in a 6–12 month period, assuming it is new demand, not recurring seasonality that is easier to predict. The need to scale up or down the end-to-end supply chain is common at product leaders. Think about the product selling 400 instead of 100 and the one

The need for a sustainable and resilient fourth generation supply chain

selling 5 instead of 100. If it is new demand instead of seasonality, it cannot be buffered in inventory. In this case the whole supply chain needs to scale up, or in the inverse situation, scale down, including key suppliers, our manufacturing and our distribution. Think about the demand corrections post-Covid, the whole supply chain had to scale down. It feels to me as if organizations are 'improvising' themselves through these swings, rather than having designed their supply chains for this type of flexibility. Needless to add, that if we design only piece per piece instead of one integrated flow, there is a risk we are suboptimal from a cost, a working capital, a fixed assets, a CO_2 and possibly also a social perspective (e.g. putting stress on the weakest link in the chain). Fourth generation supply chain design is by default considering the extended value chain, from the suppliers' supplier down to the customers' customer.

As a fifth challenge with the second generation supply chain, I talked about poorly designed service promises in Chapter 3, like promising a different lead time to different customers on a portfolio of more than 50,000 SKUs. I explained that service design is assumed to be the prerogative and decision of sales, where sales lacks the understanding of how that impacts the supply chain, and where possibly we need manufacturing and R&D to understand what could be done to redesign the product so we can come up with a reasonable make-to-order or ATO lead time. The average salesperson wants to avoid discussion with the customer and will push back in saying 'the customer won't accept this'. In a fourth generation supply chain the service design is the responsibility of a cross-functional team, and the key question becomes 'Is the customer willing to pay for this?'.

Sixth, in a second generation supply chain, it is still common to use a one size fits all instead of a segmented supply chain approach. I'm a cautious lover of segmentation, as it adds complexity, and as segmentation should not be used as an alternative for making strategic choices. As an example, I don't recommend companies to combine branded products with private label. As I discussed in my previous book at length, these are two different strategies, you don't combine Etihad with Ryanair or Southwest either. Different strategies require different cultures, who cannot be combined within one single organization. We often choose to combine branded and private label for tactical or financial reasons, we have free capacity, so we try to fill it. But it is opposite to making clear strategic trade-offs, so a recipe for disaster rather than a recipe for success.

I do accept that in larger organizations, different products in different regional markets can have a different strategic focus. In that case, think through by how far these can and need to be served by the same organization. The same customer service organization, the same logistics platform, the same planning organization. The orientation of a customer intimacy organization will be different than that of an operational excellence organization. So if you still want to do branded and private label, then do it with different organizations, with a different customer service, different supply chain all the way down to different plants and R&D teams. Private label products should be designed for quality that is 'at par' and lowest price. Manufacturing of private label products should all be about efficiency, for instance through higher automation. Branded products should be designed for premium quality and for driving premium pricing that allows for extra costs. Manufacturing of branded products will be much more driven by quality of the product, promotions, product tests, product innovations. It's a different game that needs a different team with a different skillset and a different orientation.

John Gattorna[7] has been a long-time advocate of behavioural segmentation of customers. Some customers are more price sensitive, others are more service sensitive. His idea is to segment the supply chain according to different customer behaviours. Though we greatly respect the work of John Gattorna and it is known to have been adopted by supply chain leaders like Schneider Electric, we again see a risk for a strategic conflict or a dilution of strategic focus. Strategy will tell us to choose which customers to serve. Do we want to be a price player and serve the price sensitive customers? Or do we want to be a total solution player, and serve the customers who are willing to pay for that. I believe segmentation can help to control the complexity and the chaos in larger companies, but it should never get in the way of clear and tough strategic choices.

As a seventh element, when I look at the sustainability plans of companies, they often seem to be 'separate plans' driven as 'separate projects' with 'separate objectives'. If companies present their improvement plans, except maybe for distribution projects, it is typically or with the aim to become more efficient (where the primary driver would be cost), or with the aim to become more sustainable (where the primary driver would for instance be CO_2). I don't see many plans saying these are our overall objectives, for instance across the five dimensions of service, cost, cash, environment and society, this is our improvement project list, and this is how they will contribute to achieving our 5D objectives. By separating the project portfolios, we also seem to stay away from the tougher discussions where we need to trade-off a first dimension against a second, for instance a lower CO_2 but at a higher cost or capital employed or vice versa. In general, across companies, the sustainability objectives seem ambitions rather than commitments, which is still a valuable start. As we explained at the start of this chapter, resilience seems to beat sustainability. If the service is under pressure we will start flying stuff around the world. In a fourth generation supply chain, we are more strategic about sustainability. We think through where we want to be on certain sustainability aspects, at par, differentiating or dominating. And we think through on a strategic level what is the impact on financial metrics. We reason in 5D. We will continue that discussion in Chapters 5 and 6.

Case Study: Bike industry

During the Covid pandemic, I was called into a company designing and selling high-end racing, gravel and mountain bikes. The company was suffering. Demand for bikes was booming during the pandemic, as people were stuck at home, couldn't travel for holidays, so finally wanted to buy that bike they had been longing after for many years.

The production of bikes was completely outsourced. The company was ordering from tier 1 suppliers, who were doing the bike assembly. The tier 1 suppliers were ordering from tier 2 suppliers, who were making the frames, the gear sets, the brake sets and other components. The tier 1 suppliers were delivering to two company warehouses, from which the company was supplying its dealers.

The supply chain was organized in a very traditional way. The bike company was placing orders at the tier 1 assemblers, for finished bikes, three to six months ahead. It had little or no visibility on the planning at the tier 1 assembly and no visibility or direct contact with the tier 2 component manufacturers. As long as there were no supply problems this was more or less OK, but during the pandemic everything changed.

Figure 4.4 Traditional bike supply chain

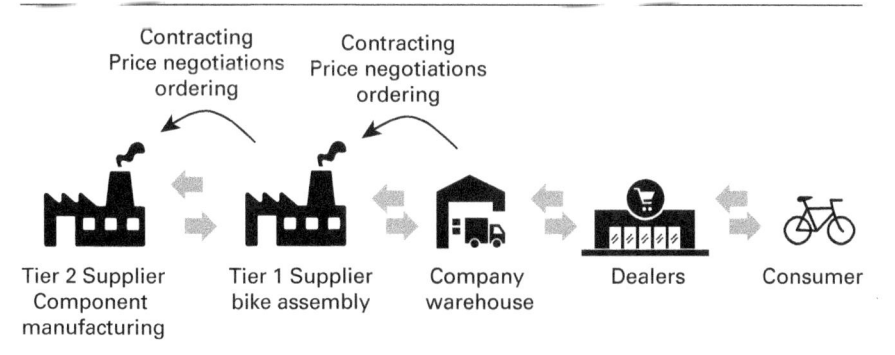

As demand was exploding, the tier 2 suppliers quickly ran out of capacity and key raw materials. That was delaying the tier 1 assemblers, who had to delay the orders of the bike company. Many of these assemblers are relatively small companies. They didn't have sophisticated planning systems to predict and communicate order lead times. The whole situation became problematic. As they were missing one or two critical components, they couldn't start the assembly, but they had to finance all of the other inventory of components. Their working capital was rising and was becoming tricky, making them cautious in the ordering process of the components. You might say that all of a sudden the heaviest burden was on the weakest link in the supply chain. When the bike company wanted to get control of its supply chain, and was asking for more details on the plans and the commitments, the tier 1 assemblers were reluctant to share this information. The information being shared was very fragmented, different spreadsheets for each assembler, leaving the bike company with a spreadsheet puzzle that was impossible to solve.

The reaction in the bike supply chain, as in many other chains, was 'order more, order further ahead'. Dealers were out of bikes so were massively ordering. The bike companies saw orders from dealers going through the roof, so were ordering more. When I came in, the bike company was placing orders with suppliers for 18 months out! Fast forward, in the second half of 2022, demand started dropping, shortages were being resolved, bike companies were flooded with the excess ordering from the Covid pandemic years of 2020 to 2021, dealers were pushing back inventories and cancelling orders, leaving the bike companies with huge and expensive inventories (the type of inverse bull whip already shown in Figure 1.4). The sector was facing a huge working capital problem, which led Giant Group, the world's largest bicycle manufacturer, to extend payment terms[8] to suppliers to 45 days.

The antiquated supply chain practices were an industry-wide problem. I was told this was simply how the industry works. Let me try to explain how this supply chain could be organized differently by starting from a question I got from the company. Despite all the operational issues and problems, the company was thinking ahead and wanted to allow their experienced bike riders (their end-users) to build their own bikes through an online portal. They would then send the individual components to the dealer and ask that dealer to do the final assembly. It could be a win-win-win: happier bike riders as they would have more options. Happy dealers, as they can add value and charge for that. And a happier bike company, as they could reduce their inventory risk by carrying inventory of components and semi-finished bikes, rather than fully finished bikes, and as the shorter lead times in this 'assemble-to-order'(ATO) model could potentially be a differentiator in the market. A win-win-win, but miles away from the current supply chain capabilities of the company.

So what would need to be done to make that ATO supply chain work? First of all, R&D and product management would need to define modular configuration options. Which type of frame could be matched with which type of brake sets, gear sets and so on. The bikes might need to be redesigned, with a final assembly at the dealers in mind. Some of the cables for gears and brakes were being pre-assembled in the frames. If different gear and brake sets would need to be mounted later on, that would have to be redesigned. R&D and product management would also need to define what would be the pre-assemblies still done at the tier 1 assembly. The goal for sure would not be to have the dealer do the full assembly, but rather a final assembly, as they were dismounting and changing brake sets and gear sets today, upon the request of the end users. It is an excellent illustration of how in a fourth generation supply chain, product design and supply chain design need to go together when we want to create agility and resilience.

Once the product design was done, we would need to create a forecasting capability on the sub-assemblies. How many of which configurations would we think dealers were going to sell? Today dealers were ordering finished products. In the future, they were going to order sub-assemblies from a website. The idea obviously is they wouldn't wait for three to six months, but that the bike company would have the sub-assemblies in stock. So, the bike company would have to make a forecast, most probably on the level of the configurations, ideally validated by its key dealers, and then break that down to the level of the sub-assemblies, so it would know which sub-assemblies to order.

To realize the ATO supply chain, the bike company would need to start direct ordering towards the tier 2 suppliers, the component manufacturers, which it currently wasn't doing. As it would start direct ordering, it would also be logical to take ownership of that tier 2 relationship, which it currently didn't have. So it would be logical for the bike company to do the contracting and the price negotiations, for its direct ordering, but also for the ordering still done by the tier 1 assemblers. Today, as shown in Figure 4.4, each of the tier 1 assemblers was contracting and negotiating prices separately. The adjusted ATO supply chain is pictured on a high level in Figure 4.5.

Figure 4.5 Assemble-to-order bike supply chain

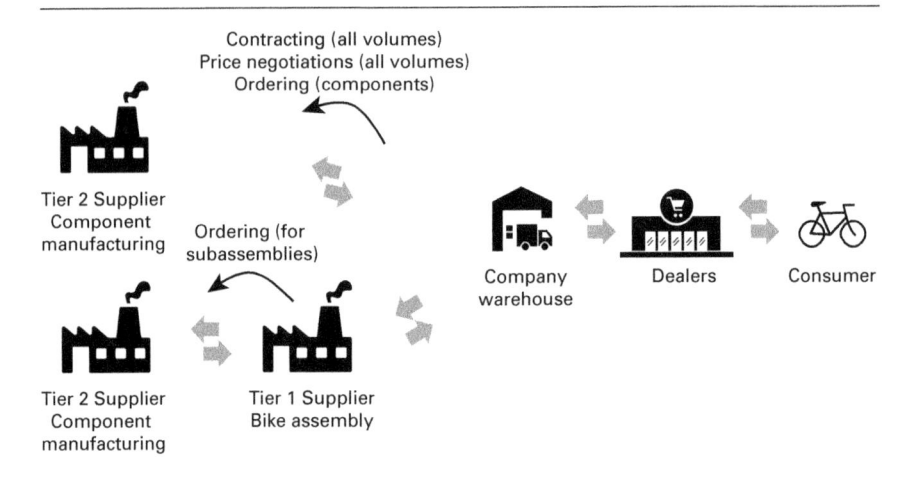

The bike company could go one step further. Next to doing the contract management and the price negotiations, with the tier 2 suppliers, on behalf of its own needs and the needs of the tier 1 assemblers, it could also start doing the actual ordering for those tier 1 assemblers, which it was not yet doing so far. To be able to do the ordering towards the tier 2 suppliers, on behalf of the tier 1 suppliers, the bike company would need to do an MRP calculation, taking its orders for the (now) semi-finished bikes, calculating the corresponding requirements for key components, and order them sufficiently ahead of time, for the tier 1 assembler to be able to assemble the semi-finished bikes on time. If the bike company would run this MRP calculation, for all the orders of semi-finished bikes it was putting on the different tier 1 assemblers, it could calculate their total requirements for key components, order these towards the tier 2 suppliers, who could deliver them to a component warehouse, owned by the bike company, from where those key components could be dispatched to the tier 1 assemblers just-in-time. That would be a next-level of control over the supply chain, requiring the bike company to have a system to do an MRP calculation based on its orders for semi-finished bikes, to do direct ordering towards the tier 2 suppliers for its own component needs and the component needs from the tier 1 assemblers, to have a component warehouse in which to receive those components and from where to dispatch it to the tier 1 assemblers. That ATO supply chain with a full control of the component supply towards the tier 1 assemblers is shown in Figure 4.6.

This approach would drastically change the collaboration model with the tier 1 assemblers. In the traditional supply chain setup, these tier 1 assemblers get orders three to six months upfront, which is giving them some

Figure 4.6 Assemble-to-order bike supply chain with full control of the component supply towards the tier 1 assemblers

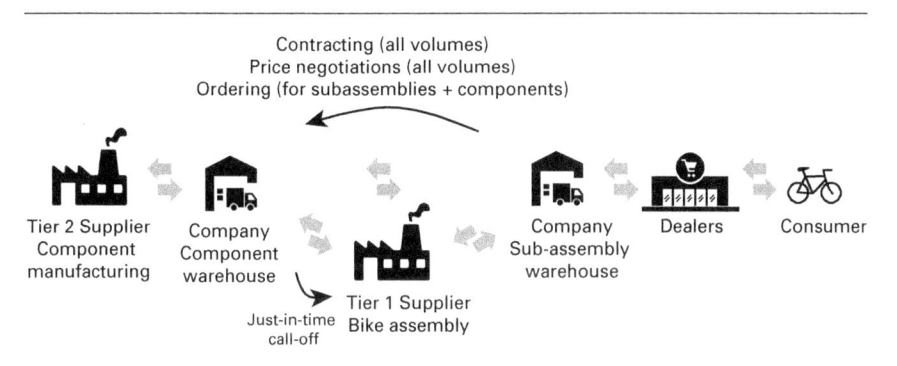

visibility on what is coming, and which is giving them the time to do the ordering towards the tier 2 suppliers. If tomorrow their components are being ordered by the bike company, and if these are available for call-off from a component warehouse, an alternative collaboration is possible. Instead of providing orders for (now) semi-finished bikes three to six months out, it would make more sense to do capacity reservations, and as the bike company, to tell the tier 1 assemblers, for the next six months, I want you to make x bikes of product group 1 and y bikes of product group 2, while specifying the exact semi-finished bike as late as possible, to keep more flexibility. It would also be logical to share a rolling schedule of which exact semi-finished products to make, for instance for the next three to six weeks, the same schedule that is used to order the components needed, and then confirm, on a weekly basis, the exact order quantities for semi-finished for the coming week. That alternative way of collaborative planning and information sharing for the ATO supply chain is illustrated in Figure 4.7.

The new supply chain requires a lot more work on the end of the bike company. They don't do direct ordering today, they don't have a component warehouse. They would need to set all of that up, and they would need to run it. That's going to cost a lot of money. They would also be taking the ownership and the risk of the component inventory. That would increase their working capital and the associated risk. Those costs and risks are with the tier 1 assemblers today, so that's where they would need to find the money to fund that. So will the assemblers be happy and willing to follow? They could be losing some of the margin they currently take on the components? Probably not all of them will like it, but if their risk gets reduced, if they can still earn a fair margin, and if they get some commitments on contracted volumes a couple of weeks and months out, then there should be a

Figure 4.7 Alternative way of collaborative planning and information sharing for the ATO supply chain

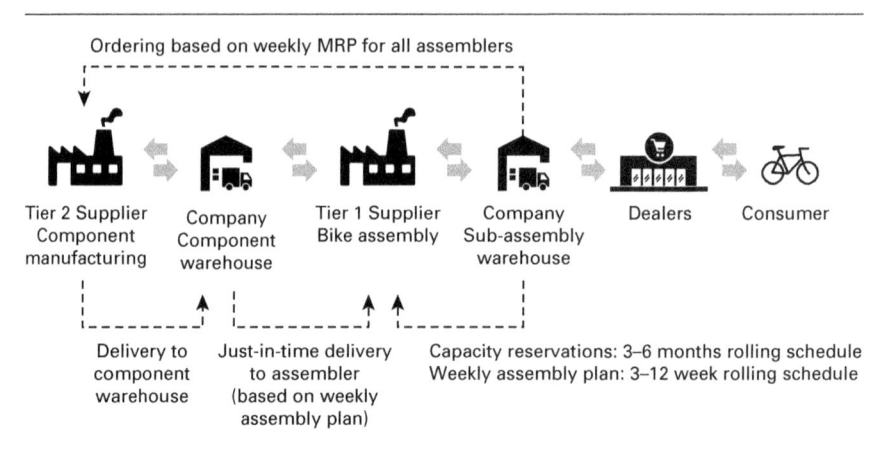

fair deal in there for them as well. Remember that they may be the weakest link in the chain, currently carrying the heaviest burden.

We believe that you will never be in control of this supply chain without deploying some or all of the processes shown in Figure 4.7. What it does is create a lot more, highly needed, flexibility. Let's start on the demand side. Instead of locking us in on a finished product level, three to six months ahead, we keep the flexibility to decide as late as possible, which semi-finished bike to make. And for the finished bike, we even put that decision into the hands of the end consumer, the bike rider, and the dealer. The lead times for the bike rider and the dealer will also be drastically reduced. They too, for specific configurations, now need to order three to six months upfront. In the ATO situation, all semi-finished and components should be available on inventory, meaning the lead for a custom configured bike would now be one to two weeks. As we specify only later which semi-finished bikes to actually produce, we also create more flexibility in which semi-finished bikes to finally produce at which assembler, assuming we do dual sourcing and each bike can be made with at least two assemblers. We also control the component inventory, so in case of constraints we can still decide where to send which component inventory, plus we rest assured that the component inventory we own will be used for our bikes only, which we don't control in the current supply chain. Finally, building this type of supply chain capabilities also creates strategic options for the bike company like starting to do some of the assembly itself. We believe this is another good illustration of how different the outcome is from a second generation supply chain thinking, focused on cost and minimal inventory, and a fourth generation supply chain thinking, which takes a view of the extended supply chain and thinks about how the supply chain can be turned into a competitive edge.

EXERCISE
Assessing your second vs fourth generation strategic – supply chain capabilities

Gather your executive team, or a cross-functional team, for a one-hour workshop, or tag this exercise onto your workshop introduced at the beginning of this chapter ('Assessing the impact of a lack of resilience'). It is important that you gather the different key functions in the company: sales, operations, marketing/product management/R&D, supply chain and finance.

Based on the second versus fourth generation strategic supply chain capabilities, summarized in Table 4.1, we have made a template where:

- For each of the capabilities we have given two extremes. For example for the first row 'designed for minimum cost' versus 'competitive advantage'.
    - The extreme to the left (linked to a second generation capability) states: Our supply chains are designed for minimum cost.
    - Extreme to the right (linked to a fourth generation capability) states: Our supply chains are designed for achieving a competitive edge.
- For each of the rows, ask the people to score twice:
    - First score is on the 'AS IS', are we closer to the statement on the left versus the statement on the right?
    - Second score is the same question but for the 'TO BE'. Where do we need to be?
- Ask people to score the seven rows, twice, once for the 'AS IS' (first bar), once for the 'TO BE' (second bar).
- Then ask people to sum up their individual scores for the 'AS IS', and put a cross in the corresponding box in the 'AS IS' summary at the bottom.
- Ask people to do the same for the 'TO BE', sum up their individual scores, and put a cross in the corresponding box in the 'TO BE' summary at the bottom.

For your convenience we have made a template available in PowerPoint on my website[9] called 'Template scoring second versus fourth generation supply chain – strategic'.

> Don't give too many explanations at the start. Let people make assumptions on what the statements exactly mean. Let people define their scores, and then ask people to share their overall score. Where are you in the second versus fourth generation in the 'AS IS'? Where does the group think you should be? Are there any manifest differences within the group? Where do these come from?
>
> You may link this back into the 'impact of a lack of resilience' analysis. Do we see any big differences between what people indicate as the 'AS IS' versus the 'TO BE' that could contribute to improving our resilience? How would that help in mitigating the negative effects from our current lack of resilience we identified?

From second to fourth generation capabilities: tactical planning perspective

Like we see important disconnects on a strategic planning and design level, we see equally important disconnects on a tactical planning level. Here as well, we see a lot of organizations that are stuck in what I call second generation supply chain thinking and capabilities, negatively affecting all of the drivers shown in Figure 4.1. Here as well, I will try to give insights into what the required fourth generation supply chain thinking and capabilities look like. They are summarized in Table 4.2. In Chapters 5 and 6 I go into more detail into what I will call 'Strategy-Driven Sustainable and Resilient Supply Chain Design' as the fourth generation capability. In Chapters 7 and 8, I will go into more detail in what I will call Integrated Value Planning as the fourth generation tactical planning capability.

Despite three decades[10, 11, 12] of Sales & Operations Planning (S&OP) or Integrated Business Planning (IBP), there are still important disconnects between sales, operations and purchasing. I still see companies where operations does not believe the forecast of sales and creates its own version of the truth. I see companies with complex matrix structures, 10 sales regions delivering 30 global product lines, where it seems impossible to have a proper validation of the demand by sales for each of the product lines. So, how do these companies plan for anything? And in that case, who is accountable for the forecast? Think about the damage done in our Supply Chain Triangle

Table 4.2 Tactical planning capabilities in a second versus fourth generation supply chain

Second generation supply chain	Fourth generation supply chain
Weak connection between sales, operations and purchasing	Connected between sales, operations and procurement
Poor portfolio and product (life cycle) management	Portfolio and product (life cycle) management as a key planning process
Disconnected from trade promotion planning	Connected with trade promotion planning
Disconnected from financial planning	Integrated with financial planning
Disconnected from key customers	Integrated with key customers
Disconnected from key suppliers	Integrated with key suppliers
Resilience eats sustainability for breakfast	We trade-off resilience and sustainability
Reluctant to invest	Fear of missing out (FOMO)

and all of the dimensions shown in Figure 4.1, financial impact, unnecessary CO_2, putting stress on our people, and breaking down relationships with customers and key suppliers. This is reckless and irresponsible behaviour.

On the supply side, I see a lot of companies where purchasing agrees on volume contracts with suppliers, based on their own assumptions of what is needed and with little to no forward visibility on whether the agreements will be adequate. Can you imagine that with all the information systems we have at our disposal in this decade? These are some of the absolute basics that need to be fixed first, before we can add any of the sophistications of the fourth generation supply chain capabilities.

In my experience, 7 out of 10 new product introductions (NPIs) are overstated, often leading to slow-moving inventory after the first order or production batch, as our supply chains have often been designed for cost instead of flexibility, as shown in the fashion and high-tech example in Chapter 3. It also means that 3 out of 10 NPIs are understated, and that we are caught by surprise, negatively affecting all of the parameters shown in Figure 4.1. Though any company introduces new products on a regular basis, it often seems that from a supply chain perspective, we keep improvising, as if every new case is different from the previous. In a fourth generation supply chain we embrace and manage the uncertainty on new products. We are prepared to scale fast or fail fast. We support the search for our next blockbuster product and understand it takes many failures to get there.

In general, companies are good at introducing new products, but bad at taking old products out. Sales will often push back, as cutting products negatively affects sales and may be a hassle for customers. But it is common sense that near the end of the lifecycle, volumes decline, there is margin erosion and we have to invest proportionally more inventory, with a bigger risk of having to write-off the inventory and destruct the product in the end. In this case the value declines and there is bigger risk of wasting resources. In a fourth generation supply chain, we understand and embrace that the health of the portfolio defines the health of the company, and that a clear accountability and process for managing the portfolio is an essential hygiene.

Another remaining struggle in the second generation supply chain is the lack of visibility on the tactical horizon. NPIs and end of life products may be known for 3–12 weeks, but there may be limited visibility further out. We see comparable challenges on the trade promotion planning, where the specific promos may be known and planned for the next 3–12 weeks, but promo volumes may be unclear further out, which may make it impossible to do proper capacity planning or ordering of long lead time materials, especially if promo volumes are important to our company. It seems we are running our company on different planning processes, that have different horizons and different objectives, but we still haven't realized that in the end all these plans are or need to be connected. In a fourth generation supply chain, we more naturally integrate product life cycle planning and trade promotion planning to our core supply chain planning.

Then comes a sensitive one. In many companies we run parallel tactical planning processes in supply chain, called the Sales & Operations Planning or S&OP process, and in finance, called the Financial Planning & Analysis or FP&A process. Both plans start from a sales forecast, need to translate that sales forecast into production volumes and purchasing requirements. The supply chain plan does it to steer the actual production and ordering and to properly define the capacity requirements over the next few months. The financial plan does it to project the P&L for the current and maybe the next quarter, to inform headquarters, analysts or shareholders about the current and future financial performance.

The two plans may be based on different assumptions, in some companies they are even based on a different forecast. I see companies where sales by day x of the month needs to submit its forecast to finance, which typically is in value and on an aggregated level, for instance product group, and by day y of the month it needs to submit its forecast to supply chain, which is typically in units (pieces, tons, m²) and on a detailed SKU level. So in some companies we make two plans based on different assumptions and a different level of detail, and then we try to align the two plans. We even have a name for that. We call it Integrated Business Planning or IBP.

In a fourth generation supply chain, we understand this is not just a waste of effort, it is also irresponsible. By starving supply chain of the correct financial information, we starve the organization from value-based decision-making. By starving finance from the appropriate level of detail (which specific SKUs are we selling within the product groups), it becomes very hard for finance to understand what is driving variances in sales values or margins. Is it driven by a volume difference, a price difference or a mix difference? Disconnecting the two plans is also known to lead to gaming by sales. The sales incentives are often linked to the financial plans and budgets, so we will have the tendency to be conservative and do sandbagging there. The actual product availability is driven by the supply chain plan, so we will have the tendency to be optimistic and less thoughtful there. That over-forecasting will drive excess inventories and an inefficient use of resources. It also undermines the trust by supply chain in the sales forecast, which is a topic we started with in this section. In the fourth generation supply chain, the financial and supply chain planning process are naturally integrated into the FSCP, financial and supply chain planning process. We will detail how this can be done in Chapter 7.

As we continue down our Table 4.2, in the second generation supply chain planning there are so many internal disconnects that we typically don't have the courage to connect to our key customers. If we are connected, it is typically not structural, we may have data from one or two customers, and as we are not connected internally, we don't know how to use the data in our internal processes to improve decision making. As discussed in Chapter 3 if we want to increase our resilience, we need to increase our visibility. With all the stocking and destocking during and after the Covid crisis, our order history is an unreliable source of information for forecasting demand. The only way to solve this is being connected. A fourth generation supply chain is connected. In Chapter 3 I introduced what we called a 'design principle', an axioma, which for customer integration states: we should have visibility on the inventories and the planned consumption (forecasted consumption) for the 20 per cent of the customers delivering 80 per cent of the volume, and with the 20 per cent of their customers delivering 80 per cent of their value. So we connect deeply into the customers' customer to get visibility on 64 per cent of the tier 2 consumption and the inventories in the chain.

It's a comparable story and situation at the supplier side. Most of the information sharing with suppliers, in most companies, is transactional. We may (or may not) have a certain contract that specifies volumes and prices, and for the rest we exchange order information. If we're lucky, it goes via electronic data interchange (EDI), if not, it even remains a manual process. It is comparable to the 'AS IS' supply chain of the bike company we discussed earlier in this chapter. This setup is failed, for the reasons described that case, but it is common. A fourth generation supply chain more intimately integrates with first and second tier suppliers. On a monthly frequency, we project and agree on aggregated volumes or capacities we are going to take. We discuss uncertainties and whether things are expected to go up or down. On a weekly basis, we give an outlook on the detailed products we will need, on any changes in our plans and inventories that are affecting our order pattern. Next, we agree on a certain horizon, where the outlook is automatically converted into orders. We agree on a certain flexibility for the suppliers to group orders, increase or decrease order sizes, based on the optimizations they see from their perspective (as in vendor managed inventory). We do this with the 20 per cent of suppliers, delivering 80 per cent of our critical raw materials and components. And we ask from our tier 1 suppliers that they do the same, and share the information from the 20 per cent of their suppliers, delivering 80 per cent of their raw materials and components. As discussed in Chapter 3, if we want to be more resilient, we need better visibility. In a fourth generation supply chain, we structurally organize for that on both the customer side and the supplier side.

As we explained in Chapter 2, sustainability is a driver for more intense collaboration as well. If we want to understand our Scope 3 emissions, we need to understand what is going into our products, and we need to understand how they are being used. Visibility and understanding will be the basis for reporting and for optimization. So once more, resilience and sustainability drive us in the same direction.

Culture eats strategy for breakfast is a famous quote of Peter Drucker, which means that you can have a good strategy, but it will fail if you don't have the right culture. Likewise I could say that, in our second generation supply chains, 'resilience eats sustainability for breakfast'. If the service and the top-line are under pressure, we make all kinds of operational firefighting costs, with negative impact on the CO_2 emissions and often less efficient resource consumptions (energy, raw materials, waste), as we are trying to close the service gap. Think about what happened during the Covid pandemic, as illustrated in Figure 1.3. The fourth generation supply chain will make more diligent trade-offs across financial and non-financial metrics. We can imagine an executive planning meeting where we trade-off top-line against CO_2. If we still ship the order via airfreight, we can still recognize revenue x in our current fiscal year. However, that would be at the expense of y extra tonnes of CO_2, which is or is not conflicting with our CO_2 target and ambition. So which option do we choose as an executive team? As we increasingly need to report on non-financials (think about the CSRD introduced in Chapter 2), and investors are increasingly concerned about non-financials, what might seem like a futuristic idea today, might be reality in the boardroom soon. Fourth generation supply chains are prepared for this debate.

In the last point in Table 4.2, I notice that companies are reluctant to invest in a proper supply chain transformation. As I described at the start of Chapter 3 it leaves me puzzled and confused. It is one of the drivers for writing this book. We invest millions in transactional processes, in ERP systems, quite often because we 'have to', because the big ERP vendor obliges us to migrate to the latest cloud-based platform, or because we see it as a 'base requirement', a 'license to operate'. At the same time, we seem to be very reluctant to invest a fraction of that in more tactical and strategic planning capabilities, which we seem to consider as 'optional'. Though the business case for this type of transformation is much more obvious, as it touches all the aspects shown in Figure 4.1. My hope is that more courageous business leaders will stand up, to trigger the supply chain revolution, the move from the second to the fourth generation, and as those companies truly leverage their supply chain capabilities as a competitive edge, others will follow suit, as there will be a fear of missing out (FOMO). As I mentioned at the start of Chapter 3, it is something psychological, we intellectually understand that this needs to be done, but something is holding us back. That makes me believe we might need to turn it into something equally psychological, the FOMO on the fourth generation supply chain.

Case Study: Nutrient additives manufacturer

A number of years ago I was working with a company active in the manufacturing of nutrient additives. The company was successful and growing, primarily by its product knowledge, and the way to package it into customer specific solutions. I would label it as a 'B2B product leader'. When their customers were designing new products, they'd call in this company to help it boost certain nutritional properties. They were adding the magic to more basic stuff.

The company was highly immature from a supply chain perspective. The planning was done in excel files. There was no MRP run. Which meant purchasing was negotiating contracts with suppliers based on their own forecast, based on what they had been using of key raw materials over the past year. Purchasing had no visibility on the planned consumption which meant that for some categories, actual consumption was way behind the contracted volumes, which meant they had to renegotiate them, which typically didn't result in better prices. Or they were surprised, by sudden and much bigger consumption, which often meant that they had to go out and do spot buys, which was typically done at significantly higher prices. Needless to say that purchasing was in big favour of better and more integrated planning processes. It's an example of a still common disconnect, and the obvious business value being lost with it. A transition to a fourth generation supply chain answers this type of misalignment.

Case Study: Outsourced manufacturing

What has struck me a number of times is how companies have different processes for managing supply for internal manufacturing, versus external manufacturing. For internal manufacturing, depending on the supply chain maturity, we might have everything: a monthly S&OP process with a demand review, a supply review, and an executive S&OP where we decide on which risks to take, on which capacities and inventories to commit. As I mentioned above, like with the bike company, when that same production is outsourced to a third party, we may have a contract that specifies a certain volume and a certain price, we may exchange orders, but we typically don't have that collaborative S&OP, we don't do a collaborative master planning. If it provides value for an internal manufacturing, we can safely assume it provides comparable value for an external manufacturing, right?

As a different example, I have witnessed a case where a company, in its internal S&OP, was seeing the demand was going much slower than planned. All manufacturing was outsourced, so when I asked whether they were going to share this with their supplier, the answer was 'Oh no, we're not going to tell the supplier'. To which I said 'euhmmm, why?'. To which they answered 'if we tell him now, he might reduce our capacity, and we don't want to give up upon it, as we may still need it at a later stage'. I was shocked. It feels like deliberate disinformation in the chain. This was not a side product for the company, but one of its key innovations. I am surprised how short-term and transactional we work with suppliers for even this type of product. By not sharing information that volumes will be lower, our suppliers will be committing capacities and inventories in raw materials they will not be able to efficiently use. In a trusted collaborative relationship we don't put the burden 'on the other', but we look for a joint optimization of costs and inventories across the two parties. That's exactly the mindset of a fourth generation supply chain. And trust comes by foot but leaves by horse. Plus trusted relationships are what helps you to weather storms. If we want to be more resilient, we will need better collaboration and more transparency and honest communication. There is no way the supplier is not going to find out if our sales volumes are significantly lower than planned!

Case Study: Retail VMI

As I described in Chapter 3, Collaborative Planning Forecasting and Replenishment (CPFR) has been around since the late 1990s. Its benefits have been well documented[13] as decreasing POS stockouts, increase of promotion effectiveness, decrease in inventory, reduced product obsolescence, reduced lead times, yet the adoption of it has been slow.

When I was talking to the logistics director of a major food retailer about VMI (Vendor Managed Inventory, which is part of CPFR), she told me that she likes to place orders herself. I was a bit surprised so I asked her to explain this. She continued, 'suppose the supplier has a problem, how will I be certain they are going to ship the product to me instead of to somebody else?' To which I answered, 'but if you place your orders, and they have a problem, how certain are you then?'

As retailers are just buying and selling, you feel the fight for the margin even more than in a manufacturing company, where we are adding value through our manufacturing process. It means that supply chains can become very transactional, which leaves huge opportunities on the table. As an example, let me talk about multi-echelon inventory optimization, my PhD at the time, which studied where to position safety stocks in the supply chain, more upstream, more downstream, and how the upstream and downstream are communicating vessels. Our typical design, in retail but also beyond, is to have stock at all echelons. We expect the supplier to deliver a 98 per cent service, we don't necessarily share a forecast, as the relationship is transactional. If, as a supplier, I have to make my own forecast, I know it will be inaccurate, so if I still need 98 per cent service, I'll need to carry a lot of safety stock. Retailers would have safety stocks in the central DC, to be able to provide good service to the stores, they would carry safety stocks in the stores, to cover the variability in the consumer demand. Multi-echelon inventory optimization will typically push stocks downstream, as that's the only point where you can score customer service, on the shelf. The added value of upstream stocks to the 'customer service' measured through the 'on shelf availability' or 'OSA' is relatively weak. The upstream stocks are just there for 'internal service levels' and 'agreements'. The upstream stocks are also consuming shelf life when they're sitting there. I even see stocks at suppliers for private label products. If the label says Carrefour, who do we think is going to sell it? Delhaize?

I give this example to illustrate how a combination of ignorance and a lack of trust are leaving value on the table. Switching to a fourth generation supply chain with true collaboration and integration will reduce inventories, save costs, increase shelf life, reduce food waste and reduce CO_2 from expediting in less than optimal quantities.

Assessing your second vs fourth generation – tactical supply chain planning capabilities

Comparable with the exercise in assessing the capabilities for the second versus fourth generation strategic supply chain capabilities, we have made a template for the second versus fourth generation tactical supply chain planning capabilities, summarized in Table 4.2, where:

- For each of the capabilities we have given the two extremes, for instance for the first row on 'weak versus strong connection between sales planning, operations planning and purchasing planning'.
    - The extreme to the left (linked to a second generation capability) states: disconnects between sales plans, operations plans and purchasing.
    - Extreme to the right (linked to a fourth generation capability) states: sales plans, operations plans and purchasing plans are always connected.

- For each of the rows, ask the people to score twice:
  - First score is on the 'AS IS', are we closer to the statement on the left versus the statement on the right?
  - Second score is the same question but for the 'TO BE', where do we need to be?
- Ask people to score the seven rows, twice, once for the 'AS IS' (first bar), once for the 'TO BE' (second bar).
- Then ask people to sum up their individual scores for the 'AS IS', and put a cross in the corresponding box in the 'AS IS' summary at the bottom.
- Ask people to do the same for the 'TO BE', sum up their individual scores, and put a cross in the corresponding box in the 'TO BE' summary at the bottom.

For your convenience we have made a template available in PowerPoint on my website[14] called 'template scoring second versus fourth generation supply chain – tactical'.

Don't give too many explanations at the start. Let people make assumptions on what the statements exactly mean. Let people define their scores, and then ask people to share their overall score. Where are you in the second versus fourth generation in the AS IS? Where does the group think you should be? Are there any manifest differences within the group? Where do these come from?

You may link this back into the 'impact of a lack of resilience' analysis. Do we see any big differences between what people indicate as the 'AS IS' versus the 'TO BE' that could contribute to improving our resilience? How would that help in mitigating the negative effects from our current lack of resilience we identified?

Conclusion

In this chapter, I have shown the impact of a mismatch between the volatility and the current supply chain resilience and capabilities. There is an impact on the core triangle of service, cost and cash, which translates into an impact on key financial metrics such a top-line, bottom-line and cash flow.

It impacts our broader sustainability footprint by affecting our people, the planet and our partnerships.

To make the gap concrete, I analysed what I see as capabilities within companies today, the typical second generation capabilities, and what I believe we need to deliver sustainable and resilient supply chains, the so-called fourth generation capabilities. I explained what that means for strategic planning and supply chain design, and for tactical planning and supply chain steering. Using the provided exercises you have mapped where you are in your second versus fourth generation supply chain capabilities. By making it concrete, by mapping the gaps, I hope to improve the understanding and to create traction for the needed supply chain transformation.

In Chapters 5 and 6 I will provide solutions for building fourth generation strategic planning and supply chain design capabilities. In Chapters 7 and 8 I will provide answers for building fourth generation tactical planning and supply chain steering capabilities.

Endnotes

1. B DeSmet, Inverse Fishbone Template, 2024. www.bramdesmet.com/rethinkingsupplychain/ (archived at https://perma.cc/3J7Y-KP54)
2. United Nations. The 17 Goals, Department of Economic and Social Affairs, United Nations, 2024. sdgs.un.org/goals (archived at https://perma.cc/U9CE-Y7LF)
3. B DeSmet, Balance in the Supply Chain Triangle, Solventure, 2024. www.strategydrivensupplychain.com/resources/surveys/balance-in-your-supply-chain-triangle/ (archived at https://perma.cc/7PC4-UFKX)
4. B DeSmet. Treacy and Wiersema, Take the Survey, Solventure, 2024. www.strategydrivensupplychain.com/resources/surveys/treacy-and-wiersema/ (archived at https://perma.cc/5ABJ-Y3L3)
5. D B Grant, W Y Chee and A Trautrims (2017) *Sustainable Logistics and Supply Chain Management: Principles and practices for sustainable operations and management*, Kogan Page, London
6. C Fine (1998) *Clockspeed. Winning industry control in the age of temporary advantage*, Basic Books, New York
7. J Gattorna and D Ellis (2019) *Transforming Supply Chains*, Pearson, London
8. R Mallon. Giant postpones payments to suppliers due to falling demand, rising inventory levels, and market "headwinds", Road.cc, 28 Dec 2022. road.cc/content/news/giant-postpones-payments-suppliers-298285 (archived at https://perma.cc/P7R2-GGH7)

9   B DeSmet, Assessing second vs fourth generation strategic supply chain capabilities, 2024, www.bramdesmet.com/rethinkingsupplychain/ (archived at https://perma.cc/2MT5-KXLU)
10 R Ling, W Goddard (1998) *Orchestrating Success: Improve control of the business with sales & operations planning*, Wiley, New Jersey. This was the basis for training given at that time by the Oliver Wight companies.
11 G Palmatier, C Crum (2002) *Enterprise Sales and Operations Planning: Synchronizing demand, supply & resources for peak performance*, J Ross Publishing, Florida
12 T Walace (2004) *Sales & Operations Planning: The How-to Handbook*, T.F. Wallace & Company, Cincinnati
13 ECR Europe. A Guide to CPFR Implementation, April 2001. www.ecr.digital/whitepaper/a-guide-to-cpfr-implementation-2001/ (archived at https://perma.cc/X5VW-8HFJ)
14 B DeSmet. Assessing your second vs fourth generation tactical supply chain planning capabilities. www.bramdesmet.com/rethinkingsupplychain/ (archived at https://perma.cc/ERQ2-HHJP)

Strategy-driven: sustainable and resilient – supply chain design

05

Introduction

In this chapter, I will start with a short recap on how to define your strategic value proposition, based on the seven value drivers of the strategy model of Crawford and Matthews. I will briefly recap how these map to the three strategic archetypes from Treacy and Wiersema: operational excellence, customer intimacy and product leadership. These have been explained in more detail in my previous books.

I extend these models, by including sustainability and resilience as two extra possible value drivers, and by formulating 'sustainability leadership' as a fourth possible option. I discuss how companies like Patagonia, Interface, The Body Shop and Tony's Chocolonely drive success by differentiating or dominating on the sustainability dimension.

I recap the seven-steps of the strategy-driven supply chain design methodology: analysing markets, defining your strategic value proposition, understanding how that drives complexity and variability, defining your supply chain response, defining the corresponding supply chain, understanding the impact on cost, capital employed and more broadly the financial structure, and then iterate and refine. I illustrate it using the ongoing strategy transformation at MediaMarktSaturn: how MediaMarktSaturn redefined its strategic value proposition, how it has impacted the underlying supply chain, how this type of transformation can be risky and how MediaMarktSaturn is managing it extremely well.

I extend the seven-step methodology to include sustainability and resilience: by including sustainability and resilience in the market analysis and your strategic positioning, by understanding the impact on and the options from product and supply chain design, by understanding the impact on financial metrics as on the social foundation and the ecological ceiling, so the full triple bottom line. I illustrate this extended approach through the case of Tony's Chocolonely, an impact company that makes slave-free chocolate, for which financial metrics like growth and EBIT are not a goal in itself, just a means to increase their impact.

The case of Siemens Smart Infrastructure talks about 'dynamic capabilities' that allow you to sense changes in the market and seize opportunities by designing and refining business models and committing resources. The related concept developed at Siemens is called the 'Strategic Diamond'. It helps your strategies to stay in sync with the changing markets and helps your strategies to stay relevant.

Further, I will provide exercises that allow you, with your executive team, to clarify your sustainability and resilience ambition, and understand the impact on your supply chain. As I will discuss, it enables your executive team to turn your supply chain into a competitive edge.

Recap: the strategic value proposition

In my two previous books, I used the strategy models of Crawford and Matthews[1] and Treacy and Wiersema[2] to introduce the need for strategic trade-offs. In *The Myth of Excellence*, Crawford and Matthews analyse the value propositions of winning companies. They observe that winning value propositions are typically based on a set of seven possible value drivers shown in Figure 5.1.

They also conclude that 'great companies never try to be the best at everything', reflecting the subtitle of their book. The best companies make strategic choices. They capture that as 'you can choose one dimension on which to dominate, you can choose a second dimension on which to differentiate, and you have to accept that at the others you will play at par'. In my previous books, *Supply Chain Strategy and Financial Metrics*[3] and *The Strategy Driven Supply Chain*[4], I explain how the model of Crawford and Matthews can be linked to that of Treacy and Wiersema, as shown in Figure 5.2.

Operational excellence players want to dominate the market on price, and will typically differentiate on psychological access, making it easy for

Figure 5.1 The seven value drivers from Crawford and Matthews

Price	Psychological access	Physical access	Service	Product breadth/ depth	Product quality	Experience
Lowest price Consistency Honesty	Easy Hassle free Succesful	Location Number of Real Estate	Advice Customization Availability	One-stop-shop Broad/ Deep range	Highest spec	Attractiveness Excitement

their customers/consumers. If it is easy, it is often also efficient, hence the match. Typical examples of operational excellence players are hard discounters like Aldi or Lidl in food retail, price players like Primark or Decathlon in clothing, low cost airlines like Ryanair or Southwest.

Customer intimacy players want to deliver the best total solution. For that they typically need a broad range of products, coupled to a specialized set of services. Think about global industrial companies like Johnson Controls, who deliver HVAC equipment and controls, security controls, building automation and controls, fire detection, and related services to deliver a 'total solution' for the next generation of smart and connected buildings. Because of the broad range of products and services, it is common for customer intimacy players to work with partners to create their total solution. Think about big retail stores that offer banking services, repair services, restaurants, under one roof.

Product leaders dominate on product quality. They simply have the best product. And they differentiate on experience, as their customers and consumers are typically proud to have and use the best product. At times, the status derived from owning the product, think about a Ferrari or Lamborghini, is bigger than the need for the high performance itself. As an example of a product leader, let's take Tesla in its early days. Tesla has disrupted the car industry by its highly innovative, high performance electric vehicles at a moment the industry was still dormant. With all of its cameras and a load of software, Tesla was coming close to the self-driving vehicle. Tesla was collecting data and could update the software through a simple wi-fi connection. The electric motors pushed the cars from 0 to 100 km/h in a couple of seconds, like the better petrol sports car at the time. And it was far ahead of other OEMs to come with an autonomy of over 400 km. All of these are clear performance parameters describing a premium product. Like Tesla, especially at the start, true product leaders don't necessarily have a broad assortment, it is primarily about boosting and boasting performance features.

The original Crawford and Matthews model considers only five value drivers. They combine psychological and physical access into one access dimension. They combine product assortment and product quality into one product dimension. I use what I call the 'extended' model, with the seven separate value drivers listed above in Figure 5.1.

From a supply chain perspective, physical access is about the density of your distribution or retail network. That has a whole different meaning from psychological access. The first requires a lot more investment in fixed assets and is increasing operating costs. Psychological access could reduce operating costs as quick, easy and efficient for the customer, is probably also efficient for us. As physical access and psychological access have a whole different impact on the supply chain, I prefer to model them as separate value drivers as shown in Figure 5.1.

A comparable story for the product dimension includes 'product breadth' and 'product quality'. The breadth of the product assortment and product quality have a completely different impact on the supply chain. Complex products, like aeroplanes, can have a very complex upstream supply chain, with many niche suppliers, many production steps with subassemblies and assemblies being done at different sites. That is something different from portfolio complexity or product breadth. That could be more linked with downstream supply chain complexity. Think about a chemical company that starts with a couple of base products, but processes them into many different, sometimes customer-specific, end products that go into many different types of packaging and end up in very different markets like construction, automotive, pharmaceuticals. As product quality, and the associated product complexity, and product breadth, and the associated product portfolio complexity, have a whole different impact on the supply chain, I prefer to model them as separate value drivers as shown in Figure 5.1.

By splitting the access and the product dimension, and using seven value drivers, I can also nicely link the model of Crawford and Matthews with the one of Treacy and Wiersema, as shown in Figure 5.2.

The idea of these two models, as of other strategy models, is that strategy is about making choices. It started with Michael Porter[5] who talked about choosing between a 'cost advantage' and a 'differentiation advantage'. Treacy and Wiersema give two specific options to differentiate: through a

Figure 5.2 Linking the strategy model of Crawford and Matthews with Treacy and Wiersema

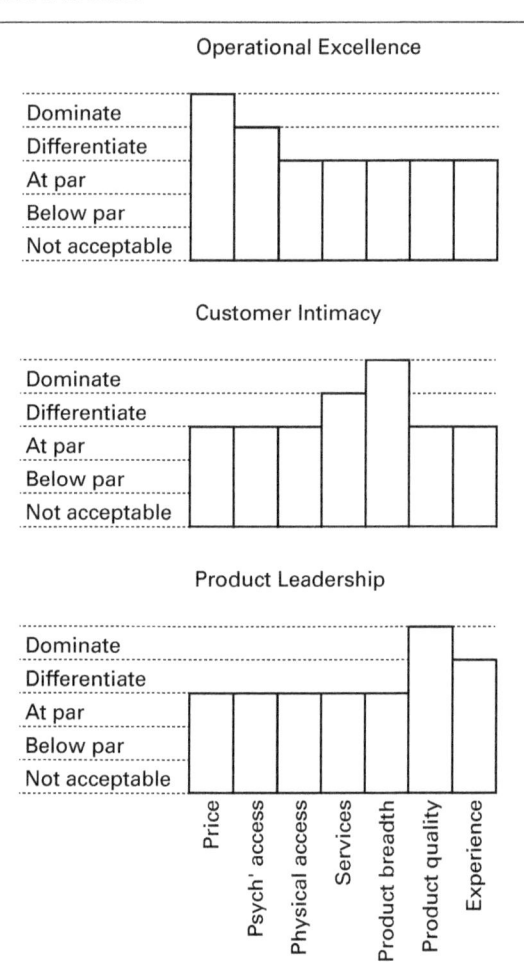

Operational Excellence

	Price	Psych' access	Physical access	Services	Product breadth	Product quality	Experience
Dominate	■						
Differentiate		■	■	■	■	■	■
At par							
Below par							
Not acceptable							

Customer Intimacy

	Price	Psych' access	Physical access	Services	Product breadth	Product quality	Experience
Dominate				■			
Differentiate	■	■	■		■	■	■
At par							
Below par							
Not acceptable							

Product Leadership

	Price	Psych' access	Physical access	Services	Product breadth	Product quality	Experience
Dominate						■	
Differentiate							■
At par	■	■	■	■	■		
Below par							
Not acceptable							

'best total solution' (customer intimacy) or 'best product' (product leadership) positioning. Strategy literature has moved on beyond Treacy and Wiersema or Crawford and Matthews, for instance into the so-called 'Blue Ocean Strategies[6]' from Chan Kim and Mauborgne. They analyse that sectors can get caught in a performance rat race on one single dimension. For example, think about delivery lead times in e-commerce. First somebody was delivering next day, until somebody delivered same day, until somebody delivered within four hours, until the German company Gorillas[7] promised to deliver your groceries to your doorstep in minutes. It creates what Chan Kim and Mauborgne call a red ocean. We overserve on one dimension to the level of irrelevance, while the market may leave other dimensions underserved, sometimes unnoticed. Blue ocean strategies encourage companies to analyse the value drivers in their markets and to look for underserved dimensions, to see if a competitive advantage can be created starting there, in a smarter way, at a lower cost, and with a higher return. Where in the model of Crawford and Matthews the value drivers are fixed, Chan Kim and Mauborgne encourage you to define the relevant drivers for your markets yourself and to look for potentially hidden gems.

Whatever strategy model you use, the key is that strategy is about making choices, and if strategy is about making choices, it means that companies, in general, are bad at strategy. This is because companies are led by humans, and as humans, we hate to make choices. Strategy literature tells us that choices create focus, and that more focused companies are more successful. If you don't make a choice, how should it be clear for the customer why they should buy from you instead of from one of your competitors? If you don't make a choice, how should it be clear for the thousands of people who work in your company what is the priority? If you don't make a choice and your competitors do, you risk being left behind with an undifferentiated positioning.

For more extensive treatments of both strategy models, Crawford and Matthews, and Treacy and Wiersema, and on strategy in general, I refer to my first two books. In what follows I will focus on linking sustainability and resilience into the strategy debate.

EXERCISE
Mapping your strategic value proposition

On the website for my second book, *The Strategy-Driven Supply Chain*, there is a free online survey that can be used to reveal your strategic profile according to Crawford and Matthews and Treacy and Wiersema. You can use the following link to launch your own survey: www.strategydrivensupplychain.com/resources/surveys/treacy-and-wiersema/.

You will be requested to select five statements from a total of 24, that most closely reflect what your business is standing for. If you are a company with multiple business units, either pick one business unit, or do the exercise twice. Comparing the outcome for different business units can be very revealing. You must select exactly five. You need to make a choice. We have adapted this exercise from Kurt Verweire.

Figure 5.3 Example output of strategic positioning survey

Product Leadership

Operational Excellence — Customer Intimacy

Figure 5.4 Example output of strategic positioning survey – split per department

— CEO + Finance

— R&D

— Sales + Cust Care

— Ops + Procurement

Product Leadership

Operational Excellence — Customer Intimacy

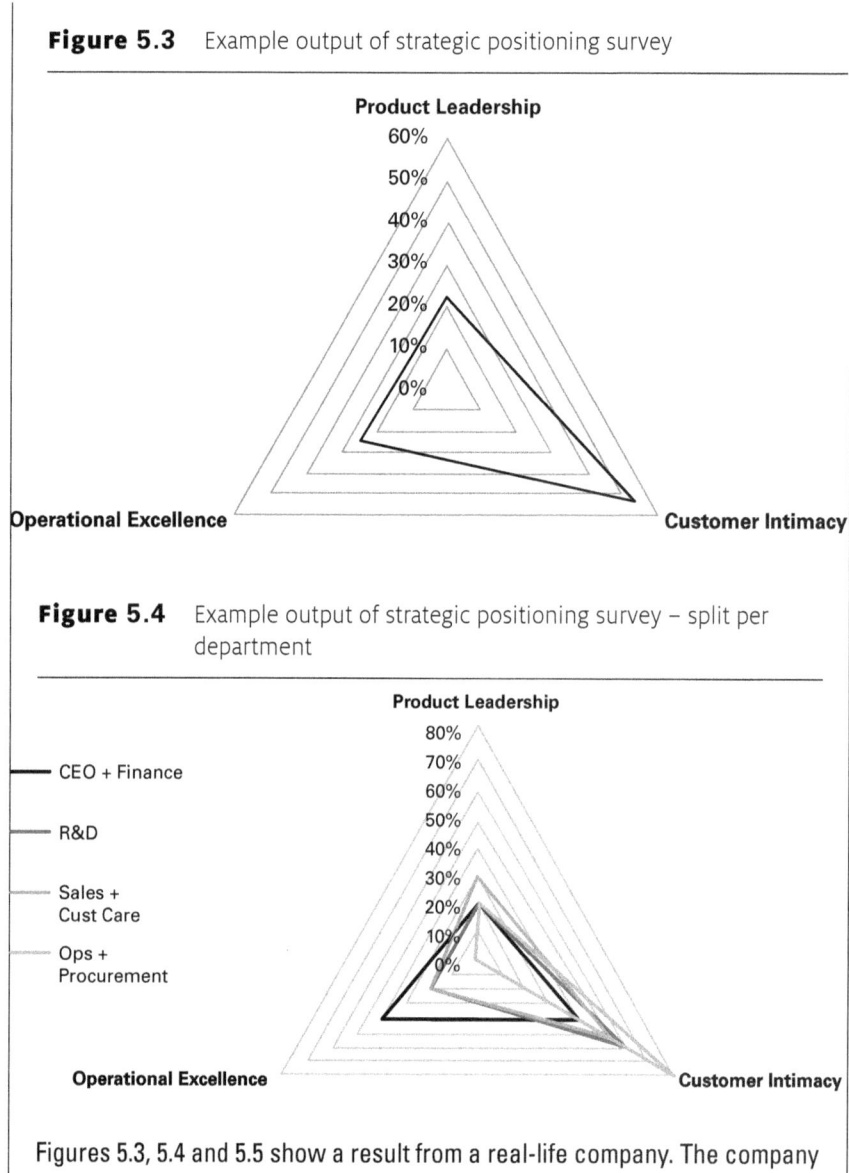

Figures 5.3, 5.4 and 5.5 show a result from a real-life company. The company is active in basic food ingredients. From the overall result in Figure 5.3, there seems to be an orientation towards customer intimacy, but as Figure 5.4 shows, there were strong underlying differences between departments with notably the general management more oriented towards price and operational excellence.

That 'split positioning' is also shown in Figure 5.5. Crawford and Matthews tell us to have one 5, one 4 and play at par for the others, but

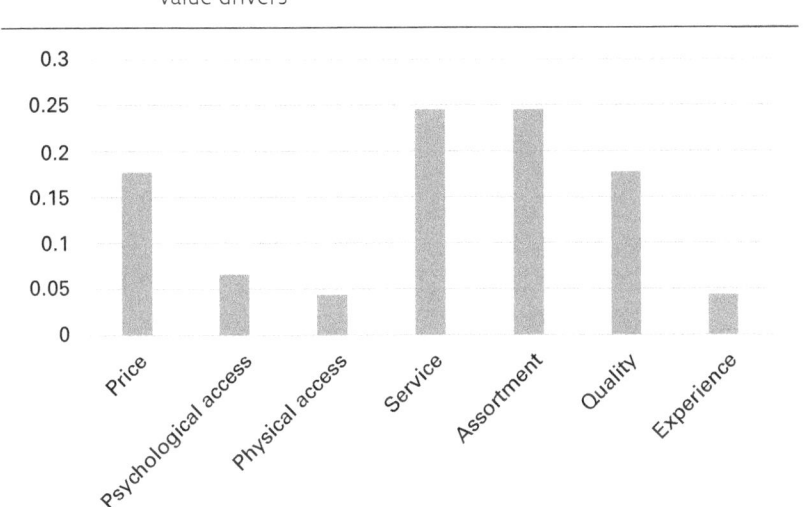

Figure 5.5 Example output of strategic positioning survey – dominance of value drivers

[Bar chart showing approximate values: Price 0.18, Psychological access 0.07, Physical access 0.04, Service 0.25, Assortment 0.25, Quality 0.18, Experience 0.04]

there is a mix of service, assortment, quality and price which leads to an undifferentiated positioning. When doing the exercise in a physical workshop setting, with the executive team, the intended positioning was clarified as 'consistent quality' (a product characteristic) and 'consistency of supply' (a service characteristic).

The company admitted that they were in a commoditizing market, which may explain some of the price votes, but they were not the cheapest in the market nor was it their ambition. They also admitted they have a complex portfolio, which they basically wanted to reduce. That could have attracted some votes for assortment, but it was not how they wanted to differentiate.

The differentiation on 'consistent quality' has to do with the fact that their smaller competitors were not always able to deliver that, and variable quality in their basic food ingredients was leading to variable quality of their customers' end product. Delivering the consistent quality was driven by consistent quality of their own raw materials and some specifics in their production process. It was as such an advantage that was not that easy to copy.

Next to the 'consistency of quality' there was the 'consistency of supply', which had to do with 'always being able to deliver'. They mentioned they are very flexible, if a customer would call them with an emergency over the weekend, they would get it solved. Consistency of supply, in combination with the complex portfolio, on the one hand required smart supply chain

> design, with some intermediates available on stock from which they could finish to order. Consistency of supply also required good forecasting and planning processes, and forecast collaboration with key customers. This example acts as a quick recap on how revealing the strategic positioning is creating focus for the supply chain.

Extending the strategic value proposition with sustainability and resilience

As I explained in Chapter 1, regional sourcing and production, as opposed to global sourcing and production, may increase resilience and improve our CO_2 footprint, but it could come at a higher capital employed (more fixed assets, requiring extra CAPEX) and at a higher cost (less economies of scale, not only producing in the lowest cost location). That is not a decision that can be left to an individual middle manager. It is a strategic decision that needs to be prepared by the executive committee and is taken by the board of directors. By adding sustainability and resilience as two extra value drivers to our list of

Figure 5.6 The extended nine value drivers from Crawford and Matthews + sustainability + resilience

Price	Psycho-logical access	Physical access	Service	Product breadth/ depth	Product quality	Experience
Lowest price Consistency Honesty	Easy Hassle free Succesful	Location Number of Real Estate	Advice Customi-zation Availability	One-stop-shop Broad/ Deep range	Highest spec	Attractive-ness Excitement

Sustainability	Resilience
Environmental and/or social impact in the extended supply chain	Consistency under volatility and disruption

Figure 5.7 Sustainability leadership as a fourth option in the world of Treacy and Wiersema

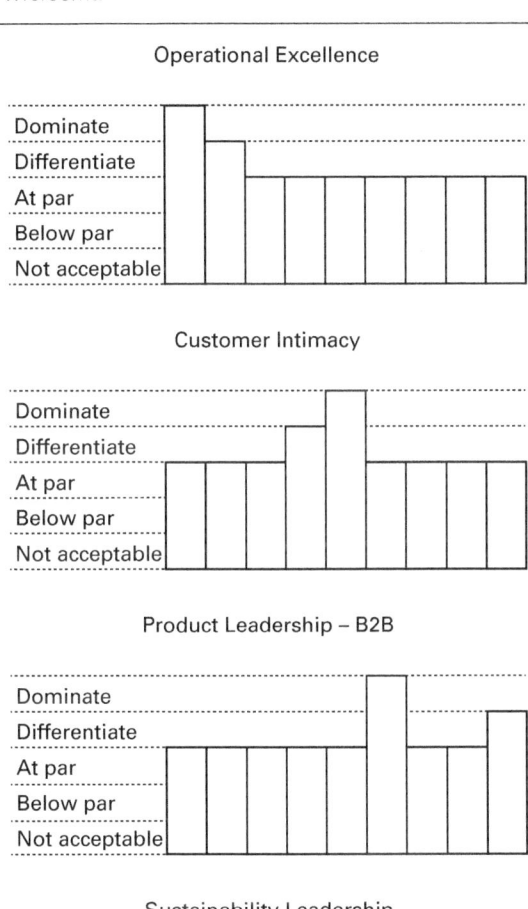

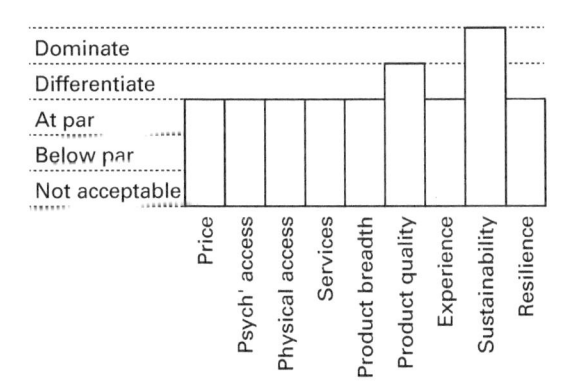

Operational Excellence

Customer Intimacy

Product Leadership – B2B

Sustainability Leadership

Categories: Price, Psych' access, Physical access, Services, Product breadth, Product quality, Experience, Sustainability, Resilience

Levels: Dominate, Differentiate, At par, Below par, Not acceptable seven value drivers as shown in Figure 5.6, we can turn sustainability and resilience into a strategic debate, trade-off and decision.

In our list of value drivers, as before, we need to decide on which driver to dominate, on which one to differentiate, and on which ones we accept to play at par. Next to operational excellence, customer intimacy and product leadership, we could add sustainability leadership as a fourth strategic option, as displayed in Figure 5.7.

Companies like Patagonia or Interface choose to differentiate or even dominate on the environmental aspect of sustainability. In 2005 Patagonia launched the Common Threads Recycling Program[8], of which the goal was to reduce the number of products customers purchased. This was done through encouraging customers to fix damaged clothing, by publishing do-it-yourself repair guides, and charging affordable fees to have garments shipped to their repair facility. Secondly, Patagonia created a second-hand market for Patagonia garments that did not fit or that were no longer worn. While most companies would encourage customers to repeat their purchases, Patagonia prides itself and its customers on waste-free purchases. Interface[9] is a global manufacturer of flooring. It prides itself on being the first global player of which all products are CO_2 neutral during their full lifecycle. They organize the reuse of flooring tiles and have designed their products for 100 per cent recycling when reuse is impossible.

Companies like Tony's Chocolonely and The Body Shop differentiate or dominate on the social aspect of sustainability. Tony's Chocolonely is a producer of chocolate bars that aims for 100 per cent slave free[10] chocolate. On their website, they explain how the chocolate supply chain is characterized by an unfair distribution of value and power. It starts with millions of farmers that produce cocoa and ends with the billions of consumers that enjoy chocolate. The bit in between is dominated by a handful of chocolate giants that profit from keeping the cocoa purchasing price as low as possible forcing farmers into poverty and leading to child labour and slavery. So how does Tony's Chocolonely make a difference? For instance by investing in long-term partnerships with cocoa farmers, making fairer price agreements and showing cocoa farmers how to be more organized and how to improve their productivity so they can achieve a decent income. The Body Shop is known as a pioneer in cosmetics, never testing products on animals, nor exploiting any in making them, working fairly with farmers and suppliers, and helping communities thrive through its community fair trade programme[11].

In Figure 5.7 I have shown 'product quality' as a typical differentiator for the sustainability leader. The products of sustainability leaders are typically more expensive, given the stronger commitments they have to make in their extended supply chain. To be commercially successful and financially viable, they need to be able to drive a premium from their customers and consumers. Differentiating on product quality, as shown in Figure 5.7, or differentiating on experience, are 'natural fits' for a sustainability leader. Think about Patagonia, their products are premium products, with a long durability, that's an extra reason to buy from them. And when you buy from Tony's Chocolonely or from The Body Shop, you may want to support their cause. That is a matter of aspiration and of experience. There is less of a fit for a sustainability leader, with for instance the lowest price dimension. Think about companies like Primark or Ryanair. In 2008, an investigation for the BBC's Panorama and *The Observer* uncovered children labouring in Indian refugee camps to produce some of Primarks' cheapest garments[12]. Children as young as 11 were sewing t-shirts costing shoppers just a few pounds on high streets across Britain. In 2009, Ryanair's CEO, Michael O'Leary, said 'Hell will freeze before we settle' in his discussions with the labour unions on working conditions at the low cost airline[13]. Several years later in 2018, he was refusing to recognize the new Polish union for cabin crew and was asking pilots to sign up to the company's local subsidiary as contractors, turning them into precarious workers without permanent employee rights[14]. In their relentless focus on cost, price fighters need to be minimalistic on each of the other value drivers. They leave the question 'whether this is still ethical' with the individual customer and consumer. But as awareness increases and as more strict regulations come into force, even companies like Primark[15] and Ryanair[16] have to start thinking about sustainability. We don't expect them to be differentiating or leading but they have to stay at or close to par.

What you may notice is that resilience is a separate dimension, so should we position something like a 'resilience leader'? I wouldn't be able to name an obvious example of a company that is trying to dominate the market on resilience. We do believe that resilience could be a differentiating dimension for a B2B product leader like 3M. Remember that in Chapter 3 I talked about the supply chain design principles at 3M to have each technology in at least three plants and in each plant at least three technologies, or the principle to have at least 80 per cent of regional needs sourced and produced locally. Because of the inherent uncertainty at product leaders on the demand of new products, the capability to scale fast or fail fast is a natural capability that serves that strategic need. But it also creates a differentiation in the resilience dimension. As 3M was already sourcing 80 per cent regional-for-regional it had less exposure to the shortage of container transport and the steep rise in container transport prices during the Covid pandemic.

> **Mapping your strategic value proposition, including sustainability and resilience**
>
> On my website, I have made available a survey that can help you define your strategic profile. The approach is comparable to the exercise and survey introduced earlier in this chapter. You will be requested to select those five statements, out of a larger set of statements, that most closely reflect what your business is standing for. The statements have now been enriched to include sustainability drivers and resilience drivers. You can use the following link to launch your own survey: www.bramdesmet.com/rethinkingsupplychain/.
>
> If you have multiple business units, that have a different strategy, choose one or repeat the survey. Contrasting the strategy of the different units can be enriching and deliver deeper insights on how and why they are different and what is the impact of that on the supply chain and operations.
>
> Results will be made available, in a comparable way as shown in Figures 5.3, 5.4 and 5.5, where sustainability and resilience will pop up as extra dimensions on which to analyse the intended positioning.

Recap: the strategy-driven supply chain

There is a double problem with strategy. The first is that we are afraid of making choices. The second is we don't understand the impact of our strategic choices on the supply chain. In the second generation supply chain thinking, we have only one recipe, that is designing supply chains for minimum cost and maximum efficiency. In my previous book, *The Strategy-Driven Supply Chain*, I show this a flawed assumption, and as shown in the fashion case in Chapter 3 often undermining our strategic position in the market. Different strategies require different supply chains. You can't have the choice and service of a traditional supermarket at the cost and inventory

Strategy-driven: sustainable and resilient – supply chain design 169

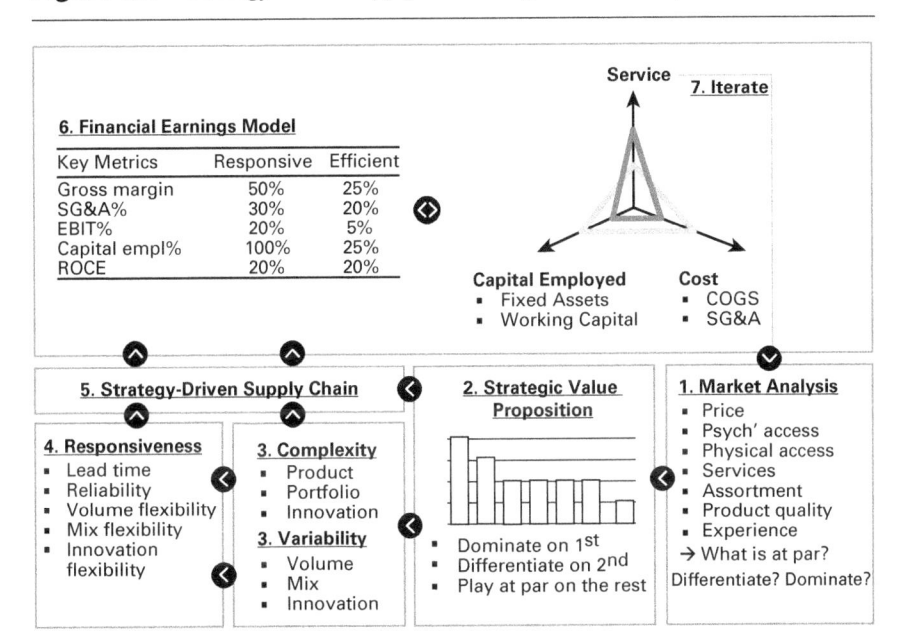

Figure 5.8 Strategy-driven supply chain design in seven steps

6. Financial Earnings Model

Key Metrics	Responsive	Efficient
Gross margin	50%	25%
SG&A%	30%	20%
EBIT%	20%	5%
Capital empl%	100%	25%
ROCE	20%	20%

Service — 7. Iterate

Capital Employed
- Fixed Assets
- Working Capital

Cost
- COGS
- SG&A

5. Strategy-Driven Supply Chain

2. Strategic Value Proposition

1. Market Analysis
- Price
- Psych' access
- Physical access
- Services
- Assortment
- Product quality
- Experience
→ What is at par? Differentiate? Dominate?

4. Responsiveness
- Lead time
- Reliability
- Volume flexibility
- Mix flexibility
- Innovation flexibility

3. Complexity
- Product
- Portfolio
- Innovation

3. Variability
- Volume
- Mix
- Innovation

- Dominate on 1st
- Differentiate on 2nd
- Play at par on the rest

levels of a hard discounter. As long as we don't understand the supply chain to fulfil our strategic value proposition, we don't understand the level of cost and capital employed, so we don't know how we will drive financial value, neither do we know the environmental and social impact. So as long as we don't know the supply chain, there is no strategy. The strategic value proposition and the corresponding supply chain are like the yin and yang of the business strategy. They need to be designed together and in harmony.

In my previous book I have developed a methodology for strategy-driven supply chain design that allows us to connect the supply chain, and the business strategy, with the corresponding financial value model. It goes along seven steps which I will briefly recap and which are illustrated in Figure 5.8. We will start with the base model, explained in the last book, focused on financial value creation and in a next section expand it to include sustainability and resilience.

Step 1: We start from analysing the market. In our market, what does it mean to play at par, to differentiate or to dominate on the different value drivers. In the base version we look at the seven value drivers of Crawford and Matthews: price, psychological access, physical access, service, product assortment, product quality and experience.

Step 2: Define our strategic value proposition. Within the defined market environment, what is our position? Where do we (want to) dominate, differentiate and where do we accept to play at par?

Step 3: Understanding your complexity and variability is key in understanding your level of cost and capital employed. Our strategic value proposition translates into complexity and variability. Complexity and variability are important drivers for operational costs and for buffers. Typical buffers are inventories and capacity, so extra complexity and variability typically translates into extra working capital and/or fixed assets. Lowest price players typically don't want complexity and variability as these kill efficiency. They go for simplicity and stability. Think about how Walmart started with Every Day Low Price (EDLP) as opposed to being promotion driven. Customer intimacy players will differentiate through total solutions, which creates product portfolio complexity and mix variability. Product leaders will differentiate through more innovative and advanced products, which creates product complexity and volume variability and uncertainty, with not just changes in the mix, but the total sales volume being much higher or lower than expected.

Step 4: In the face of the complexity and the variability, we need to define our supply chain response. What is the targeted customer order lead time? And what is the target delivery reliability, as measured through the on-time in-full (OTIF) delivery performance? What is the required flexibility? Let's take the example of volume flexibility. Should we be able to double the production in three months' time, 12 months' time or 24 months' time? Product leaders require a higher volume flexibility compared to operational excellence players. What do you think is the appropriate supply chain response for your strategic value proposition? Step 4 basically links back into step 1. What does it mean to be at par, differentiating or dominating in the market? Product leaders typically can afford a longer lead time, as customers are willing to wait for their products. Operational excellence players typically try to play at par, as shorter lead times and a higher flexibility are driving up cost. It is typically the customer intimacy players that may be differentiating or dominating on lead time and reliability.

Step 5: Once we understand the complexity, the variability and the desired supply chain response, we can design the supply chain. Being able to double the supply in three months' time will lead to different design choices compared to delivering a 25 per cent YoY growth. It leads to different decisions on the fixed assets (for instance capacity to install), the choice of suppliers (for instance cost versus flexibility). The different designs will lead to a different level of operating cost and a different level of capital employed (= working capital + fixed assets).

Step 6: Once we understand the costs and the capital employed, we can derive the financial value model. Strategic differentiation drives extra costs and capital employed but if done well drives a premium from the consumer. So based on our supply chain design we should be able to understand at least the gross margin. From my first book, *Supply Chain Strategy and Financial Metrics*, we expect product leaders to drive gross margins of 50 per cent or more, and luxury goods players of 60 per cent or more. Operational excellence players can go all the way down to 20 per cent. Customer intimacy players will be positioned somewhere in between with 30–40 per cent. As illustrated in the table in Figure 5.8, different strategies are basically different ways to drive the same ROCE.

Step 7: Iterate. It could be expected that we don't, immediately, get to the appropriate gross margin or ROCE. When that happens, we may need to iterate through steps 1–6 and adjust the value proposition, our price point in the market, the supply chain response, until we do get to the appropriate gross margin and ROCE level.

I understand the methodology proposed in Figure 5.8 can feel a bit 'high-level'. The focus of Figure 5.8 is in making the connection between the different steps. I see companies redesigning the distribution network or manufacturing footprint without taking the strategic value proposition as a starting point. What we end up with in that case is a cost minimization and efficiency maximization, which can be conflicting with the strategic requirements. In nearly all distribution or manufacturing footprint studies I see an exclusive focus on cost and CAPEX. We don't question what would be the impact on sales or on pricing and hence on gross margin. In that way we don't spot the strategic opportunities.

Take the following example of a high-tech company. To reduce costs and CO_2 supply chain was considering to shift more goods from airfreight to ocean transport. That is increasing lead times and is conflicting with the time-to-market objectives of a product leader. Regional sourcing and production could be an alternative but was not considered as it was increasing costs and required significant extra CAPEX. Regional production could offer a unique advantage of localized products or last minute differentiation, capabilities the company currently didn't have. Only by considering the strategic value proposition and understanding what this could bring as extra revenues or increased price points, can we truly do the supply chain design. So yes, it is high-level, but it captures the essential connections, those that are often ignored in the second generation supply chain thinking discussed in Chapter 4.

Case Study: MediaMarktSaturn – transforming a traditional bricks consumer electronics retailer into an omnichannel consumer experience and service provider, by Joeri Kuik, VP Supply Chain Management

MediaMarktSaturn Retail group[17] is Europe's leading consumer electronics retailer and provider of related services. Before 2017, it was part of the Metro group, together with Metro Cash & Carry and Real hypermarkets. MediaMarktSaturn is operating over 1,000 stores in 11 countries. In 2021/22 it generated sales of €21.8 billion and employed around 50,000 people. Joeri Kuik, the VP Supply Chain Management, came on board in October 2019, for an ambitious strategy and supply chain transformation programme. Four years down the road, he is happy to share his story and experiences with us.

Joeri comments:

The model of electronics retail in the 1980s, was all about price, assortment and physical access, to use the terminology of Crawford and Matthews. The physical access was delivered through the 1000 plus stores. The price and the assortment were delivered through a push model. We would agree on quantity discounts for big volumes with suppliers, and push the inventory to the stores, to get it sold to consumers. We would have a lot of inventory, compensated by long payments terms towards our suppliers, and immediate payment by customers. It was a high volume / slim margin / low capital employed business model.

Then from the 2000s, clouds were packing in the sky. There was an increasing competition from e-commerce and cloud computing companies with wide assortments and new business models, which was eroding margins, eroding bottom-line profits, and creating pressure on sales. There was an obvious need to re-invent consumer electronics. Utilizing our stores as assets and knowing that customers start their exploration online, omnichannel was the obvious approach for MediaMarktSaturn. However, omnichannel retail requires a different set of systems, with inventory visibility throughout the entire network including cross store shipments, potentially dark stores or e-fulfilment centres. Important investments had to be made, but from razor thin margins. And you know that the costs always come upfront, while the benefits come later. We were about to cross the, infamous, valley of death.

He continues that:

in 2020, a new management was gathered, that defined and embarked on the new strategy. Next to catching up in the omnichannel dimension, where we were significantly below par, we decided to change our strategic value

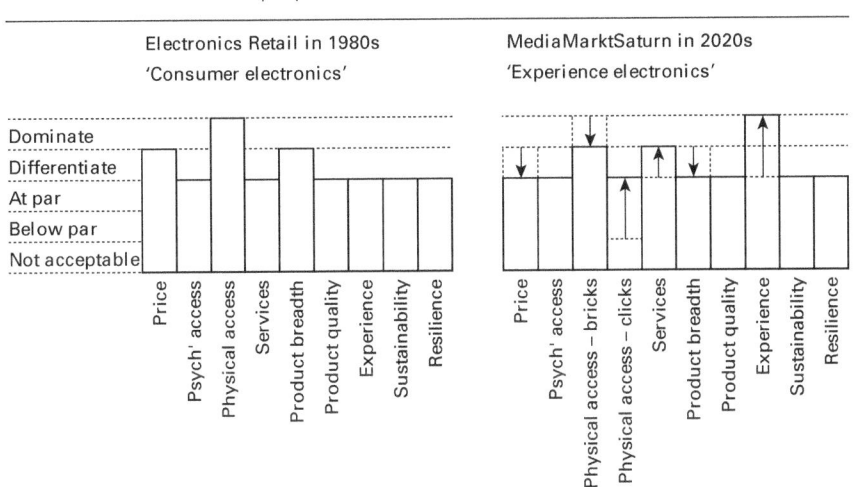

Strategy-driven: sustainable and resilient – supply chain design

Figure 5.9 The old 'consumer electronics' versus the new 'experience electronics' value proposition

	Electronics Retail in 1980s 'Consumer electronics'	MediaMarktSaturn in 2020s 'Experience electronics'
Dominate		
Differentiate		
At par		
Below par		
Not acceptable		

Categories (both panels): Price, Psych' access, Physical access (bricks / clicks on right), Services, Product breadth, Product quality, Experience, Sustainability, Resilience

proposition, by differentiating on experience and service, while playing at par on cost, product assortment and product quality. We decided to switch from 'consumer electronics', which was product-centric, store-driven and supplier funded, to 'experience electronics', which focused on customer-stickiness, was platform-centric, and data-driven. Changing the value proposition is all encompassing, as it was about to change the way we position and operate our stores, our supply chain behind it, our organization model, and our financial model.

We have summarized the switch in strategic value proposition in Figure 5.9. In the TO BE, shown at the right of Figure 5.9, we have split the physical access in a 'bricks' and a 'clicks' dimension. Just looking at the number of arrows going up and down gives an impression of the impact and the difficulty of the transformation that MediaMarktSaturn was about to embark upon.

'To step into the modern omnichannel world, and to enable that new "experience electronics" strategy, our supply chain had to be drastically reformed', Joeri comments.

> At the heart of it, is a new network structure, with city hubs, regional hubs and country hubs. Where in the past all the inventory was in the stores, we decided to centralize the inventory, for instance by only having 'showcase' models in the stores, and by centralizing most of the inventory in the city or regional hubs, from which we can deliver to the store, or to the door front. Keeping less stock

in the stores, was creating space to enable the 'new shopping experience.' The store as an amusement park[18], it was coined in the press, where consumers can game with the newest gear, get their hair styled or taste a cappuccino. Centralizing the inventory allowed to reduce the inventory and was delivering savings to suppliers, as they were now delivering to hubs versus in-store. This allowed us to negotiate price reductions.

A second element of the strategy change was putting less emphasis on the portfolio and more on services. In a country like Germany, we reduced the number of stock keeping units from 300,000 to 30,000. You can imagine how drastic this is as a change. Coming from an era where we were very decentralized and the stores were having a high autonomy on the assortment, the deals, even the pricing… switching to a more centralized approach is an 180 degree turn. It is an integral part however of the strategic repositioning and transformation. In parallel to reducing the portfolio, we have been adding more services, like TV calibration, offering guarantees and insurances…

Joeri comments:

As a part of the more centralized approach, we also had to build a central supply chain staff and organization, and build up new and more centralized supply chain planning capabilities. We were basically poor in demand forecasting, inventory control, complexity management, supplier performance as in the old push model these were not needed. One of our major steps has been to introduce a sales & operations planning (S&OP) process that fits the retail business, where we try to understand the market demand, translate that into supply from suppliers, and then adequately deploy the inventory into our omnichannel network. We have been supporting these new processes with the appropriate IT systems, and have been clarifying roles & responsibilities of the central organization versus the stores. We are currently in the process of reviewing the responsibilities of supply chain versus category management, centrally and in the countries, to better understand and manage the complexity of our winning portfolios.

And on the physical access, Joeri comments, 'the idea is not to have less. The plan is to maintain or grow the number of physical stores but reduce the average floor space per store, in combination with different store formats, for instance "Lighthouse" stores in bigger cities versus "Smart" stores in neighbourhoods. The aim is to increase the sales per m² with local entry. Our new sweet spot will be click and collect.'

Joeri expands:

> All of this is a huge cultural change. Our culture is very commercial driven, and the sales is highly influenced by pricing and by promotions. It is a very competitive and very dynamic market, where product life cycles are very short. For long we have been very much driven by sales and by that short term dynamic. Now we have a strategy for 3 to 5 years out. That exerts a forward pull on the organization. It isn't always easy to bridge between that strategy and the day-to-day operation. With 1000 stores this is a tanker that doesn't turn overnight. There is also no golden bullet that easily takes us there. It is a totally different, new way of working, that requires belief, determination and perseverance.

'One of the opportunities of the new distribution model,' Joeri comments, 'is to add services for suppliers. For some of them, we could act as a delivery platform for their direct e-commerce solutions, and increase their coverage.' A recent publication by ChannelX[19], a news specialist on marketplaces, comments that by the end of July 2023, MediaMarktSaturn had around 1,060 third party resellers on its platform, offering nearly 1.2 million products. With the marketplace live in Germany, Austria and Spain it is fuelling growth.

Despite all the challenges and all the market uncertainties, results are moving in the right direction. CECONOMY, the holding above MediaMarktSaturn reports[20] strong performance in the third quarter for the year 2022/23. With sales increasing by 7.4 per cent year-on-year, to €4.5 Billion in Q3 2022/23, to €16.9 billion in the first nine months (+5.9 per cent), customer satisfaction – Net Promotor Score – reaching 55, the highest-ever, EBIT significantly improving by €43 million to €149 million over the first nine months, and free cash flow increasing by nearly €1 billion year-on year in the first nine months. From these results, it seems that MediaMarktSaturn is finding its way through the valley of death and will succeed in reinventing itself. Changing strategy is about changing the DNA of the company. As this case illustrates it has a deep impact and as such is hard to achieve. Courage, a strong belief in own capabilities, dedication, determination, building teams and convincing people are all needed ingredients but never a guarantee for success. We are impressed with the transformation that MediaMarktSaturn is realizing, and judging by the dedication, determination and conviction of the people I talked to, I am convinced that the company will succeed in repositioning for a new profitable growth journey, driven by an omnichannel electronics experience!

Strategy-driven sustainable and resilient supply chain design

The strategy-driven supply chain design methodology, explained in Figure 5.8, connects strategy, supply chain and finance. It seems obvious (which is good, obvious things stick better), but it's not. As already explained and illustrated through many examples in Chapter 4 in practice we (think we can) design value propositions in isolation of the supply chain, and we optimize supply chains for cost and efficiency without giving (thoughtful) consideration about their strategic purpose.

I see the same disconnects with sustainability. We have sustainability plans and ambitions, but they are often separate plans, driven by separate teams and a separate end responsible, often a Chief Sustainability Officer. Separate plans lead to disconnects. We may not have a clear view on the financial impact (cost and capital employed) and the strategic impact of our sustainability initiatives. Our different plans in different areas might well be conflicting. If we're not considering the three simultaneously, strategy, financial impact and sustainability, we may also leave the best options unexplored. Think about the example of the high-tech company introduced before. Regional sourcing and production will lower CO_2 but it will increase cost and capital employed, hence it is less likely to be proposed from a sustainability perspective. If we add the strategic perspective, we realize it could sharpen our strategic edge, with a capability to create localized products and for instance do some customization. The extra revenues and the higher price point that could bring might cover the extra costs and the extra CAPEX. The best and most courageous options may only be considered by taking a natively integrated view.

Figure 5.10 shows how to include sustainability and resilience at the core of what I call 'strategy-driven, sustainable and resilient supply chain design'. Let's discuss how it works step by step.

Step 1: Market analysis

We need to analyse what it means to be at par, to differentiate and to dominate on different value drivers, now firmly including sustainability and resilience. As we explained in Chapter 1, John Elkington[21] describes that, in the

Figure 5.10 Strategy-driven sustainable and resilient supply chain design in seven steps

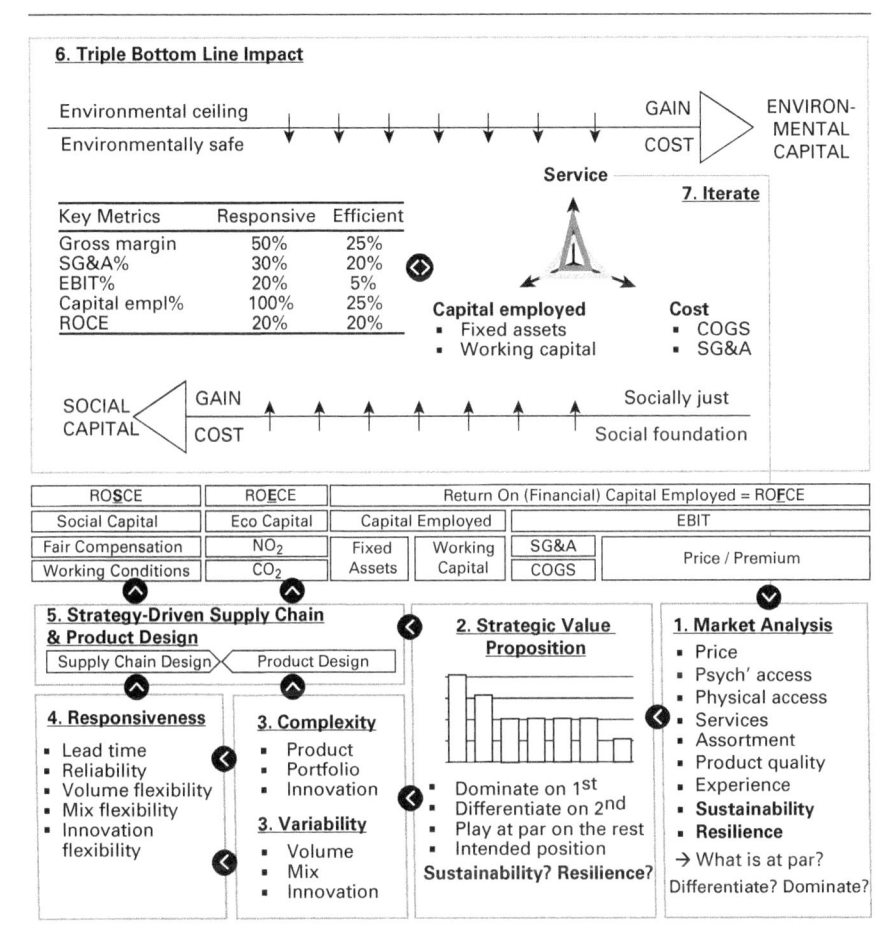

6. Triple Bottom Line Impact

| Environmental ceiling | | | | | | GAIN | ENVIRON- |
| Environmentally safe | ↓ | ↓ | ↓ | ↓ | ↓ | COST | MENTAL CAPITAL |

Service

7. Iterate

Key Metrics	Responsive	Efficient
Gross margin	50%	25%
SG&A%	30%	20%
EBIT%	20%	5%
Capital empl%	100%	25%
ROCE	20%	20%

Capital employed
- Fixed assets
- Working capital

Cost
- COGS
- SG&A

| SOCIAL CAPITAL | GAIN | | | | | | Socially just |
| | COST | ↑ | ↑ | ↑ | ↑ | ↑ | Social foundation |

ROSCE	ROECE	Return On (Financial) Capital Employed = ROFCE
Social Capital	Eco Capital	Capital Employed — EBIT
Fair Compensation	NO_2	Fixed Assets / Working Capital / SG&A / COGS — Price / Premium
Working Conditions	CO_2	

5. Strategy-Driven Supply Chain & Product Design
Supply Chain Design × Product Design

4. Responsiveness
- Lead time
- Reliability
- Volume flexibility
- Mix flexibility
- Innovation flexibility

3. Complexity
- Product
- Portfolio
- Innovation

3. Variability
- Volume
- Mix
- Innovation

2. Strategic Value Proposition
- Dominate on 1st
- Differentiate on 2nd
- Play at par on the rest
- Intended position
- Sustainability? Resilience?

1. Market Analysis
- Price
- Psych' access
- Physical access
- Services
- Assortment
- Product quality
- Experience
- Sustainability
- Resilience

→ What is at par? Differentiate? Dominate?

1980s, a common corporate tactic for sustainability was 'secrecy'. If we could stay below the radar of activist groups, and if we could avoid major accidents, profit maximization was a common single and primary goal. In around 40 years, that reality has changed, and it has changed drastically.

Companies, investors and owners have been leading, taking their environmental and social responsibility serious. Some of them may have been greenwashing initially, but many are now in a real competition of how green and how social companies can be. It has become an integral part of the competitive game.

Customers and consumers have become increasingly aware and are changing their buying behaviour. Younger consumer generations are still using low cost airlines to travel, but when they buy for their daily living, they are more critical on whether they really need a product, whether they can buy it second hand, and where and how a product was made. With the younger consumers, we seem to be passed the heydays of consumerism.

Governments have been following, slowly, but firmly. In 2019, the European Commission brought forward bold objectives on fighting climate change in its Green Deal[22] which includes no net emissions of greenhouse gases by 2050, economic growth decoupled from resource use and no person and no place left behind. In 2022, the Biden administration launched the Inflation Reduction Act[23], which aims at reducing US greenhouse gas emissions by 50–52 per cent below 2005 levels by 2030. The same focus on inclusion here with the Justice40 Initiative, which commits to delivering 40 per cent of the overall benefits to disadvantaged communities, including Tribes, communities with environmental justice concerns, rural areas and energy communities.

Regulators are sharpening the required disclosures on Environmental and Social risks. As introduced in Chapter 2, in January 2023, in Europe, the Corporate Sustainability Reporting Directive or CSRD has entered into force. The CSRD modernizes and strengthens the rules concerning the social and environmental information that companies have to report. A broader set of large companies, as well as listed SMEs, will now be required to report on sustainability – approximately 50,000 companies in total. The days of secrecy and 'staying below the radar' are gone forever.

So the new strategic playing field does include sustainability drivers, and any strategic analysis should start with understanding what it means to be at par, to differentiate and to dominate on the environmental and the social aspects of your business. The forced disclosure of sustainability information will make it more transparent on how good or bad we are in those aspects, to an increasingly sensitive ecosystem. Regulators will also define minimum thresholds, to create a level playing field. Knowing that the push towards more sustainability is coming, what is your preference? Will you wait and be a fast follower? Or do you want to take a leap forward, and become leading in your sector? In the fourth generation supply chain capabilities, the strategic positioning in the sustainability space has become an integral part of the broader strategic trade-offs to be made.

We have again focused less on the resilience dimension as I feel less of a burning platform. As supply pressure has declined at the time of writing this book, we seem to be postponing our resilience concern until the next crisis. The drive for sustainability seems the better change agent for further maturing and ensuring the resilience of our supply chain capabilities at the moment. And as discussed in Chapter 4, increasing sustainability and increasing resilience often go together.

Step 2: Strategic value proposition

Here, we need to define our strategic value proposition. Within our competitive landscape, including the sustainability aspects, where do we want to be? Do we want to be at par? Do we want to be differentiating, or dominating? Take the story of Tony's Chocolonely[24]. It all started in 2003 with a popular Dutch TV programme called 'Keuringsdienst van Waarde' ('Value Inspectors'), and one of its journalists Teun van de Keuken who investigated the human rights abuses, including modern slavery and child labour, in the chocolate supply chain. The investigating team was outraged and followed up with multiple episodes through the years that followed. The investigating team gathered eyewitness accounts from victims of modern slavery and brought a case before a public prosecutor in the Netherlands. Teun, an avid chocolate fan, suggested he was complicit in the crimes of the chocolate industry after filming himself eating a chocolate bar, in an attempt to set a legal precedent. Thousands of consumers got the message. In 2005 an initial edition of 5,000 fairtrade bars was produced and they flew from the shelves. Another 8,000 were made and sold off. It was the starting point of Teun – Tony's – lonely charge, to change the norm in the chocolate industry and prove to big choco that treats, free of modern slavery, could be possible. It was the start of Tony's Chocolonely. Even today, Tony's Chocolonely states they are 'an impact company that makes chocolate'. They pursue 'to make 100% slave free the norm in chocolate, not just their own, but all chocolate worldwide'. In 2011 the company had €1million turnover, in 2022 that was €133 million[25] with a 50 per cent gross margin. That can count as an illustration that differentiating or dominating on a sustainability dimension should not conflict with financial objectives like growth and gross margin. This type of disrupter may appear in any market. As they grow their success with environmental or socially sensitive customers, they are gradually raising the bar for the rest of the industry.

Step 3: Complexity and variability

Next, we need to understand our complexity and variability. To start with, differentiating or dominating on sustainability may drive product or process complexity. If we continue the example of Tony's Chocolonely, as a small company, Tony's needs to get a grip on the unequally divided cocoa supply chain. In its 2022 annual 'fair' report[26], the company reports that around 60 per cent of the world cocoa is produced in two countries, Côte d'Ivoire and Ghana, by around 2.5 million smallholder farmers and that around 1.56 million children work under illegal conditions because their parents are unable to earn a living income. In its fight for zero slavery chocolate, Tony's has defined five sourcing principles. First, traceable cocoa beans, by not buying from a heap, but trading directly and on equal footing with cocoa farmers and co-ops. Second, a higher price, paying a price that enables cocoa farmers to earn a living income and run healthy farms. That requires paying an extra premium, above the fairtrade premium, to get to the living income of $1.96 per person per day in Ghana and $2.45 in Côte d'Ivoire (Living Income Community of Practice, 2022). Third, strong farmers, working with cocoa co-operatives to professionalize and make the work of cocoa farming safe and sustainable. Fourth, improved quality and productivity, investing in agricultural knowledge and skills related to growing cocoa and other crops together with the partner co-ops. Fifth, the long-term engagements, ensuring that farmers and partner co-ops receive five year commitments (at least) to buy beans at a higher price, providing income security, and allowing to make choices about future investments and recouping costs.

Next in its fight for zero slavery chocolate, Tony's monitors, detects and remediates child labour, under the Child Labor Monitoring and Remediation System (CLMRS). In 2022 it has reported 736 cases at the long-term partner co-ops, or 4.4 per cent of the long-term partner co-ops, and 1,939 cases at the newer partner co-ops, or at 58.2 per cent of the newer partner co-ops. This can be seen as a proof that the approach works.

Next to the deeper integration with the farmers, Tony's needs to ensure a full traceability throughout the value chain, 'from bean-to-bar' as they call it. From the farmers that deliver to the co-ops, the co-ops who send it to SACO in Abidjan who makes cocoa butter, and to Barry Callebaut who makes Tony's liquid chocolate, before it goes to De Laet International NV and Kim's who make the chocolate bars, before they send them to retailers and wholesalers who sell them to consumers.

One could call all of these 'process complexities' as opposed to 'product complexities'. We tend to consider them under one single name and umbrella of 'product complexity'. It is obvious from the description that this complexity is driving up costs and capital employed.

We see a lot of similarities with product leaders, that, because of the premium quality of their products, need to be very selective in the suppliers they work with and that may need a detailed quality control of the chain to be able to guarantee the quality of the output, and to ensure that there is no fraud or cheating going on in the chain. Sustainability leaders need to ensure, just like product leaders, that they can drive a premium from their customers and consumers to cover these extra costs and investments. Sustainability leaders, as opposed to traditional product leaders, may not have the financial performance as a single or primary criterion of success, but nevertheless, they will need to generate sufficient money to support their existing business and be able to grow it.

Growing the business is important for a sustainability leader, not necessarily to grow its profits, but primarily to grow its impact. Tony's reports that their current impact is 0.3 per cent of the West African cocoa bean market. Growing their business allows growing their impact. They are also trying to grow their impact through their so called 'Open Chain' initiative. That is a collaborative initiative that makes it possible and efficient for other companies to adopt Tony's five sourcing principles for their cocoa supply chains. Tony's Open Chain is the invitation to do things differently and create impact together. It is looking to create a snowball effect that will change the norm, with the help of what they call their 'Mission Allies', which is what they call the companies that join them in their fight. Ben & Jerry's became a Mission Ally in August 2022 by committing to and sourcing cocoa via Tony's Open Chain. That is obviously a major brand name and a major win for Tony's Open Chain initiative.

To complete step 3, differentiating or dominating on sustainability may also drive variability. Take the example of Interface, the flooring company, that prides itself on being the first global player of which all products are CO_2 neutral during their full lifecycle. As part of that ambition, Interface works a lot with recycled yarns. That creates significant variability on the raw material side. Variability on how much and when the recycled yarns come in. Variability on the quality of these yarns. That will require more complex planning and production processes which drives up cost and may drive up capital employed, for instance through more variable raw material stocks and more complex production equipment.

Step 4: Supply chain response

Interface and Tony's Chocolonely, as other flooring manufacturers and chocolate bar manufacturers, will need to define their targeted supply chain response. In my experience, product leaders don't need to have the shortest lead times or the highest reliabilities, if your product is differentiating enough, your customers or consumers will wait to have the best. I believe the same holds true for sustainability leaders. Under the umbrella of lower

CO_2, reduced waste, your customers or consumers may be willing to accept a longer lead time. As these have an important impact on the supply chain cost and capital employed, which is already high, it is important to think this through, and not go over this too lightly (as is often the case today, in the second generation supply chains).

Because of the specific characteristics of the (socially) sustainable supply chain, it can become vulnerable as opposed to resilient. This is again witnessed by the supply chain of Tony's Chocolonely. The company reports in its 2022 Annual FAIR Report that their processor, Barry Callebaut, experienced salmonella contamination in its factory in Wieze in 2022. As a result they have not been able to make any chocolate for two months (!), missing the production of Sinterklaas (Saint Nicolas) bars, and leading to a postponed launch of the Ben & Jerry's bars. So (socially) more sustainable supply chains are not always more resilient, environmentally sustainable supply chains are, from the examples we have seen so far.

Step 5: Supply chain and product design

This is our strategy-driven, sustainable and resilient, supply chain and product design. As I discussed in Chapter 4, integrated supply chain and product design is key from a CO_2 perspective. The product design locks in a lot of the scope 3 emissions, by selecting the materials, deciding how the product will be used, whether it is fit for recycling etc. The supply chain locks in a lot of the scope 1 emissions when we decide where to buy, where to produce and how to transport goods. Understanding and reducing CO_2 is a major imperative for any company I talk to. I believe that as such it is an important driver for a more close joint design of the products and their supply chains.

Let's zoom out from the CO_2, and take examples of companies that want to differentiate or dominate on the environmental aspect of sustainability, for instance Interface, the flooring company, or take Ricoh, a case we'll describe in Chapter 6. If these companies want their products to be recyclable, they'll need to design them to be recyclable, and they'll need to design the supply chain to recycle the products. We will need to set up the reverse logistics to get used products back to our factory, and set up the tools and machines that allow us to recover the basic materials in them. Think about recycling yarns at Interface, or recycling core components of multi-functionals at Ricoh. And if our ambition is to be CO_2 neutral, as in the case of Interface, we'll also have to think through how all of this can be done with minimal CO_2. It is a broader illustration of how product and supply chain design are intertwined in (environmentally) sustainable supply chains.

And when we take socially sustainable supply chains, think about Tony's Chocolonely, or The Body Shop, or fashion companies that want to pay fair wages to the people stitching the garments, there may be a bit more focus on setting up the right partnerships, the transparency and control of the supply chain. But if we bring in durability of our product, like with Patagonia, or taste, as with Tony's Chocolonely, the link with product design will again be more obvious.

Step 6: Triple Bottom Line Impact

The next step in designing our product and supply chain, is further understanding and detailing the financial and the non-financial, more specifically the environmental and the social, impact. In the second generation supply chain thinking, we often focus on minimizing financial costs and investments. In the 3D generation supply chain, we try to model the full triangle impact, including the top-line impact, and understand the financial return, through a metric like ROCE (think about the case of H&M in Chapter 1). In the fourth generation supply chain, we also want to understand the non-financial impact, as for sustainability leaders, these non-financials may play a leading role.

In its 2022 Annual Fair Report, Tony's reports impact across three dimensions called: 'create awareness', 'lead by example' and 'inspire to act'. By 'creating awareness', amongst consumers, amongst farmers, it comes closer to its goal of zero slavery chocolate. It has defined and reports KPIs such as: percentage of Choco Fans who are aware of the existence of modern slavery on cocoa farms, number of participants in CLMRS awareness raising sessions, number of cocoa growing households who participate in the CLMRS (CLMRS = Child Labor Monitoring and Remediation System). In the 'lead by example' dimension, it tracks performance on number of child labour cases detected and remediated with the CLMRS, US dollars amount of premium paid, per metric ton of cocoa to reach LIRP (Living Income Reference Price[27]). It also tracks metrics such as percentage growth, US dollars net revenue and percentage gross margin, as it is important to show to other chocolate producers that a non-financial purpose doesn't withhold successful financial performance. On the 'inspire to act', Tony's reports on the number of metric tons of cocoa sourced via Tony's Open Chain, and the number of Tony's Open Chain conversations with potential mission allies. These metrics are what Tony's reports as actuals in its Annual Fair Report.

Tony's has been certified as a 'B corp' already in 2013[28]. B Lab[29] is a non-profit that is certifying B corporations, which are companies that meet high standards of social and environmental performance, accountability and transparency. It started in 2006 with the idea that a different kind of economy was not only possible, but necessary – and that business could lead the way towards a new, stakeholder-driven model. The primary objectives of B corporations may lie outside of the financial objectives, they may see the financials more as a result, and financial parameters like growth and profit merely as ways to grow their impact. Tony's states they are 'an impact company that makes chocolate', so what they try to measure is that broader impact. When B corporations design their supply chain, they need to understand how it contributes to that broader impact. Many of us may not be B corporations today, but it gives an idea in which direction many of us are going.

Step 7: Iterate

It is also important to understand the ambitions and growth targets when we design our supply chains and products. If Tony's want to double its volume organically and double its volume through mission allies, how can that be realized? How many extra farmers and co-operatives will they need to onboard? Will they stick to the single sourcing with Barry Callebaut as a liquid chocolate processor? These type of questions brings us into step 7 in Figure 5.10, where we need to iterate, starting with refining the intended strategic positioning, for instance how far do they want to go with their mission allies? Do they stick to supplying the raw materials or do they want to become a supplier of liquid chocolate or even private label finished products for retailers? As we refine our strategic value proposition, we need to iterate all the way over the supply chain impact, the financial and non-financial impact, until we feel our value proposition, our supply chain and our strategic plan are solid, integrated and robust enough to move forward with the implementation.

Case Study: Siemens Smart Infrastructure – from resilience to robustness through the strategic diamond – by Alexander Tschentscher, Head of Supply Chain Strategy, Sven Markert, Head of Supply Chain & Logistics

The strategic diamond of Siemens is rooted in a strategy field that is called 'dynamic capabilities', which itself builds on the 'resource based perspective'. One of the important authors in the field is David J. Teece[30]. 'Dynamic capabilities' and the 'resource based perspective' are alternatives or at least complement the 'competitive perspective' that goes back to the 'competitive forces' model from Michael Porter[31]. That competitive forces model defines industry attractiveness and profitability by the interaction of five forces: entry barriers, threat of substitution, bargaining power of buyers, bargaining power of suppliers and rivalry among industry incumbents. In this 'competitive perspective', strategy is all about influencing these five forces, for instance by creating entry barriers to competitors, or by industry consolidation to increase bargaining power. In the 'competitive perspective', the profitability is defined on the market level. Teece argues this cannot be the full truth, by indicating there are significant differences in profitability within the same industry. According to Teece, we need to understand what is driving competitive advantage at a company level, rather than an industry level, as the differences in profitability are bigger within the same industry than across industries. The 'resource based perspective' analyses what type of strategic assets and competences companies have. The 'dynamic capabilities' perspective analyses how companies can reconfigure these assets and competences to respond to changing market conditions.

In a recent paper[32] from 2018, published just before the Covid crisis, Teece further defines dynamic capabilities as the capability to 'sense', identifying threats and opportunities, to 'seize', by designing new or refining existing business models, and then finally 'transform' the organization and culture in line with the refined business model. This is illustrated in Figure 5.11. Teece comments that 'the strength of a firm's dynamic capabilities determines the speed and degree of aligning the firm's resources – including its business model(s) – with customer needs and aspirations'. He mentions that 'an enterprise with strong dynamic capabilities will be able to profitably build and renew resources, assets, and ordinary capabilities, reconfiguring them as needed, to innovate and respond to (or bring about) changes in the market'. In his 2018 paper he comments that this approach is relevant for companies active in fast changing markets, for instance technology companies. One can question whether today not all companies are living in fast changing markets. The disruptions from Covid-19, the Russia-Ukraine war, the resulting inflation, partly driven by exploding energy prices, the war in Israel, the arrival of ChatGPT and generative AI, the obvious question to ask is 'what's next?'. In the current market circumstances, probably all companies can benefit from strategy models that enable 'dynamic capabilities'.

At the bottom of Figure 5.11 we see the changes in the business model are fed with the strategic context. Teece comments that 'strategy maps out in broad terms how the company will compete, which market segments, which go-to-market approach, which strategic value propositions based on a thorough strategic analysis'. How I interpret this is, that where the strategy defines the longer-term trends and business model choices, the 'dynamic capabilities' provide a more continuous basis for sensing, seizing and transforming them. If your dominant DNA is that of a product leader, you'll recombine some of your process, market, technology capabilities, to sense opportunities and seize them. The strategy is the breeding ground on top of which we develop the dynamic capabilities.

Siemens has organized its dynamic capabilities around its strategic diamond, introduced in Figure 5.12. The strategic diamond is meant to continuously check the relevance of the strategy and the strategic plans with the market and customer environments in which we are operating.

It starts on the left with triggers and trends. The triggers and trends can come from any of the volatility drivers we introduced in Chapter 3, in Figure 3.1. Trends and triggers are evaluated on a regular basis, for instance quarterly. They are clustered into focus areas for which we check whether we have ongoing strategic activities, and if not, we create them. Not all trends and triggers or focus areas need to be addressed with strategic activities. At each step, we question whether they are relevant to the strategy. It is like a two-layered filter. As an example, a breakthrough in medical technology may have a strategic impact for Siemens Healthineers, but may be neutral for Siemens Smart Infrastructure. By applying the filters, there is less noise or disturbance which means the strategic plans are basically implemented faster.

Figure 5.11 Schematic overview linking dynamic capabilities with business models and strategy

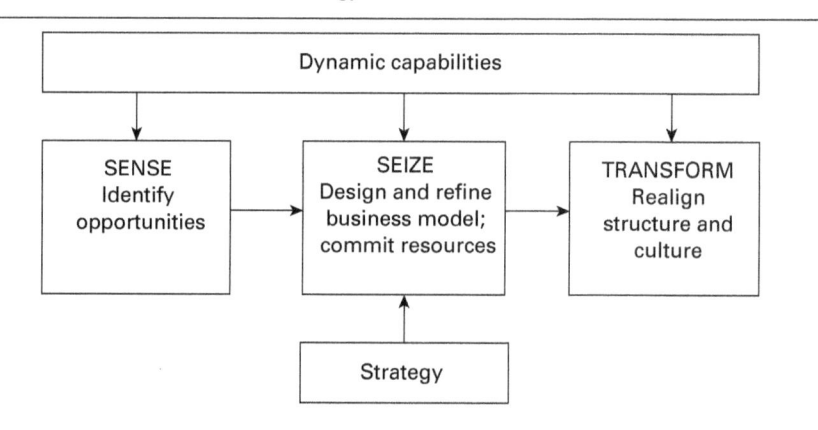

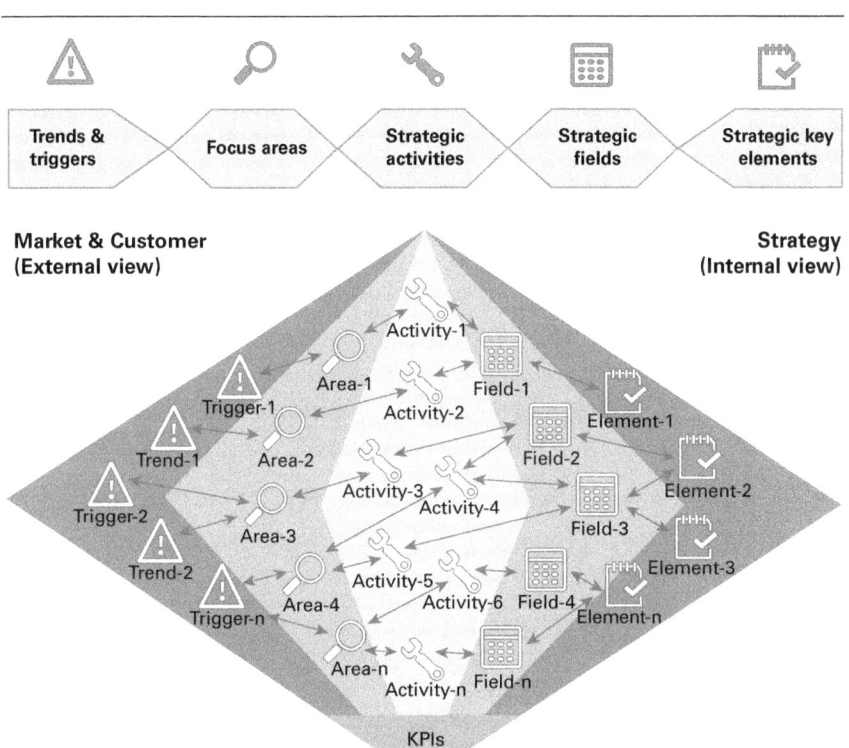

Figure 5.12 The strategic diamond at Siemens

Continuing to the right in the strategic diamond, strategic activities are grouped into strategic fields that address strategic key elements from the strategic plan. The strategy side of the diamond is called the 'internal view', as opposed to the 'external view' from markets and customers. Strategic activities are connecting the external and the internal view. They keep the strategy relevant in continuously changing market circumstances.

Figure 5.13 shows a fictitious example, with sustainability trends coming from different angles: customers, financial markets, government regulations and the talent market. Trends can be combined into focus areas such as 're-ducing CO_2 in the supply chain', which can be addressed by strategic activities such as reshoring and increasing multi-modal transports. These are fictitious, not Siemens examples. The strategic actions can get combined into strategic fields such as 'redesigning the EU distribution network', which supports a key strategic element such as 'turning the logistics service offering into a key differentiator'. Once more, this is a fictitious example, not a Siemens example.

'The approach is simple,' Alexander Tschentscher, head of supply chain strategy, comments. 'It doesn't require hundreds of hours of consultants to set it up. You start writing your trends and triggers on the left hand side, you start writing your strategic fields and key elements on the right hand side, and then you start connecting the two. But it is very powerful,' he continues.

'It helps you to move from resilience to robustness. Resilience is all about bracing for impact, and then recovering from the impact. Some people like to stay in the resiliency mode, but recovering from one impact after the other is not sustainable. The end goal is to become robust, or resistant. The strategic diamond will help you achieve robustness in two ways. First, it will identify gaps or white spaces in your strategic activities and strategic fields. As these get addressed, you will get more robust. Second, it will question the market relevance of your strategic fields or key elements. We might have defined

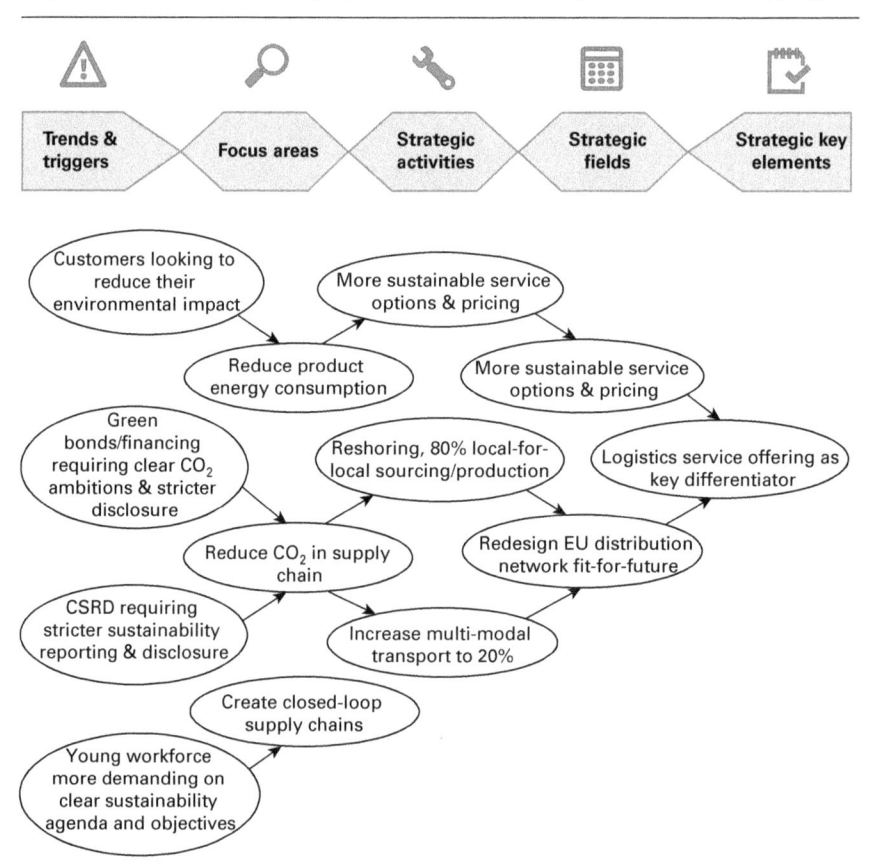

Figure 5.13 Siemens supply chain diamond: example end-to-end mapping

initiatives around using more robotics in our warehouses, but how does that support the focus areas and the key trends and triggers in the market? If there is no link to the market perspective, then maybe we don't need these strategic fields or key elements. So a second way the diamond builds robustness is in creating focus and speeding up implementations.'

I asked Alexander about his view on the 'reconfiguration of the business models' from Figure 5.11, how actively do they change their strategic fields or strategic key elements? He comments that

'as a start, we decided to focus on the visualization. In a big global organization like Siemens the better way is to create the visibility on disconnects and that something has to change, but leave it up to the local teams to define what needs to be done. It is also about repetition, repetition, repetition. If we see trends and triggers that are not being addressed and their relevance and impact is growing people will automatically start addressing it and be building more robustness. In big organizations like Siemens it doesn't work to steer that from a central perspective, it is the local teams that need to use the diamond to keep their strategies in sync with the markets.'

In summary, when asked for what he sees as the main impacts of the strategic diamond, Alexander comments that

'first, it is connecting the external market side and the internal strategy side. That enables Siemens' supply chain executives in making better strategic decisions while having a detailed view of the interconnected elements of the strategic diamond. Second, it safeguards the organization as it helps selecting which triggers and focus areas are key to the strategy. That speeds up strategy implementation and keeps it more focused. Third, it keeps the strategy relevant through this adaptable framework. It provides the flexibility needed in today's market circumstances. And fourth, it provides intra-organizational transparency. Through the strategic diamond, every member of the logistics community at Siemens has the accessibility to know the impacts of their job-related activities on the strategy. It enables leaders to initiate the projects crucial to fulfilling the strategic goals and further manage the interdependencies of the activities throughout the organization.'

Clarifying your sustainability ambition and its impact on the supply chain

Gather your executive team, or a team of cross-functional experts. Ensure the different functions such as sales, marketing, R&D, operations, supply chain, procurement, finance, HR, IT are represented.

In the exercises from Chapters 1 and 2, you may have been mapping your sustainability risks, where is your material impact and which metrics you already have on the social foundation and the ecological ceiling. From the exercise earlier in this chapter, you may have gathered input from the online survey on how your strategic value proposition looks like, and in which way sustainability (or resilience) is part of the competitive positioning. You could consider these exercises a more bottom-up data gathering, increasing insights in where you currently are.

Give an introduction to the strategy-driven sustainable and resilient supply chain design framework shown in Figure 5.10 and then take 60 minutes to do a first iteration of steps 1–6 by giving a first pass to the following questions. Choose one business unit or product group to simplify the answers, as needed.

- In our market, what does it mean to play at par, differentiate or dominate on sustainability?
- What is our intended strategic position on sustainability: play at par, differentiate or dominate?
- How will our intended strategic position on sustainability influence the complexity and/or variability within our supply chain?
- What is our intended supply chain response (if needed, independently from your positioning on sustainability)?
- What will be key characteristics of our supply chain, given our positioning on sustainability?
- How does that influence our key financial and non-financial metrics? (Note: your intended strategic position will define your key metrics, take the example of a B corporation like Tony's Chocolonely).

After the 60 minutes, ask to the group what they see as the biggest 'blind spot that has been revealed'? Was our sustainability positioning clear? Was it clear how that was influencing the level of complexity or variability and the setup of our supply chain? Was it clear how that is affecting financial and non-financial parameters? Are the non-financial parameters and intended outcome on them clear?

Depending on the outcome, you may plan extra iterations, to iterate and refine the supply chain design, which is the 'iterate' step from Figure 5.10.

Clarifying your resilience ambition and its impact on the supply chain

Comparable exercise but then focused on resilience. So gather your executive team, or a team of cross-functional experts. Ensure the different functions such as sales, marketing, R&D, operations, supply chain, procurement, finance, HR, IT are represented.

In the exercises from Chapters 3 and 4, you may have mapped what are your drivers for volatility, what are options to improve resilience and what is the impact from the lack of resilience. You could consider these exercises a more bottom-up data gathering, increasing insights in where you currently are.

Give an introduction to the Strategy-Driven, Sustainable and Resilient Supply Chain Design framework shown in Figure 5.10 and then take 60 minutes to do a first iteration of steps 1–6 by giving a first pass to the following questions. Choose one business unit or product group to simplify the answers, as needed.

- In our market, what does it mean to play at par, differentiate or dominate on resilience?
- What is our intended strategic position on resilience: play at par, differentiate or dominate?
- How will our intended strategic position on resilience influence the complexity and/or variability within our supply chain?
- What is our intended supply chain response (your level of resilience defines how consistent you are in delivering it)?
- What will be key characteristics of our supply chain, given our positioning on resilience (think about the examples from 3M)?
- How does that influence our key financial and non-financial metrics? (Note: your intended strategic position will define your key metrics, take the example of a B corporation like Tony's Chocolonely).

After the 60 minutes, ask to the group what they see as the biggest 'blind spot that has been revealed'? Was our resilience positioning clear? Was it clear how that was influencing the level of complexity or variability and the setup of our supply chain? Was it clear how that is affecting financial and non-financial parameters? Are the non-financial parameters and intended outcome on them clear?

Depending on the outcome, you may plan extra iterations, to iterate and refine the supply chain design, which is the 'iterate' step from Figure 5.10.

Conclusion

In this chapter I have integrated sustainability and resilience into our strategic trade-offs, through our strategic value proposition and into the strategy-driven design of our supply chains, by understanding the impact on complexity and variability, the product and supply chain design, and the full triple bottom-line impact, including financial, social and environmental impact.

The case of MediaMarktSaturn shows the impact of changing your strategic value proposition on your physical supply chain and your supply chain organization. The case of Tony's Chocolonely shows how differentiating or dominating on sustainability can trigger extra complexity, which can trigger extra costs, but if the consumer is willing to pay for that, can lead to a successful financial outcome, being high growth and high profitability. The hope of Tony's is that this will trigger 'big choco' to follow suit and take a comparable social responsibility. The case of Siemens shows how to keep your strategies up-to-date and relevant in fast changing markets. I hope the exercises have helped you to gain insights into your sustainability and resilience ambition: do you want to play at par, differentiate or dominate, and what is the impact on your supply chain.

In the next chapter, I will further deepen the strategy-driven, sustainable and resilient, supply chain design by looking into circularity, supply chain segmentation and scenario management, all extra tools to design your supply chain for a competitive edge.

Endnotes

1. F Crawford and R Mathews (2001) *The Myth of Excellence, Why great companies never try to be the best at everything*, Three Rivers Press, New York
2. T Treacy and F Wiersema (1995) *The Discipline of Market Leaders*, Basic Books, Cambridge
3. B DeSmet (2018) *Supply Chain Strategy and Financial Metrics: The supply chain triangle of service, cost and cash*, Kogan Page, London
4. B DeSmet (2001) *The Strategy-Driven Supply Chain, Integrating Strategy, Finance and Supply Chain for a Competitive Edge*, Kogan Page, London
5. M Porter (1996) What is Strategy?, *Harvard Business Review*
6. K Kim Chan and R Mauborgne (2005) *Blue Ocean Strategy*, Harvard Business Review Press, Boston
7. Gorillas. Groceries at your door in minutes, 2024. www.gorillas.io/en (archived at https://perma.cc/4W4V-B7VH)

8   Z Doss and F Szekely. Patagonia's sustainability strategy: Don't buy our products. IMD—International Institute for Management Development (2015).
9   Interface. Celebrating 50 years: Our next journey starts here, Interface Blog, 2024. www.interface.com (archived at https://perma.cc/GJ7F-JQXV)
10 Tony's. 100% slave free the norm in chocolate, Tony's our mission, 2024. tonyschocolonely.com/nl/en/our-mission (archived at https://perma.cc/MCV4-Y2PV)
11 The Body Shop. Our Story, 2024. www.thebodyshop.com/en-gb/about-us/our-story/a/a00002 (archived at https://perma.cc/Z3LS-Y6AD)
12 D McGougall. The hidden face of Primark fashion, The Guardian, 22 Jun 2008. www.theguardian.com/world/2008/jun/22/india.humanrights (archived at https://perma.cc/XU7G-7QGF)
13 D Michaels. A Robin Hood for inconvenienced fliers in Europe, The Wall Street Journal, 13 Aug 2009. https://www.wsj.com/articles/SB10001424052970203612504574344832790197904 (archived at https://perma.cc/SS9P-BBU7)
14 J Spero, J Shotter. Ryanair turns Polish pilots into precarious workers, Financial Times, 1 Nov 2018. www.ft.com/content/b8f77f16-d865-11e8-ab8e-6be0dcf18713 (archived at https://perma.cc/D6DD-DTGX)
15 Primark. Primark pledges to make more sustainable choices affordable for all as it unveils extensive programme of new commitments, 14 Sep 2023. corporate.primark.com/en-gb/a/news/primark-cares/primark-pledges-to-make-more-sustainable-choices-affordable-for-all (archived at https://perma.cc/WQ7R-37US)
16 Ryanair Group. Sustainability, 2024. corporate.ryanair.com/sustainability/ (archived at https://perma.cc/F6BC-AGXZ)
17 Media Markt Saturn. About us, 2024. www.mediamarktsaturn.com/company (archived at https://perma.cc/MBS8-FMPL)
18 Media Markt presents: Experience 2.0, Retail Detail, 24 Apr 2017. www.retaildetail.eu/news/electronics/media-markt-presents-experience-20/ (archived at https://perma.cc/SKM3-6PHH)
19 C Dawson. MediaMarkt marketplace growth in 2023, Channel X, 17 Aug 2023. channelx.world/2023/08/mediamarkt-marketplace-growth-in-2023/#:~:text=Ceconomy%2C%20Europe's%20leading%20consumer%20electronics,positive%20in%20the%20third%20quarter (archived at https://perma.cc/HWN3-V7Z7)
20 Media Markt Saturn. Good prospects for MediaMarktSaturn: CECONOMY issues positive outlook for full year 2022/23 based on strong performance in the third quarter, 10 Aug 2023. www.mediamarktsaturn.com/taxonomy/term/14 (archived at https://perma.cc/87VM-28XF)
21 J Elkington (1999) *Cannibals with Forks: The Triple Bottom Line of 21st Century Business*, Capstone, London

22 European Commission. The European Green Deal, Striving to be the first climate-neutral continent, 2024. commission.europa.eu/strategy-and-policy/priorities-2019-2024/european-green-deal_en (archived at https://perma.cc/84BQ-658X)

23 The White House. Inflation Reduction Act Guidebook, 2024. www.whitehouse.gov/cleanenergy/inflation-reduction-act-guidebook/ (archived at https://perma.cc/5RHP-BTKW)

24 Tony's Chocolonely. Annual report 2020/2021, Nov 2021. tonyschocolonely.com/nl/en/annual-fair-reports/annual-fair-report-2020-2021 (archived at https://perma.cc/7KNX-URZX)

25 Tony's Chocolonely. Annual report 2020/2021, Nov 2021. tonyschocolonely.com/nl/en/annual-fair-reports/annual-fair-report-2020-2021 (archived at https://perma.cc/9E2B-CXT8)

26 Tony's Chocolonely. Annual report 2020/2021, Nov 2021. tonyschocolonely.com/nl/en/annual-fair-reports/annual-fair-report-2020-2021 (archived at https://perma.cc/KF93-6CUS)

27 A Living Income Reference Price (LIRP) indicates the price needed for an average farmer household with a viable farm size and an adequate productivity level to make a living income from the sales of their crops

28 B Lab Global. Tony's Chocolonely, 2024. www.bcorporation.net/en-us/find-a-b-corp/company/tonys-chocolonely/ (archived at https://perma.cc/U7SQ-P7RK)

29 B Lab Global. Make Business a Force For Good. www.bcorporation.net (archived at https://perma.cc/C394-8GWG)

30 DJ Teece, G Pisano and A Shuen. Dynamic capabilities and strategic management, *Strategic management journal* 1997, 18(7), 509–533.

31 M E Porter (1980) *Competitive Strategy*, The Free Press, New York

32 DJ Teece. Business models and dynamic capabilities, *Long range planning*, 2018, 51(1), 40–49

Including circularity, segmentation and scenario management

06

Introduction

In this chapter, I deepen the strategy-driven – sustainable and resilient – supply chain design. I start by discussing concepts from circularity, such as the value hill, and how to narrow, slow and close the loops through the 10Rs, such as refuse, reduce and reuse. I show how to integrate them into the strategy-driven – sustainable and resilient – supply chain design.

The case of Ricoh on the one hand illustrates another strategy transformation. Ricoh has changed its strategic value proposition. From historically being focused on leading products and innovations, being a product leader, it is now centred on delivering the best total solution, or being a customer intimacy leader. The case illustrates the impact on the supply chain and the supply chain organization. The case also discusses how circularity is becoming a possible differentiator for the core printer business of Ricoh. The new MF5 is for 80 per cent built out of older MF4s. Strategy changes are notoriously difficult. The case shows the commitment from Ricoh as a group which gives confidence it will drive success. It shows how sustainability techniques like circularity can help creating a competitive edge.

As a second addition, we explore the segmentation of markets and supply chains. I start with a caveat that supply chain segmentation should not be an excuse for not making strategic choices. The culture of the lowest price and the best product blend like oil and water. Nevertheless, different regional markets may provide different playing fields and require different value propositions which require different supply chains. I will discuss how the supply chain design can include a segmented approach and which supply chains archetypes are available to respond to the different market segments.

As a third addition, I will discuss scenario capabilities. If we look 5–10 years ahead, the future is per definition uncertain. I introduce a technique, developed at MIT, on how to prepare for different world views. Based on these, we can analyse what is common, what could be different, what we can act upon now, what we might want to postpone. This approach is illustrated in the case of Infineon, where they understand that seeing is believing. Once you've seen how the future could look like, you start acting upon it and behaving accordingly. The case discusses that the approach is important. People will only believe if they have imagined themselves. To get them in the right mindset some preparations are needed.

The case of Colruyt group shows the importance of education. Through a 'Strategy-driven supply chain lab', Colruyt group is building strategy-driven capabilities at the top of its organization. Whether it is about scenario thinking, strategic modelling or mapping the impact on the supply chain, these are not standard topics at universities nor business schools. Colruyt group believes that developing these capabilities within the senior management are essential to deal with the upcoming challenges in the dynamic retail market.

Near the end of the chapter I introduce 'Strategy-Driven Supply Chain Maps' as a practical tool to translate strategic trade-offs into their supply chain impact, in analogy to the strategy maps once introduced by Kaplan and Norton. They may be especially helpful to increase supply chain understanding with non-supply chain professionals.

We close the chapter by doing the cross check on whether our strategy-driven – sustainable and resilient – supply chain design, as developed in Chapters 5 and 6 answers the needs of the fourth generation supply chain introduced in Chapter 4.

Strategy-driven circular supply chain design

Let's dig a bit deeper in sustainability through a 'philosophy' called 'circularity' or 'circular supply chains'. One of the key concepts in circularity is the 'value hill' elegantly described by Ed Weenk and Rozanne Henzen in their

Including circularity, segmentation and scenario management

book 'Mastering the circular economy[1]'. In the so-called 'linear' business model, we take raw materials from earth, make products out of them (going up the hill), we use them (being on top of the hill) and then dispose of these products through incineration or landfill (going down the hill). In Chapter 3 I introduced the massive waste problem created by fast fashion companies, which Bloomberg[2] reports is 'choking developing countries with mountains of trash'. In a different sector, 'Waste Electrical and Electronic Equipment' or 'WEEE' is reportedly still leaking[3], through illegal exports, to developing countries, where it ends up in landfills. This 'leaked' electrical and electronic waste contains various substances – including lead, mercury and flame retardants – that pose considerable environmental and health risks if improperly treated.

Low cost production in Asia has fuelled consumerism and the linear business model. A hundred years ago equipment was repaired and reused over multiple generations. Because of the low cost of the equipment we are tempted, and encouraged, to buy more of it, and when it is out of fashion or when it breaks down, to dispose of it and buy the latest and greatest. There is debate about so-called 'planned obsolescence[4]' – do companies deliberately make products to break down so they can sell more? Or are they merely satisfying consumer requirements to have access to cheap products and frequent updates? Whatever the drivers are of consumerism and faster obsolescence, the corresponding linear model of take-make-dispose is unsustainable.

It is not sustainable as we take more than the earth can generate. The so-called 'earth overshoot day[5]' in 2023 was 2 August. It means that the amount of ecological resources that the Earth is able to generate, in 2023 was consumed by 2 August. If you consume more than is being generated, it means you are depleting resources, which de facto cannot be sustained. A second reason the linear model is unsustainable is because of the pollution it creates. Leakage from poorly controlled landfills is creating pollution and killing biodiversity. We are turning our oceans into plastic soups. Even if we had all the resources to sustain our current way of life, we would simply kill the very planet we live on, including ourselves. If this sounds gloomy, then add the projected growth of the world population, and the prospect that a bigger share of it has access to a consumerist lifestyle then it becomes a real issue which we will need to act upon now, rather than within a couple of decades.

Next in their book, Weenk and Henzen introduce the 'circular' version of the value hill. It starts by trying to extend the 'use' phase of the product by the user. That may require a different product design and different supply chains. First of all we'll design the product for durability as opposed to planned obsolescence. Second, we probably want products that can more easily be disassembled when something is broken (try that with a mobile phone) and a service supply chain that makes the service parts available and potentially the repair services. As we go down the value hill, if customers or consumers are no longer using the product, we may try to find extra ways to bring it into the hands of other customers or consumers. Think about the second hand initiative taken by Patagonia introduced in Chapter 5. Or think about Interface, the flooring company introduced earlier in this chapter, that takes back used flooring tiles and redistributes them to be reused by charities and other organizations that can use support[6]. If products are worn-out, circular strategies try to refurbish or remanufacture them before going into recycling. Circular supply chains try to close the loop and avoid any landfill or incineration.

The value hill is linked to the so-called R-ladder, also elegantly described in the book of Ed Weenk and Rozanne Henzen. The R-ladder contains 10Rs that together need to result in fully circular supply chains. It is a ladder in the sense that we try to stay on top and we try to stay away from the lower levels of the ladder. These need to be seen as a last resort.

- R0 = Refuse, consume less
- R1 = Reduce, use less materials
- R2 = Resell, Reuse, second-hand market
- R3 = Repair, extend lifetime, same user
- R4 = Refurbish, extend lifetime, new user
- R5 = Remanufacture, of components, in new, similar product
- R6 = Repurpose, of components, in other function
- R7 = Recycle materials, downcycle, recycle, upcycle
- R8 = Recover energy, incinerate, but store/use energy
- R9 = Re-mine, mining of landfills and waste plants

Weenk and Henzen talk about stages R0–R2 'narrowing the loop', as on the one hand they try to reduce the need for products and materials and on the other hand, for those in use, maintain the usage as long as possible. It is trying to ensure there is less product entering the system, and once it is there, less product flowing down the value hill. For stages R3 to R6 they talk about R3 to R6 'slowing the loop'. As product starts flowing downhill, we try to push it back up via the value side and insert it 'back into the loop' with as little effort as possible. For stages R7 to R9 they talk about 'closing the loop'. If we can no longer recuperate the product itself (refurbish, remanufacture) or key functions of the product (repurpose), we start focusing on the materials inside, the recycling step in R7. Finally, R8 and R9 foresee that if, against the principles of circularity, things are incinerated or go to landfill, we try to recuperate whatever energy we can, or we start mining landfills as a new source of raw materials.

Circularity is more than an approach, it is a way of life, with a heavy focus on what the European Green Deal calls 'decoupling economic growth from resource use'. When using less, using longer, by re-using and recycling to 100 per cent, we will have to extract less. We may still see economic growth, from extra extractions from the earth or for instance in services, but without necessarily putting our planet and ourselves at risk.

Circularity is another good example of where product design and supply chain design need to go hand in hand. Instead of the presumed 'design for obsolescence' or 'planned obsolescence', we will need to 'design for longevity' and 'durability'. We will also need to design the products for easy refurbishment, remanufacturing and recycling. At the flip side of this we will need to construct the supply chains that support that. The supply chains that support the redistribution, the refurbishment, the remanufacturing or the repurposing of components. Circular product and supply chain design need to go hand in hand.

That brings us back to our Strategy-Driven Sustainable and Resilient Supply Chain Design. In Figure 6.1 we have replaced the 'Supply Chain & Product Design' with 'Circular Product & Supply Chain Design'. When thinking about circularity, it becomes obvious to put product design before supply chain design. The arrows from the use and end-of-life stages to the deliver and make stages represent the different R-strategies discussed previously.

Circular products and supply chains should be as strategy-driven as any others. Circularity is one of the options to become more sustainable, specifically on resource usage. A company like Tony's Chocolonely chose a social dimension to dominate the playing field. A company like Interface chose circularity as a way to dominate the playing field. Being circular doesn't make you CO_2 neutral. So in our strategic positioning we'll need to balance circular objectives against other objectives. Who do we want to

Rethinking Supply Chain

Figure 6.1 Strategy-driven circular product and supply chain design in seven steps

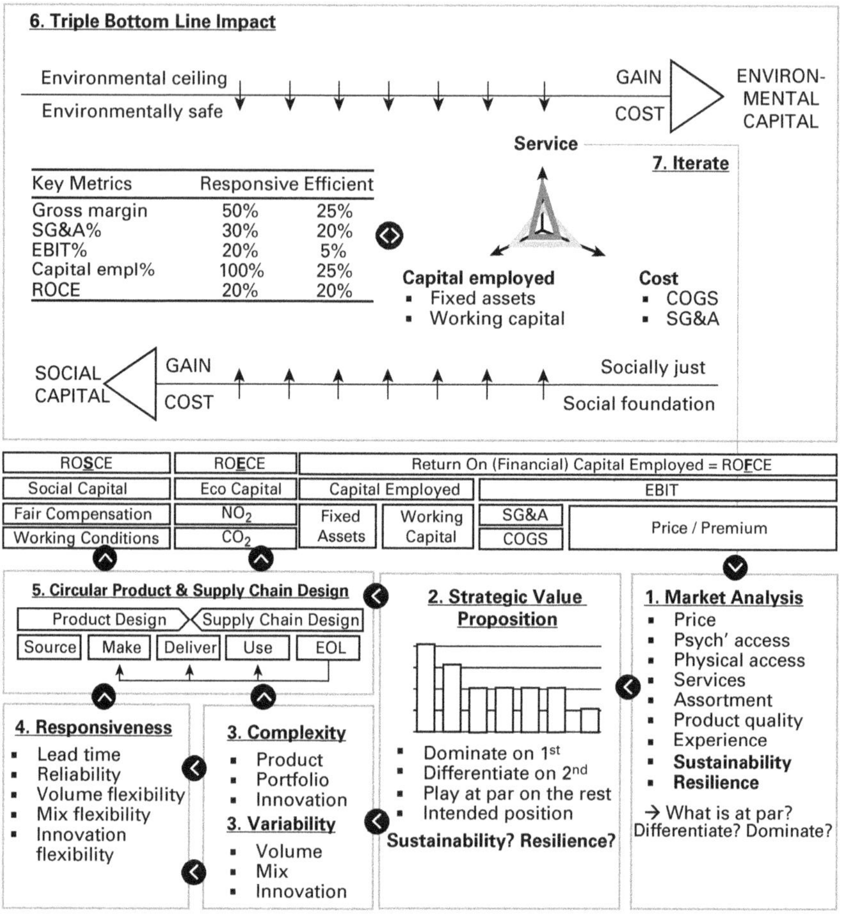

6. Triple Bottom Line Impact

Environmental ceiling / Environmentally safe — GAIN / COST — ENVIRONMENTAL CAPITAL

Key Metrics	Responsive	Efficient
Gross margin	50%	25%
SG&A%	30%	20%
EBIT%	20%	5%
Capital empl%	100%	25%
ROCE	20%	20%

Service

7. Iterate

Capital employed
- Fixed assets
- Working capital

Cost
- COGS
- SG&A

SOCIAL CAPITAL — GAIN / COST — Socially just / Social foundation

ROSCE	ROECE	Return On (Financial) Capital Employed = ROFCE
Social Capital	Eco Capital	Capital Employed	EBIT
Fair Compensation	NO_2	Fixed Assets	Working Capital	SG&A	Price / Premium
Working Conditions	CO_2			COGS	

5. Circular Product & Supply Chain Design
Product Design / Supply Chain Design
Source | Make | Deliver | Use | EOL

2. Strategic Value Proposition
- Dominate on 1st
- Differentiate on 2nd
- Play at par on the rest
- Intended position
Sustainability? Resilience?

1. Market Analysis
- Price
- Psych' access
- Physical access
- Services
- Assortment
- Product quality
- Experience
- Sustainability
- Resilience

→ What is at par? Differentiate? Dominate?

4. Responsiveness
- Lead time
- Reliability
- Volume flexibility
- Mix flexibility
- Innovation flexibility

3. Complexity
- Product
- Portfolio
- Innovation

3. Variability
- Volume
- Mix
- Innovation

be? For which type of customers? Where do we want to stand out? Where do we want to differentiate? Where do we want to play at par. Pick your battles wisely, and then fight them all the way. That's the principle of being strategy-driven.

> **EXERCISE**
>
> **Clarifying your circularity ambition and its impact on the product and the supply chain design**
>
> Gather your executive team, or a team of cross-functional experts. Ensure the different functions sales, marketing, R&D, operations, supply chain, procurement, finance, HR, IT are represented.

In the exercises from Chapters 1 and 2, you may have been mapping your sustainability risks, where is your material impact and which metrics you already have on the social foundation and the ecological ceiling. From the exercises in Chapter 5 you may have gathered input from the online survey on how your strategic value proposition looks like, and in which way sustainability (or resilience) is part of the competitive positioning, you have done a follow-up exercise to clarify your sustainability ambition by analysing what it means to be at par, differentiating or dominating in your market, what is your intended strategic position, how that impacts the complexity and variability of your supply chain and what type of key characteristics it drives into your supply chain.

With the group, think through by how far circularity is needed or can help to achieve your sustainability objectives. Which aspects of narrowing, slowing and closing the loop and relevant for your market? Which of the 7Rs introduced above can make a difference in your market? Are customers or consumers sensitive to this? Could circularity lead to a differentiating position in your market? Is circularity the goal or is circularity a means to an end? What is our vision? If it is a means to an end, what type of goals could it support? Can we clarify our ambition? Can we translate it into an action plan? How does that fit into the broader strategic plan?

By going through these discussions, you should align within the executive team on what is your company vision on circularity. Is it part of the goals or is it supporting objectives? What is the action plan and how does it fit within the broader strategic plan?

Case Study: RICOH – From product leadership to customer intimacy, by Mark van Abeelen, Director Finance, Strategy & Business Excellence at Ricoh Europe SCM

Changing strategy is changing the DNA of the company. Needless to say that it is hard and prone to failure. Your DNA, whether it is product leadership, customer intimacy or operational excellence, exerts a gravitational pull. Any initiative into a new strategic direction needs to overcome that gravitational pull, like a rocket needs to overcome the gravitational pull of our planet Earth when it is launched into space.

In my book *The Strategy-Driven Supply Chain*[7], Chapter 4 is all about 'strategy fails'. One of those fails is 'we changed our strategy', and I give two cases to illustrate that. A first is how Barco, a product leader, tried to venture into mass markets by making products that were 'good enough', to revert back to its product leadership position after a decade. A second case discussed how Casio, originally an operational excellence player, switched to a product leadership position, how it was determined to get there, but how it was struggling from a financial perspective to drive the appropriate return on the significantly increased capital employed. Changing strategy is not for the 'faint at heart'.

However difficult it is, an impressive story of changing strategy is being written by Ricoh. Ricoh is a Japanese multinational, founded in 1936 as a spin out of the sensitized paper business of Rikagaku Kogyo, itself founded as a spin-off of the Institute of Physical and Chemical Research in Tokyo in 1927[8]. The company was originally named Riken Kankoshi Co. and changed its corporate name to Ricoh Company, Ltd. in 1963.

With its roots in a research institute, Ricoh was born as a product leader. Throughout different technological waves, from analogue to digital, from black and white to colour, from standalone to networked solutions, Ricoh was known for being the first on the market with cutting edge products. 'Everybody wanted Ricoh products,' comments Mark, 'whether it were cameras, copiers, fax machines, multi-functionals. So selling in a certain way was simple. The products were that innovative and appealing to the market that the products were selling themselves. The regional markets were primarily box moving the products that were developed and produced primarily in Japan.'

Fast forward to the 2000s where the world is increasingly becoming digital and as such paperless. Fast forward to the 2020s where any transitions in work environments and working habits, such as more hybrid working, have been greatly accelerated by the Covid-19 pandemic. With declining unit placements and page counts in the printer and copier industry, Ricoh evaluated its strategic options and decided to transform itself into a 'digital services company', culminating in reformulating its mission and vision into 'Fulfilment through Work', in 2023. The new mission is based on the foundation of its corporate values and its founding principles called 'The Spirit of Three Loves', which are to 'Love your neighbour', 'Love your country' and 'Love your work'[9], which were formulated as the Ricoh Group's Founding Principles in 1946.

Including circularity, segmentation and scenario management

The digital services business model is explained in detail in the 2023 Integrated Report. Mark Van Abeelen, director finance, strategy & business excellence at Ricoh Europe SCM, comments that

> 'the company is transforming into a leading value-added workspace integrator. The mind shift is enormous', he says. 'In the digital model, the growth is largely coming from the sales regions rather than the mother organization. In Europe, for example, we have done a lot of acquisitions to create that new digital capability. It requires the development of a lot of new processes in the region. Take procurement as an example. In the past, Japan had a procurement capability, but Europe didn't, as Europe had a portfolio that was delivered from Japan. Marketing was focussed on the models created by R&D, it wasn't starting from the needs in the market but rather from the products that had been developed.' Mark continues that 'one of the keys in this new business model is to understand how to integrate acquisitions into service propositions towards the market, knowing we have different types of acquisitions. Take Apex, which is producing lockers[10]. That is another hardware company, which is relatively easy to integrate from a portfolio and supply chain perspective. You could say it is just another supplier of a hardware product. Then we acquired Docuware[11] which is a workflow solution, which is again relatively easy to integrate, as an extension of the existing portfolio. We also acquired networking and cybersecurity companies, which is more about the expertise. These companies don't necessarily have an own developed product. How to integrate these? How do you keep and nurture that expertise?'

Ricoh Europe did around 20 acquisitions over the last five years. That is impressive. It shows that Ricoh is implementing the new strategy full force. 'It increases the complexity', Mark comments.

> 'We used to have two main product lines: production print and office print. We now have eight, including audio-visual, cybersecurity, networking, managed document services. It creates a lot of pressure on the operating companies, the countries, to sell more and more. At the same time there is a pressure on costs, as margins are lower than in the old, product leader, world. It has led us to think and act more on a regional level, for instance in the budgeting cycle. Also within supply chain, everyone is now part of a regional supply chain organization, meaning the resources in every country are also available for another country. We can deploy somebody from Germany on a project in Austria without having to ask permission to the MD of Germany. If you want to come to one portfolio, there is almost no alternative. The consistency of

that portfolio across countries is also a major sales argument to our bigger customers. If you are an SME, you may find local players that can do the same as Ricoh. But if you are a global player, providing the same service across the region makes Ricoh into a preferred partner.'

When moving from product leadership to customer intimacy, one of the challenges I have seen before is the 'doubling' of the complexity. We still have the 'old' product leadership business, with complex products, based on complex supply chains, for instance long lead time components coming from niche suppliers. And to that we then add 'portfolio' complexity. Knowing that the customer intimacy business doesn't drive the same premium margins as the product leadership business, that delivers a double hit on the Return On Capital Employed. So I asked Mark how they deal with that.

'First of all', Mark comments, 'not all of the products from our total workspace solution are on stock, that would be impossible. We do have good contracts and agreements with players like Ingram Micro, a distributor of information technology products and services. We act as an integrator and an installer. The margin may not even come from the installation but from the management that follows afterwards. We also see that customers may have specific requirements like for meeting rooms. Relying on partners provides a lot more flexibility in responding to that. At the same time, we have been reducing complexity in the old core. The idea is that we still offer Ricoh products as part of the total solution, but price plays a more important role. So we will have to review and reduce the assortment and we have reduced the flexibility. As an example, we used to do postponement in Europe for production print, but that has been pushed back into the manufacturing organization, with the associated longer lead times. We have also announced a joint venture with Toshiba[12]. More scale should help us to improve our price competitiveness in the core markets of production printing and office printing.'

Mark continues that 'from an innovation perspective, he is seeing a shift towards sustainability aspects. Sustainability has always been in the DNA of Ricoh, as witnessed by the three loves introduced above.' As an example, he talks about the focus on circularity. 'Our new MF5,' he comments,

'is for 80 per cent built from existing MF4s. The MF4 had more recycled components than the MF3, but the MF5 really reuses the MF4 as the base. That introduces new trade-offs. Should we extend the contract of an MF4, knowing that is attractive from a margin perspective? Or should we replace it with an MF5, as we need the MF4s to produce the MF5s, and the MF5 may have advantages like a lower energy consumption, supporting the customer in their sustainability objectives? Shifting towards more sustainable solutions is a potential source of competitive advantage',

Mark believes. 'We see that competitors are currently buying market share by playing on price. We may have a differentiating positioning here.'

As impressive as this strategic transformation journey at Ricoh is going, Mark does admit that 'at times it is tempting to revert back to the old model. If margins are under pressure, you will see suggestions to push some more of the A3 printing solutions, which is a higher margin business. As in any transformation, it goes in steps, and some steps are backwards.' But overall, when talking to Mark and his colleagues, I sense the excitement, about this courageous journey. The flag has been firmly planted on where Ricoh wants to go. Half of the recipes seem to be clear, like building a portfolio of hardware, software and competences to deliver that ambition of the digital services company and the vision and mission of 'Fulfilment through Work'. Half of the recipes are being defined during the journey, like how do you assemble this into winning portfolios and solutions, and how do you harmonize that across operating companies? Half of it is building the bridge as you walk on it. How sceptical I remain on strategy changes, how impressed I am by the story that Ricoh as a company is writing. It is clear, it is bold, it is courageous and above all it is firm. It also shows how deep the impact of a strategy change is, in the supply chain, but far beyond. If strategy literature tells us that sharper strategies lead to more successful companies, I believe Ricoh holds a challenging though bright future!

Segmenting markets and supply chains

I have never been a big fan of segmented supply chains. Why? Because I believe that, on average, they are used as an excuse not to make needed strategic choices. An easy example is combining branded products and private labels under the same roof. Can we do that? Yes we can, but is this what we want? I get pushed back by supply chain managers who tell me 'this has been decided by the board'. Well, OK, but maybe then the board has taken the wrong decision. Strategy literature tells us that strategy is about making choices, as choices create focus. I often use the example of taking someone from the low-cost airlines Ryanair or Southwest and putting that person at a premium quality carrier like Etihad Airways. What happens? Well, that person would be completely disorientated, as all of the focus would be on premium service and quality instead of cost. Or likewise, take somebody from Etihad and put that person at Ryanair or Southwest. That person would also feel like arriving on a different planet, where premium service and quality have disappeared, and where it is all about cost-cost-cost. Still, this is exactly what we do when combining private label and branded products. So, on Monday and Tuesday the focus is all on cost and efficiency and a quality which is at par. Wednesday till Friday it is all about innovation, experimentation, creating emotions, ensuring top-notch quality in a premium brand-selling-packaging. And we're doing that with the same R&D people? The same production operators? The same production equipment? Strategy literature is consistent in telling us this doesn't work.

Another example explained in my previous book *The Strategy-Driven Supply Chain* is that product leaders tend to keep products and technologies on board even when they commoditize. This is a comparable story. The market may have commoditized, so price is more important here. If the DNA of your company is that of an innovator, then maybe you don't want to be in commodities. Some companies like 3M are known to sell off businesses before they commoditize. 3M once was in VHS cassettes, which is logical, as it requires coating technology, which is one of its core competences. But that doesn't oblige 3M to stay on board when the market commoditizes. Sometimes we are afraid of losing the sales, as it conflicts with our growth objectives. However, this is thinking tactically, not strategically. If we sell the business early enough and at the right price, it can provide the funding to create two new businesses that each have the potential of the old. That is the more bold and courageous choice that product leaders should follow.

With these caveats, I can accept that in global companies, as an example, not all regional markets behave the same way. The playing field in Asia may be different as we don't have a strong brand or market penetration. Or markets in Africa may be more price-driven than those in Europe or the US. Or different channels may have different needs, such as OEMs, distributors and project-driven markets. Let's start with the first questions, which are more strategic in nature. I will come back to the channel question near the end of this section.

If needed, we indeed need to segment different regional or application markets. As shown in Figure 6.2, it is a kind of pre-phase, prior to the market

Figure 6.2 Strategy-driven market and product/supply chain segmentation

6. Triple Bottom Line Impact

Environmental ceiling
Environmentally safe
GAIN / COST → ENVIRONMENTAL CAPITAL

Service
7. Iterate

Key Metrics	Responsive	Efficient
Gross margin	50%	25%
SG&A%	30%	20%
EBIT%	20%	5%
Capital empl%	100%	25%
ROCE	20%	20%

Capital Employed
- Fixed assets
- Working capital

Cost
- COGS
- SG&A

SOCIAL CAPITAL ← GAIN / COST

Socially just
Social foundation

ROSCE	ROECE	Return On (Financial) Capital Employed = ROFCE
Social Capital	Eco Capital	Capital Employed / EBIT
Fair Compensation	NO₂	Fixed Assets / Working Capital / SG&A / COGS / Price / Premium
Working Conditions	CO₂	

Product/Supply Chain Segmentation
Efficient | Intimate | Innovative | Sustainable

Market Segmentation (Geography, Product, Channel...)

5. Circular Product & Supply Chain Design
Product Design × Supply Chain Design
Source | Make | Deliver | Use | EOL

2. Strategic Value Proposition
- Dominate on 1st
- Differentiate on 2nd
- Play at par on the rest
- Intended position
Sustainability? Resilience?

1. Market Analysis
- Price
- Psych' access
- Physical access
- Services
- Assortment
- Product quality
- Experience
- Sustainability
- Resilience
→ What is at par? Differentiate? Dominate?

4. Responsiveness
- Lead time
- Reliability
- Volume flexibility
- Mix flexibility
- Innovation flexibility

3. Complexity
- Product
- Portfolio
- Innovation

3. Variability
- Volume
- Mix
- Innovation

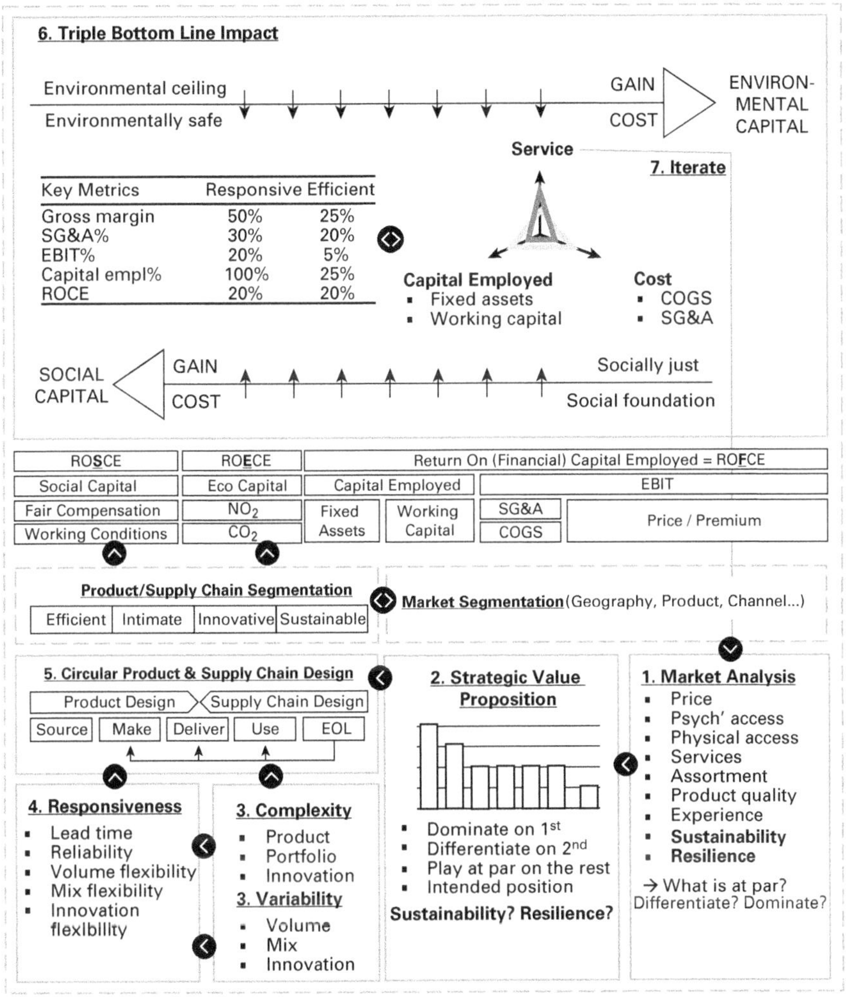

analysis, or it can go in parallel to the market analysis, when we realize that the needs are different, for instance as regional markets are not the same. As you can see mirrored in Figure 6.2, different market segments may need different types of supply chain, and most probably not just supply chains, but different products as well. Think about the example of the high-tech company in Chapter 4. In the pursuit of growth, they wanted to offer a high performance piece of technology for a desalination application in the Middle East. There were questions on how to create a service supply chain and organization around that, but one of the concerns was also this was more a price-driven market as opposed to a performance-driven market. The company was probably not going to make the right margins with its existing high-performance equipment. So it's another example where product and supply chain design naturally get intertwined.

In Figure 6.2, I have mirrored the market segmentation with a supply chain segmentation and named four archetypical supply chains. It is another topic I have long resisted, as I believe real-life supply chains are too complex to be captured in be it, 3, or 4, or even 16 supply chain types, as proposed by John Gattorna in his latest book *Transforming Supply Chains*[13]. The reason I have added them in this book, as opposed to the previous books, is that I see it resonates with people. It improves our understanding. It gives us some grip on what is otherwise a dark and amorphous mass. It also helps us to explain there are different types of supply chains, that serve different purposes, and come with a different level of cost and capital employed. I have defined four types of supply chains, the 'efficient', the 'intimate', the 'innovative', and to provoke you, the 'sustainable' supply chain. I briefly describe them bullet-wise:

- Efficient:
  - no complexity but simplicity (pareto is the rule of law), no variability (e.g., Every Day Low Price as opposed to promotions)
  - trim service to the basics, no madness or special treats, basic but honest and reliable service
  - focus on efficiency-efficiency-efficiency and cost-cost-cost.
- Intimate:
  - portfolio and service complexity, a lot of SKUs and a lot of different services, leading to mix variability, which means it is hard to define where the demand will be coming
  - short lead times and high reliabilities are typically part of the offering, which is difficult on a complex portfolio, so ABC/XYZ segmentation and differentiating lead times across segments is common sense
  - the motto could be 'whatever the customer wants' but the underlying and true motto should be 'whatever the customer is willing to pay for'.
- Innovative:
  - product complexity, specific components or raw materials coming from niche suppliers, and volume variability, hard to predict which one of the innovations will be highly successful

- volume flexibility is important, if not just from a customer perspective then for sure from a financial perspective, out of the 10 NPIs, only one or two will be successful, it is key to be able to scale as the margin of these needs to pay for the eight or nine failures
- the motto could be 'fail fast or scale fast', the high margins are paying for 'fast-fast-fast whatever it takes'.

- Sustainable:
  - product and process complexity, driven by the sustainability requirements, organize for 100 per cent recycling, use raw materials from qualified and controlled sources only
  - traceability is key, auditing, certification, we don't want to be compromised on our key sustainability promises
  - the motto is 'mastering a different (social, environmental) dimension', higher margins are paying for 'whatever it takes to master in the different dimension'.

I hear you saying, 'do you mean that an efficient supply chain cannot be sustainable and vice versa? We want our supply chain to be both efficient and sustainable!'. Well, the truth is that not all supply chains will be equally sustainable, just like not all supply chains are equally efficient. Think about the supply chain of Tony's Chocolonely introduced in this chapter. If we want to be truly socially responsible, we will pay a premium price for our cocoa beans, which is not just above the market price, it is above the fairtrade price, in order to get to the living income of $1.96 per person per day in Ghana and $2.45 in Côte d'Ivoire. So if you are a private label chocolate manufacturer, what are you going to do? Are you going to pay the same price as Tony's Chocolonely and join their 'Open Chain' initiative to become a truly sustainable supply chain? Or are your private label customers not willing to pay for that, and will you go for the lowest cost and highest efficiency supply chain? Will you buy at market prices (which is the price at which people buy on average)?

This triggers two considerations. First, just like with strategy, we may be tempted to have a bit of everything. However, just as with the strategic value proposition that may not be what you want. Being focused and clear on the supply chain objectives brings clarity to all stakeholders in the supply chain. And we may extrapolate from the strategy field, that more focused supply chains will simply be more successful. A second consideration is that the supply chain doesn't stand on its own. So whether we want to be more efficient or more sustainable depends on the company strategy, for which the corresponding four supply chain archetypes have been shown in Figure 6.2.

John Gattorna has been a long-standing author and practitioner in the domain of supply chain segmentation. He worked with leading supply chain companies like Schneider Electric to help them organize and orchestrate their complex global supply chain networks. Instead of a 'strategy-driven' approach, Gattorna uses an 'outside-in' and 'customer-driven' approach which shows similarities with classifying people according to MBTI. You can be more introvert or extrovert, more thinking or feeling, judging or perceiving, and sensing or intuitive, leading to 16 possible types of personalities. Gattorna has developed a comparable approach of classifying customers into 16 possible types.

Gattorna says that the most frequently seen segments were 'collaborative', 'transactional' and 'dynamic', which, if you read the description, align closely with the 'intimate', 'efficient' and 'innovative' supply chains defined above. Personally, I prefer a strategy-driven approach. The reason is that the strategy-driven approach allows asking the question 'do we really want to serve these three segments of customers' where the behavioural approach does not. In the behavioural approach we just accept that the different customer segments exist. The behavioural approach fits better in the second generation supply chain thinking, where the supply chain is not expected to ask strategic questions, and to 'just get it organized'. The strategy-driven approach, is obviously at the heart of the third and fourth generation supply chain thinking. Think about the example of the branded versus private label customers. Behavioural segmentation will create two types of supply chains. The strategy-driven approach will question whether we want to serve both.

Further on in his book, Gattorna adds a fourth 'common' supply chain type which he calls the 'project accumulation' supply chain. That brings us to the question of OEMs compared to dealers and compared to the project-driven customer segments at the start of this section. Obviously, these different segments have different needs and behaviours. With OEMs we may have contracts for the next three to five years (think about automotive) and regular updates on the changes in their production plans and the inventories they have on the ground. Project or tender-driven business could be completely different. Your customers may for instance be installers that are bidding themselves for big construction projects. It is typically uncertain for them, and for you as a supplier, if and when they will get the project. Specifications on the project and which products to deliver could still change. You may even have different customers bidding for the same construction project, which in a certain way increases your chances you will be a part of it. So these are obviously two very different needs, requiring different supply chain approaches, but I would call them 'tactical' or 'functional' segmentations as opposed to 'strategic' segmentations. Whether I'm in a project-business, an OEM business or both, the strategic question is whether I will differentiate based on cost, total solution, product quality or sustainability. Our strategic choice will define how we make trade-offs in our OEM and project-driven business which will obviously be organized differently.

Preparing for uncertainty using scenarios

In their book *Strategic Planning for Dynamic Supply Chains*[14], Phadnis, Sheffi and Caplice introduce a technique to deal with the uncertainty inherent in many strategic supply chain decisions. If we design our supply chains, we design them for the next 3–5 or potentially 10–20 years. If we decide to do reshoring and build extra manufacturing plants in Europe or in the US, it is not a decision we are likely to revert two or three years from now. When we look into the future, there is an inherent uncertainty in what the world will look like. Instead of assuming just one version of the truth, Phadnis, Sheffi and Caplice introduce a technique for proper scenario management. I will shortly summarize it here and then include it in our strategy-driven design approach.

They start from a so-called 'focal decision', which is the key strategic question we are trying to answer. It could be 'how to organize our global footprint and flows', in a retail context it could be 'how do we conquer the city' or how do we win the battle with the competition for the city consumer, knowing they shop differently and environmental and social regulations in cities are increasingly more strict. For the focal decision, I list what the authors call 'local factors' and 'driving forces'. The 'local factors' are factors that more directly impact the focal decision and that we more directly control. For the 'conquer the city', some examples are shown in Table 6.1. There may be consumer-related factors like how many people will live in the cities, what will be their primary concerns, or traffic-related factors like what will the congestion be like, what about road taxes, or labour-related factors like the cost of labour in these city centres, depending on where these factors go, we may come to different outcomes on how to best conquer the city. Next to the local factors, we list 'driving forces'. These 'driving forces' are broader forces, which we don't control, and which influence the direction of the local factors. The examples for our 'how to conquer the city' focal decision in Table 6.1 are urbanization, migration flows, sustainability, digitalization. As driving forces the PESTELE part of our volatility fishbone shown in Figure 3.1 is a good checklist.

After listing the local factors and the driving forces, we can start scoring them. We first score the local factors. The authors suggest to first ask different people to individually score the local factors on a scale of 1–5, from a lower to a higher impact, on the focal decision. It is shown in the second column of Table 6.1. The people involved could be part of a project team, that is studying

Table 6.1 Local factors and driving forces for our focal decision on how to conquer the city

Local factors	Scoring local factors	Urbanization	Migration	Sustainability	Digitalization
Consumer-related	>	>	>	>	>
- number of consumers living in city areas	2	2	2	0	...
- consumers being more price sensitive	2	0	2	0	...
- consumers being more concerned about health	3	0	0	2	...
Traffic-related	>	>	>	>	>
- increasing congestion	3	2	2	2	...
- road taxes	3	0	0	2	...
...	...	>	>	>	>
Labour-related	>	>	>	>	>
...	...	>	>	>	>
Sum product	>	10	14	18	...

Table 6.2 Four example scenarios for our focal decision on how to conquer the city

Sustainability = HIGH	Migration = LOW	Migration = HIGH
Urbanization = HIGH	'BIG AND WEIRD' • Green • WEIRD • Expanding	'THE MELTING POT' • Green • Multi-cultural • Expanding
Urbanization = LOW	'THE ELITE FEW' • Green • WEIRD • Shrinking	'EXODUS' • Green • Multi-cultural • Shrinking

the focus decision. The authors suggest to go sufficiently broad in involving, obviously relevant people, to ensure a sufficiently broad perspective is developed. We then ask that group to individually score how the driving forces impact the local factors, with 0 being no effect, 1 being a weak effect and 2 being a strong effect. If we understand the impact of the driving forces on the local factors and the impact of the local factors on the focal decision, we can calculate the relative impact of the driving forces on the focal decision by calculating the sum of the products as shown in the bottom row of Table 6.1. If we have a longer list of driving forces, the relative scores will highlight which ones are the more relevant for our focal decision at hand. Next we think through which of the driving forces are more or less uncertain. Taking the examples from Table 6.1, we might say that there is less uncertainty on whether the future will be more or less sustainable. If we would ask ten experts, they would probably all agree that the future of the cities will be greener and more sustainable. That's why we will consider this to be a 'trend', that needs to be addressed in any of the scenarios we put forward. That could be different for the urbanization and the migration flows. If we ask ten experts the answer could be 'it depends '. If the future state is uncertain, we talk about uncertainties. For the uncertainties, for instance urbanization, we try to come up with two scenarios, two possible outcomes, typically a 'high' and a 'low' scenario. The probability of the scenarios is not important, even if something is highly unlikely, it still is important to understand what the world would look like and how we would organize for it. If we have two possible outcomes for our two uncertainties, for instance urbanization and migration, we try to combine the scenarios as shown in Table 6.2.

EXERCISE
Defining scenarios for future supply chains

Gather your executive team, or a cross-functional team, for a two hour workshop. It is important that you gather the different key functions in the company: sales, operations, marketing/product management/R&D, supply chain, finance.

Ask your team 'what they consider as the big drivers for how the future supply chain will or should look like'. Ask them to list the drivers on a sheet of paper. If they pick two of those drivers, what are two possible outcomes for each of them, a 'high' scenario, and a 'low' scenario. Let them combine the high and the low into four different world views as show in Table 6.2. Ask them think about names that capture the essence of the world view, as we have tried to show in Table 6.2. Ask the team to think through what are the scenario dependent supply chain design questions (and answers), and what are scenario independent supply chain design questions (and answers). It could be that you say 'the supply chain will always be more digital' but 'whether it is more regional depends on the scenario'.

I did exactly this exercise with my book council in a short timeframe of approximately one hour. The result is shown in Table 6.3. In the four groups that did the exercise, three drivers came up: the evolution of AI, and the question whether it will really take over or remain supportive, the political stability, will trade-wars with China intensify, will that break down and revert the trend of globalization, and the resource scarcity, will the economy be driven by a scarcity of and a fight for resources? In Table 6.3, I combined the political stability and resource availability, assuming that in a politically stable world, global trade will keep the access to resources open and vice versa, that political instability will expose us to a scarcity of resources.

At the bottom of Table 6.3, we look at a first scenario, where political stability is high and that keeps resources available. In this scenario, depending on whether AI takes over, we may see a primary focus on resources or a focus on resources and cheap labour. The more jobs are taken over by AI, the more the focus will exclusively be on where the resources are. In the scenario of political instability, where the world is shrinking, global trade breaks down, we may see the rise of regional trading blocks, where companies will need to reinvent themselves to work around structural shortages of key raw materials or components. The question whether AI will take over results in a different level of disintermediation of the labour force by potentially massive automation. It could face governments with the question how to deal with that and whether to subsidize labour to avoid societies from collapsing. If this disintermediation

Table 6.3 Four example scenarios for our exercise on what the future supply chain will look like

TRENDS: • SUSTAINABILITY • AUTOMATION (INDUSTRY 4.0)	AI TAKES OVER	Human Intelligence CONTROLS
RESOURCE SCARCITY / POLITICAL INSTABILITY	**'Artificially made in Europe'** • REGIONAL TRADING BLOCS • INNOVATION BORN OUT OF NECESSITY • AUTONOMOUS • STILL GOING GREEN? • AUTOMATED vs SUBSIDIZED LABOUR?	**'Make America Great Again'** • REGIONAL TRADING BLOCS • INNOVATION BORN OUT OF NECESSITY • ORCHESTRATED • STILL GOING GREEN? • UPGRADED WORKFORCE
RESOURCE AVAILABILITY / POLITICAL STABILITY	**'Chasing the Source'** • GLOBAL FREE TRADE • FAIL FAST OR SCALE FAST • AUTONOMOUS • GREEN & CLEAN • AUTOMATED vs SUBSIDIZED LABOUR?	**'Chasing Cheap Labour'** • GLOBAL FREE TRADE • FAIL FAST OR SCALE FAST • ORCHESTRATED • GREEN & CLEAN • UPGRADED WORKFORCE

happens to a lesser extent, there will still be needed a massive upgrade of the workforce capabilities to deal with this new digital and more automated reality. The prospect of political instability and resource scarcity for sure is more gloomy. Though sustainability currently looks like a trend that cannot be stopped, it raises the question whether it would stay centre stage or whether more basic needs would be prioritized in this world scenario.

Whichever of the scenarios would happen, there seems no way around 'letting AI take over'. In that sense, experimenting with topics where it seems safe to run our supply chain in a more automated way, upgrading our people's capabilities to understand and embrace this new technology, all of these seem safe bets. The same for building capabilities

> to design, deploy, reconfigure and redeploy modular supply chains, a bit like the 'dynamic capabilities' introduced in Chapter 5 in Figure 5.11. Whichever scenario would come true. Good strategy-driven product and supply chain design capabilities seem key to deal with the future uncertainty. Maybe it will be more driven by access to cheap labour, as it has been over the last three to four decades, maybe it will be more driven by the access to key raw materials, maybe we'll be forced into regional organizations, whatever the driver or the direction will be, excellent capabilities to reconfigure and redeploy our supply chains, in a modular way, will be one of the assets to swiftly navigate through the upcoming changes in how the global economy works.

In Figure 6.3 I have included this scenario management in our Strategy-Driven Sustainable and Resilient Supply Chain Design. The scenario management adds complexity. If we have four scenarios and would have four market segments, we would theoretically have to design 16 different supply chains. That could be a bit too much. However, see it as a robustness test. As discussed in the exercise output of our book council, across the four possible scenarios, what seems like the 'safe' thing to do and what choices are really scenario dependent? Is there a way to postpone some of these scenario dependent choices until we have more insight which direction the world is going? Use the scenario technique as a way to enrich your insights and improve the robustness of your supply chain design. Don't assume that you 'know' what the future looks like, embrace the uncertainty by evaluating different scenarios.

Case Study: Infineon – imagining the unimaginable, by Konstanze Knoblich, VP Supply Chain Engineering

It was at a conference in Munich that I started talking with Konstanze Knoblich, VP Supply Chain Engineering at Infineon, about what I felt was a life changing experience, for her, and for her colleagues involved in the process. They had imagined what they previously assumed was unimaginable, namely the future, and they started acting upon it.

Konstanze got inspired by a technique from Jane McGonigal[15], a director of game research and development at the Institute for the Future. The IFTF is a non-profit based in Palo Alto, California, that supports businesses, governments and social impact organizations with foresight, including global forecasts, custom research and foresight education.

Including circularity, segmentation and scenario management 217

Figure 6.3 Including scenario management in our Strategy-Driven, Sustainable and Resilient Supply Chain Design

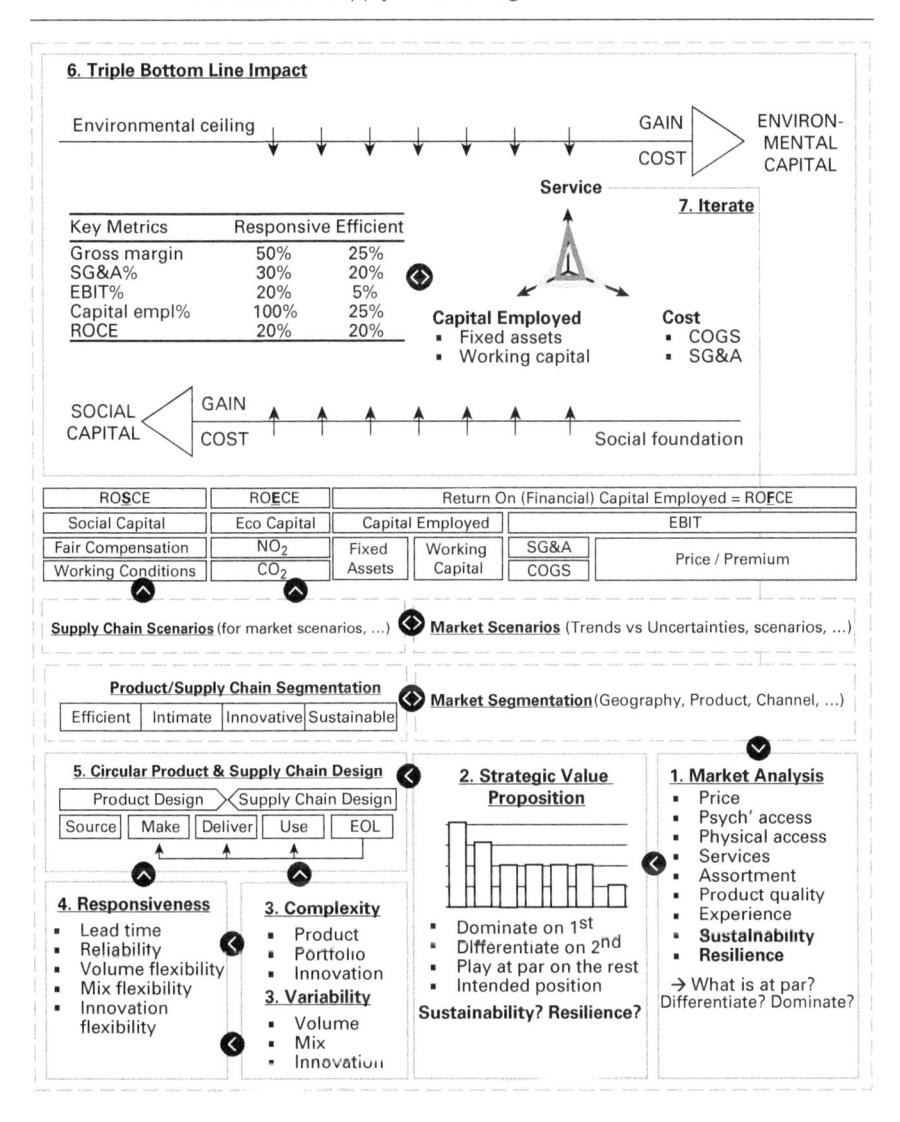

6. Triple Bottom Line Impact

Environmental ceiling → GAIN / COST → ENVIRONMENTAL CAPITAL

Service

7. Iterate

Key Metrics	Responsive	Efficient
Gross margin	50%	25%
SG&A%	30%	20%
EBIT%	20%	5%
Capital empl%	100%	25%
ROCE	20%	20%

Capital Employed
- Fixed assets
- Working capital

Cost
- COGS
- SG&A

SOCIAL CAPITAL ← GAIN / COST → Social foundation

ROSCE	ROECE	Return On (Financial) Capital Employed = ROFCE
Social Capital	Eco Capital	Capital Employed	EBIT
Fair Compensation	NO_2	Fixed Assets	Working Capital	SG&A	Price / Premium
Working Conditions	CO_2			COGS	

Supply Chain Scenarios (for market scenarios, …) ⇔ **Market Scenarios** (Trends vs Uncertainties, scenarios, …)

Product/Supply Chain Segmentation ⇔ **Market Segmentation** (Geography, Product, Channel, …)
Efficient | Intimate | Innovative | Sustainable

5. Circular Product & Supply Chain Design
Product Design × Supply Chain Design
Source | Make | Deliver | Use | EOL

2. Strategic Value Proposition
- Dominate on 1st
- Differentiate on 2nd
- Play at par on the rest
- Intended position
Sustainability? Resilience?

1. Market Analysis
- Price
- Psych' access
- Physical access
- Services
- Assortment
- Product quality
- Experience
- Sustainability
- Resilience
→ What is at par? Differentiate? Dominate?

4. Responsiveness
- Lead time
- Reliability
- Volume flexibility
- Mix flexibility
- Innovation flexibility

3. Complexity
- Product
- Portfolio
- Innovation

3. Variability
- Volume
- Mix
- Innovation

Konstanze's goal was to create a vision for supply chain 2030. She was a believer herself in the proposed techniques, but feared she was not going to be taken seriously in an engineering company like Infineon. It turned out to be a huge success, and we'll try to explore why and how this happened. Though I tell the story from her perspective, Konstanze wanted to stress that she didn't do this alone. She had active support from Mara Memmel, a student in psychology, from Maike Wiechmann, the executive assistant to the global head of corporate supply chain, and from Mario Müller, the senior director IT for the customer ecosystem. Also the blessing from her boss, Klaus Buchwald, the global head of corporate supply chain, was crucial.

One of the success factors she believes was opening up people's minds with two half-an-hour sessions, some five to six weeks before the two-day 'think tank' session. Managers are so stuck in today's issues that we need to create the mental space to think out of the box. In the first half-an-hour session she started from a game-like setting where she stated 'Imagine you're at home. You realize that the internet is out. You have no cell phone service. You notice there is no broadcasting on TV or radio. There is no electricity. All telecommunications seemed to have suddenly stopped working.' To then ask 'What do you do in the first five minutes? How do you feel? What do you think happened?' Konstanze comments that different people react differently. The digital natives are in panic, whereas other people stay totally calm under the assumption this will only last half an hour. If you relate that to the future supply chain, then there are two conclusions. A first is that different people will have different assumptions and views, which is a reason to think about the future together. A second thing Konstanze noticed is that the digital natives get comforted by the less dramatic views. If the scenario were now to happen, it would increase the chances they would react more calmly. So scenario thinking makes you better prepared.

The second half-an-hour exercise was to imagine yourself in 10 years' time. What will your future look like? Where will you live, work and play? How will the world be different? Konstanze and team created a Webex space where people could post their ideas. 'I was nervous', she says. 'I was unsure whether people would actually start sharing their vision. Again, as an engineering company people might have found this too esoteric. But then the first person started sharing, and then a second, and the different stories were enriching the views on how the world could look like 10 years from now.'

In that second session she also gave the assignment to start collecting signals from the future. 'At Infineon we are already very good at reviewing our supply chain trends', she comments. 'We are evaluating each year which ones are affecting us most.' But she indicated to the team that we also have news, social media, so she invited all of them in the coming weeks to keep their eyes and ears open, when they were following the news, when they were driving their car, when they were reading an article. She invited people to collect their observations on 'Signals for the Future' in another Webex chat.

The signals were an extra input to a two-day 'think tank' session. The group she and her team gathered was around 10 senior executives from supply chain, operations and IT, one or two levels below the executive committee. They also added a number of young talents, which were bringing in a different and fresher perspective. 'To make it successful, make it feel exclusive,' Konstanze comments. 'Tell people why you have invited them to be part of this experiment.' By calling it an experiment, Konstanze also tried to manage the expectations, as she was unsure about how the two-day think tank session would go and what would be the outcome.

'On day 1', she comments, 'we identified five key aspects about Infineon we know are true, and we flipped them to the inverse, as a possible starting point for scenarios. As an example, we have big production sites, so we flipped that around and said, OK, let's assume we have small production sites, for instance because there is a water shortage, and that water shortage led into a decentralization. In doing so, before you realize, what you thought was unimaginable starts to sound reasonable.' As you break people in different groups, you get different stories, which is further opening up people's minds.

The second day, they went through the collected trends and signals from their homework, clustered them, identified the most critical ones and compiled them into scenarios. One scenario was more people and customer oriented, one scenario more digital and environmental. 'An example of a scenario could be the following,' Konstanze comments. 'A first critical element could be that one of our main competitors like Intel builds a new, big, manufacturing site close to one of ours. A second critical element could be working habits further change and the four-day work week becomes mainstream. What if we would now couple the two, Intel builds a big plant next to ours and offers a four-day work week. What do we do?'

'Once you get immersed in those new realities, you start to embrace them and act upon them', Konstanze comments. One of the examples she describes is a possible response to changing attitudes to work and a shortage of skilled labour. 'Instead of assigning people to roles, we thought about creating a marketplace for jobs. Younger people may be eager to learn and go the extra mile, but as they get a first child or construct a house, they may prefer a slower pace. A problem in the current allocation of resources is that managers safeguard their teams. They are reluctant to share talent as they don't want to lose them. If through a market place we can advertise the skills required for a project, and people can apply, it may lead to a better allocation of talent. It could also solve the question around work-life balance and help people in developing their purpose. This is one which was eye opening for me,' Konstanze comments, 'and we can take this into action. We are developing an online platform where we can show all supply chain projects. The idea is that from wherever in Infineon you can have access, see what roles are needed, which skills and whom to contact.'

'Translating into action is important', Konstanze says. So they ended the two-day workshop by asking 'What is in your target for next year? What should we take as a joint team/group target? What is in our responsibility to get prepared? What do I decide today to do tomorrow or next week in order to get started?' By translating it into practical actions, putting it really into the short-term, we ended by getting the people back in the here-and-now.

The two days were an unimaginable success. 'How afraid I was in the beginning, how overwhelming were the positive reactions afterwards', Konstanze comments. 'In the end it was only two days and two warming up sessions. One of the keys is in the emotional aspect,' she continues. 'As the group jointly gets immersed into a scenario, there is an unimaginable sense of urgency that comes up. If someone would simply explain pre-defined scenarios, you'd never have that emotional connection. The excitement of envisioning the future as a group makes all the difference.'

Konstanze concludes by giving examples on how the ideas from the exercise are now getting embedded into their roadmaps. She also comments how the technique was picked up by other departments, like the sales and marketing board, and how it could be integrated into the standard management trainings at Infineon. In the end, as a manager or leader, envisioning the future needs to be a regular management task, a management task that needs to be learned, as one of the many others.

Case Study: Colruyt Group – developing strategy-driven supply chain capabilities through a strategy-driven supply chain lab

Colruyt Group is a family business that has grown over three generations into a retail group with over 33,000 employees and a diverse portfolio of food and non-food formats, in Belgium and abroad[16]. The biggest activity remains the supermarket Colruyt, which has delivered on its brand promise 'Lowest Prices' day after day for 50 years. Over the last half a century, the group has diversified its activities substantially, however, remaining true to retail, which still accounts for 80 per cent of the revenues. Today, the group is active in retail with around 10 businesses formats, with both physical outlets and online shops in Belgium, Luxemburg and France. In addition, it operates in foodservice and wholesale, for instance as a dedicated partner for the independent Spar stores. In recent years, the group has also grown as a producer and supplier of renewable wind and solar energy. The Colruyt group continues to do many things itself. It possesses a wealth of experience and expertise in areas such as technology, IT and communication, as well as production and packaging of meat, coffee, cheese and wine.

Colruyt group has been investing for long in the development of supply chain knowledge and competences through educational programmes. It started 10 years ago with the development and delivery of a 'strategic' supply chain education program, focused on the senior management. For eight consecutive years, I delivered, together with a team of relevant experts, an 11-day training programme, to a selected group of 16 people, coming from different functional backgrounds, and different food and non-food brands. Next to a yearly programme in Dutch, over the eight year period, three programmes were run in French, leading to 11 cohorts in total, or 176 people. Topics treated have been strategy models, how strategy impacts the supply chain, balancing the Supply Chain Triangle through better forecasting, planning, inventory management, purchasing and network design. Next to building knowledge and competence, one of the goals was also to build an internal network of cross-functional and cross-brand supply chain champions. Champions of end-to-end supply chain thinking, that are willing to break the unavoidable silos that you find in big organizations, with a focus on 'creating sustainable added value together through value-driven craftsmanship in retail', which is the group's purpose.

In parallel to the 'strategic programme', focused on the senior management, we also launched a 'tactical programme', focused on the middle management. That tactical programme has been running for five years now, in Dutch and in French, with 16 participants each, leading to another 160 people trained. The tactical programme is centred around the cross-functional processes that have been developed within the Colruyt group, processes like 'forecast-to-availability' or describing the return flows from the store network. For eight years we have also provided 'in-depth' training, to functional specialists, on topics such as forecasting and forecasting algorithms, inventory management and inventory algorithms, or network design and available optimization techniques and technology. If we take another 20 people trained on a yearly basis through these 'in-depth' trainings, that adds another 160 people trained leading up to a total of 500 people, being trained in supply chain knowledge and competences, at different levels, and from different angles.

In these 10 years, it has helped Colruyt group to develop a common language on how to address supply chain challenges, from a market and strategy perspective. Models like Treacy and Wiersema and Crawford and Matthews have become part of how Colruyt group defines and understands the strategic positioning of the different retail brands, and how a different positioning impacts the underlying supply chain. It has also developed a cross-functional understanding of how one function, be it procurement, central logistics, store logistics or marketing, is impacting the other functions or the end-to-end supply chain. It has helped to clarify how all functions need to be aligned to deliver the strategic value proposition to the consumer, at the lowest possible cost-to-serve, and how to do so in a consistent and sustainable manner.

The practical organization of the trainings is supported by the Colruyt Group Academy. The content of the programme has been developed by Solventure, in supervision by myself, in close cooperation with the Supply Chain Centre of Excellence, led by Dirk Leemans, and with the help of internal Colruyt experts. The overall approach is governed by a steering committee, consisting of the logistics directors of the major retail brands.

In 2022, after eight years of driving the strategic programme, the steering committee decided to take a step back and rethink the intended outcome and approach. One of the observations was that in the current 'strategic' programme, it was increasingly difficult to involve the top management of the organization, their peers from marketing, sales, procurement, in the management committees of the different retail branches. At the same time, it was where the steering committee saw the biggest need and the biggest added value. So the question was, whether we could define a new or adjusted format targeted towards the top 60 of the company. That was nuanced in a couple of iterations to the members of the top 60 active in the food retail brands, and extended with members of the management teams and talents that formally are not a part of the top 60.

To validate the need and the approach, we started interviewing the general managers of the major brands. From those interviews the need was confirmed. 'People who think that the retail market in five years will be the same as that of today have it wrong,' one of them commented. And 'painting a picture of the world, five years from now, and understanding the impact on our supply chain and logistics setup, is a key capability to develop within the top management of the group. We have a lack of people that can do exactly that,' another stated.

What has been developed since is what we termed the 'Strategy-Driven Supply Chain Lab'. The lab is built around the Strategy-Driven Supply

Chain Design shown in Figure 6.3. To make it practical and hands-on, the training starts from a practical case, sponsored by the TCFR, the Tactical Committee Food Retail, which includes the general managers of all food retail brands. It will then construct scenarios of how the world will look like five years from now. What are the main uncertainties? To which type of scenarios could that lead? We will follow the approach outlined earlier in this chapter and of which a possible outcome is shown in Table 6.3. Once we have different scenarios of how the world will look like, we will dive into value propositions. How well are we equipped with the retail brands we have today? Should they be adjusted? Should we create new brands with a completely new value proposition? Once we understand what is needed from a strategic positioning perspective, we will map that to the existing supply chains. How does it affect our complexity? The volatility? What is our desired supply chain response? And how does that affect our physical supply chain setup? The stores? The DCs? The transport? And how does that affect our financial metrics? And how does it affect our environmental ceiling and our social foundation? This is where we will use the 'Strategy-Driven Supply Chain Maps' shown in Figure 6.4. The strategy-driven lab will be a mix of delivering 'concepts' that can be used to analyse supply chain transformation, and applying them to a concrete case. At the end of the programme, the individual teams will debrief their results and findings to the TCFR, the council gathering all general managers from the different retail brands.

Driven by the volatility introduced in Chapter 3 and the increasing complexity of the 5D supply chain, introduced in Chapter 4, there is a huge need within companies to enhance supply chain knowledge and competences. Though the need is obvious, most companies are hesitant to properly invest in it. As a family owned group, that firmly believes in the power of its people, Colruyt group has consistently done so over the last 10 years and stays committed to extend this towards the future. Supply chain is the essential backbone of a retail company. Better understanding how to build or adapt that backbone based on market evolutions and strategic value propositions is key to the company purpose of 'creating sustainable added value together through value-driven craftsmanship in retail'. It has been a pleasure and a privilege to be part of that development journey over the last 10 years. My knowledge and understanding has grown alongside, in a mutual win-win partnership. Some people and companies are life changing. Colruyt Group has been life changing for me, and for all the people that have followed these training programmes over the last 10 years.

Strategy-Driven Supply Chain Maps

One of the common problems supply chain managers are confronted with is that their commercial counterparts don't understand the impact of their commercial decisions on the supply chain and the related costs and capital employed. I remember seeing a logistics director of a non-food retailer with sheer panic in his eyes when the commercial team had decided to lower the ceiling in the stores to improve the shopping experience, but what they had overlooked was that in one go they eliminated a lot of storage space above the shelves, which was needed to do a proper stock build-up for seasonal events like the back-to-school campaign or Saint Nicolas Day on 6 December. Less storage space in the stores meant more just-in-time deliveries, for which logistics currently didn't have the capacity. Any decision is good, as long as it is a conscious decision, across the three corners of the triangle (service, cost and cash), when we understand the environmental and social impact, and when it is aligned with the strategy. Companies do struggle with that, because of a lack of end-to-end understanding.

To help managers, supply chain and non-supply chain, better understand the impact of their decisions, I have developed what I have called 'Strategy-Driven Supply Chain Maps', referring to the well-known strategy maps[17], proposed two decades ago by Kaplan and Norton. Just like the strategy-maps of Kaplan and Norton had as an objective to visualize interdependencies across core processes and supporting processes, the Strategy-Driven Supply Chain Maps want to visualize the impact of commercial decisions on the broader supply chain, and their impact on financial and non-financial metrics.

Figure 6.4 contains a 'blank' map. The first column lists the possible value drivers of Crawford and Matthews, in this case focused on a retail environment. Notice I have included sustainability and resilience as possible value drivers at the bottom, in correspondence with what I introduced earlier in this chapter. The second column allows us to map the impact of our strategic moves and trade-offs (in the first column) on the complexity and variability, which from our strategy-driven methodology we know are important drivers of cost and capital employed. The third column contains our desired supply chain response, again something we need to decide upon. That links into supply chain network decisions such as (for a retail context) type, location and size of stores, type, location and size of distribution centres (DCs), our inventory policies, insourcing/outsourcing decisions, supplier base and related inbound logistics activities (again, in this form, to be used in a retail context). The fifth column maps this to capital employed (fixed assets and working capital) and to operating costs. The sixth column maps this to the environmental and social impact.

Figures 6.5 and 6.6 use a Strategy-Driven Supply Chain Map to illustrate the impact of portfolio decisions. Sales, marketing, category management may be eager to expand a certain category, for instance to increase the choice on offer for the growing group of flexitarians. Figure 6.5 shows this has a potentially broad impact, amongst others on shelf space and store size, on number of picking slots and DC space, on number of suppliers and the corresponding inbound logistics, which has a potential impact on fixed assets, on inventory, and on operating costs such as indirect cost of procurement (number of people in the purchasing department), inbound logistics cost, cost of reordering (depending on the level of automation), warehousing cost (because of longer picking distances). This has a potential impact on food waste, as an environmental impact. Figure 6.6 tries to illustrate that the financial and non-financial impact depends on the desired supply chain response, such as targeted on-shelf-availability. Is the philosophy to push a certain quantity and sold-is-sold, or do we want to guarantee a certain availability in some or all of the extra items of the assortment? That decision will influence the inventory levels, the food waste risk, the amount of shelf space needed and so on.

Figure 6.7 shows another illustration of the Strategy-Driven Supply Chain Maps. As a food retailer, we may decide to differentiate or even dominate on sustainability. Local products and shorter supply chains are one of the common value propositions. Within our strategic discussions we may consider to no longer offer blueberries that have been on ocean or airfreight. The biggest producers of blueberries are[18] the US, Canada and Peru[19], which together produce 10 times what is being produced in Europe. Given the strategic intent, we can use the Strategy-Driven Supply Chain Map to explore the broader supply chain impact. On the service side, we may not be able to guarantee the same availability given the much smaller production in Europe compared to that overseas. From a price perspective we will have to investigate whether European producers, which are smaller in scale, can deliver at the same price point or not, so local berries may become more expensive. If from a sustainability perspective we want to show the country of origin, to convince customers this is local product, not product that we have been flying in, that might require the creation of extra SKUs and may require extra picking places in the warehouse. From a supplier perspective, we may have to deal with many more and smaller suppliers compared to

Figure 6.4 Blank Strategy-Driven Supply Chain Map

Inputs from strategic planning			Design decisions	Financial impact	Impact analysis
Value proposition	Complexity & variability	Supply chain response	Supply Chain Network Design		Environmental and social impact (across the extended supply chain)
Price	Portfolio complexity	Lead time Reliability (OSA targets)	**Proximity to customers** (store count/location, dark store count/location, pickup-point count/location)	**Fixed assets**	CO_2 emissions (extended supply chain)
Psychological access (reduced stress of choice, easy parking)	Product complexity	Volume flexibility (ability to respond to peaks)	**Store size** (m3, shelf space, storage space, buffer for peaks, operating hours, in store operations bake-off/butcher)	• DC footprint, racking, shelving, automation,	Energy consumption
Physical access (count, location of stores, eCommerce)	Innovation complexity (e.g., certifications)	Mix flexibility (ability to respond to mix changes)	**Outbound logistics** (supplier to store, cross-dock, 1-1 from DC, milkrounds, temperature-controlled, pallet/kart/)	• Store footprint, racking, shelving, special storage	Water consumption
Service (service counter, traiteur, dining, on-shelf-availability)	Volume variability (intra-day, day on day, month on month)	Innovation flexibility (ability to respond to changes in the portfolio)	**Inventory policy** (on-shelf vs on-order, central stock yes/no, 1SKU-1DC?.)	• Material handling equipment	Food waste
Product breadth/depth (regional assortments, holiday assortments)	Mix variability (product mix, channel mix)		**DC capacity** (m3, pick slots, pallet/layer/ box/piece/ operating hours, level of automation, temperature/safety requirements, peak capacity)	• Truck/trailer assets	Waste flows (packaging)
Product quality (premium, specialty)	Innovation variability (renewal rate, seasonal assortments)		**Insourcing/outsourcing**	**Working capital**	Labour conditions (extended supply chain)
Experience (tasting, inspiration, in-store butcher, bake-off)			**Supplier base** (supplier type, count, location)	• Account payables (supplier type/size)	Fair compensation (extended supply chain)
Sustainability (local products, fair trade)			**Inbound logistics** (#goods receipts, pick-up vs delivery, consolidation, returns)	• Inventory	Diversity (extended supply chain)
Resilience (failsafe service)				• Accounts receivables	
				Operating costs	
				• Purchasing cost	
				• Cost of procurement	
				• Inbound logistics cost	
				• Cost of reordering	
				• Warehousing cost	
				• Outbound logistics	
				• Store operations	

Figure 6.5 Strategy-Driven Supply Chain Map illustrating impact of expanding the product portfolio

Inputs from strategic planning		Design decisions	Impact analysis	
Value proposition	Complexity & variability	Supply chain response	Supply Chain Network Design	Financial impact	Environmental and social impact (across the extended supply chain)
Price			**Proximity to customers** (store count/location, dark store count/location, pickup-point count/location)	**Fixed assets** • DC footprint, racking, shelving, automation • Store footprint, racking, shelving, special storage • Material handling equipment • Truck / trailer assets	CO_2 emissions (extended supply chain)
Psychological access (reduced stress of choice, easy parking)	Portfolio complexity	*Impact* Lead time			Energy consumption
Physical access (count, location of stores, eCommerce.)	Product complexity	Reliability (OSA targets)	**Store size** (m³, shelf space, storage space, buffer for peaks, operating hours, in store operations bake-off/butcher)		Water consumption
Service (service counter, traiteur, dining, on-shelf availability)	Innovation complexity (e.g., certifications)	Volume flexibility (ability to respond to peaks)	**Outbound logistics** (supplier to store, cross-dock, 1-1 from DC, milkrounds, temperature-controlled, pallet/kart)		Food waste
Decision Product breadth/depth (regional assortments, holiday assortments)	Volume variability (intra-day, day on day, month on month)	Mix flexibility (ability to respond to mix changes)	**Inventory policy** (on-shelf vs on-order, central stock yes/no, 1SKU-1DC?)	**Working capital** • Account payables (supplier type/size) • Inventory • Accounts receivables	Waste flows (packaging, etc.)
Product quality (premium, specialty)	Mix variability (product mix, channel mix)	Innovation flexibility (ability to respond to changes in the portfolio)	**DC capacity** (m³, pick slots, pallet/layer/box/piece/...., operating hours, level of automation, temperature/safety requirements, peak capacity)	**Operating costs** • Purchasing cost • Cost of procurement • Inbound logistics cost • Cost of reordering • Warehousing cost • Outbound logistics • Store operations	Labour conditions (extended supply chain)
Experience (tasting, inspiration, in-store butcher, bake-off)	Innovation variability (renewal rate, seasonal assortments)		**Insourcing/outsourcing**		Fair compensation (extended supply chain)
Sustainability (local products, fair trade)			**Supplier base** (supplier type, count, location)		Diversity (extended supply chain)
Resilience (failsafe service)			**Inbound logistics** (#goods receipts, pick-up vs delivery, consolidation, returns)		

Triple Bottom-Line Impact

Figure 6.6 Strategy-Driven Supply Chain Map illustrating reinforcing impact of lead time decisions

Inputs from strategic planning		Design decisions	Impact analysis	
Value proposition	Complexity & variability	Supply chain response	Supply Chain Network Design	Financial impact	Environmental and social impact (across the <u>extended supply chain</u>)

Price

Psychological access (reduced stress of choice, easy parking)

Physical access (count, location of stores, eCommerce,)

Service (service counter, traiteur, dining, on-shelf availability)

Decision
Product breadth/depth (regional assortments, holiday assortments,.)

Product quality (premium, specialty)

Experience (tasting, inspiration, in-store butcher, bake-off)

Sustainability (local products, fair trade)

Resilience (failsafe service)

Portfolio complexity

Product complexity

Innovation complexity (e.g., certifications)

Volume variability (intra-day, day on day, month on month)

Mix variability (product mix, channel mix)

Innovation variability (renewal rate, seasonal assortments)

Impact

Lead time

Reliability (OSA targets)

Volume flexibility (ability to respond to peaks)

Mix flexibility (ability to respond to mix changes)

Innovation flexibility (ability to respond to changes in the portfolio)

Proximity to customers (store count/location, dark store count/location, pickup-point count/location)

Store size (m^3, shelf space, storage space, buffer for peaks, operating hours, in store operations bake-off/ butcher)

Outbound logistics (supplier to store, cross-dock, 1-1 from DC, milkrounds, temperature-controlled, pallet/kart)

Inventory policy (on-shelf vs on-order, central stock yes/no, 1SKU-1DC?)

DC capacity (m^3, pick slots, pallet/layer/box/piece/... operating hours, level of automation, temperature/ safety requirements, peak capacity)

Insourcing/outsourcing

Supplier base (supplier type, count, location)

Inbound logistics (#goods receipts, pick-up vs delivery, consolidation, returns)

Fixed assets
- DC footprint, racking, shelving, automation
- Store footprint, racking, shelving, special storage
- Material handling equipment
- Truck / trailer assets

Working capital
- Account payables (supplier type/size)
- Inventory
- Accounts receivables

Operating costs
- Purchasing cost
- Cost of procurement
- Inbound logistics cost
- Cost of reordering
- Warehousing cost
- Outbound logistics
- Store operations

CO_2 emissions (extended supply chain)

Energy consumption

Water consumption

Food waste

Waste flows (packaging)

Labour conditions (extended supply chain)

Fair compensation (extended supply chain)

Diversity (extended supply chain)

Triple Bottom-Line Impact

Importance of impact depends on the desired Supply Chain Response

Figure 6.7 Strategy-Driven Supply Chain Map illustrating impact of a sustainability-driven decision

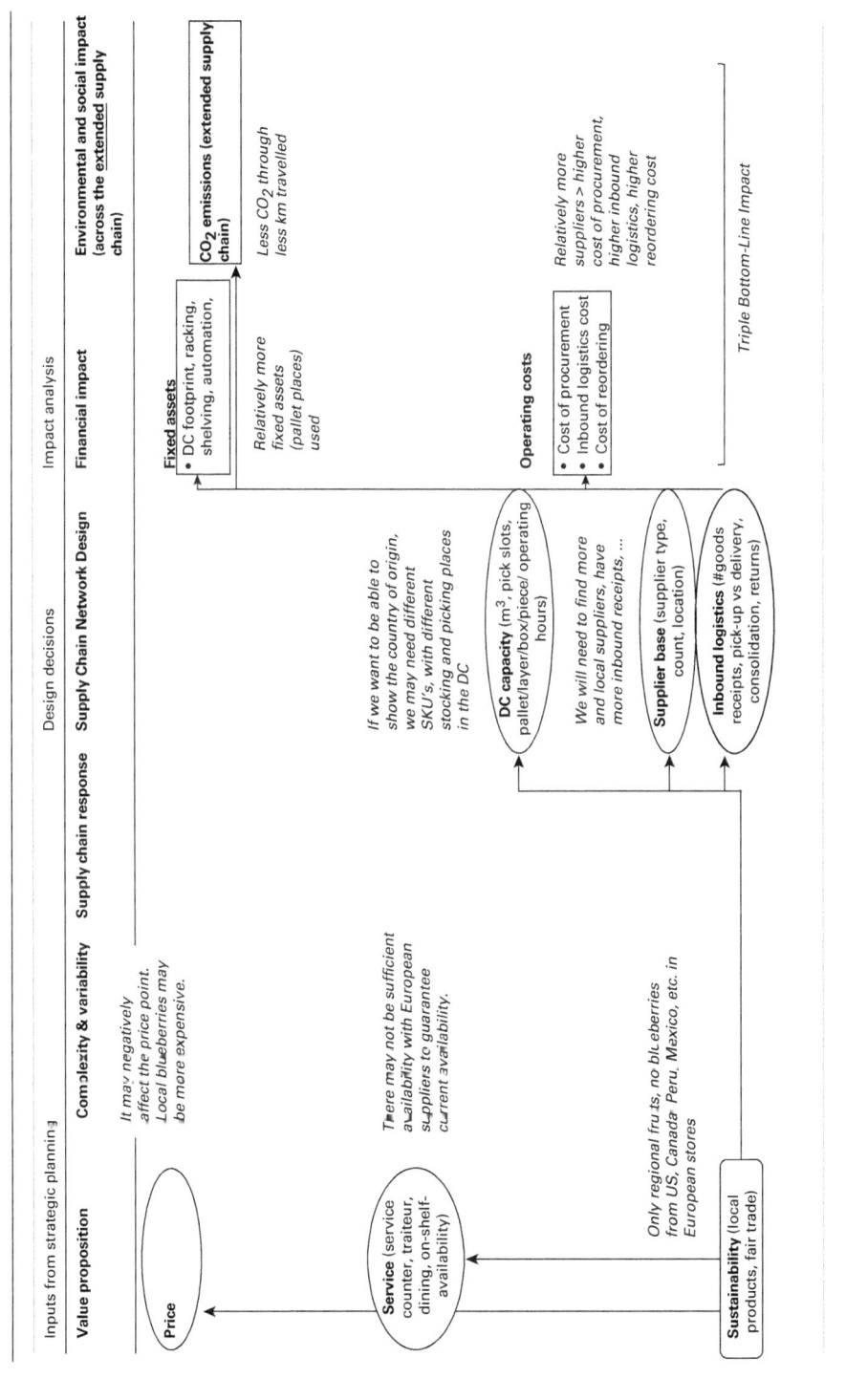

Inputs from strategic planning		Design decisions	Impact analysis	
Value proposition	Complexity & variability	Supply chain response	Supply Chain Network Design	Financial impact	Environmental and social impact (across the extended supply chain)

Price — It may negatively affect the price point. Local blueberries may be more expensive.

Service (service counter, traiteur, dining, on-shelf availability) — There may not be sufficient availability with European suppliers to guarantee current availability.

Sustainability (local products, fair trade) — Only regional fruits, no blueberries from US, Canada, Peru, Mexico, etc. in European stores

If we want to be able to show the country of origin, we may need different SKU's, with different stocking and picking places in the DC

We will need to find more and local suppliers, have more inbound receipts, …

DC capacity (m^3, pick slots, pallet/layer/box/piece/ operating hours)

Supplier base (supplier type, count, location)

Inbound logistics (#goods receipts, pick-up vs delivery, consolidation, returns)

Fixed assets
- DC footprint, racking, shelving, automation, …

Relatively more fixed assets (pallet places) used

Operating costs
- Cost of procurement
- Inbound logistics cost
- Cost of reordering

Relatively more suppliers > higher cost of procurement, higher inbound logistics, higher reordering cost

CO_2 **emissions (extended supply chain)**

Less CO_2 through less km travelled

Triple Bottom-Line Impact

some of the bigger global ones we have today. More picking places may impact our DC and our fixed assets, more suppliers might impact our indirect purchasing cost. On the sustainability side, the local supply should positively impact our CO_2 emissions.

Though the consequences from the above examples seem obvious, I frequently encounter that the obvious is overlooked by non-supply chain executives. I hope the Strategy-Driven Supply Chain Maps will be used as a tool by both supply chain and non-supply chain executives to map the obvious and what is beyond obvious, and that they ensure our decision making is considering the different dimensions of the triangle, the environmental and social impact, and the strategic context.

Analysing decisions using the Strategy-Driven Supply Chain Map

Download a blank Strategy-Driven Supply Chain Map from my website[20]. Think about a recent example where your feel that 'the business' or 'sales' or 'commercial' has been forcing a decision without having the full understanding of the end-to-end impact. Think about the examples shown in Figures 6.5, 6.6 and 6.7. Use the Strategy-Driven Supply Chain Map to visualize the impact. See the example of how more sustainable products might drive more SKUs as you want to show the country of origin to convince consumers this is a product that has not been airfreighted. Try to show the impact on the supply chain, like number of picking places in the warehouse, number of suppliers, and how it impacts financial and non-financial metrics.

If you're happy with the result, take a blank Strategy-Driven Supply Chain. Plan a meeting with the responsible business, sales or commercial colleague that has made the decision. Give some explanation on how the Strategy-Driven Supply Chain Map works. Ask the person to draw what they see as the impact, on complexity, variability, supply chain design, financial and non-financial metrics. Let the person think and draw 10–15 minutes. You can provide clarifications on what the different elements in the map mean, but don't give your opinion on where you think the impact is. After 15 minutes, compare both results and discuss the joint assessment of the impact. As you're discussing a decision that has been made, avoid sticking to the analysis. The key question to your colleague is whether they would be open to pre-discuss based on the Strategy-Driven Supply Chain Map, the potential impact of future related or comparable decisions, before the actual decision has been made.

Cross check second versus fourth generation strategic supply chain design capabilities

To close this chapter, let's go over our second versus fourth generation strategic supply chain design capabilities introduced in Chapter 4, as a checklist, and see whether the methodology developed in Chapter 5 and 6 meets the fourth generation criteria. I have recapped Table 4.2 as Table 6.4 below.

By starting from the market analysis and our strategic value proposition, we ensure that proper strategic trade-offs have been made, and that these are translated into the corresponding supply chain trade-offs. Supply chains are now designed for a competitive advantage, and we explain that may be different from designing for the lowest cost. Instead of a waterfall approach, we explained how the strategic value proposition and the corresponding supply chain are designed together in an iterative approach. Throughout Chapters 5 and 6 I have introduced how closely intertwined product and

Table 6.4 RECAP – second versus fourth generation strategic supply chain design capabilities

Second generation supply chain	Fourth generation supply chain
Designed for minimum cost	Designed for competitive advantage
Waterfall: first business, then supply chain	Integrated: strategic value proposition and corresponding supply chain
Disconnected from product design	Integrated product and supply chain design
Focus on distribution network	Focus on extended supply chain
Poorly designed service promise	Smartly designed service promise
One-size-fits-all	Supply chain segmentation
Separate sustainability plans and metrics	Integrated sustainability plans and metrics
Unclear trade-offs of sustainability vs financial metrics	Integrated design of sustainability and financial metrics

supply chain design are. This was advocated many years ago by Charles Fine[21] who focused on increasing the innovation speed of our supply chains. He considered any competitive advantage by default to be temporary. That same question around integration of product and supply chain design naturally surfaces when we want to optimize our Scope 1, 2 and 3 emissions, or when we want to use the principles of circularity to reduce our material footprint. These same sustainability drivers oblige us to look into the extended supply chain, from our suppliers' suppliers to our customers' customers. Think about how Tony's Chocolonely had to get a grip on its tiny part of the millions of small farmers growing cocoa beans in Côte d'Ivoire and Ghana. Transparency and control of the extended supply chain is key to Tony's to achieve its mission of zero-slavery chocolate. Smart decisions on lead times, reliability, flexibility are an integral part of the approach. If we have complex products and portfolios and want to have all of it available on stock with a high reliability, we will quickly find out it is a supply chain we cannot afford. This supply chain design process is inherently cross functional which avoids that one function or department monopolizes any design decision. It will be a joint outcome for the better of the company, not an individual KPI like sales revenue. We also discussed supply chain segmentation and the limits of supply chain segmentation. Put simply, you can't be both Ryanair and Etihad. That simply will not work. We also discussed how our sustainability objectives should be an integral part of one strategic positioning exercise, not something separate. There will be trade-offs with costs and investments to be made, so it is important we trade them off in our single strategic positioning exercise. In that strategic trade-off exercise, we should balance our financial and non-financial metrics. Think about the three impact areas defined by Tony's Chocolonely: create awareness, lead by example and inspire to act. Tony's has incorporated the financial metrics in the 'lead by example' category, in the sense that proving to others we can have a social impact while also driving financial results may potentially move big chocolate to follow suit.

Conclusion

In this chapter, we have deepened the strategy-driven – sustainable and resilient – supply chain design method by including circularity, market and supply chain segmentation, and scenario capabilities. The case of Ricoh has illustrated that a strategy transformation and circularity can go hand in hand. The case provides another illustration of the deep impact a change in value proposition has on the supply chain, its organization and its capabilities. The case of Colruyt group witnesses that companies need to invest in building these capabilities as they are needed, but are not being taught as a standard part of curricula at universities or business schools.

I introduced the strategy driven supply chain maps as a practical tool to map changes in the strategic value proposition into their supply chain impact. I hope it will be a useful tool to engage non supply chain executives into the importance and relevance of mapping that impact.

I have closed the chapter by confirming that, yes, the developed strategy-driven – sustainable and resilient – supply chain design answers the needs of the fourth generation supply chain. I obviously hope it will help companies to change what they are doing today and align it with this fourth generation capability template.

In Chapters 7 and 8 I will analyse our new and broader supply chain ecosystem, develop a new approach for integrated tactical planning and steering, that goes beyond the supply chain, covering the full business and our broader ecosystem. At the end of Chapter 8, I will again check whether the developed approach meets the needs of the fourth generation supply chain.

Endnotes

1. E Weenk and R Henzen (2021) *Mastering the Circular Economy: A Practical Approach to the Circular Business Model Transformation*, Kogan Page, London
2. N O Pearson, F Dontoh, D Pandya. Fast-fashion waste is choking developing countries with mountains of trash, Bloomberg 2 Nov 2022. www.bloomerg.com/news/features/2022-11-02/h-m-zara-fast-fashion-waste-leaves-environmental-impact (archived at https://perma.cc/TC9D-SWFS)
3. A Tidey. EU e-waste 'illegally' exported to developing countries: Report, Euronews, 7 Feb 2019. www.euronews.com/my-europe/2019/02/07/eu-e-waste-illegally-exported-to-developing-countries-report (archived at https://perma.cc/P4BX-PG9B)
4. A Hadhazy. Here's the truth about the 'planned obsolescence' of tech, BBC, 12 Jun 2016. www.bbc.com/future/article/20160612-heres-the-truth-about-the-planned-obsolescence-of-tech (archived at https://perma.cc/GA6X-FR6M)
5. Earth Overshoot Day, 2024. www.overshootday.org (archived at https://perma.cc/54SY-37M4)
6. Interface. Hergebruik en recycling, Een nieuwe bestemming voor uw oude vloeren, 2024. www.interface.com/EU/nl-NL/sustainability/recycling.html (archived at https://perma.cc/H9AA-G4GQ)

7   B DeSmet (2021) *The Strategy-Driven Supply Chain: Integrating Strategy, Finance and Supply Chain for a Competitive Edge*, Kogan Page, London
8   Ricoh. Company History, 2024. www.ricoh.com/about/history (archived at https://perma.cc/2QX3-D3DW)
9   Ricoh. Corporate Philosophy "Ricoh Way", 2024. www.ricoh.com/about/ricoh-way (archived at https://perma.cc/6U7F-TNUD)
10 Ricoh. Ricoh grows smart locker capabilities with acquisition of apex's European business, 3 Sep 2021. www.ricoh-europe.com/news-events/news/ricoh-grows-smart-locker-capabilities-with-acquisition-of-apexs-european-business/ (archived at https://perma.cc/7EKP-8EDC)
11 Ricoh. Ricoh completes acquisition of DocuWare, 6 Aug 2019. www.ricoh.co.uk/news-events/news/ricoh-completes-acquisition-of-docuware/ (archived at https://perma.cc/X46L-Z328)
12 J McIntyre. Ricoh and Toshiba Tec to merge MFP development & manufacturing, The Imaging Channel, 5 Jun 2023. theimagingchannel.com/ricoh-toshibatec-merge-mfp-development-manufacturing/ (archived at https://perma.cc/KM67-NLL4)
13 J Gattorna and D Ellis (2019) *Transforming Supply Chains*, Pearson, London
14 S S Phadnis, Y Sheffi, and C Caplice (2022) *Strategic Planning for Dynamic Supply Chains: Preparing for Uncertainty Using Scenarios*, Palgrave Macmillan, Cham
15 J McGonigal (2023) *Imaginable*, Spiegel & Grau, New York
16 Colruyt Group. Annual report with sustainability reporting 2022/2023, 2024. www.colruytgroup.com/en/invest/annual-report-with-sustainability-reporting (archived at https://perma.cc/SC47-LAHV)
17 R S Kaplan and D P Norton (2004) *Strategy Maps: Converting Intangible Assets into Tangible Outcomes*, Harvard Business Press, Boston
18 World Blueberry Production by Country, Atlas Big, 2024. www.atlasbig.com/en-us/countries-blueberry-production (archived at https://perma.cc/3DUS-FQYT)
19 World Blueberry Production by Country, Atlas Big, 2024. www.atlasbig.com/en-us/countries-blueberry-production (archived at https://perma.cc/83EC-Y844)
20 B DeSmet. Template Strategy-Driven Supply Chain Map, 2024. www.bramdesmet.com/rethinkingsupplychain/ (archived at https://perma.cc/9MKJ-K7XY)
21 C H Fine (1998) *Clockspeed. Winning Industry Control in the Age of Temporary Advantage*, Basic Books, New York

Our evolving supply chain ecosystem and the new concept of Integrated Value Planning

07

Introduction

I start this chapter by studying and mapping our evolving supply chain and business ecosystem, and by clarifying, based on that ecosystem, that we lack integration of planning processes and planning systems. Today, in companies, we primarily take a functional view when defining planning processes and implementing planning systems, as opposed to a 'systems' view. 'Systems' not referring to IT systems but to an 'ecosystem' view, trying to plan the whole 'system' instead of individual aspects of it in isolation of each other.

I map the five-stage Gartner S&OP maturity to our Supply Chain Triangle and use it to illustrate the lack of ambition when it comes to integrated planning. We don't feel like we need level 5 maturity. I will discuss why this is wrong. It also illustrates the long road towards integrated planning, knowing that many companies are currently at level 1 or 2 maturity.

I then introduce a new concept of 'Integrated Value Planning' or 'IVP', starting from the 'systems' (or 'ecosystem') view. At the foundation of the Integrated Value Planning is a full integration of financial planning and supply chain planning into Financial and Supply Chain Planning or FSCP. Next, I natively integrate Marketing Planning, Product Planning, Sales Planning and Resource Planning, by defining the interfaces upfront: which information flows from which process into which process and correspondingly in the underlying systems. Third, I integrate key customers and suppliers, in a comparable way: we define the collaboration in the form of which information flows from which processes and we prepare our systems on both ends to capture the corresponding data flows. Fourth, I integrate social and environmental metrics into all of our planning and decision making processes. All four elements are needed and they together define Integrated Value Planning.

In this chapter I define the basic building blocks of Integrated Value Planning or IVP. In the next chapter I elaborate on the IVP process, how to make decisions based on an IVP dashboard, how to organize for successful IVP, I develop an eight-stage IVP maturity model that shows you how to build IVP, and I do the cross check on whether IVP delivers us with the required fourth generation tactical planning capabilities.

Case Study: CPG – the changing ecosystem of CPG companies, by Martijn Lofvers, CEO & Chief Trendwatcher of Supply Chain Media

Supply Chain Media is a trend-watching company that is informing, is visualizing and is connecting professionals in supply chain management. It publishes *Supply Chain Magazine*, in Dutch, *Supply Chain Movement*, in English, that has ten thousands of readers in Western-Europe, the United States and in the rest of the world, and it brings over thousands of delegates together in its online and on-site events yearly. Apart from the numerous interviews with supply chain executives and directors at manufacturing, wholesale and retail companies, Supply Chain Media is known for its creative visualizations of complex topics into concept maps, subway maps and compasses. Martijn Lofvers is the CEO, the chief trendwatcher and a creative brain, an energizer, a challenger, an advocate and a thought leader in the global supply chain community.

Martijn recently made a visualization of how the ecosystem of household products is evolving. The result is shown in Figure 7.1. The supply chain of consumer packaged goods (CPG) used to be linear, with raw materials flowing from ingredient suppliers, to the brand manufacturers, who were selling to the retailers, from their distribution centres or via wholesalers. Via mass advertising (TV adds, billboards), the CPG companies would seduce consumers, to become repeat buyers of their products, in

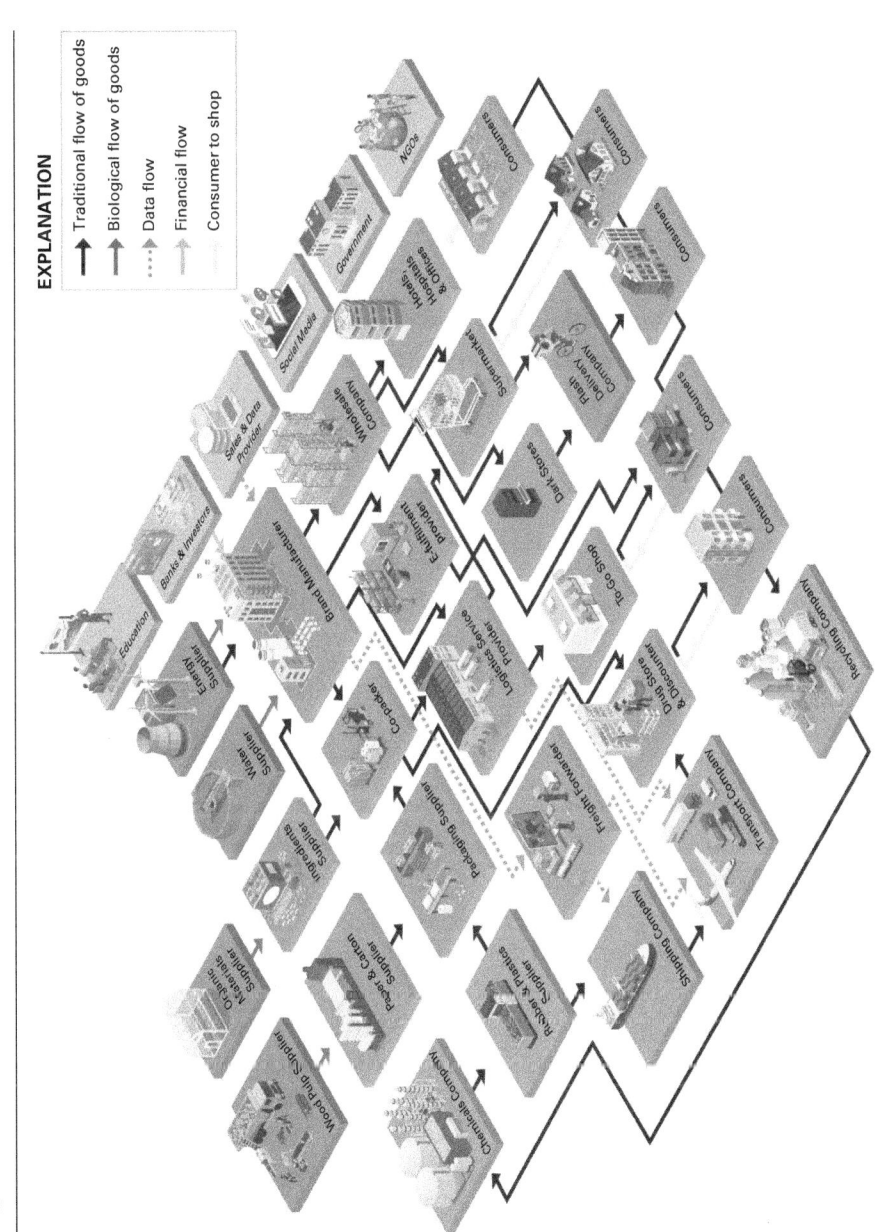

Figure 7.1 The evolving CPG ecosystem

store. Though that seems long ago, in the 1980s and the 1990s the CPG supply chain was essentially this.

The CPG ecosystem has dramatically changed in numerous ways. Products are increasingly delivered to the consumers' doorstep. Orders may come in through our own website, be picked at an outsourced e-fulfilment provider, to be delivered to the consumers' doorstep through a 'flash delivery' company like Gorillas[1]. Or orders may be received online by the retailer, who may pick and deliver from a dark store, and who may offer in store pick-ups. In 20 years' time, downstream supply chains for CPG companies have become truly omnichannel. Delivering on the high service expectations of consumers, while managing the associated costs, inventories and CO_2 has sharpened the challenges in the downstream CPG supply chain.

In the CPG ecosystem, stakeholders like banks, investors, governments, NGOs and social media companies play an increasingly active role. Banks and investors want to understand your sustainability agenda when they deliver financing solutions. They want to know whether you are exposed to any specific risks that could be detrimental to the financial health of the company. They may couple interest rates to sustainability targets in so-called 'green bonds' or 'green financing'. Governments, driven by the European Union, provide increasingly strict regulations, on food safety, on the use of packaging materials, on the disclosure of health-related information. They are continuously reshaping the competitive landscape. And NGOs will use social media to influence your consumers around any behaviour that conflicts with their agenda. It could be the use of child-labour in your upstream supply chain, protection of animal rights, any negative effects on people's health like obesity. Whereas in the 1980s, big multinationals may have been powerful and in control, with a lot of influence on the media, by powerful lobbying within politics, the playing field seems to have been levelled, with different stakeholders increasing pressure, and with an active stakeholder engagement left as the only option.

Supply chains have also become more circular. Think about the 7Rs introduced in Chapter 6. We want our products and/or its packaging to be re-used, re-distributed, re-paired, re-furbished and if all of that doesn't work we want them to be recycled and re-injected into the upstream manufacturing processes. That fully transforms the linear flows we started with into circular flows across different steps in the value chain. Also in planning, it is not just about planning what consumers will buy, it's also about what consumers will return, and how much returns we may need to reach our circular objectives.

As answers to that changed and the ecosystem becoming more complex, Martijn Lofvers sees digitalization and collaboration as the two biggest opportunities. 'Since 2018,' Martijn comments, 'our company organizes our inNOWvate Supply Chain Event, with the European supply chain start-up and scale-up contest. We also compile our analysis of over 250 emerging young companies into a yearly maturity matrix of supply chain start-ups. The power of the cloud, in combination with AI, is creating many solutions to the challenges of the new expanded ecosystem. Whether it is about capturing trends from unstructured social media data and turning that into a forecast, or about tools that help in capturing Scope 3 CO_2 data, there are dozens of startups and scale-ups addressing the needs of our new, more complex, supply chain realities. A second key element is collaboration. In today's volatile markets, it is important to understand the key challenges of your key suppliers and key customers, and to be open and transparent about them. Smart companies have understood that being willing to help and focusing on a long-term relationship as opposed to a short-term opportunity, provides the basis for jointly delivering results, not as individual companies, but as collaborative supply chains.' More information on these[2] and other trends can be found through the website of supply chain media.

Modelling the supply chain and business ecosystem

For a basis on how to model the supply chain and the business ecosystem, I return to the work of Geary Rummler and Alan Brache. Thirty years ago, they wrote their influential book *Improving Performance: How to Manage the White Space on the Organization Chart*[3]. They introduced 'process thinking' and 'process management' as the way to 'break the organizational silos', or in their terminology 'to manage the white space on the organization chart', which is the white space in between the silos. As we will see later on, the work from Rummler and Brache also reveals a completely new and different view on fourth generation 'integrated planning', a question from Chapter 4 which is still to be answered.

Figure 7.2 is guided by what Rummler and Brache call the 'system view' of the business, as opposed to the common hierarchical or functional view. At the heart, it shows how the different functions in an organization interact to deliver value to its customers. It starts with marketing, that detects

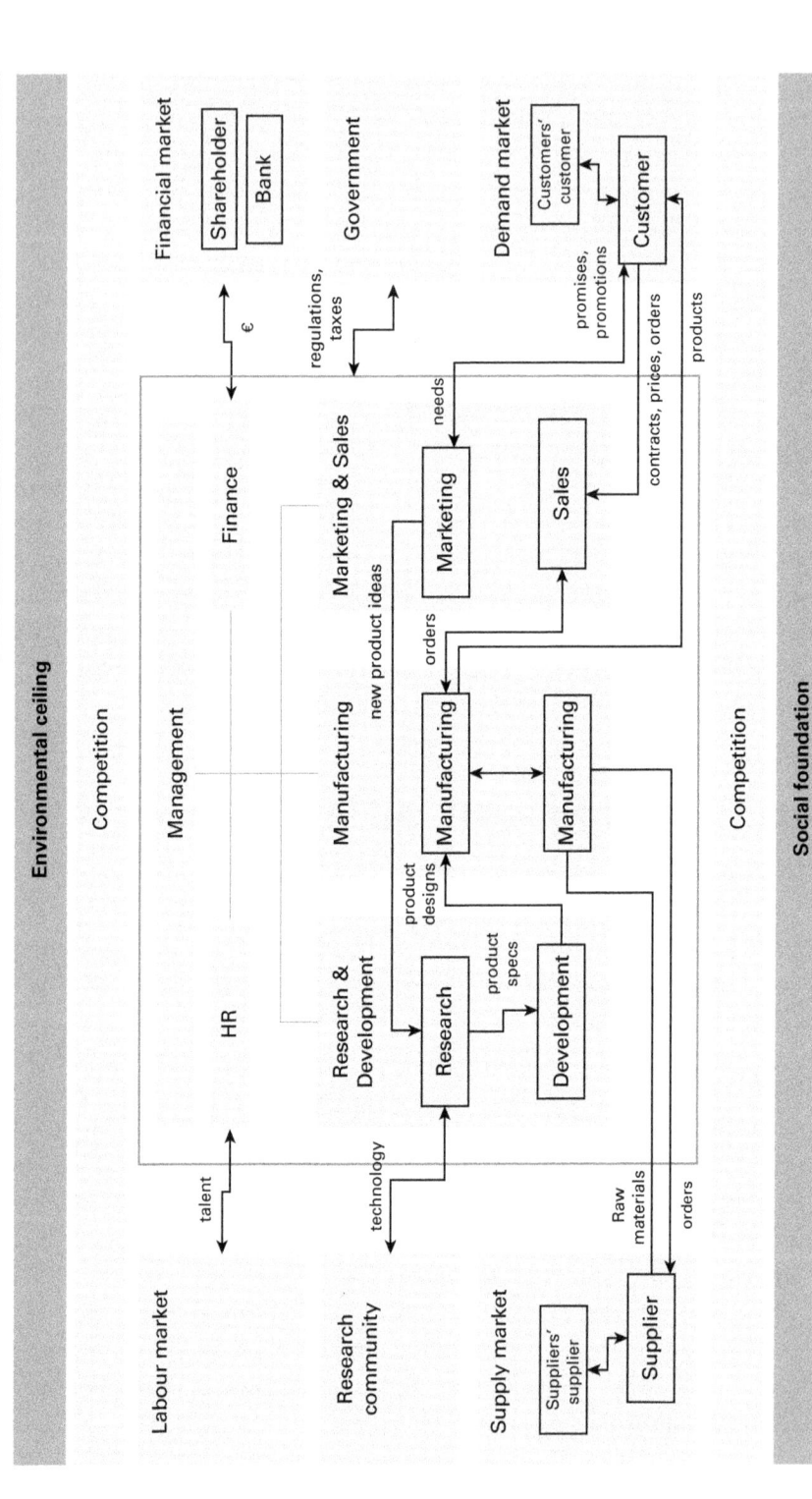

Figure 7.2 Modelling the supply chain and business ecosystem – guided by Rummler and Brache, 1995

customers' needs and delivers them product promises and promotions. Marketing provides product ideas to Research which turns them into product specs for Development. Development turns the product specs into product designs for manufacturing who will first test and then scale manufacturing. Sales makes contracts, negotiates prices and receives orders from customers, for which goods are delivered by manufacturing. Manufacturing will place orders on suppliers. Suppliers will deliver the required raw materials to manufacturing. In your company you may have more or less functions involved, but from a high level, these connections together are the base and the heart of the value generation in the business, the primary value stream of Michael Porter.

Figure 7.2 also describes the broader ecosystem around the core value stream. Rummler and Brache simply call it the 'system view' of the business. On the right, I have mapped our need to deliver financial value to our financial stakeholders. When we have financing needs, we can also draw funding from them. I also show the government, which is shaping our ecosystem by driving all kinds of regulations and taxation. On the left, I show we are competing in a market for labour, the so-called war for talent. We try to stand out by providing attractive jobs at an attractive remuneration. I also show the research community in which we are embedded, and from which we may draw knowledge for our innovations. And we are not alone, our competitors are operating in the same markets. They fight for the same customers, the same financing, the same talent and are probably buying from the same suppliers. As explained in Chapters 5 and 6 differentiating is key to be focused and drive success in this competitive environment.

To put things into the correct sustainability perspective, building on our sustainable supply chain zone from Chapter 2, we need to manage this ecosystem not just for financial profit, but also within the limits of a social foundation and an ecological ceiling. The sustainability perspective requires us to take an extended view of our value chain, from the suppliers' supplier down to the customers' customer, which we've called 'supply markets' and 'demand markets' in Figure 7.2. We could further extend our ecosystem by adding NGOs or pressure groups, or by adding specific communities on which we have an impact, think about the cocoa farmers in the example of Tony's Chocolonely in Chapter 5. I believe the ecosystem mapping is just a basis from which you could derive yours.

EXERCISE
Mapping your supply chain and business ecosystem

Gather your executive team, or a team of cross-functional experts. Ensure the different functions sales, marketing, R&D, operations, supply chain, procurement, finance, HR, IT are represented.

In analogy to Figure 7.1 and Figure 7.2, the idea is to map your supply chain and business ecosystem.

As in the approach with Rummler and Brache, start by drawing your organization structure. In Figure 7.2 we have six main functions: marketing, sales, manufacturing, R&D, finance and HR, you may have more or less. Then focus on mapping the key processes: discovery of market needs and how they translate into product and service innovation; the capturing of orders and the delivery process; the manufacturing and the supply of key raw materials.

As in Figure 7.1, feel free to map your extended value chain in more details. You may want to specify key second tier suppliers (such as the 'organic material suppliers' in Figure 7.1), key first tier suppliers, key first tier customers (for instance wholesaler or retailers) and key second tier customers (for instance the end consumer in Figure 7.1).

Make sure that it is clear how the value flows from your suppliers' supplier to your customers' customer and how key functions in the organization cross-functionally contribute to it. You may have a complex matrix structure of regional sales organizations and global product organizations and one common manufacturing back-end. The more complex your organizational chart, the more important to understand how the value flows across the functional silos.

Then enrich the value stream and turn it into your supply chain and business ecosystem by mapping financial stakeholders, governments, the labour market and any other stakeholder you believe is relevant to your ecosystem. Try to find logical 'spots' to add the stakeholders. The community of cocoa farmers for Tony's Chocolonely may be an extra circle around its upstream suppliers. You may employ a big portion of the people in your head quarter area and have an important impact on the local community. Then you may draw a circle that intersects with your labour market square in Figure 7.2.

On the social foundation and the ecological ceiling you may define some of the key metrics for your organization. What is key to us as an organization? Are we profit driven or are we purpose driven? How important are the non-financial metrics to us? Look for inspiration in the examples of Vandemoortele from Chapter 2 and Tony's Chocolonely from Chapter 5.

Once your work is done, have it processed by a professional designer, so you can come to a result like the one shown in Figure 7.1. Stick it against the wall in your offices. A better understanding of how the value flows and which ecosystem you're trying to manage will help people understand both the need of a sharp strategic profile and an aligned supply chain, as the need to coordinate the different aspects of this ecosystem through a more advanced form of integrated planning.

The lack of integration in planning processes and systems

In Chapters 5 and 6, I have outlined an approach to do an integrated, strategy-driven, sustainable and resilient supply chain design. Though a lot of companies don't do a proper job on that today, as discussed and illustrated at length in Chapter 4, it is still relatively easy to convince people that on the strategic level an integrated approach is needed, across the commercial value proposition, the product and supply chain design and that we need to understand the financial and the non-financial impact of our strategic choices. Visualizing your supply chain and business ecosystem should only support that. Seeing the complexity, the dynamics and the competitiveness of the ecosystem in which you need to thrive, makes you understand that sharp strategies and good alignment of the supply chain are needed for success. Better strategic or strategy-driven design capabilities are a first element of the fourth generation supply chain.

The need for a cross-functional, integrated approach, seems a lot less obvious when it comes to tactical planning. In Chapter 4 I discussed at length the differences between second and fourth generation tactical planning capabilities, and all of the negative effects of managing a fourth generation supply chain with second generation planning capabilities as shown in the fishbone in Figure 4.1. As an example, I see frequent disconnects between the financial plan and the supply chain plan, starting from different assumptions and a different level of detail. I see companies where sales needs

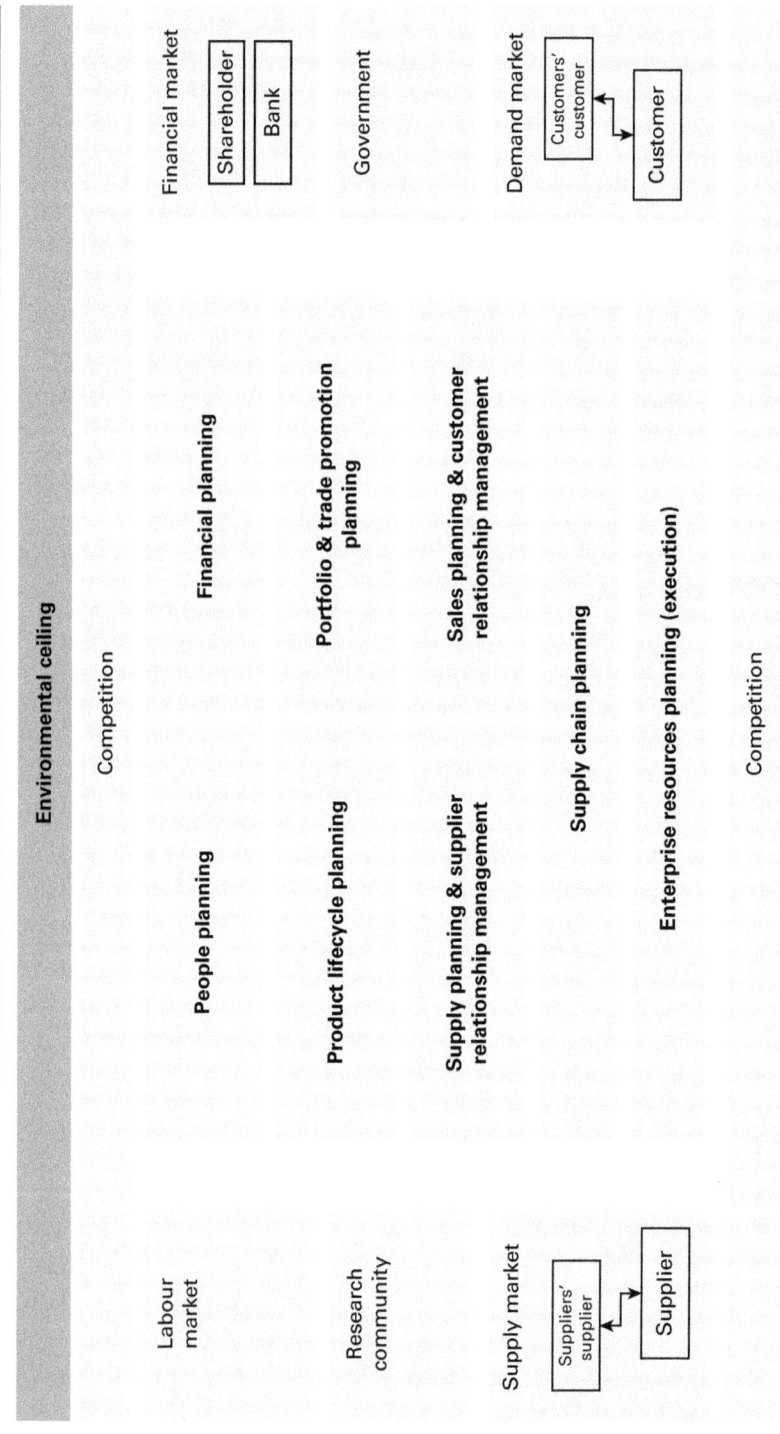

Figure 7.3 Integrated Value Planning as a need for managing the 'system'

Environmental ceiling

Competition

Labour market — People planning

Financial market
- Shareholder
- Bank

Research community — Product lifecycle planning

Financial planning

Government

Supply market — Supply planning & supplier relationship management
- Suppliers' supplier ↔ Supplier

Supply chain planning

Portfolio & trade promotion planning

Sales planning & customer relationship management

Demand market
- Customers' customer ↔ Customer

Enterprise resources planning (execution)

Competition

Social foundation

to submit two forecasts, 1 to finance, in value, on an aggregated level, focused on the current quarter, and 1 to supply chain, in units, on a detailed level, focused on the next 12–18 months. The problem becomes even more apparent when we look at the myriad of disconnected tools supporting the different planning processes in the company. Though the need for integrated planning should be obvious, we tend to find ways to resist the required transformation.

I started using the adapted ecosystem from Figure 7.2 to start mapping planning processes and planning systems. It helps in understanding where we are, and it provides the basis for a new and better vision on integrated planning. In Figure 7.3 I have mapped the different planning processes I see in companies today. Financial planning, often referred to as Financial Planning & Analysis or FP&A, is about creating financial plans for the company, creating a projected top-line, bottom-line and cash-flow. The primary user of these reports are senior managers, the board of directors, shareholders and investors. The 'People' or 'Workforce' planning is an important input to the financial plan, as the cost of resources is typically an important driver. On the revenue side, the financial plan will obviously depend on the sales plan (what to sell to which customers at which price), on the portfolio plan (how will the portfolio evolve) and for FMCG companies on the 'Trade Promotion Plan' (what type of promotions will be do). R&D will need to back up the portfolio plan with a product life cycle plan. It will need to come up with the product specs that need to be delivered to either internal or external manufacturing. Our 'cost of goods sold' or 'COGS', next to the people resources, will be driven by the supply chain plan (what to produce where and how to transport it) and the purchasing plan (what to buy where and at which prices).

In essence, there is no way to disconnect, as an example, the financial plan from the sales plan. The only way to separate the two is to make assumptions on the financial side which are per definition less accurate. Likewise we can't disconnect the financial plan from the supply chain plan. The only way to separate the two is make assumptions on what will be produced and what inventories will be built, which, especially in volatile markets, is again per definition less accurate. Still this is what we do, and we even believe it is appropriate. Disconnects create the inverse of agility. It creates slower and less precise information flows. It is the inverse of what we need in the volatile times. The lack of agility has all the consequences we analysed in Figure 4.1. It burns cash, it adds CO_2 and it burns people. Again, still we think it is appropriate to do. I believe that our main hurdle, as de-

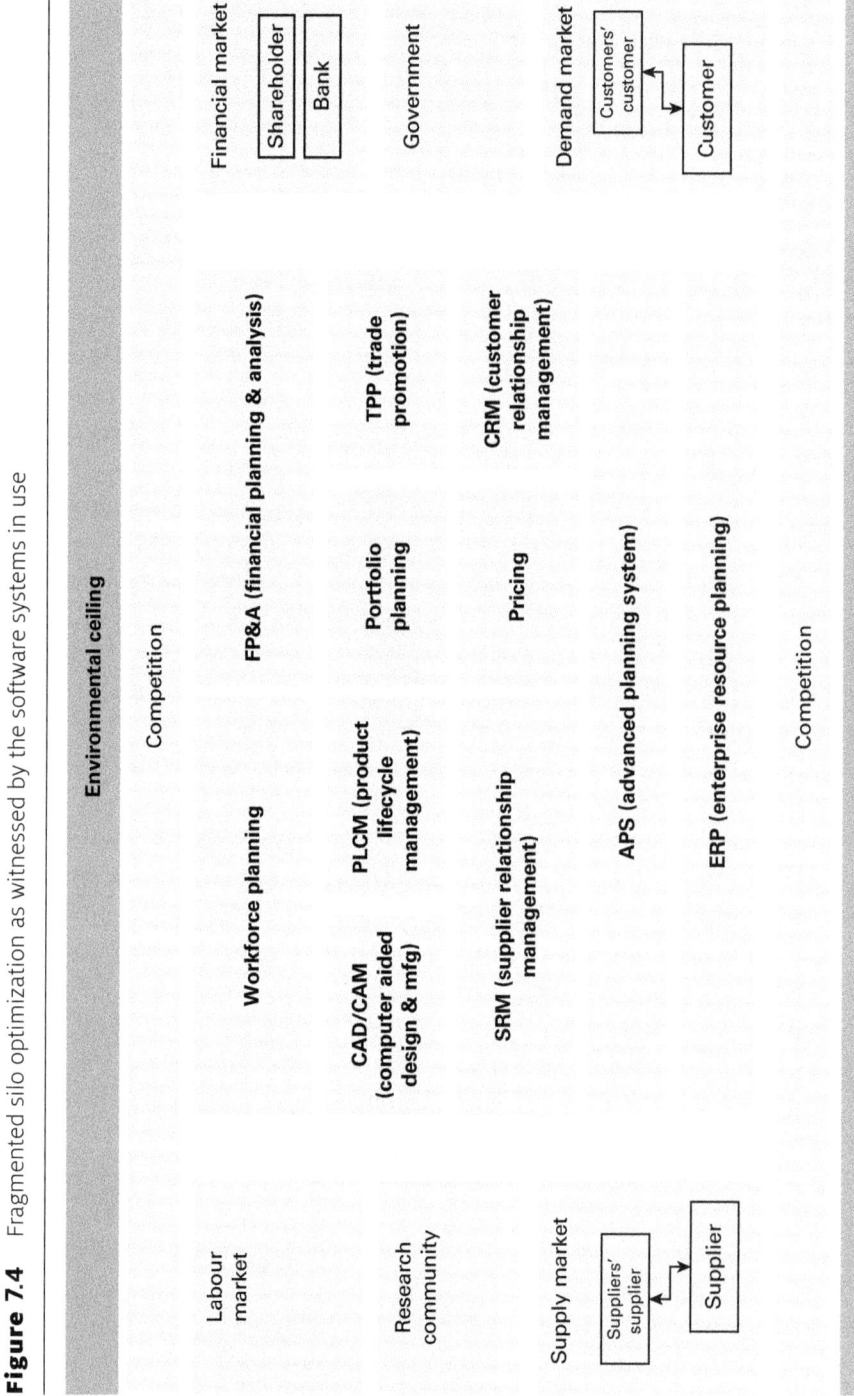

Figure 7.4 Fragmented silo optimization as witnessed by the software systems in use

scribed by Rummler and Brache, is to let go of our outdated hierarchical and functional organizations.

The lack of process integration is also witnessed by the fragmentation of the IT systems supporting the ecosystem. I have mapped the typical systems I find in companies in Figure 7.4. Finance typically has its own FP&A system (Financial Planning & Analysis) to cover the financial planning needs of the company. Marketing has its own TPP (Trade Promotion Planning) system to manage and optimize its marketing spend. R&D may have its own PLCM (Product Life Cycle Management) system that manages the lifecycle of its products (often based on a stage-gate process for the new product introductions or NPIs). Sales will have a CRM (Customer Relationship Management) system that allows it to manage and optimize its customer base and the associated opportunities. Sales may also have a separate system for pricing, that supports defining and keeping track of prices. Operations and Supply Chain will have their APS (Advanced Planning System). The APS typically has sales forecasting capabilities, to generate statistical forecasts and drive a collaborative process with sales, to collect their adjustments, typically in parallel to the information gathering in the CRM or the input needed for the financial forecast (creating both inefficiencies and confusion). Purchasing will have its SRM (Supplier Relationship Management) to be able to professionally manage its supplier base.

The imperative from the 'system view of the business', as Rummler and Brache call it, is clear. In the 'system view' of the business, the whole 'system' needs to be managed, in an integrated way. However, in practice, I see disconnected puzzles of best-of-breed systems. Situations where supply chain planning, promotions planning and financial planning are implemented in separate systems are common. They are often the result of separate implementations by separate teams as the result of separate investments and RFP processes. Only in the odd cases, IT will have a business information architect that asks questions on how these things should interact with each other. I have never seen a solution architect on the business side that oversees how the processes should interact with each other. The sponsor of these individual projects will typically be a functional VP, the VP of Sales or the VP of Supply Chain, or a VP of finance. These sponsors will try to optimize their turf, and given the complexity of the task at hand, refrain from taking a broader cross functional or 'system view' perspective. IT is often pre-occupied with the technical aspects of integrating the software, and will boast about its new middleware or data lake, that can connect anything to anything, without having a vision on what needs to be connected and in which way. As we launch all of these initiatives in parallel, we seem to improvise ourselves through this integration question, which means that it often falls off the overloaded agenda, and the resulting integration is lacklustre, the inverse of what we need from the 'systems view'. As introduced a couple of times, the fragmentation is slowing us down, it creates the inverse of agility. It is duplicating unaligned versions of information like the sales forecast. It is a source of confusion, extra work and imprecision.

Mapping your business planning processes and the corresponding systems

Gather your executive team, or a team of cross-functional experts. Ensure the different functions sales, marketing, R&D, operations, supply chain, procurement, finance, HR, IT are represented.

In analogy to Figure 7.3 and Figure 7.4, the idea is to map your business planning processes and business planning systems. A good way to start is give people 10–15 minutes to individually write down what they see, within their department and their daily operations as planning processes and ask them by which type of tooling it is currently supported. Any decision making process that needs to make assumptions about the future can be seen as a planning process. So yes, treasury makes assumptions on future cash in and outflows, so this can safely be said to be a cash planning.

To map the processes and systems, build on your supply chain and business ecosystem map that you derived in the first exercise from this chapter. That ecosystem map should show all the relevant functions in your organization which can be the place-holder for your planning processes and the corresponding systems. Make two big brown-papers, one to gather the planning processes, a second to gather the planning systems being used. In general, I expect more systems than processes, as different countries or regions may be using different systems to perform the same or a comparable planning process.

The number of plans may be overwhelming at the start but try to cluster them and consolidate them until you have the big blocks. When the big blocks are there, spend 10–15 minutes to understand how integrated these planning processes are and what are possible consequences of a lack of integration.

Note: I have made a template available for download from my website[4]. You may print it on an A0, in which case you can use it as a visual support for a sticky note exercise. It shows the broader ecosystem but has left the planning processes empty. You could use one print for the processes and one print for the systems.

The long road to integrated planning

One of the models that has been used intensively to measure how far companies are in their process integration, is the five stage Gartner S&OP maturity model[5]. In Figure 7.5 I have summarized and mapped it to our Supply Chain Triangle. While Gartner is not necessarily precise in its definitions, I usually interpret and define the five stages as follows:

- **Stage 1 – React:** there is a clear lack of cross-functional integration. These are the situations where production, behind the back of sales, modifies the forecast going into the production planning because sales is always

Figure 7.5 The five stages of the Gartner S&OP maturity linked to the Supply Chain Triangle

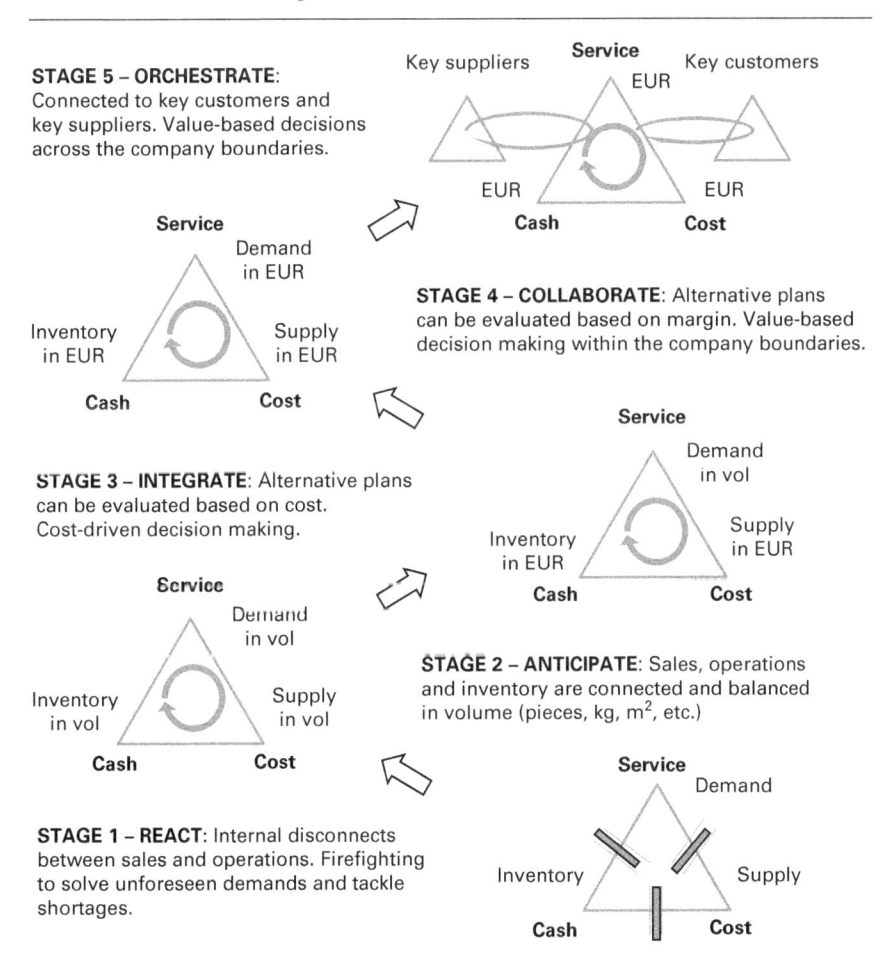

STAGE 5 – ORCHESTRATE: Connected to key customers and key suppliers. Value-based decisions across the company boundaries.

STAGE 4 – COLLABORATE: Alternative plans can be evaluated based on margin. Value-based decision making within the company boundaries.

STAGE 3 – INTEGRATE: Alternative plans can be evaluated based on cost. Cost-driven decision making.

STAGE 2 – ANTICIPATE: Sales, operations and inventory are connected and balanced in volume (pieces, kg, m², etc.)

STAGE 1 – REACT: Internal disconnects between sales and operations. Firefighting to solve unforeseen demands and tackle shortages.

over-forecasting. Or situations where there is no sales forecast on a granular level at all, so production has to make it up by themselves. Or situations where procurement is not ordering based on an MRP result, because it is so unreliable, but based on its own forecast and assumptions. I unfortunately see many of these happening still today.

- **Stage 2 – Anticipate:** there is a base balancing of sales, production and inventory. This means that production takes into account inventory targets (typically defined by supply chain on a granular level, as an iteration of an overall inventory value or turns target from finance). The balancing and the discussions are primarily volume based.
- **Stage 3 – Integrate:** we now have good cost information in the planning. This means we can start analysing the cost impact of different planning scenarios and look to balance service, cost and cash.
- **Stage 4 – Collaborate:** next to good cost information, we also have the revenue information. This allows us to do margin based planning.
- **Stage 5 – Orchestrate:** at this stage we are connected to key customers and key suppliers. We can sense shifts on the customer side and know how to translate that to the supplier side. We can sense shifts on the supplier side and are able to translate that into impacts on the customer side. We are able to orchestrate the full network to drive the optimal response, in the traditional sense that would be sales revenue, margin and inventory (cash) optimization.

The Gartner model is a supply chain model. It means that it focuses on what it believes supply chain as a function needs, to do a proper job for running the supply chain. The Gartner model doesn't have the ambition nor the potential to deliver a fully integrated planning for our broader ecosystem introduced in Figure 7.3. Nevertheless, it provides us with a lot of insights on where companies are today, in their integrated planning journey, as it is common to assess and report on current and desired maturity levels.

Though I have not come across any public statistics, if you ask companies, many of them will indicate to be somewhere between 1 and 2, with an ambition of level 2–3. The more mature ones may be somewhere around 3, with an ambition of level 4. Unfortunately, I haven't met any company that candidly told me the ambition is level 5. Given the recent experiences of Covid that leaves me puzzled.

Level 5 is about integration with key customers and key suppliers. I have seen many, if not all companies, struggle with separating the 'true demand' from the 'hoarding' (stocking) or the 'stock build-off' (de-stocking) by customers. We have all complained about highly disturbed demand patterns, through these inventory effects, but as well, for instance, due to customers starting dual sourcing. So, tell me how you will get a structural grip on your supply chain, if you don't collaborate with your key customers to clarify these questions?

At the same time, all companies during Covid have been struggling with their supply of raw materials and components. Lead times were increasing with little to no visibility on where this would go. Any promises we got, we knew were highly unreliable. What did we do as a result, we ordered more, and more and more. Then, all of a sudden, lead times started to decrease and suppliers started delivering everything we ordered, at a time that our demand was collapsing. As a result, we were left with expensive overstocks, that took us months to consume. So, tell me how you are going to properly manage the shortages or the overstocks without an intense collaboration with your key suppliers?

Level 5 maturity is also about being able to translate the upstream and downstream signals into a financial impact. That is the true meaning of 'orchestrate'. Well, if we don't think we need level 5 maturity, tell me if you think it is appropriate to take supply chain decisions in the current market situation, without knowing the financial impact? Do you believe not understanding the financial impact is a sufficient level of maturity given the complexity and volatility of our current supply chains?

In Chapter 8, I will extend the Gartner model from 5 into 8 stages, to create a step-by-step roadmap to get to our 'full' vision of 'integrated planning' (which I will further elaborate in the next section). What the current Gartner model shows us that even on a scale of 1–5, many companies still struggle with the absolute basics, and there is a clear lack of ambition on where we want to be.

Integrated Value Planning or IVP

In Figure 7.6 I have a proposal on how to integrate the different plans needed to effectively control the 'system view' of the business introduced in Figure 7.2. In Figure 7.7, I also define possible steps to follow, which should help you to realize this integrated planning. I will call the result 'Integrated Value Planning' or 'IVP', where with value I mean both financial value and non-financial value, as indicated by the social foundation and the environmental ceiling shown in Figure 7.6 and Figure 7.7.

Figure 7.6 Integrated Value Planning or IVP

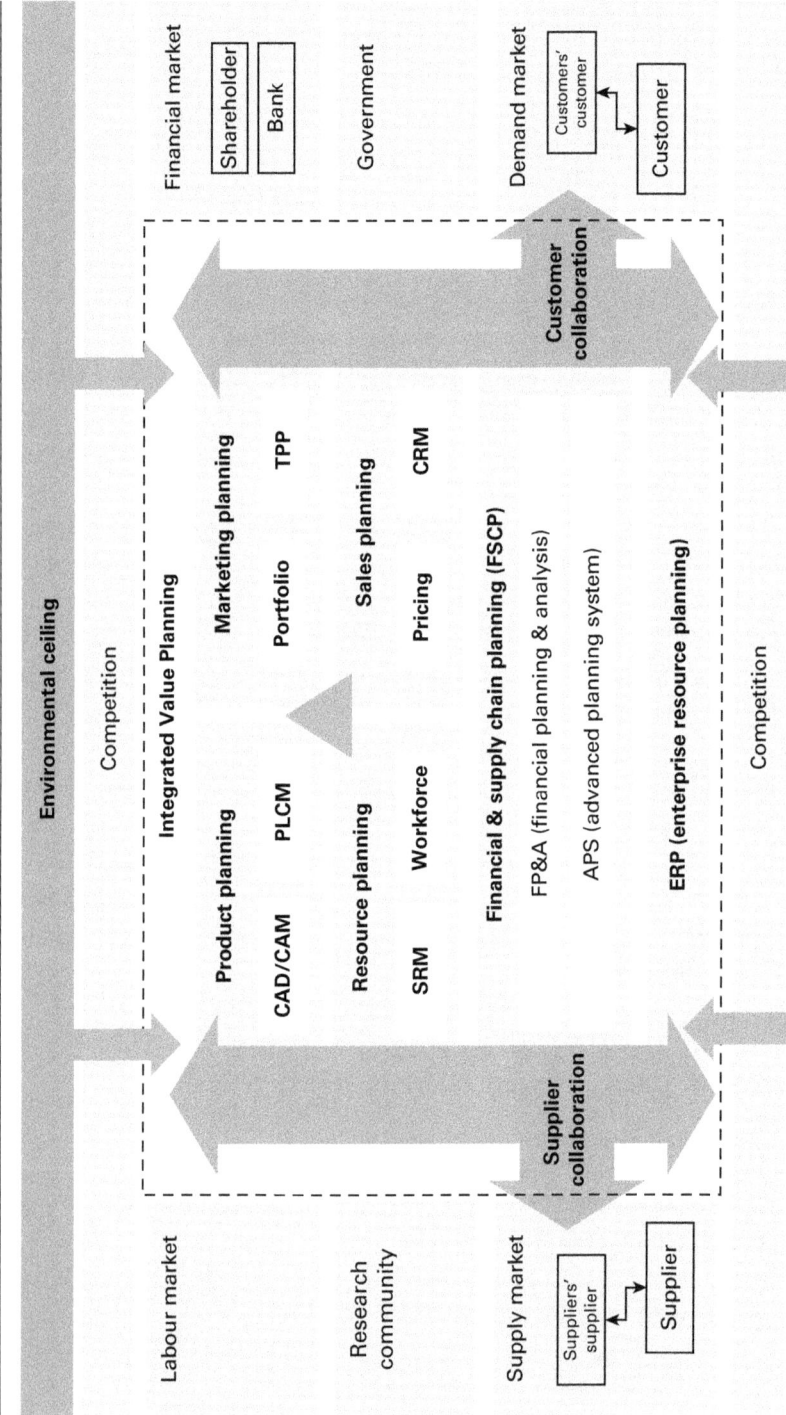

Figure 7.7 Four steps to get to Integrated Value Planning (IVP)

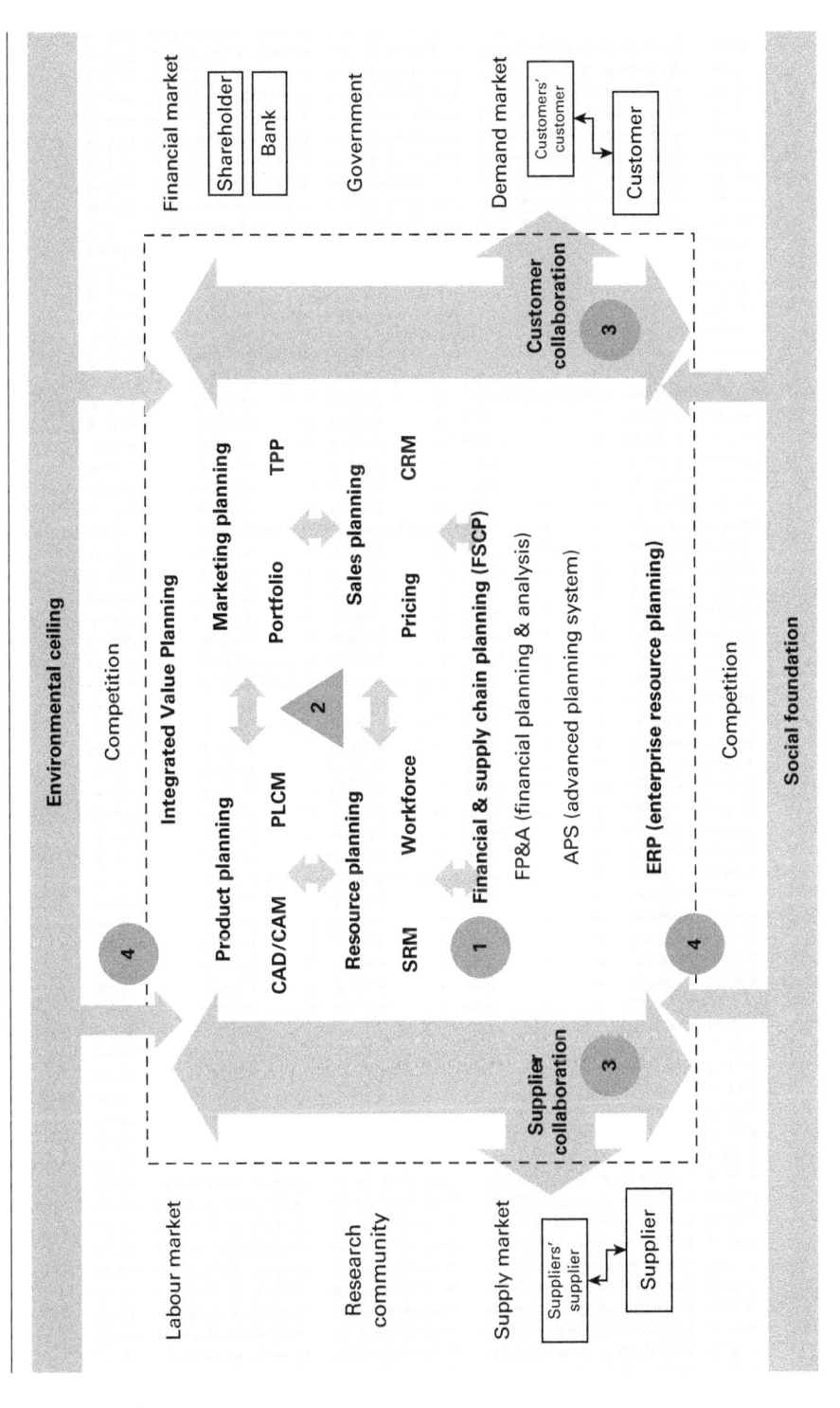

People told me to consider 'Integrated Business Planning' as alternative terminology for the integrated planning vision. Where on the one hand that would be logical, as for sure we are addressing the different planning activities needed to steer and control a business, the problem I see with using Integrated Business Planning or IBP is that it has been used by Oliver Wight for a more narrow version of the integrated planning shown in Figure 7.6. As an example, Oliver Wight never questioned whether it is OK to have two separate planning processes in supply chain and finance, it merely looked for aligning the two. In that sense, the IBP from Oliver Wight also takes a supply chain perspective. Like the Gartner S&OP maturity model, it questions 'what does supply chain as a function need to properly run the supply chain' and 'how can it contribute to the business'. If we want to properly and structurally answer the needs from the 'system view' of the business, as introduced in Figure 7.2, we need to take a 'system view' or a 'business view' as opposed to the more limited 'supply chain view' of the Oliver Wight IBP. If I want to point out that I take a different perspective, I believe it is better to use a new terminology, and hence I have opted for 'Integrated Value Planning' or IVP.

One of the challenges of the term 'Integrated Value Planning' might be that people associate value exclusively with financial value, or basically think about the shareholder as the main stakeholder in the company. That may be exactly what we're looking for. The challenge at hand, in any case, within companies and within peoples mind, is to broaden the concept of value, from financial value to non-financial value, including what we do with the natural and the human resources we are provided with, and to broaden our perspective to the non-financial stakeholders, including the individuals, families, communities and societies with whom we work and on whom we have an impact.

Finally, I believe that Integrated Value Planning is also more output oriented than Integrated Business Planning, which is more input oriented. Yes, it is about planning and coordinating the activities within the business, but the goal of planning is to optimize the value we generate, both financial and non-financial value, for both shareholders and non-financial stakeholders.

Coming back to 'what to do' and 'in which sequence', as shown in Figure 7.7, I believe the first step is integrating financial planning and supply chain planning as a new basis for Integrated Value Planning. The financial plan and the supply chain plan are the two plans that connect the end-to-end value chain, from the customer down to the supplier. Both need input from sales and marketing, both need assumptions on new product introductions,

Our evolving supply chain ecosystem and the new concept of Integrated Value Planning

both need to translate it to production volumes (and costs), and both need to translate it to raw material volumes (and costs). As, in any case, we try to make our financial plans more granular and our supply chain plans more financial, given all the overlap, I will argue in a next section it is due time to integrate the two into 1 planning process into 1 planning tool and make it into the base engine for our Integrated Value Planning, as shown in Figure 7.7.

The newly integrated Financial and Supply Chain Plan (FSCP) can be the platform on which to further integrate the sales plan, the marketing plan, the product plan and the resource plan in a second step. In a next section I will document which type of interfaces I see, and which type of functionality could reside where, in which type of planning process and/or tool.

Third, it is key, mandatory, obligatory and non-negotiable that we are integrated with key customers and key suppliers. The days that we were guessing what key customers were going to buy from us are passed. The days we had no idea of how much capacity a supplier had reserved for us have been left behind. As we need to extend our impact beyond the traditional service, cost, cash to embrace environmental and social impact, we have to extend our reach to key customers and suppliers. Not only will the extended reach unlock currently hidden value, both financial and non-financial, it is also needed to be more consistent, resilient and agile in our complex and volatile markets.

Fourth, and this doesn't need to be sequential, we need to integrate non-financial metrics into our core planning processes. As witnessed by the case of Schneider Electric in Chapter 2, sustainability is not a side process or project, sustainability is in the daily trade-offs we make in each of our planning processes. In a following section I will give extra examples of which metrics should be integrated where.

From a systems perspective, ERP will not do the job. The ERP landscape will talk about WMS, TMS, EDI, MRP, which clarifies that ERP is and will remain a transactional system that is used to steer and follow-up the execution. That is an important task, so ERP is and will remain very relevant. However, planning is a different world. You are dealing with uncertainty instead of the known and certain world of transactions. If you plan 12–18 months out, you are dealing with incomplete master data such as incomplete bill-of-materials for new product introductions. ERP vendors have tried to integrate planning functionality by buying and integrating existing software packages. However, they have never succeeded in bringing comfort to the planner. The ERP planning suites have only been used because planners were forced to by IT or by finance, because it looked natively integrated (IT) or because buying the total license with one vendor was cheaper (finance). The planning suites of the ERP vendors were never chosen because they were fit for the task at hand or because planners liked them. So don't make this mistake. Integrated Value Planning is way too critical to do it with second-best systems. Companies need specialized planning tools that can cover one or multiple aspects, and they need specialists that can help them define the required process and systems integration.

In my previous two books, I used the term 'Integrated Value Planning & Execution' or IVP&E to indicate the integration of strategic planning, the tactical financial and S&OP planning, and the operational planning which Gartner calls S&OE (Sales & Operations Execution). As I explained at the start of this chapter, I believe it is intuitive for people that on the strategic planning we need to better integrate the strategic value proposition (the business side) and how we are going to deliver that (the operating model or the supply chain). It is less obvious for people that we need to have the same integration at the tactical level. To identify that need and give the solution a name, I chose to use the term Integrated Value Planning to indicate the needed integration on this tactical level (rather than focusing on the integration between strategic, tactical financial, tactical S&OP and operational S&OE). Based on the experiences of the last three years, including but not limited to the Covid period, I believe the bigger challenge and opportunity for companies is on properly integrating that tactical level.

Step 1: Integrating financial and supply chain planning

In Figure 7.8 I recap the analysis from my previous book *The Strategy-Driven Supply Chain*, on how financial planning and S&OP planning are based on the same core and why integration is more a mental rather than a technical problem. Figure 7.8 takes the financial plan as the starting point. I will indicate where it interferes with the supply chain plan or how the supply chain plan is often doing comparable calculations. At the end of the analysis, it should be clear that a native integration is not a problem but rather logical. Duplicating the process and the effort, and basically tripling the effort as we consequently try to align the two, that is the illogical thing to do.

The sales piece is relatively easy. We start from a sales forecast in units, multiply with a standard sales price, and will get to a volume forecast and a top-line (gross sales) forecast. When I discuss the integration with sales planning, I will explain how to get to a net sales forecast. The supply chain plan will define whether we need to produce more or less than the sales forecast. We may decide to produce more, to anticipate a plant shutdown or because the demand in the high season exceeds our capacity. We may decide to produce less to consume inventories that have been built up earlier or because we want to temporarily reduce inventory to generate cash. Notice that there is a potential difference between the sales forecast and the production plan, the difference is in the stock build-up or build-off.

To calculate the cost of goods sold, we need to understand how much direct material and labour we are consuming and how much indirect costs or so-called overhead to allocate. The direct material and labour are taken from the bill of material and the routing. The same information is used by supply chain to ensure sufficient raw materials or components are purchased and sufficient direct labour is available. If one of these becomes a constraint, the supply chain plan will come up with solutions, like buying more from an outsourcing partner, or propose to 'constrain' the demand so the resulting plan is always 'feasible'. When allocating overhead costs like machine depreciation, we may look at the volumes produced or the run-times of the product (which would be more accurate). The production times can be calculated from the routings. Note that the supply chain plan generates the shift planning and as such the direct labour requirements. This interlinks with the workforce planning I will come back to later.

So, next to the 'gross sales' topline and sales volume forecast, we now also have a production plan, we know how much direct material we will use (material requirements), how much direct labour (labour requirements), we know the variable costs (allowing us to calculate a margin over variable cost or MVC) and we know the fixed cost allocation (allowing us to calculate the cost of goods sold and the resulting gross margin). I see no reason why not every S&OP or supply chain planning tool should not deliver this projected gross margin and provide the organization with the related scenario capabilities. The core engine of the two planning processes, FP&A and S&OP is the same. It is indicated as the grey area in Figure 7.8.

Once we have calculated the raw material or component requirements, we need to decide on a purchasing plan. If there are no constraints, the two may be equal. We may decide to purchase more to build up stocks or for instance because of an anticipated price increase. Likewise, we may decide to order less than needed to reduce inventories and/or to generate cash. As such, as is shown in Figure 7.8, from the supply chain plan, we can typically derive increases and decreases in finished goods inventories, in any intermediates and in raw material inventories. From the financial plan we have the cost of goods and the purchasing cost, which allows us to project inventory evolutions in both volumes and values. If we link in the payment terms for customers and suppliers, we can also project the accounts receivable and the accounts payable. So basically, from this combined plan we can derive a working capital forecast. That is something that finance currently doesn't have, as it is lacking, for instance, a good visibility on the inventory piece. It is something that supply chain currently doesn't deliver as an output of the S&OP process, as it is typically lacking the appropriate financial data, like the proper cost information. By combining the two processes into one single process, this becomes a net extra output. Cashflow forecasting is highly relevant to the 'business system', so we really shouldn't wait with this integration.

If we continue in Figure 7.8 when adding the planned SG&A (which, except for logistics costs, is beyond the sphere of influence of supply chain), we can come to a projected EBIT. When we account for the planned CAPEX (which is a financial planning thing), we can come to a projected Free Cash Flow. How does that sound? Generating a Free Cash Flow forecast on a monthly basis. One that is actually accurate, as it accounts for any capacity constraints, for any increase in in shifts and associated costs, for any stock build-ups, all things that are not accessible to finance when we have disconnected processes and systems.

One of the holy grails of S&OP and IBP has always been 'one set of numbers'. We need one set of numbers that tell us where the company is going. I believe that is a false goal. There will always be a difference between the ambition (currently the budget), the best guess (currently the supply chain plan) and the commitment (what we are willing to communicate towards shareholders or the group, currently the latest financial estimate). Financial markets are risk averse, so it is more rewarding to under-promise and over-deliver. You don't want to push this into one plan or one set of numbers:

- we don't want to put the ambition in the (current) supply chain plan that risks we will be left with unsold products, excess inventories and potentially write-offs
- we don't want to put the communicated plan in the (current) supply chain plan that risks we will face shortages and will not be able to capture the real potential of the market because of a lack of product availability.

If we want to move into an integrated 'Financial & Supply Chain Plan' (FSCP), we need to enable different versions of the same truth, the ambition, the best guess and the commitment. A good 'Financial & Supply Chain Plan'

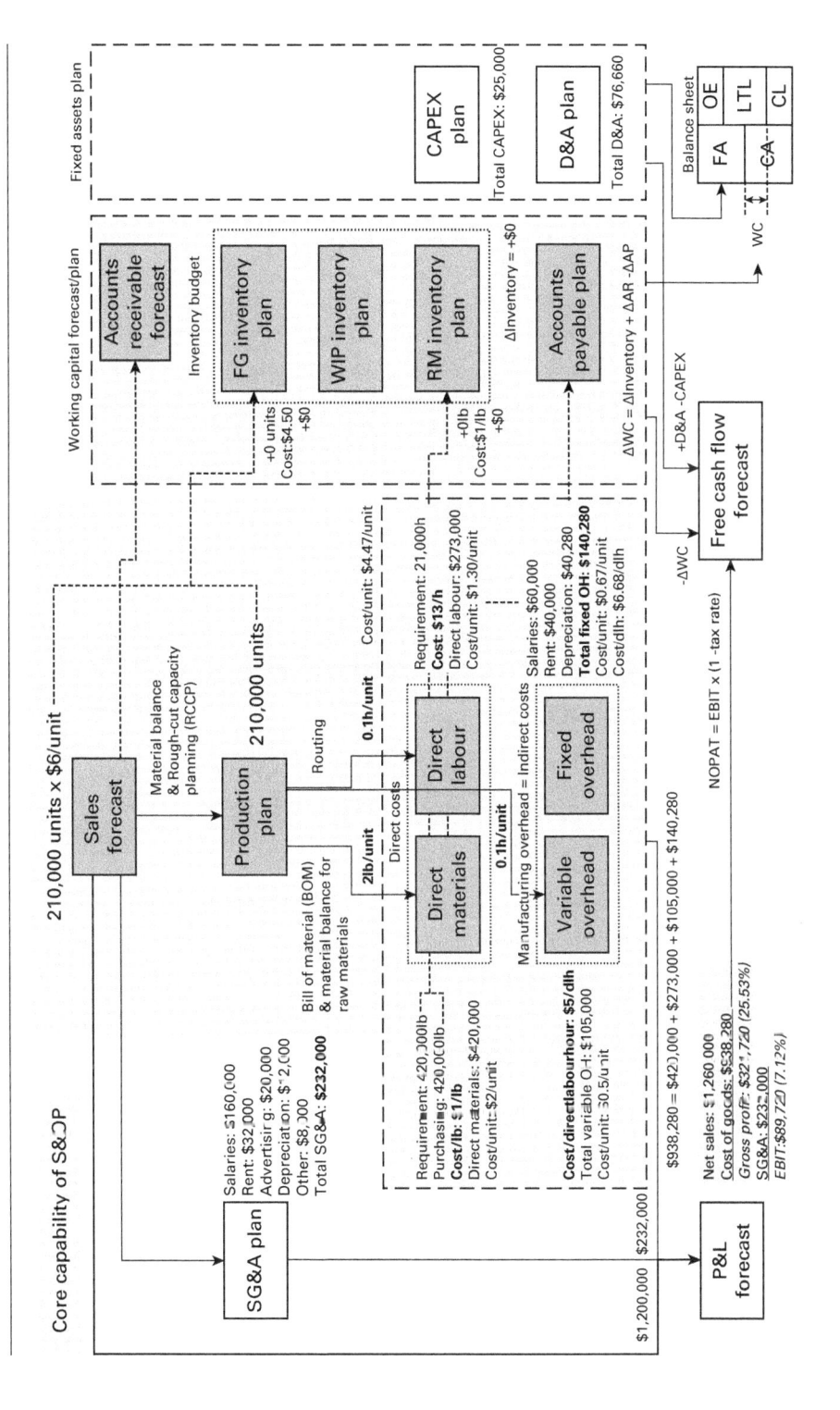

Figure 7.8 Integrating financial planning and supply chain planning

(FSCP) understands the differences and is able to contrast them. For instance, at the end of Q1, we see we are lagging behind the sales ambition (currently the budget). We also see the gap is increasing with our best guess sales plan in Q2 and Q3. This will trigger questions such as 'what can be done to close the gap'? If we can't close the gap on the sales side, do we want to or need to cut costs to protect the EBITDA and the cashflow? If yes, where do we think this can be done? What type of cut brings us to where we need to be? What is a fair distribution of the pain? Can we implement this in the organization and follow up this scenario during Q2? And what do we do in the meantime? Do we stick with the realistic plan, or do we plan for a potential upside from a supply perspective? In which type of products and markets are we willing to take the associated inventory risk? What is the potential working capital impact if we produce but the upside doesn't materialize? And what is our corresponding commitment towards HQ or the shareholders? These are the questions that should be reviewed during the executive meeting of the IVP cycle. This is how steering from the cockpit should look like.

Step 2: Integrating sales, marketing, product and resource planning

Once we have integrated our financial and supply chain planning, we need to integrate the rest of the plans in the company. We are talking about the sales planning, the marketing planning, the product planning and the resource planning, shown as step two in Figure 7.9.

Let's start with the marketing planning. Marketing will make decisions on the current and the future product portfolio. It may have a product portfolio tool in which it tracks the efficiency of the portfolio (not a lot of them exist), or their analysis may be based on BI reports and excel files (the more common situation). In any case, when we make a financial and supply chain plan for the next 12–18 months, we'll need to have an understanding on what moves marketing plans to make. Will there be any phase-outs? Any new product introductions (NPIs)? Do we plan any cost-downs on certain products? Do we plan any price increases? Or do we on the contrary expect price pressure and potential price decreases? So, as a minimum, the information on new-product-introductions, end-of-lifes, and list prices and list price changes, needs to flow into the financial and supply chain plan.

A second aspect of marketing planning is the trade promotion planning, for which marketing may have a separate TPP system. When we make a financial and supply chain plan for the next 12–18 months, marketing will need to define how much money it plans to spend on promotional activities and what will be the expected impact on the demand of which type of products and product groups. In many companies the supply chain plan has a good visibility on the promotions for the next 3–12 weeks, as these are the promotions where the planning has been fixed, but has limited or no visibility on the promotions thereafter, as for example the promotions are retailer specific and no concrete plans have been agreed beyond that horizon. However, supply chain planning doesn't work like that. No promos beyond 12 weeks means the demand drops after 12 weeks. It means there is no visibility on the longer-term capacity requirements and the longer-term key raw material requirements. So, we need to realize this longer-term visibility is not optional but mandatory, and that it needs to come from marketing. So as a second minimal input from marketing we note: promotion plans, associated costs, and associated volumes, per product and product group, in detail for the next 3–12 weeks, indicative for key raw materials and capacity consumption, for the next 12–18 months.

Let's continue with the product planning in Figure 7.9. The product planning will make the portfolio planning of marketing more concrete. Where the portfolio outlook for months 4 – 18, will come from marketing, the short-term outlook, let's say month 1-3, will be refined by R&D. R&D typically has a stage-gate process that tracks where individual NPIs or end-of-lifes are. That feeds the short-term financial & supply chain planning with specific details on the bill-of-material (BOM), the routings and the like. So, a minimum we need from R&D is: detailed short-term plan (e.g. next 3 months) for phase-ins, phase-outs, cost-downs and the associated detailed BOMs and routings.

Let's next continue with the sales planning in Figure 7.9 and more specifically pricing. If marketing defines the 'list pricing', it is typically sales that negotiates the actual prices with customers, based on those list prices. When we want to project the net sales 12–18 months out, sales will need to tell us what type of price reductions it expects on which types of customers and products. Sales might currently be doing this in a CRM system, in the ERP, or in all kinds of excel files. We need to ensure this information is integrated. So, what sales for sure needs to deliver is: price reductions on the list prices, so we can calculate net sales.

A second thing sales will need to do is validate the forecasts that have been generated in the financial and supply chain planning tool. These tools can typically generate forecasts for combinations where we have a certain history, but if we expect customers are going to buy more or less products, or if we expect to win new or lose existing customers, this will may be a manual input into the financial and supply chain plan. If this information would be available in the CRM in a structured way, it can be managed and taken from there. More often it is not, in which case it will be a direct manual input into the financial and supply chain planning system. So minimal, typically direct, input from sales: changes in the product mix of existing customers, changes in the customer portfolio (attrition versus new).

A third thing we may need from sales is a 'sales pipeline'. If we are a project-driven or tender-driven business, we typically have a pipeline of 'potential new projects or tenders we may win'. That type of sales pipeline is often managed in a CRM system rather than a financial and supply chain planning system. A bit like with promotions, our pipeline may be quite accurate for the next two to three months, but quickly degrade beyond that horizon as there is less concrete projects or tenders beyond that horizon. As with promotions, both are important. We need to have an accurate detailed view on the shorter term horizon, but equally important is to have an accurate view for the next to 12–18 months, which will be more indicative on which key raw materials and capacities to provide. So, in a project or tender-driven business, extra things we need from sales are: project/tender pipeline, in detail for the next two to three months, indicative for key raw materials and capacity consumption, for the next 12–18 months.

If we continue our journey in Figure 7.9, last but not least, we need to integrate with the resource planning. On the one hand, we have the workforce plan. When it is about the direct labour, that should follow from the supply chain plan. In the so-called 'Rough Cut Capacity Plan' or RCCP, we typically plan how many shifts we will need for the next 3–12 months. So, for the direct labour, the workforce planning should be fed by the financial and supply chain plan. When it is about indirect labour, or SG&A, we may rely on what has been budgeted for, in the current separate workforce plan. When moving to the integrated Financial and Supply Chain Plan (FSCP), we can consider the resource plan would be fully integrated into the FSCP, following the same logic of the 'ambition' (or budgeted), the 'realistic' (will we be using more or less resources based on our latest plan) and 'committed' (based on what assumptions do we communicate to the outside world). But, for now, let's note as interactions with the workforce planning that: for direct labour, the workforce plan is fed by the supply chain plan, for indirect labour and SG&A, the workforce plan is feeding the financial and supply chain plan (FSCP), with as an option to fully integrate it into the FSCP.

Our evolving supply chain ecosystem and the new concept of Integrated Value Planning

A second aspect of the resource plan is the plan we agree with suppliers. In many companies I see that procurement is contracting volumes with suppliers without having a decent view on where these are going. Procurement may have purchase orders and requirements for the next 1–12 weeks (the MPS horizon), but the requirements beyond that horizon may be inaccurate, for instance because the longer-term portfolio, trade promotion or project/tender forecast is inaccurate. On a longer horizon, 3–18 months out, procurement may also, instead of showing requirements for individual raw materials or components, rather focus on expected volumes in certain categories, or for instance, in case of outsourcing, rather reserve certain capacities at the outsourcing partners and commit to certain raw materials. This information should be fed, from the financial and supply chain plan, for instance as an output of the so-called RCCP plan. Procurement from its side, will need to give a view on the expected evolution of key raw material and component prices. Are they expected to go up, when and by how much, or are they expected to go down, by when and by how much. This price information may be stored in a separate system, in excel files or in the ERP system. Procurement, from its side, will also need to input in the financial and supply chain plan, whether it plans to pre-buy, for instance based on anticipated shortage or a price increase, or whether it proposes to build-off inventories as we are beyond a certain critical point. The expected inventory increase or decrease could be a direct input into the financial and supply chain plan, a bit like sales is validating plans on the sales side. So in summary, when linking into procurement and external supply: the financial and supply chain plan needs to feed procurement with the raw material and component requirements for the next 12–18 months, procurement needs to feed the financial and supply chain plan with expected price increases or decreases on key raw materials and components, and procurement will need to give as a direct input to the financial and supply chain plan, whether it plans to pre-buy, for instance based on expected price increases, or suggests to build off inventories, for instance because we are beyond a critical point.

At the heart of this step, you will see we have put a triangle, which is our Supply Chain Triangle. Companies today work with disconnected processes and systems, and they believe that is a feasible option. That is a false assumption. Disconnected plans lead to gaps in the financial performance, as we are making decisions based on incomplete or incorrect information. It creates the inverse of agility, and it leads to all the issues I have described in Figure 4.1. The level of integration shown in Figure 7.9 is not optional, it is mandatory.

Figure 7.9 Information flows with the sales, marketing, product and resource plan

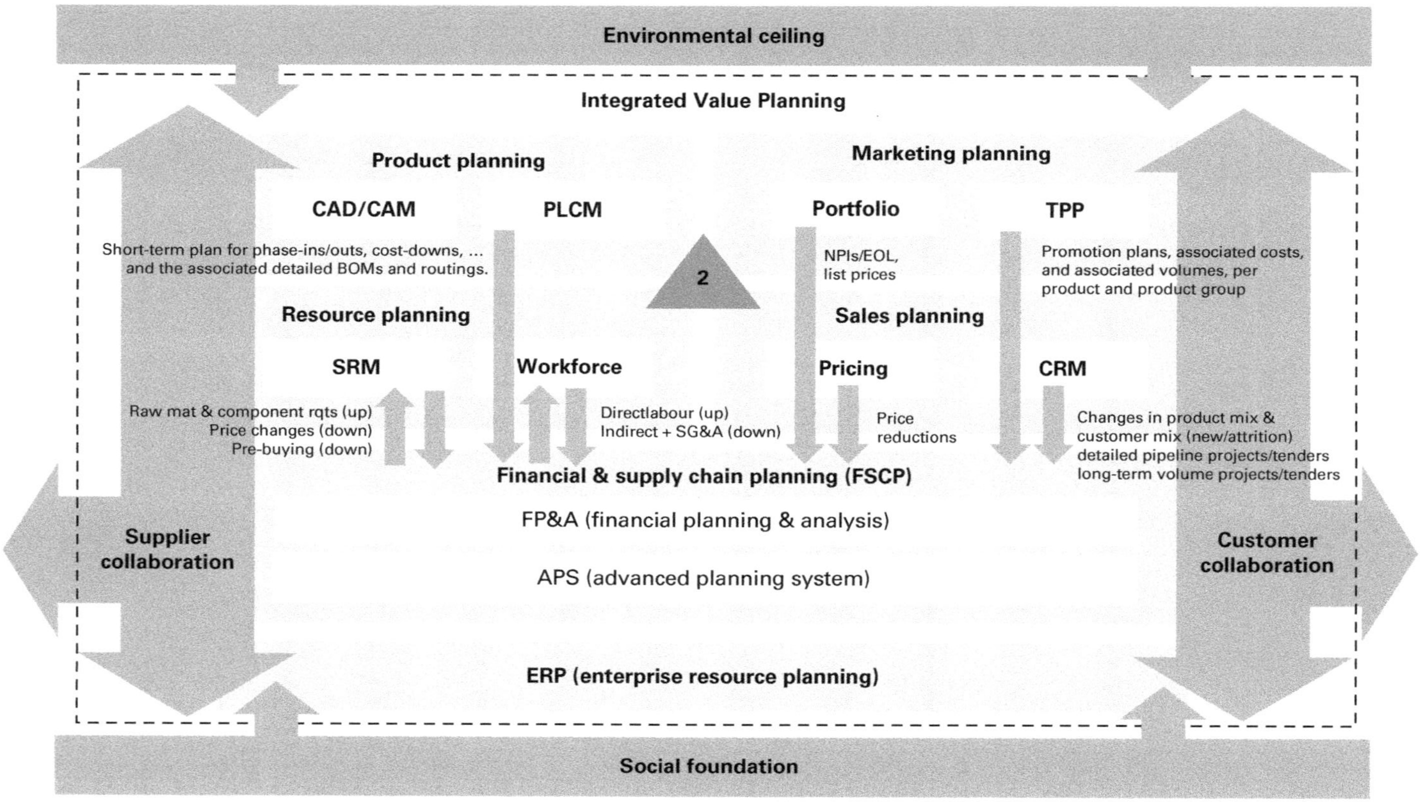

Step 3: Integrating key customers and key suppliers

We all know that, today, we compete, not companies against companies, but value chains against value chains. This saying is attributed to the late Peter Drucker already decades ago. Still, as companies we underinvest in integrating and collaborating with key customers and key suppliers. The integration we do have, is often on the transactional level. We may have an EDI connection that allows for an automatic transmission of orders, or we may send advanced shipping notes, which explain what we are going to deliver when, but we seem to have overlooked an integration or collaboration on the more tactical planning level.

In Figure 7.10, I have indicated which type of integration we need with key customers and with key suppliers. The integration with key customers starts on the 'marketing planning' side. CPFR (Collaborative Planning Forecasting and Replenishment), as first created by VICS (Voluntary Interindustry Commerce Solutions), and now managed by GS1[6], has been around for 20 years. It advocates collaboration between FMCG companies and retailers not just on the forecast or the replenishment, but also on the assortment planning. What is the current assortment, how will it evolve, what will be the new product introductions (NPI), what will be the end-of-life products (EOL), next to what will be the promo plans per product and product group. If you are a branded goods manufacturer you may control the promotions yourself. When you do private label, the customer typically controls the promotions. I had many discussion with companies on their portfolio. I had to explain many times that 'if something is slow moving for the manufacturer... it's typically moving even slower for the retailer. If it doesn't make sense to keep it in the assortment for you, it typically makes even less sense for the retailer, it may just be consuming shelf space and working capital, without a proper margin return. The last thing you want to do for slow movers is 'double stock' in the supply chain, which is exactly what may happen, as customers may try to push back inventories, and expect you to keep a safety stock for the unlikely event they would sell a bit more. Somebody needs to take the end-to-end supply chain perspective and say 'stop, this doesn't make sense'. If, together, you think it through, you may find alternatives, for instance products which are better selling at other customers. The portfolio management and the planning of promotional peaks easily extends into B2B companies. In B2B many products may be customer specific. Also here you want to avoid 'double stocking'. Discussing the 'health of the portfolio' with your customers is part of a proper customer development. In B2B instead of 'promotional peaks' we may have 'events' such as a major shutdown, which may create a temporary drop in demand. Or your customers may be tender-driven and may want to communicate which type of tenders they have in the pipeline and how they could affect you. In the B2B portfolio discussion, you might also discuss technology evolutions, how your customers should gradually move from an existing onto a new technology platform. All very needed discussions and integrations, in our complex and volatile supply chain world.

We continue in Figure 7.10 with the sales interaction. Sales will (try to) get a customer forecast, showing where the customers demand is going and how it affects the demand of your products. During the high inflation of the post-Covid energy crisis, sales also spent a lot of effort in increasing sales prices at customers and renegotiating contracts. Supply chain will discuss capacity reservations with customers or the procurement of customer specific raw materials. It will also communicate a delivery schedule for the next 3–12 weeks. Whether you are in FMCG or in B2B, you basically want to avoid you having to wait for your customers to order on you, you want to have visibility on their inventory, on their planned consumption and be able to do a Vendor Managed Inventory (VMI).

If we continue at the supply side, like we do portfolio planning with our key customers, our key suppliers want to do portfolio planning with us. What are any new product introductions or end-of-life plans on our side? The supplier may have its own view on which type of technologies it wants to phase in and which ones it wants to phase out. If we have big promotions or other events like projects or tenders that may impact our key suppliers, we will communicate the information to them. Just like we reserve capacities for key customers, we provide a longer-term forecast and agree on capacity reservations at key suppliers. We may commit on critical raw materials that our key supplier needs to buy. We discuss planned price increases and expectations on a longer horizon. Like we communicate a planned delivery schedule for the next few weeks to our customers, we request the same from our key suppliers. Just like we don't want to wait for customers to order, our key suppliers don't want to wait for our orders but prefer visibility on our inventory and the planned consumption so they can replenish our inventory in time.

As introduced above, most of the integration today is stuck on the operational level and not enough effort is spent on the tactical level. I can only repeat that, today, we compete as supply chains, not as companies, so integrating key customers and suppliers is not optional but mandatory. Not

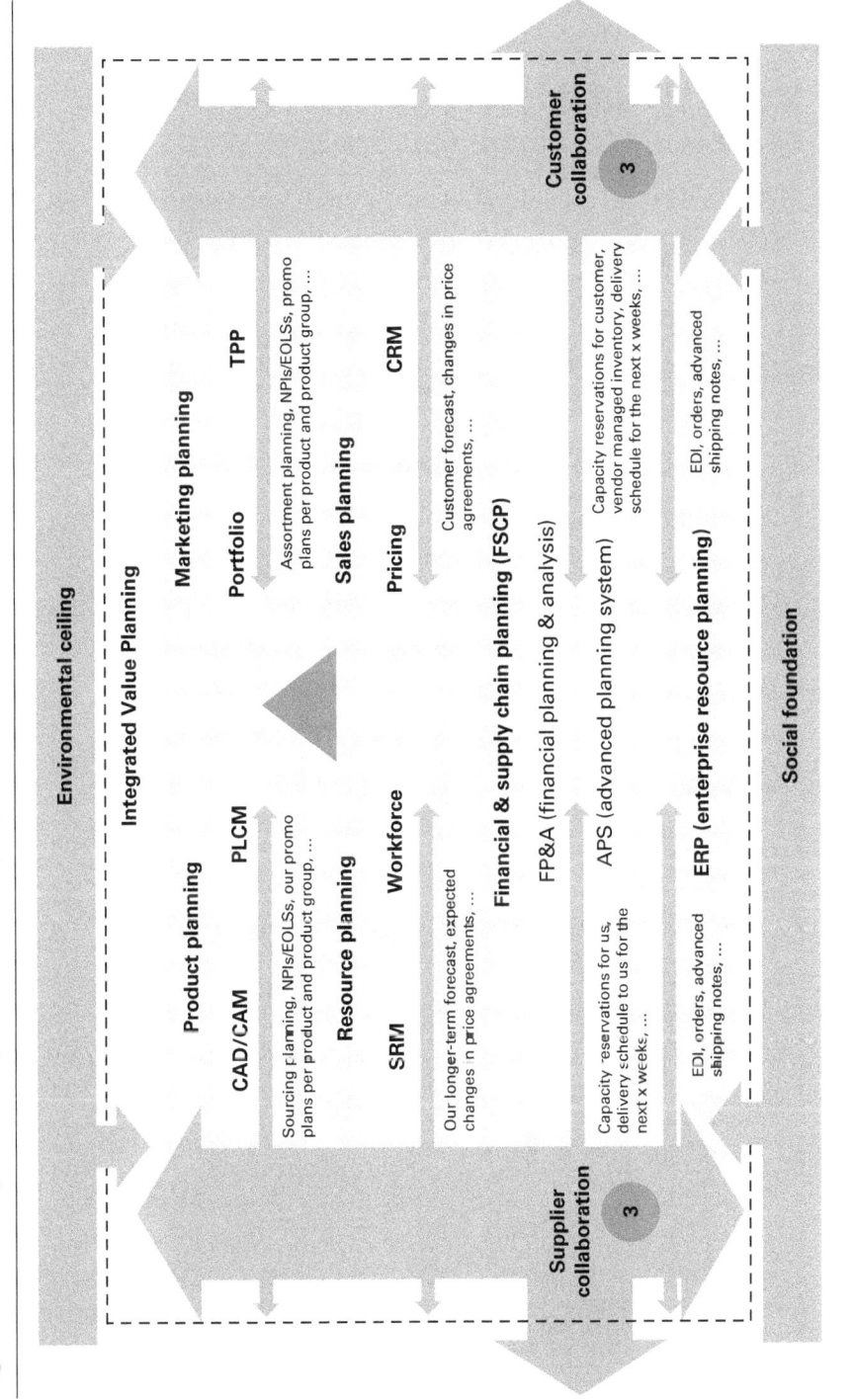

Figure 7.10 Integration of key customers and key suppliers into our planning process

doing so is, once more, the inverse of agility, which leads to all the negative consequences introduced in Figure 4.1.

Step 4: Integrating sustainability into the core of our business planning processes

In Figure 7.11, we continue our journey to see how to natively integrate the sustainability dimensions into our planning processes. We can start from the marketing planning at the top right. Marketing will analyse the sustainability trends and needs in the market and think through the impact on product options, cost and on pricing. Are consumers willing to pay more for healthier or environmentally friendly products? Are they willing to wait longer or pay extra for environmentally friendly transport options? Should we be a first mover, a fast follower, or wait for the masses to convert? What is our resulting product and pricing plan?

The moves on the marketing side, will obviously translate in moves on the R&D side or the 'product plan', filling the pipeline with product changes and new product ideas. From their side, R&D may come up with new options or new technologies. Healthy alternatives for unhealthy habits, options to reduce consumption of energy, water or other scarce resources, in the production process (Scope 1) or during the product lifetime (Scope 3).

Depending on our strategic objectives, defined during the strategic trade-offs introduced in Chapter 5, we will trade-off the sustainability impact with the financial impact. Think about how Vandemoortele chose to gradually reduce the sugar and fat content in its products. As it is affecting taste, and consumer taste changes slowly, moving aggressively could significantly impact sales, and to have a lasting positive impact, it is key your company stays financially healthy.

Let's continue at the bottom right with sales. How should we account for CO_2 and food waste in our customer contracts? Should we oblige customers to order in full trucks? How to deal with food waste that was caused by inaccurate forecasts? Our sustainability objectives should translate into this type of decisions.

Continuing at the bottom left, sustainability translates into our resource planning. From an environmental perspective it triggers the question of regional sourcing and auditing suppliers on their sustainability plans. From a social perspective, it is about ensuring well-being of employees, about safety, education and diversity within our company walls, and extending into first and second tier suppliers.

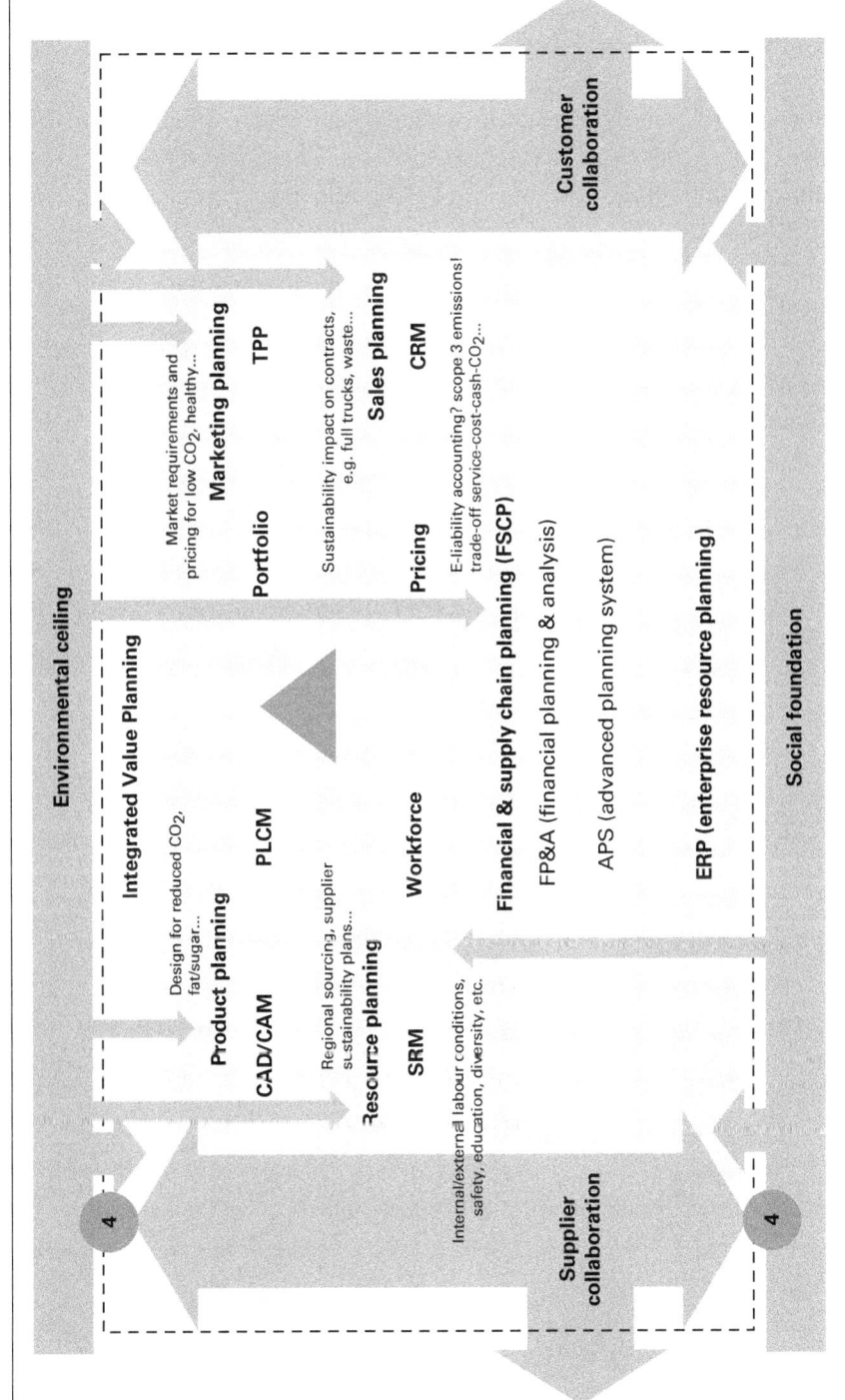

Figure 7.11 Integration of sustainability metrics into all of our planning processes

In our core 'financial and supply chain planning', it is important that instead of balancing service, cost and cash, we now firmly include environmental metrics like CO_2 and social metrics like overtime. If we need to rush an order because of an inaccurate customer forecast, are we willing to produce in overtime and expedite goods making extra costs and CO_2? Or will we deliver within the standard agreed lead time? That answer used to be simple, and what if it makes the difference between recognizing the revenue still in this fiscal year versus next fiscal year, knowing we are lagging behind the plan? Or what if it is about having the order or losing it?! The only way to make integrated decisions, is centralizing all the information into one tool and one process.

In our ERP system, we might want to add CO_2 information to the Bill-of-Materials (BOMs) and Routings to understand how much CO_2 we are adding through raw materials/components and through the manufacturing processes. This implements the 'e-liability accounting' promoted by Robert Kaplan and introduced in Chapter 2. As Kaplan states, the only CO_2 that is being emitted is Scope 1, so if each company does a proper accounting of its Scope 1 liabilities, we will have a full transparency of how CO_2 accumulates throughout the chain, just like financial costs accumulate and get passed on. Once this data is in the ERP system, using it in scenarios in the financial and supply chain planning tool becomes relatively straightforward.

Conclusion

In this chapter, I have defined the new concept of 'Integrated Value Planning' or 'IVP', with an integrated 'Financial and Supply Chain Planning' or 'FSCP' at the core, with native integration of marketing planning, product planning, sales planning and resource planning, with native integration of key customers and key suppliers, with native integration of social and environmental metrics into the heart of our planning and decision making processes.

This Integrated Value Planning or IVP addresses the needs from our evolving supply chain and business ecosystem. It takes the 'system' perspective, guided by Rummler and Brache, as opposed the current dominant 'functional' perspective.

In the next chapter I will build on this, by defining how an IVP process could look like, how to make decisions based on an IVP dashboard and how to organize for successful IVP. I develop an eight-stage IVP maturity model that shows you how to build IVP step by step. And I finish by doing the cross check on whether IVP delivers us with the required fourth generation tactical planning capabilities.

Endnotes

1 Gorillas. Groceries at your door in minutes, 2024. www.gorillas.io/en (archived at https://perma.cc/R69G-5TJF)
2 Supply Chain Movement, Ecosystem for household products, 29 Sep 2022. www.supplychainmovement.com/ecosystem-for-household-products/ (archived at https://perma.cc/GR2B-ZRW9)
3 G A Rummler, A P Brache (1995) *Improving Performance. How to manage the white space on the organization chart*, Jossey-Bass, San Francisco
4 B DeSmet. Template Supply Chain Ecosystem, 2024. www.bramdesmet.com/rethinkingsupplychain/ (archived at https://perma.cc/39HF-JW9F)
5 Gartner. The 5 Levels of S&OP Maturity, 2024. www.gartner.com/en/supply-chain/trends/sales-operations-planning-sop-maturity (archived at https://perma.cc/F67U-J2P7)
6 GS1 US. The GS1 US Solution, 2024. www.gs1us.org (archived at https://perma.cc/YFT4-T6FA)

Implementing Integrated Value Planning through an eight-stage maturity model

08

Introduction

In this chapter, based on the building blocks define in the previous chapter, I define the Integrated Value Planning or IVP process, with its different steps for reviewing the marketing and product planning, the sales planning, rolling this up into a Financial and Supply Chain Plan or FSCP, translating the impact on the resource plan, and comparing the ambition, the most realistic and the committed plan in the Executive IVP meeting, making decisions based on scenarios, assessing the impact on the triple bottom-line, financial, social and environmental metrics. The IVP process defines a continuous collaboration with key customers and key suppliers, validating the assumptions on latest outlooks for demand or consumption, capacity reservations and ordering of specific components or raw materials. The resulting supply chain is highly collaborative and highly connected.

Next I introduce the Integrated Value Planning or IVP dashboard that complies metrics in a logical way: service, cost and capital employed metrics, leading to sales, bottom-line and return metrics, changes in capital employed leading to cash flow metrics, but all of these now captured within a social foundation and environmental ceiling, and with process metrics like forecast accuracy or first pass yield so-called causal or diagnostic metrics for all the other 'downstream' metrics. As I will show, it is the dashboard for the Executive IVP meeting. It is the way we should compare scenarios to the ambition and the commitment, to make better informed decision from a more holistic perspective.

The case on the supply chain planning transformation at Reckitt summarizes an impressive four-year planning transformation. It confirms some of the difficulties in getting planning transformations sold, on how to natively connect and integrate with others planning processes. In a first step, the integration with financial planning will be there but the integration with trade promotion planning or sales planning will be done only later. This doesn't detract from how impressive the transformation is. It will bring Reckitt to a solid stage 3 to stage 4 maturity, which is way further than many companies are today. The scope of transformation and the timeline within which it happens make it impressive. The case also highlights the process and the organizational aspect, next to the systems aspect. It is truly an impressive job done very well.

Next I will continue exploring how to organize for IVP success. I make a specific proposal on how to complement the strong functional focus, with an equally strong cross-functional focus, namely by introducing a new role, called the Chief Value Planning Officer (CVPO). That Chief Value Planning Officer will have Integrated Value Planning as a core responsibility, next to the strategic planning and the Strategy-Driven Sustainable and Resilient Supply Chain Design. It will have a balancing financial metric like ROCE and key metrics on the social foundation and environmental ceiling as the compass for guiding cross functional teams in decision making.

In this chapter, I will also share some insights from organization theory, namely Henry Mintzberg, on how to organize for complex and dynamic environments. Mintzberg points us in the direction of 'decentralized' and 'organic' structures where 'mutual adjustment' is used to coordinate activities. 'Decentralized' means delegating power vertically, down the line (for instance into regions or product lines) and horizontally, to the relevant experts in support functions (for instance a supply chain analytics team). 'Organic' means structures should flexibly adapt in need of the circumstances (for instance a temporary team to respond to the Ever Given blocking the Suez Canal). 'Mutual adjustment' means no single person holds the decision, we mutually align and adjust. Based on these findings I will propose more decisions to be left to knowledgeable cross-functional teams, creating a 360° view, rather than leaving them to an individual and potentially biased function. Using examples I will try to make it concrete.

Near the end of the chapter I will propose an eight-stage maturity model for Integrated Value Planning. Stages 1 to 4 will take a supply chain view, and are basically solving the supply chain needs, which is closely related to what the traditional Sales & Operations Planning (S&OP) and Integrated Business Planning (IBP) are doing. Stages 5 to 8 take a systems view, and is solving the broader business and ecosystems needs. It is where Integrated Value Planning or IVP differs from the earlier models for integrated planning.

I close the chapter by cross checking wither Integrated Value Planning solves the tactical planning needs of our fourth generation supply chain, as defined in Chapter 4.

The Integrated Value Planning process

If we structurally want to get the information flowing, we need to define a monthly process, that connects the different elements of IVP. Figure 8.1 proposes how to connect the different processes from Figure 7.6.

We start with a monthly marketing and product planning review. We review changes to the product portfolio, new product introductions, end-of-life products, cost-downs, (list) price increases. We review trade promotion plans with associated costs and volumes, as shown in Figure 7.9. What is important is that we are specific on the shorter horizon, for instance, anything that is within a 6 or a 12 week horizon needs to be 'fixed and agreed', whether is about product changes or promotions. The lead time will depend on your time needed to properly process, prepare and execute. Yes, for sure you want to become more agile, so you may be happy to start with 10 weeks and then gradually try to bring that down. Beyond the agreed horizon, we should validate the outlook on portfolio changes and promotions, and how they will impact key capacities and key raw materials. These are important to do proper planning in the next steps of the IVP process.

Second step is a monthly sales review, which looks at changes in the customer and product mix, any changes in pricing, how the changes from the product and marketing review will be implemented. The sales review includes the more traditional demand review, where we update and validate the forecast. If we are tender driven or project driven business, as before, it is important we agree on a horizon, 6 weeks, 12 weeks, within which these need to be 'specified in detail'. The lead time will depend on your time needed to properly process, prepare and execute, for instance the buying of tender/project specific raw materials or components. Beyond the agreed

Implementing Integrated Value Planning through an eight-stage maturity model

horizon, we should validate the outlook on project and tenders, and how they will impact key capacities and key raw materials. Do we expect the volumes to go up? Is the market in an upturn? Or do we expect the volumes to go down? Are we in downturn? This is where leading indicators, as discussed in the case of Solvay in Chapter 3 can help. Having the longer-term outlook is important to do proper planning in the next steps of the IVP process.

In parallel, we run 'customer collaboration' reviews with our key customers. At the table from our side are the key account manager, a product manager or specialist and a customer supply chain manager. From the customers' side there is the procurement manager, an R&D manager or product specialist and a supply chain manager. On the agenda are a review of the customer product and/or service assortment, any expected changes from the customers' side or our side (for instance because of technology changes). As relevant are a review of the promotions plans with associated budgets, timings and volumes. Validation of any forecast assumptions we currently have, the inventory situation at the customer. Review of projects or tenders with agreed horizons within which things are specific versus indicative for key capacities and key raw materials beyond that. We can try to be prescriptive on when exactly these customer reviews need to happen, for instance before the sales review meeting, but it's probably wiser to insist that it happens, on a monthly basis, and with all key customers, rather than being too restrictive in which week it actually should happen.

Step three in the cycle is the FSCP, the Financial and Supply Chain Plan, where we make a capacity constrained plan for the next 3–18 months. As the outcome, we show a projected net sales, a projected gross margin, a projected working capital, and a projected EBIT and free cash flow, based on assumptions of the SG&A, the D&A and the CAPEX. We explained how this can be done in more detail in Chapter 7 based on some key understandings summarized in Figure 7.8. The FSCP is also steering the full material planning in volumes. As shown in Figure 8.1, it is scenario based, which will be needed to support our Executive IVP meeting.

Step four, is the resource planning, which on the one hand will be our workforce planning and at the other hand will be the collaborative planning with our key suppliers on key capacities and key raw materials to reserve. A bit as with the customer collaboration, we can try to be prescriptive on when exactly the supplier collaboration needs to happen, but we believe it is more important to insist it happens, on a monthly basis. From our company side we will have our procurement manager, an R&D or product specialist,

Figure 8.1 The monthly Integrated Value Planning (IVP) Cycle

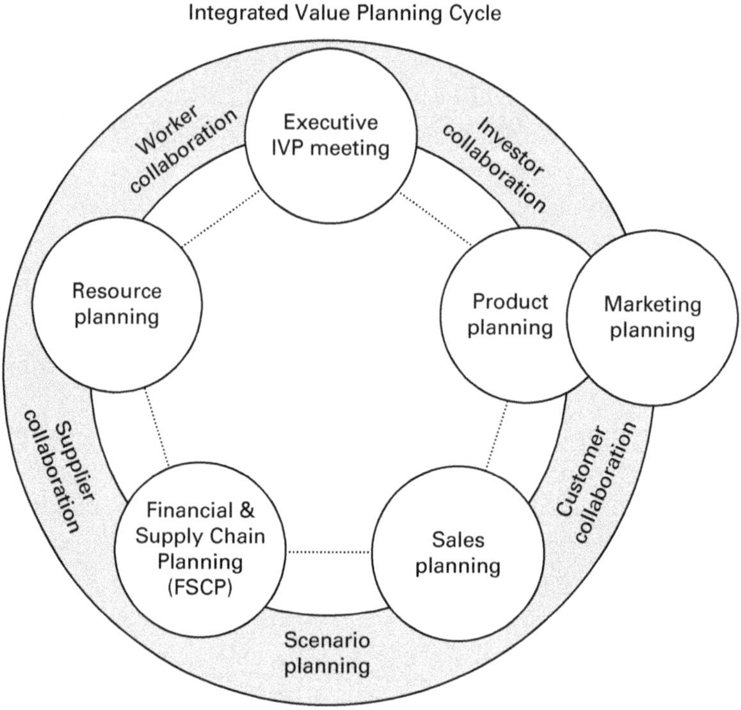

Integrated Value Planning Cycle

- Executive IVP meeting
- Product planning
- Marketing planning
- Sales planning
- Financial & Supply Chain Planning (FSCP)
- Resource planning
- Scenario planning

Worker collaboration, Investor collaboration, Customer collaboration, Supplier collaboration

and a supply chain manager. With our key suppliers, we will review what we are currently buying, any anticipated changes in the portfolio from our side or the suppliers' side, any expectations in key capacities and key volumes to be reserved and any specific commitments our key supplier has to make like purchasing of his raw materials. By ensuring all of this information is shared and updated at least monthly, we keep our key suppliers in sync.

The process rolls up into the Executive IVP meeting. In this meeting we compare the ambition (the budget), with the most realistic plan (based on steps 1 to 4), we compare scenarios and alternatives on what can be done to close any gaps, and we finally decide on the committed plan, which is the plan we can submit to headquarters or financial stakeholders. As is shown in Figure 8.1, the insights from the Executive IVP meeting will also be the basis for regular reviews with other stakeholders like investors, or the works council. The IVP process supports us in managing our broader supply chain and business ecosystem.

At least once per year, we define a new ambition or budget. As our FSCP is a rolling plan, there should be a solid base on which can easily be built. In

Implementing Integrated Value Planning through an eight-stage maturity model 277

Figure 8.2 Fixing a new 'ambition' or budget every six months

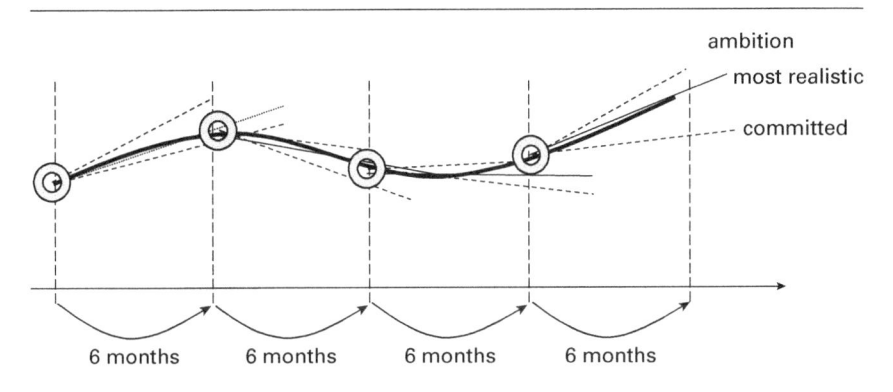

the ambition we may for instance add extra growth, which could come from new products or new regions, for which we add extra OPEX in R&D or in SG&A. All of these should easily follow as scenarios from our most realistic FSCP. Some people talk about 'rolling budgets' or question the added value of a budget all together. I'm a believer in taking a step back from the most realistic plan and adding an ambition now and then. It is a normal way of planning, committing resources, following up the progress and correcting course as needed. I do believe that doing it every 6 months, with a 6–9 months horizon, as shown in Figure 8.2, makes more sense than doing it every year, with a 12–15 month horizon. In many companies the next 6–9 months can be predicted with a reasonable accuracy, anything that goes beyond may not be accurate enough to take any serious commitments.

There may be two main reasons why we have run yearly budgets so far. A first is that our fiscal years are also years. But that shouldn't really play a role. The budgets are forward looking, our accounting is backward looking. Our board of directors may be used to approve one budget per year, but if we believe we'll be more accurate by approving a budget every six months, what would be holding us back? A second reason we run yearly budgets might be that it is such a lengthy and painstaking process. With the new FSCP capabilities we believe running it twice a year should be easy.

> **EXERCISE**
> Mapping and aligning your existing IVP meetings
>
> Gather your executive team, or a team of cross-functional experts. Ensure the different functions sales, marketing, R&D, operations, supply chain, procurement, finance, HR, IT and so on are represented.

Review the pentagon shown in Figure 8.1 and for each of the blocks ask the question:

- Which meetings do we have around these topics? What is the agenda? Who is involved? What are inputs? What are outputs? What is the frequency?
- What do we have for product management? What do we have for promotion planning?
- What do we have for sales planning?
- What do we have for supply chain planning? For financial planning?
- What do we have for workforce planning? For resource planning at key suppliers?
- What do we have as an executive decision-making meeting?
- And what can be done to better connect the different steps?

Note: I have made a pentagon available for download from my website[1]. You may project it or print it on an A0, in which case you can use it as a visual support for a sticky note exercise.

The Integrated Value Planning dashboard

In the IVP meeting, we report and decide based on an integrated set of financial and non-financial metrics. The dashboard template is shown in Figure 8.3. We have service metrics that are driving sales or top-line metrics, top-line minus costs driving margin metrics, margin over capital employed driving return metrics, margin plus changes in capital employed driving cash flow metrics. All of these have been explained in detail in my previous two books. Next, we add our social foundation and environmental ceiling, to include our sustainability focus. And we add process metrics that monitor our core processes and can act as causal or diagnostic metrics, as I will shortly illustrate.

Figure 8.4 shows a more elaborate version of the same dashboard template. For service I have listed the value drivers of Crawford and Matthews, including resilience, but excluding sustainability as these have been added as the social foundation and the environmental ceiling. On the social foundation I have added examples we encountered in the case of Vandemoortele in

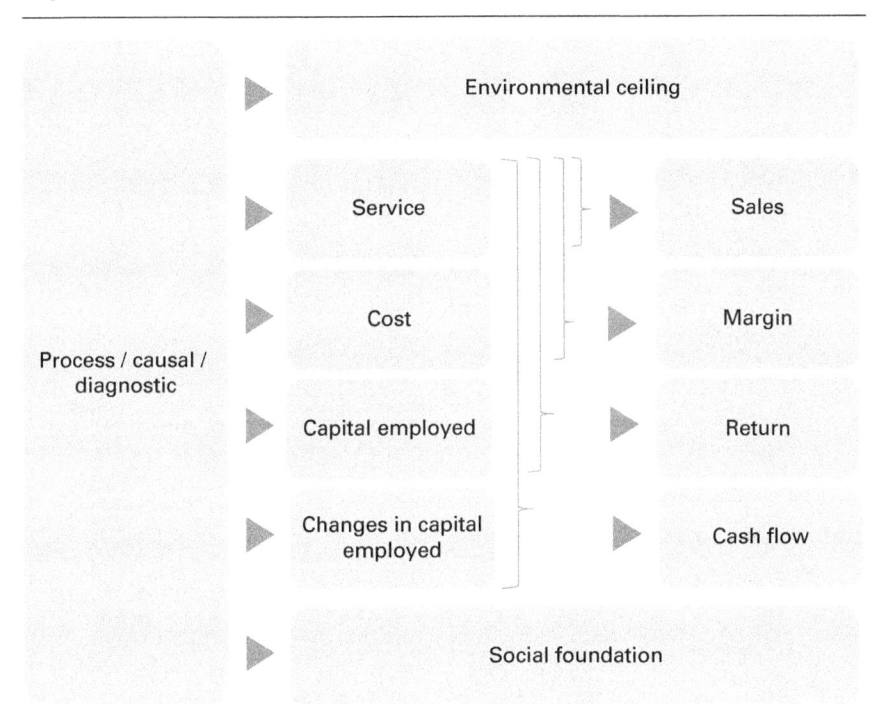

Figure 8.3 The Integrated Value Planning (IVP) dashboard

```
                          ▶  Environmental ceiling

                          ▶  Service          ▶  Sales

                          ▶  Cost             ▶  Margin
Process / causal /
diagnostic
                          ▶  Capital employed ▶  Return

                          ▶  Changes in capital  ▶  Cash flow
                             employed

                          ▶  Social foundation
```

Chapter 2. The company wanted to sustainably source key raw materials like soy beans, it wanted a bigger proportion of its products receiving a healthier quality label, and it was looking to improve its employee engagement score on a number of elements like gender equality. On the environmental ceiling I show CO_2, the food waste we encountered at Vandemoortele and the per cent of reused materials which we saw in a case like Ricoh in Chapter 6, to add an example from a different sector. The cost, cash and financial metrics are all relatively standard, as are the process metrics.

Figure 8.5 shows an example of how a process metric, like forecast accuracy, can have a negative effect on all metrics to the right. During and post-Covid, forecasting has become harder, because of stocking and destocking at customers, dual sourcing at customers, and more variability in the market in general. As our forecast error goes up, it will typically negative impact our on-time, in-full (OTIF) delivery performance, and as such, it may negatively affect sales. Either customers will just buy from a competitor that has availability, or prolonged service issues, are leading to customer churn. When we have service issues, we will have operational firefighting costs, like last minute change-overs, which increases our manufacturing overhead, and

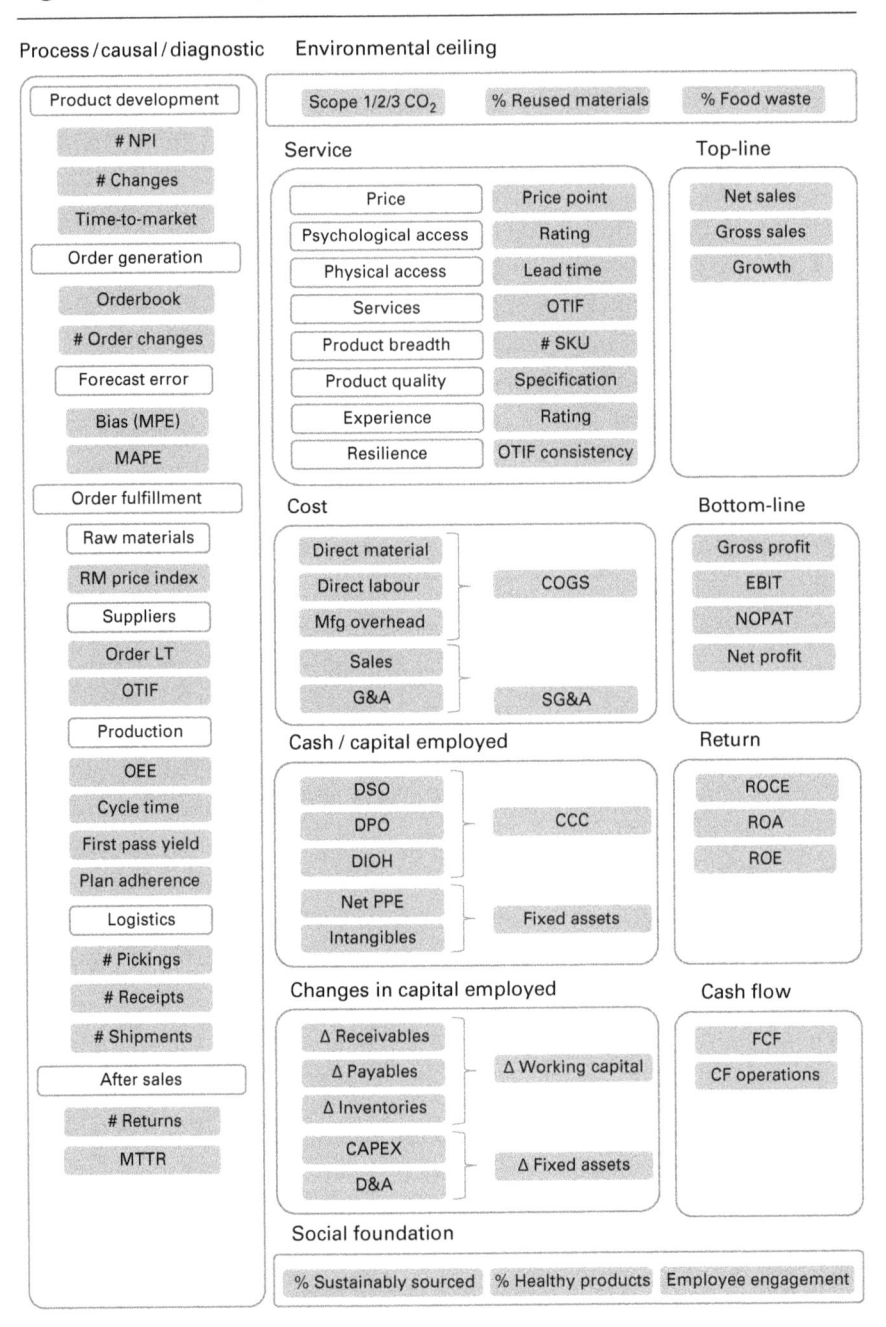

Figure 8.4 The Integrated Value Planning (IVP) dashboard – example metrics

Process / causal / diagnostic

Product development
- # NPI
- # Changes
- Time-to-market

Order generation
- Orderbook
- # Order changes
- Forecast error
- Bias (MPE)
- MAPE

Order fulfillment
- Raw materials
- RM price index
- Suppliers
- Order LT
- OTIF
- Production
- OEE
- Cycle time
- First pass yield
- Plan adherence
- Logistics
- # Pickings
- # Receipts
- # Shipments

After sales
- # Returns
- MTTR

Environmental ceiling

| Scope 1/2/3 CO_2 | % Reused materials | % Food waste |

Service

Price	Price point
Psychological access	Rating
Physical access	Lead time
Services	OTIF
Product breadth	# SKU
Product quality	Specification
Experience	Rating
Resilience	OTIF consistency

Cost

Direct material	
Direct labour	COGS
Mfg overhead	
Sales	
G&A	SG&A

Cash / capital employed

DSO	
DPO	CCC
DIOH	
Net PPE	Fixed assets
Intangibles	

Changes in capital employed

Δ Receivables	
Δ Payables	Δ Working capital
Δ Inventories	
CAPEX	Δ Fixed assets
D&A	

Social foundation

| % Sustainably sourced | % Healthy products | Employee engagement |

Top-line
- Net sales
- Gross sales
- Growth

Bottom-line
- Gross profit
- EBIT
- NOPAT
- Net profit

Return
- ROCE
- ROA
- ROE

Cash flow
- FCF
- CF operations

Implementing Integrated Value Planning through an eight-stage maturity model

Figure 8.5 Impact of less accurate forecasts on the Integrated Value Planning (IVP) dashboard

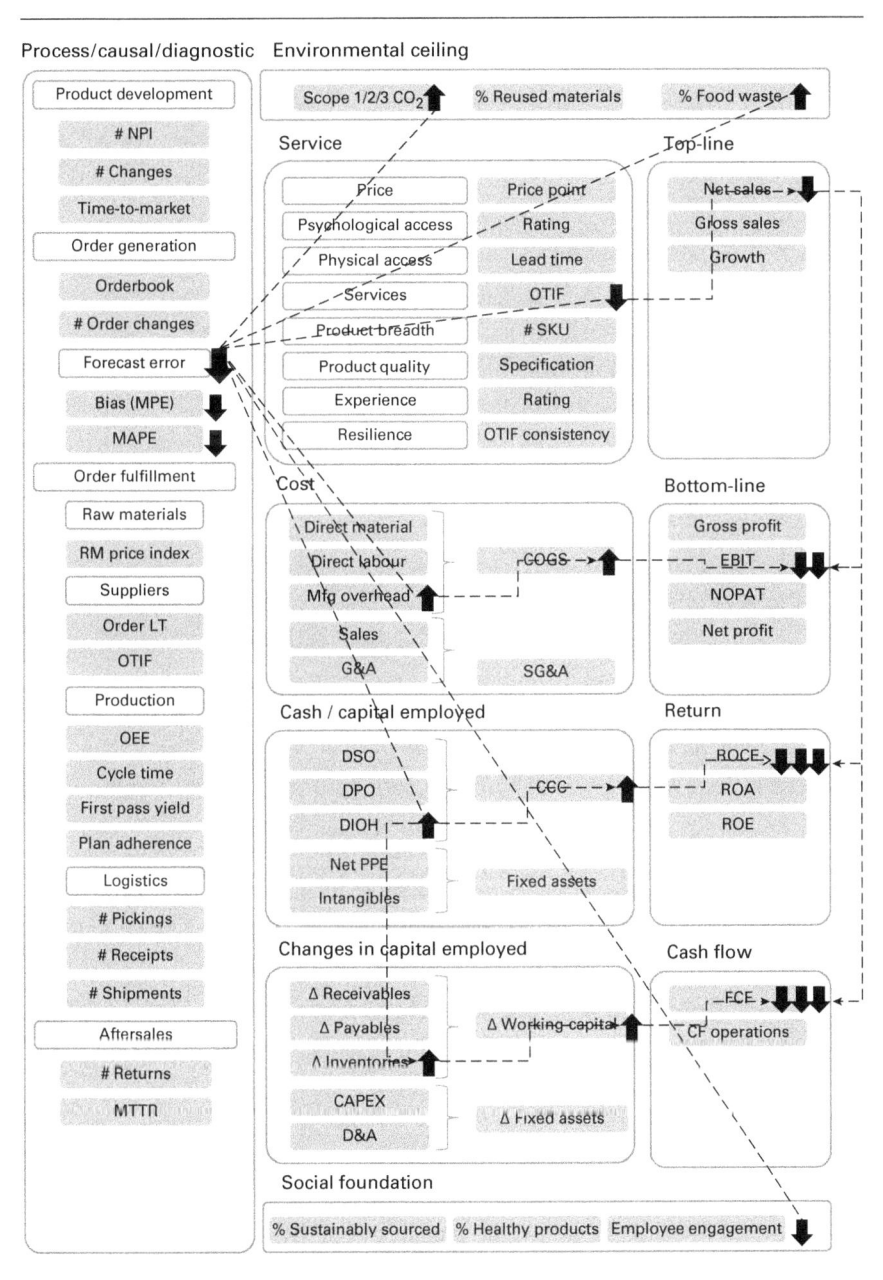

as such our cost of good sold. It implies that our costs are going up, while our sales is going down, so we have a double negative impact on the margin. Last minute expediting may negatively impact CO_2. The firefighting may negatively impact morale and employee engagement. If some forecasts are too low, others may be too high, negatively impacting our food waste. The forecast error clearly goes beyond service or financial metrics.

As we continue our analysis of the impact on the financial metrics, bigger forecast errors will result in higher safety stocks, trying to keep the OTIF service level at the target. This means that on the short term we will have less margin, but at a higher level of capital employed, or we have a triple impact on the return. At the moment we are increasing the safety stocks, we will also consume cash, at a moment that the margin is less than expected, or we take a triple impact on the cashflow. We believe this example shows how connected these different metrics are. Improving our understanding starts with compiling the metrics into one dashboard. This type of dashboard should also be the 'report out' of the scenarios supporting the Executive IVP meeting.

Mapping and designing your executive dashboard

Gather your executive team, or a team of cross-functional experts. Ensure the different functions sales, marketing, R&D, operations, supply chain, procurement, finance, HR, IT are represented. You can couple this exercise to the earlier exercise of mapping and aligning your existing IVP meetings.

Review the IVP dashboard shown in Figure 8.4. You can start from an empty template, just showing the placeholders, like the one from Figure 8.3. Write down on sticky notes which KPIs you are following from which blocks. If you work with a large brown paper, you may try to cluster KPIs and indicate in which type of reports they are currently being captured. Once you have an overview of KPIs and reports, try to define in which meetings they are, or are not being reviewed.

Now ask yourself the question: do we have all of these metrics in one integrated overview? If no, do we see value in compiling them into one integrated overview? What do we lose by not having an integrated overview? What would be the challenges of interpreting one integrated overview?

Note: I have an empty dashboard template available for download from my website[2]. You may project it or print it on an A0, in which case you can use it as a visual support for a sticky note exercise.

Strategy-Driven Integrated Value Planning

So IVP is a key process that helps us to connect the different planning processes needed to manage our supply chain and business ecosystem introduced in Chapter 7 in Figure 7.2. It is also natively equipped to balance financial and non-financial metrics as captured in the IVP dashboard shown in Figure 8.3. To visualize that triple-bottom-line capability, I have added a Triple Triangle at the heart of the IVP process as shown in Figure 8.6. Instead of putting 'governance' at the heart, I have put 'strategy' at the heart, as I believe it is the strategy, above all, that defines how to trade-off these different metrics. Do we want to be at par, differentiating or dominating? And on which metrics? Hence I think it is fair to call the version shown in Figure 8.6 the 'Strategy-Driven Integrated Value Planning'.

The illustration in Figure 8.6 is comparable to an illustration I made 10 years ago on Sales & Operations Planning, with the typical steps of S&OP and the traditional Supply Chain Triangle at the heart. Though this illustration looks similar, it has a completely different meaning and impact, as we continue to explore after the case of Reckitt.

Figure 8.6 Strategy-Driven Integrated Value Planning

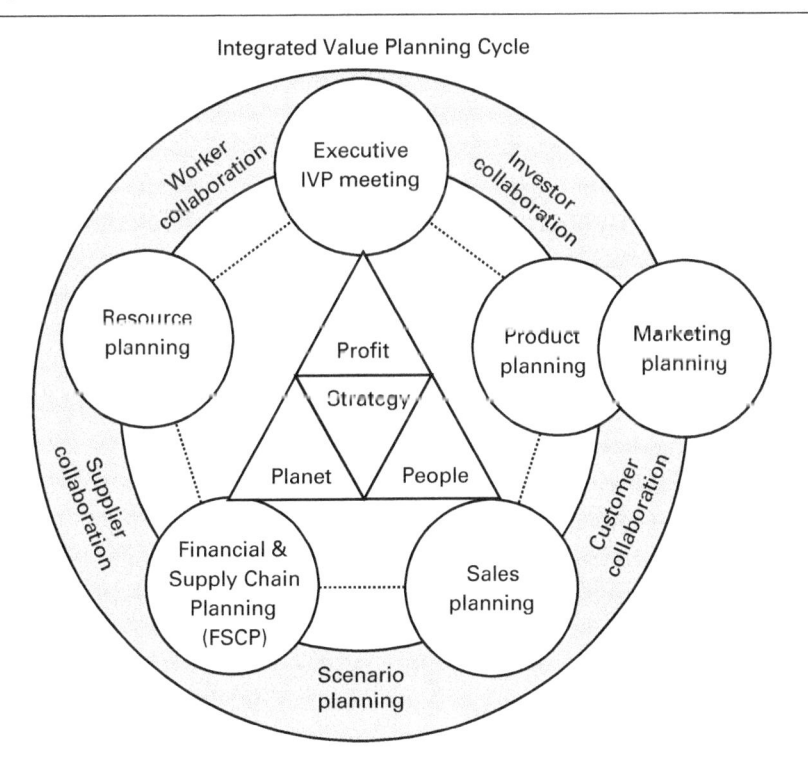

Case Study: RECKITT – Four-year supply chain planning transformation – as described by Alberto Lupano, SVP Group Supply Services Transformation

Reckitt exists to protect, heal and nurture in the pursuit of a cleaner, healthier world. It is the company behind some of the world's most recognisable and trusted consumer brands in hygiene, health and nutrition, including Air Wick, Dettol, Durex, Enfamil, Finish, Harpic, Lysol, Mucinex, Nurofen, Nutramigen, Strepsils, Vanish and more.

Reckitt undertook a major transformation of its supply chain planning processes, operating model and systems from 2020 through mid-2024, and is now leveraging its benefits to the business.

'Supply Chain Planning in general is an overlooked area of supply chain,' Alberto comments. 'It is not usually a big budget so it doesn't achieve a strong overall focus. Many companies didn't realize, pre-Covid, that planning is actually influencing a majority of their cost of sales.'

But the world has changed in recent years. 'Given issues such as Covid, geopolitics, climate change and extreme weather, there is now more risk in being slow to react. You need clarity on decision-making and cannot depend on weekly or monthly manual integration of processes and information flows.'

'Across industries people now understand the need for visibility and scenario planning. It is no surprise you see a lot of digital transformations in planning these days.'

When Alberto and his team defined the scope of the transformation, they decided to go big. 'There are not many opportunities to do this type of transformation within an organization, so we wanted to take it at full scale. The business case was built on driving growth through improving service, improving margins through reducing costs, generating cash through reducing inventory and improving asset utilization.'

All the elements you can find in the Supply Chain Triangle.

'Other elements included becoming more resilient by taking faster and better planning decisions, and working to be more sustainable by reducing the use of resources like water, CO_2 and energy that could be wasted through unoptimized inventory levels.'

The scope of Reckitt's transformation was end-to-end, considering short-, medium- and long-term planning horizons, from suppliers to customers and from raw materials to finished goods.

Implementing Integrated Value Planning through an eight-stage maturity model

What Alberto notices is that 'not many companies include the production scheduling and MRP in the plants, either because they already have a legacy system or they see it merely as a way to execute production, without optimizing it. Reckitt wanted to include it as we wanted to have the E2E connection, being able to simulate capacity constraints you have in each factory.'

Also not commonly included is the link to financial planning and commercial planning, which Reckitt wanted to align.

'The output of the S&OP/IBP process, the volumes, are the input for the financial planning process. This is to ensure that if volumes are committed in the supply chain planning tool and S&OP/IBP process, there is visibility on the financial impact through metrics like gross sales and gross margin. By connecting trade promotion management and optimization tools with supply chain planning systems, for example, you can increase intelligence for more efficient promotions.'

By extending the horizon of the S&OP/IBP, and by automating the connection between the supply chain and the financial plan, you get a seamless process.

About the integrated approach, Alberto comments that 'the idea of the transformation was not just a technology replacement. Technology is an enabler of new processes and a new operating model. So, the ambition is to install the processes of the future, the operating model of the future, supported by the system of the future, as the three are interlinked.'

An example of new process capabilities is scenario management.

'An enterprise scenario can be created where the planner can simulate a higher or lower forecast or capacity, and, when the planner is authorized, with the press of one button, the scenario can become the new enterprise scenario,' Alberto said.

A second example of how technology can support more advanced processes is 'concurrent planning'.

'Instead of the traditional waterfall approach, where you first run your demand plan through a DRP engine before passing it on to a supply planning engine, concurrent planning looks at the integrated supply chain at the same time through a concurrent planning model. In the waterfall you may realize only in step 2 or step 3 that what you've decided downstream as a plan doesn't fit with the upstream capacity.'

Regarding the operating model, Alberto talks about how Reckitt aimed to connect demand planners in markets with supply planners in factories by creating so-called connected planning control towers that link the two and facilitate communication and production allocations.

'Another role of the connected planning control towers is to specialize in certain tasks of demand planning. The "hard" side of demand planning – the number crunching, the statistical algorithms, the data science, is organized in the control tower. The relationship side of connecting with finance, with commercial people, remains in the countries, together with the enrichment of the statistical forecast with the local sales and marketing inputs. Reckitt has defined a segmentation on which SKUs, for instance low variability, are forecasted in the control tower, and which SKUs, for instance the higher variability, need to be forecasted in the countries.'

Next to the planning control towers, Reckitt has also created a group-level centre of excellence (CoE) with geographic hubs around the world. Alberto explains that the CoE supports the control towers with: 1) a focus on the system, to ensure that it is fully exploited and utilized with new functionality, 2) process compliance, to ensure that all processes are followed, and 3) data management, to ensure that Reckitt delivers the appropriate data quality, for the systems and processes to function properly.

'The CoE is the insurance policy of our transformation program,' Alberto says.

The planning transformation at Reckitt went through three phases. Alberto explains 'a first one was the thinking phase, where Reckitt designed the operating model, selected the new planning software, and designed the new processes. This phase started in early 2020, and went well with strong support across the company, as Covid made clear the difference that planning can make.'

He continues that

'the second phase is the deployment phase, which started mid-2022.

The deployment consisted of three workstreams. Demand planning, which is deployed per country or group of countries, and which after one year, covered around 75 per cent of global net revenue. The second stream is Supply planning, the process which calculates the net requirements for the plants, which is complex given how many countries and plants we have. Stream three is the factory planning deployed in each internal and external production unit.

Clear benefits already achieved include forecast accuracy improvements, inventory reductions, and better assets utilization due to the integrated planning approach,'

Alberto says.

The third and final phase of the transformation is adoption of the implemented changes in processes, systems and operating model. It is important to focus on this on an ongoing basis, in order to continue to sustain the benefits into the future.

Implementing Integrated Value Planning through an eight-stage maturity model

When it comes to the integration with key customers and key suppliers, Alberto comments that 'in the choice of the system, it was important to have connectivity options, to be able to give access to customers and suppliers to their parts of the data. In general, wherever Reckitt finds support from customers, we will move toward collaboration with projects like VMI or other forms of continuous replenishment. The customers upload their forecasts into their system as another element that can help to improve forecast accuracy.'

On the topic of sustainability, which is becoming more important for Reckitt and its customers and suppliers, Alberto says that he is 'intensively working on logistics-related sustainability metrics such as the CO_2 footprint from transport operations.' This is part of Reckitt's measurement across its business of metrics such as consumption of energy and water.

When looking at the case of Reckitt through the lens of our Integrated Value Planning model summarized in Figure 7.6, it confirms a number of findings true of many companies. First, that there has historically been room to increase investment in supply chain planning and business planning, especially after Covid increased awareness on the need for supply chain maturity.

Second, it confirms how important it is that different functions have well-connected processes and tools. With many other companies still lacking an overall business planning architecture that defines the overall data model and how data should flow between the pieces of the puzzle, integrations still risk being manual, which can lead to unwanted mistakes, delays or costs.

Mapping Reckitt to our eight-stage maturity model, I believe Reckitt is currently moving itself into a solid level 5 maturity, with elements of the higher levels, like integration with sales planning, or connecting with key customers and suppliers. The achievement of the Reckitt team is impressive. Getting to a level 5, is today best in class. However, as we have argued previously in this chapter, we believe it is not the industry's end point, and we hope the models introduced here will help manufacturers such as Reckitt envision where to go next.

The drag of functional organizations and functional silos

When re-reading the book of Rummler and Brache, I understood that what I was seeing in the Supply Chain Triangle was very real, insidious and even pernicious. How different functions with their different objectives are pulling different sides of the triangle and causing unbalance and financial value loss. Think about the examples shown in Figure 1.2 all the way at the start of this book.

When they talk about 'managing the white space on the organization chart', Rummler and Brache make the implicit point that as companies, we seem to have forgotten that value flows across the silos. We seem to be in a situation where the silos have 'taken over'. They have taken over to pursue their own objectives, starting from their 'own reality', and the impact that they directly control. It seems like we got used to the conflicts and unbalances that it creates. We don't seem to consider them harmful, nor do we feel the need or urge to move away from this conflict model into something more balanced and more harmonious.

The increased volatility we discussed in Chapter 3 and the impact of the lack of agility discussed in Chapter 4 doesn't seem to be a major concern. It makes me think of the apologue of the boiling frog in the following way. First, I would have expected us to jump out of the boiling water during the heavy volatility and disturbances of the Covid-19 pandemic, i.e., change the way we plan and run our business. Second, as volatility and temperatures have cooled down a bit, we seem to think it is actually quite cozy and familiar. As mentioned earlier in Chapter 3, I'm puzzled by the lack of action within companies.

Figure 8.7 shows an update of the 'functional metrics and responsibilities' and in Figure 8.8 we show how they lead to tension in the triangle. These were introduced in my first book *Supply Chain Strategy and Financial Metrics*[3] as a basis to capture the behaviour observed in Figure 1.2. Next to functional service-cost-cash or financial metrics, I have now also added some functional social and environmental metrics I increasingly see popping up.

The sustainability metrics can conflict with the financial metrics or the core Supply Chain Triangle. Think about last-minute change-overs, leading to extra food loss, overtime and work pressure to close a service gap because of an unplanned promotion. The sustainability metrics are potentially also conflicting on their own. Developing healthier and or eco-friendly products may temporarily create more waste or require overtime as my plants are being fully utilized.

In Figure 8.9 we have added the functional planning processes discussed in Figure 7.6. They further strengthen the functional silos and the functional focus. On the one hand it may feel safe as in this way 'everybody knows what to do and what is expected'. At the same time, you feel it is full of inherent though hidden conflicts that will pop up on a continuous basis and continuously derail you from your targeted outcome.

Implementing Integrated Value Planning through an eight-stage maturity model

Figure 8.7 Functional metrics and responsibilities in a traditional organization chart

Environmental ceiling:	Waste reduction	CO_2 from transport	Eco-friendly products	Increase return flows

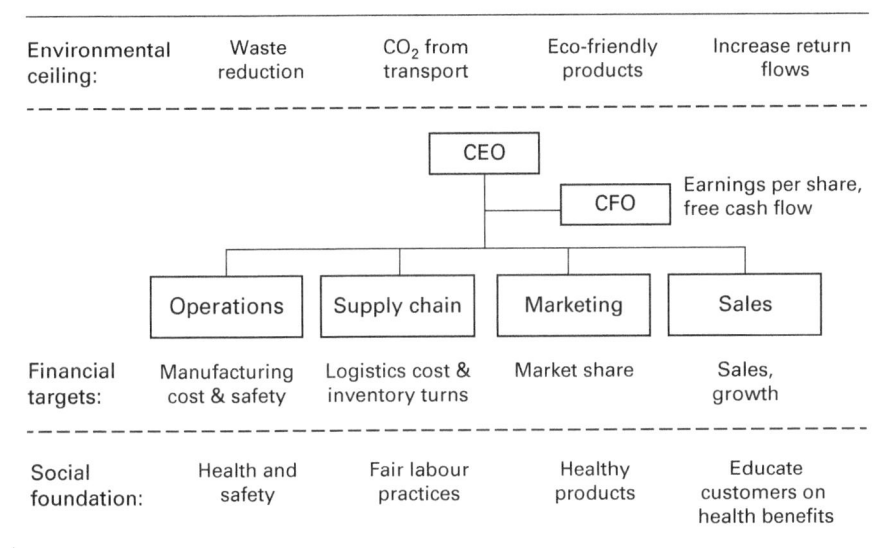

```
                    CEO
                     |
                    CFO  —  Earnings per share, free cash flow
     ┌──────────┬────┴─────┬──────────┐
 Operations  Supply chain  Marketing    Sales
```

Financial targets:	Manufacturing cost & safety	Logistics cost & inventory turns	Market share	Sales, growth

Social foundation:	Health and safety	Fair labour practices	Healthy products	Educate customers on health benefits

Figure 8.8 Functional metrics leading to imbalance in the triangle, the social foundation and the environmental ceiling

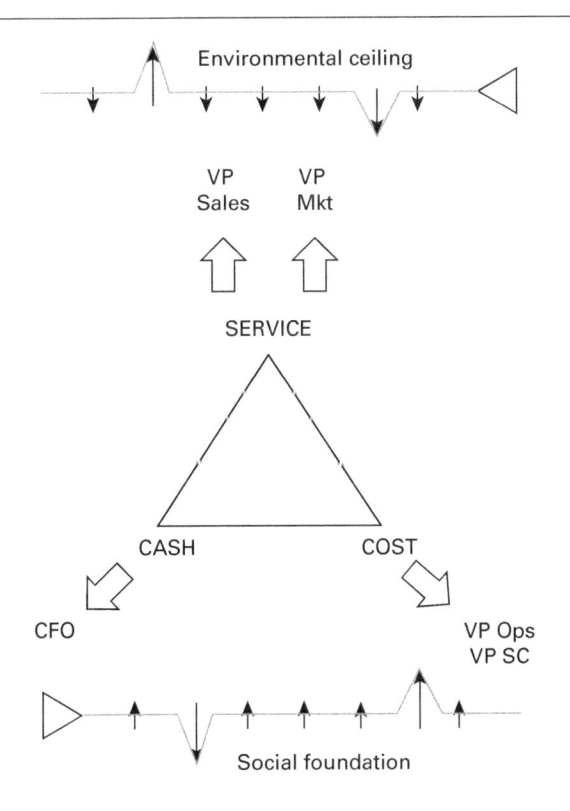

Environmental ceiling

VP Sales VP Mkt

SERVICE

CASH   COST

CFO   VP Ops
                       VP SC

Social foundation

Figure 8.9 Functional metrics and planning processes leading to imbalance in the triangle, the social foundation and the environmental ceiling

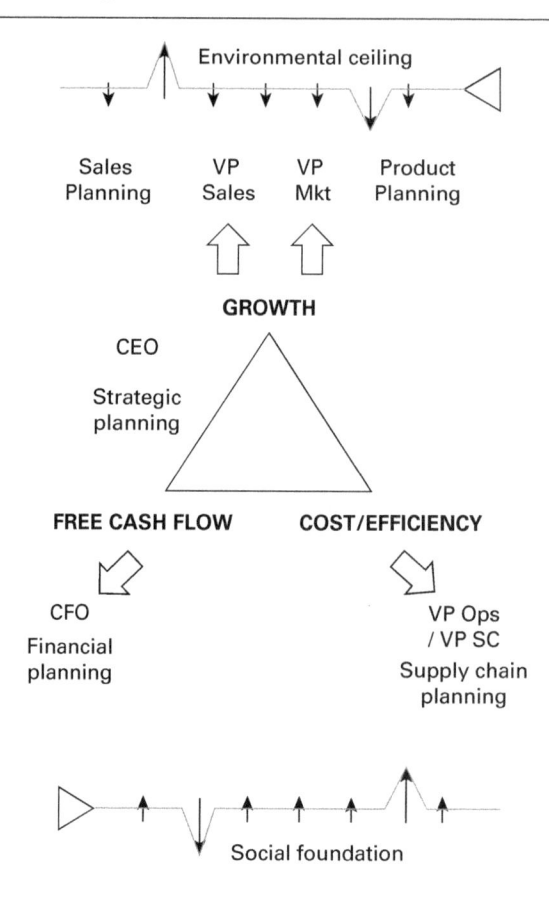

Cross functional balance and the Chief Value Planning Officer

In Figure 8.10 we show an alternative for the 'conflict-driven' model, namely a more 'strategy and value-driven' model. It retakes some elements I first proposed in my second book *The Strategy-Driven Supply Chain*[4]. A first is that balance doesn't come by itself. If we want balance, we'll need to organize it. One of the possible ideas is to have shared targets. In practice I have seen that when everybody is responsible for inventory, basically nobody is responsible. If sales has 20 per cent of its variable compensation linked to inventory or forecast accuracy, they'll disregard it as they don't think they control it anyway. They'll focus on those elements where they think they have the bigger impact. So my conclusion was and remains that it is OK to have functional targets and strong functions. It is OK for sales to wake up in the morning and being concerned about the top-line growth and our market share, or for procurement to wake up and think through how we can buy more sustainably but at a lower overall cost. But we need to build something that bridges the functions and shows us the broader impact of our intentions and our decisions, as those considerations clearly don't happen automatically.

So in the 'strategy and value-driven' model, I have created a new role called the 'Chief Value Planning Officer'. That CVPO is running the strategic planning, ensuring that the necessary trade-offs between financial metrics like gross margin and capital employed are being made, and ensuring that trade-offs between financial, resilience and sustainability objectives are being made. The CVPO ensures that all of this is integrated into a strategy-driven sustainable and resilient supply chain design, our story of Chapters 5 and 6, and that we follow that through with our Integrated Value Planning introduced in Chapter 7. As a basis for the Integrated Value Planning, the CVPO runs the integrated Financial and Supply Chain Plan or FSCP introduced in Chapter 7 as well. Functional strength is good, but it needs to be balanced by a strong role that is running cross-functional balancing processes.

There are three important evolutions from what I first presented in my second book. A first is obviously that the set of metrics the CVPO takes into account have expanded from Return On Capital Employed, as a balancing financial metric, to whatever key ambitions we have defined on our social foundation and our environmental ceiling. The CVPO will ensure that strategic trade-offs are properly addressed, for instance, do we want to be more resilient and sustainable through regional sourcing and production if that requires extra CAPEX and OPEX and at least temporarily negatively impacts ROCE. The CVPO will bring those discussions to the table, including the full sustainability aspect.

Second, I have called it the CVPO instead of the CSCO. Though supply chain is a good candidate to balance the triangle, defining a new role is less controversial. It focuses the discussion on 'do we think this role makes sense and what type of capabilities would be needed' rather than trigger a political debate about the untamed ambition of supply chain.

Third, I believe more decisions should be made by cross-functional committees rather than being the presumed prerogative of one single department. I have two concrete examples, but I intend to gradually expand the list. A first is the decision on 'customer order lead times' and 'make-to-stock/make-to-order'. As introduced in Chapter 3, I see many companies where this is decided by sales, as sales is in touch with the client, and where the rest of the organization has to accept. As sales cannot judge the impact of this on costs or inventories, the decision should not be left to sales alone. I already suggested making it the decision of a 'service design committee', with representatives from marketing, sales, customer service, supply chain, manufacturing and R&D. They should analyse what is common in the market, what is the customer willing to pay for, what type of MTO lead times make sense for manufacturing, what are the options to reduce MTO lead times for instance by redesign products for postponement and last-minute differentiation. The committee should make a proposal, that can be validated by the CEO. The CVPO and his office would be good candidates to chair these committee meetings and moderate the debates.

A second example is deciding on the target inventory level. I see many companies where this is decided by finance and where the rest of the organization must simply accept. As finance cannot judge the impact of this on costs or on service, the decision should not be left to finance alone. Here again I propose a cross-functional committee that evaluates the options and makes a proposal to be validated by the CEO.

If we design our service promise poorly, it is a drag on the financial and non-financial performance of our triangle. Think about the earlier mentioned case of a company promising different lead times to different customers on a portfolio of 80,000 stock keeping units. There is no way you can reliably deliver upon that promise so it will be a continuous drag on your financial and non-financial performance. The same for unrealistic or high-level inventory targets. Cutting 10 per cent across the board can never be the optimal solution, though it is very common. If we really need to cut 10 per cent, then let a cross-functional team propose where exactly to take the impact and where to protect the business and clarify any trade-offs with cost or with service upfront.

So, in summary, we should balance the functional drag created by our historically strong functions, with a cross-functional counter-weight, the Chief Value Planning Officer or CVPO. That CVPO is the person that can run the strategy-driven, sustainable and resilient, supply chain design from Chapters 5 and 6. It is the person that can run the Integrated Value Planning or IVP process defined in Chapters 7 and 8. As we will continue to explore in a next section, in complex and dynamic environments, we need to ensure we bring the relevant experts together to get a 360° view of the situation at

Implementing Integrated Value Planning through an eight-stage maturity model

Figure 8.10 Complementing functional metrics and planning processes with cross-functional metrics and planning processes to improve balance

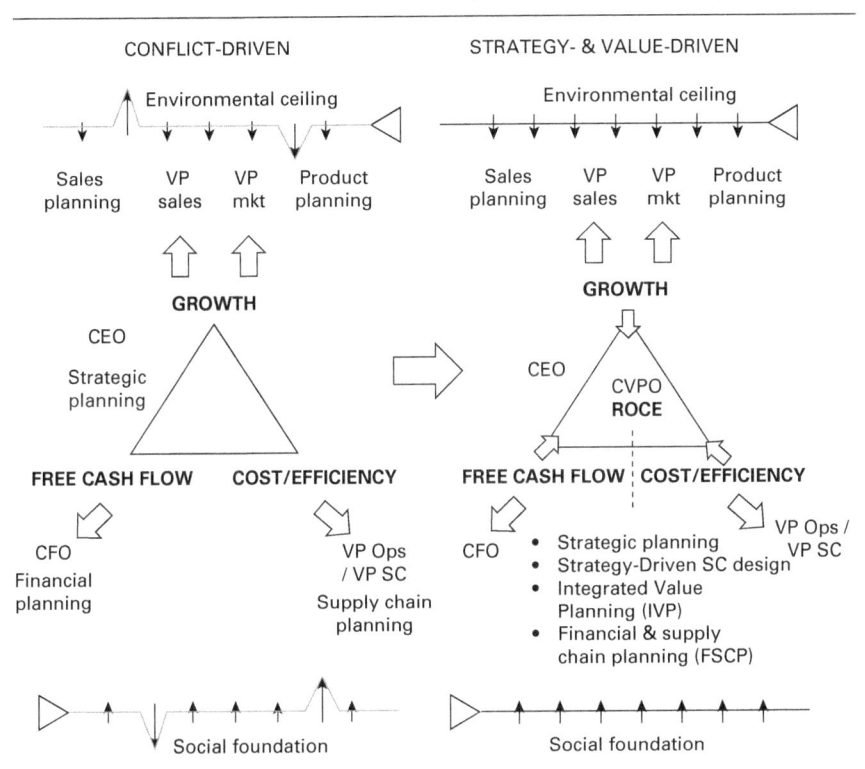

hand and come to joint decisions, for the best possible outcome of the 'system', not the 'functions'. Think about the examples of service design and setting inventory targets. Anything cross-functional would beneficially be driven by that new CVPO office.

Organizing for complex and dynamic environments

Henry Mintzberg is one of the founding fathers of organization theory and organizational behaviour. Table 8.1 is taken from his book *The structuring of organizations* from 1979[5]. Mintzberg comments that simple, stable environments give rise to centralized, bureaucratic structures. The classic organizational type that relies on standardization of work processes as the

Table 8.1 Four basic organizational environments according to Henry Mintzberg

	Stable	**Dynamic**
Complex	Decentralized Bureaucratic (standardization of skills)	Decentralized Organic (mutual adjustment)
Simple	Centralized Bureaucratic (standardization of work processes)	Centralized Organic (direct supervision)

'coordinating mechanism' (ensuring that people know what is expected from them to do or decide). Complex, stable environments lead to structures that are bureaucratic but decentralized. These organizations try to standardize skills, for instance by standardizing knowledge through formal training programmes. They are decentralized, which means they pass authority down the line, to the managers of the line functions, and horizontally, to support staff, your experts, think about your supply chain analytics team.

When an environment is dynamic but nevertheless simple, the organization requires the flexibility of an organic structure, but its power can remain centralized. Think about an entrepreneurial firm where the organization structure can quickly change but the chief executive maintains tight, personal control. But as you can imagine, the most relevant for many companies today is what to do when the dynamic environment is complex. On that Mintzberg states that 'the organization must decentralize to managers and specialists who can comprehend the issues yet allow them to interact flexibly in an organic structure so that they can respond to unpredictable changes. And, mutual adjustment emerges as the prime coordinating mechanism.'

In his book Mintzberg describes how in a complex and dynamic environment the traditional 'machine bureaucracy' as he calls it doesn't work. As too many ad hoc issues fall outside of the written procedures and need to pass often all the way up the chain of command for discussion and approval, the 'strategic apex' as he calls it, the top management, becomes a gigantic bottleneck. It also withholds that 'strategic apex' from its strategic discussions. In that sense it is slowing down decision making in the here and now, and withholding thinking and decision making for the future success of the company. A more appropriate organization form for complex and dynamic environments is called the 'adhocracy'. It is more decentralized: puts the power in the hands of managers and specialists who can comprehend the issues, it is more

Implementing Integrated Value Planning through an eight-stage maturity model

organic: build structures as needed to respond to unpredictable changes, and it looks for mutual adjustment: we continuously align our decisions with those of our peers as to maximize the overall output.

When I was looking for extra academic backup or input on 'how to get organized' for a complex and dynamic environment, I was surprised that I could not readily find more recent or better information. How to deal with functional versus shared cross-functional targets in incentive plans? How do we come to decisions as an executive team? How does that depend on the environment we're operating in? All obvious and important questions but when talking to colleague HR professors I didn't necessarily get clear answers.

I did want to share what Henry Mintzberg gives as an indication as I believe it supports the case for 'decision making through cross functional teams'. Some teams or committees could be relatively fixed, like reviewing our service design or inventory targets on a yearly basis. Some teams or committees could be ad hoc like how to deal with the Ever Given blocking the Suez Canal, or how to deal with a big competitor opening a new plant close to ours with the promise of a four-day work week (thinking back of one of the scenarios from the Infineon case in Chapter 6). A combination of different functions and different experts will help us to get a good 360° view. If we have good integrated metrics like ROCE from a financial perspective and our key priorities are clear from a sustainability perspective, that should enable people to make firm recommendations for CEO and/or exco approval.

From 5 to 8 maturity stages and from S&OP to IVP

As introduced in Chapter 7, for many companies it is a long road towards properly integrating planning. Many companies are stuck on the level 1 or 2 of the 5 stage maturity model shown in Figure 7.5. Moreover, we are lacking momentum or a burning platform, even after all the issues we have seen in the turbulent Covid period. To clarify the challenge on hand and to provide a roadmap for companies, I have extended the five-stage maturity model into an eight-stage maturity model based on the integrated planning framework shown in Figure 7.6. The eight stages are summarized in Figure 8.11 and Figure 8.12.

Stage 1 till 4 are the same as in Figure 7.5, they are about getting the basic information together to do a proper supply chain planning, not based on volumes and cost, but based on margins. Sales & Operations Planning (S&OP) or Integrated Business Planning (IBP) never had the ambition nor the courage to integrate Financial Planning (& Analysis, FP&A) and Supply

Chain Planning (SCP) into one single Financial & Supply Chain Planning (FSCP). They were rather talking about aligning the two worlds. As discussed in Chapter 7, we believe this is not just inefficient, it is also ineffective, as we keep starving supply chain from the proper financial information and finance from the proper operational information to steer the business in volatile times. Splitting the two processes is the inverse of agility, it creates delays and disconnects. We have shown in Figure 7.8 that the core of the planning processes overlaps. The systems are capable of doing it, the data is there, it is primarily due to the lack of understanding and the lack of willingness in both worlds. It is time to set aside egos and make a step forward in professionalizing our planning processes.

In Figure 8.11 we define an integration of financial and supply chain planning as the stage 5 maturity. It should be the solid base on which we build next steps. It doesn't make sense to integrate sustainability (stage 6) if we can't properly control and trade them off against financial metrics. It doesn't make sense to integrate key customers or suppliers (stage 8) if we don't first connect the internal processes. We wouldn't be able to properly leverage the effort we put in from both sides. The illustration for the FSCP we have used in Figure 8.11 is the triangle linked to financial metrics such as ROCE, with the integrated SCP and FP&A at the heart. The financial metrics go beyond the ROCE show in the illustration and for sure include for example the working capital forecast and free cash flow forecasts introduced in Figure 7.8.

Once we have a proper integration of the financial and operational view of the world, in stage 6, we can add the sustainability dimensions and start trading off decisions based on service, cost, cash and sustainability metrics like CO_2. In Figure 8.11 we have shown the triangle between its environmental ceiling and its social foundation. As advocated above, we are in favour of creating an 'e-liability accounting' capability. Just like we accumulate costs when we produce, we accumulate e-liabilities like CO_2. If we want to truly understand and control our scope 1 emissions, this is a needed core capability at stage 6.

In stage 7, we start properly connecting the product, marketing, sales and resource plans. In stage 6, when the proper connection is not there, we either simply miss information or we make assumptions that are either validated ad hoc or on a recurrent basis through for instance a product management review meeting. At level 6 however, the information is either not updated or it is updated manually which makes it slow and prone to error. Improving our agility, flexibility, accuracy and resilience, will require the more proper

Implementing Integrated Value Planning through an eight-stage maturity model

Figure 8.11 From five to eight maturity stages and from S&OP to Integrated Value Planning – 1

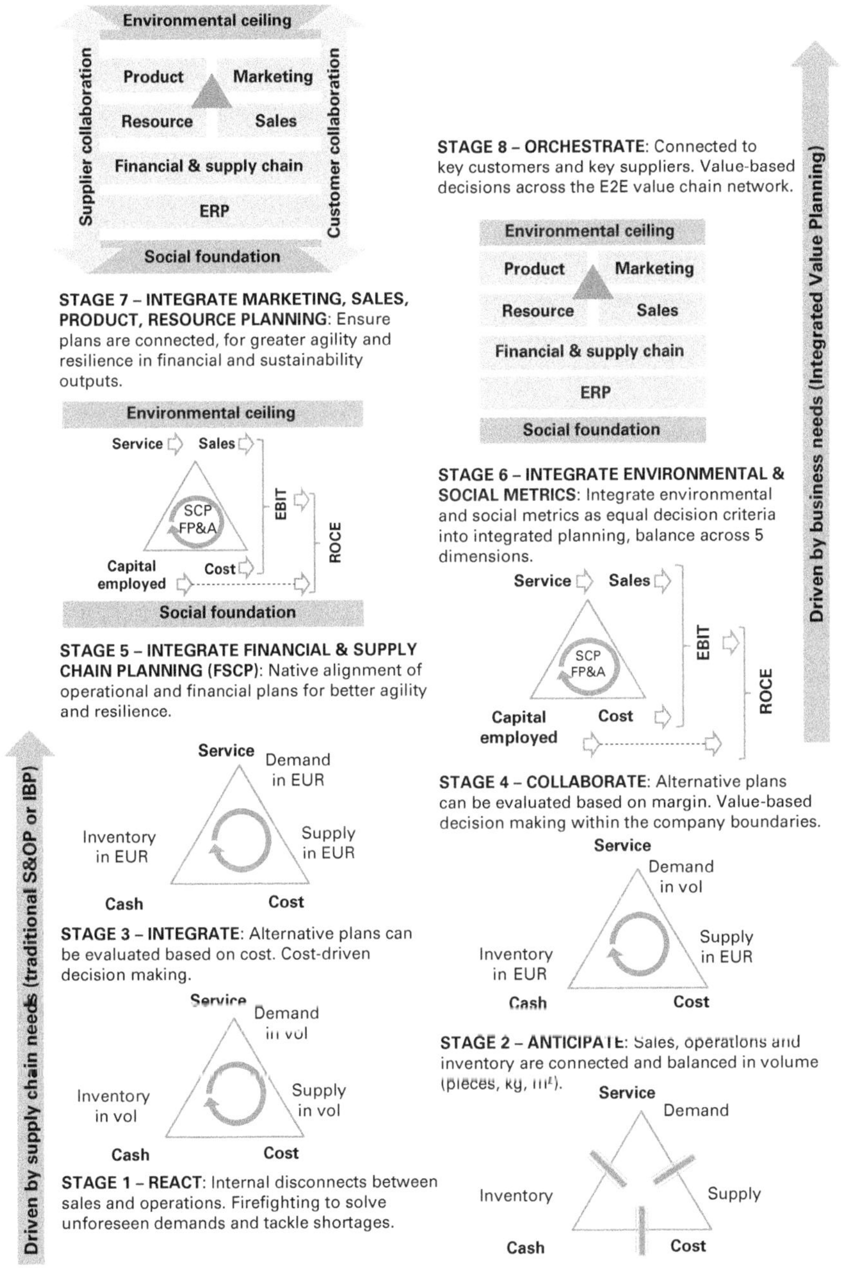

STAGE 8 – ORCHESTRATE: Connected to key customers and key suppliers. Value-based decisions across the E2E value chain network.

STAGE 7 – INTEGRATE MARKETING, SALES, PRODUCT, RESOURCE PLANNING: Ensure plans are connected, for greater agility and resilience in financial and sustainability outputs.

STAGE 6 – INTEGRATE ENVIRONMENTAL & SOCIAL METRICS: Integrate environmental and social metrics as equal decision criteria into integrated planning, balance across 5 dimensions.

STAGE 5 – INTEGRATE FINANCIAL & SUPPLY CHAIN PLANNING (FSCP): Native alignment of operational and financial plans for better agility and resilience.

STAGE 4 – COLLABORATE: Alternative plans can be evaluated based on margin. Value-based decision making within the company boundaries.

STAGE 3 – INTEGRATE: Alternative plans can be evaluated based on cost. Cost-driven decision making.

STAGE 2 – ANTICIPATE: Sales, operations and inventory are connected and balanced in volume (pieces, kg, m³).

STAGE 1 – REACT: Internal disconnects between sales and operations. Firefighting to solve unforeseen demands and tackle shortages.

Driven by supply chain needs (traditional S&OP or IBP)

Driven by business needs (Integrated Value Planning)

and structural integration introduced in Figure 7.9. That is the work to be done at stage 7. In Figure 8.11, we have used a simplified version of Figure 7.9 as the illustration for stage 7.

In stage 8, we can structurally connect key customers and key suppliers and start to 'Orchestrate' the extended value chain. Orchestrate is the current level 5 of Gartner as shown in Figure 7.5. We believe there are important steps to be made in between to be able to truly orchestrate. Integrating key customers and suppliers will increase complexity, so it is import we first simplify our internal complexity, for instance by natively integrating financial and supply chain planning. We believe that creating a capability to trade-off a broader set of financial and non-financial metrics is more critical as an organizational capability than improving the information inflow going into it, hence the introduction of stage 6 as a step in between. If we want to structurally capture the collaboration with key customers and suppliers, it is important that we first properly integrate the internal planning processes in stage 7, before indeed connecting and orchestrating the extended value chain in stage 8. We might say that the Gartner version of orchestrate in Figure 7.5 is the 'supply chain version', what do we need to be able to run our supply chain. The version of orchestrate we have shown in Figure 8.11 is the 'business version', what do we need to be able to run our modern day business.

We believe the fundamental shift when we extend from 5 to 8 maturity stages, is that we extend the maturity from a supply chain to a business view. As shown in Figure 8.11, the stages 1 to 4 are driven by supply chain needs, what information do I need to run my supply chain. It has been the traditional view of supply chain centred processes like Sales & Operations Planning (S&OP) or Integrated Business Planning (IBP). The stages 5 to 8 are driven by business needs, what information do I need to run my business. It makes us feel uncomfortable as it tries to structurally bridge the silos and connect the previously disconnected islands. The problem is not technical, the systems and the data are basically there. The problem is psychological, it has to do with letting go of our illusion of control when we are on our disconnected islands, and letting go of our egos, and become just one small part in the bigger picture rather than a bigger part in our smaller functional picture.

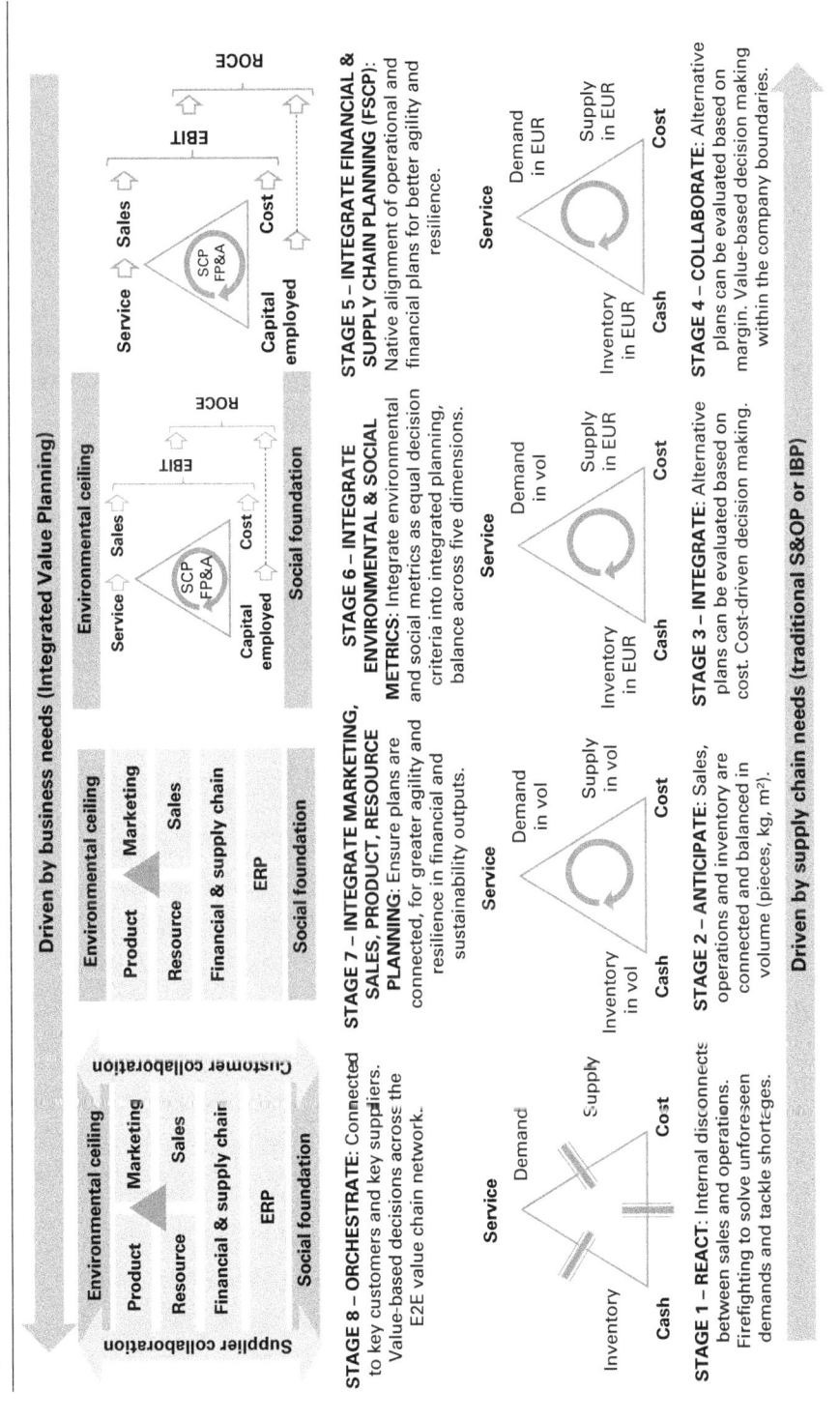

Figure 8.12 From five to eight maturity stages and from S&OP to Integrated Value Planning – 2

EXERCISE
Assessing your stage 1 to 8 IVP maturity

On my website, I have made available a quick survey (5–10 minutes), that can help you assess where you are in your level 1 to 8 maturity. The survey is built as such that we try to define one level on which you have a 'firm' performance, knowing you may have notions of the higher levels. We may run into inconsistencies, where based on the questions you think you are firm on one of the higher levels while still lacking maturity at one of the lower levels. We will reveal those inconsistencies and would be happy to follow-up with you where they come from. The survey is available from: https://www.bramdesmet.com/rethinkingsupplychain/.

In preparation of a workshop with your executive team, or a team of cross-functional experts, send the survey to the corresponding group. As before, ensure the different functions sales, marketing, R&D, operations, supply chain, procurement, finance, HR, IT are represented. This can be done through the website, we will provide you with the compiled results before your actual workshop.

Download an infographic on the eight-stage IVP maturity model from my website[6] and print it on A0. Use the 'pentagon' from Figure 8.6 to explain the IVP process (template also available for download) and then use the infographic to explain the different maturity levels.

Before you show the survey results, hand-out three colours of sticky notes or stickers: green, orange and red. Ask people to sticker each of the maturity levels, with their assumption on whether you are 'firm' (green), 'have notions' (orange) or it is currently 'absent'. Ask people to think through individually, and then have them start stickering. Interpret the results. Are they consistent? Are there important differences? Allow people to explain why they believe something is green, orange or red. Part of the discussion will be about definitions. What does it take to be a 'firm' level 4 or a level 5? Those discussions are OK, aligning on the definitions is part of the exercise. Different people may have a different understanding of what is already done and what is not. These are relevant insights to be brought forward in the discussion.

Then contrast with the survey results. Do they point in the same direction? Where do they? Where not? Do the same differences pop up amongst people? More discussions on definitions and different understandings of what is or is not happening already can be expected.

Implementing Integrated Value Planning through an eight-stage maturity model

Then close off with the question on whether this is an issue? Are we OK with where we are or do we believe we need to improve? Which of the levels is most appealing to us? Where do we see the biggest benefit?

If you have done the earlier exercises from Chapter 4, especially the one on 'the impact of a lack of agility', the inverse fishbone from Figure 4.1, remind people what Integrated Value Planning is trying to solve and how it contributes to more financial and non-financial value generation and better realizing our strategic value proposition.

From second generation to fourth generation supply chain

As a cross check, and to close this chapter, let's revisit whether we have answered the questions raised in Chapter 4 when we introduced the tactical planning capabilities in second versus fourth generation supply chains. We have recapped Table 4.2 as Table 8.2 below.

Connecting sales, operations and procurement, is the stage 2 in our maturity model shown in Figure 8.11, the full integration with financial planning we defined as stage 5. Including of sustainability metrics to be able to trade them off against financial or any other metrics is part of stage 6, and in stage 7 we integrated the other internal plans like portfolio and product lifecycle and the trade promotion planning. In stage 8 we connect key customers and key suppliers into our extended ecosystem view. So yes, we can confirm that the concept of Integrated Value Planning tackles the challenges described in Chapter 4, as is apparent from the different maturity stages, it is something that may need to be built in steps rather than going all the way from maturity level 1 to maturity level 8. Along the way we'll also need to change our organization model and create a stronger cross-functional role which we called the Chief Value Planning Officer, and we will need to take more decisions with cross-functional teams instead of relying on 1 function in the assumption that is needed to better understand the full 'system' impact.

The bottom of Table 8.2 leaves us with 'reluctant to invest'. As I repeated throughout this chapter, I miss a sense of urgency within executive teams to really get this moving. Managing conflicts in the triangle seems to be our comfort zone. The only organization form we have learned is the machine bureaucracy and we don't see how it is holding us back. My last resort

Table 8.2 Tactical planning capabilities in a second versus fourth generation supply chain

Second generation supply chain	Fourth generation supply chain
Weak connection between sales, operations and purchasing	Connected between sales, operations and procurement
Poor portfolio and product (life cycle) management	Portfolio and product (life cycle) management as a key planning process
Disconnected from trade promotion planning	Connected with trade promotion planning
Disconnected from financial planning	Integrated with financial planning
Disconnected from key customers	Integrated with key customers
Disconnected from key suppliers	Integrated with key suppliers
Resilience eats sustainability for breakfast	We trade-off resilience and sustainability
Reluctant to invest	Fear Of Missing Out (FOMO)

creating a burning platform has been the extension of the Gartner maturity model and defining 8 as opposed to 5 stages. Realizing that you are a level 1 or 2 may still be acceptable on a total of 5, but being a 1 or 2 on a scale of 8 becomes really embarrassing. So instead of fear of missing out (FOMO) it might trigger a GOOTDZ (Get Out Of The Danger Zone) and it may create a push for companies to at least become a 5 or a 6, which would already be a huge step forward.

We can also only hope that the clarification of where 'supply chain stops' and 'where the business needs take over', will help people to stop seeing this as a supply chain (only) process. Supply chain is where it comes from, as supply chain is today linking the pieces in the operational Supply Chain Triangle. But it is a broader business need and obligation, to better balance that triangle, better understand how it balances with our sustainability objectives, how to trade it off with resiliency needs. It is also an obligation to be more responsive, by being more integrated in our planning, and by being more organic and decentralized and looking for 'mutual adjustment', to respond to our complex and dynamic environments. We hope all of these ingredients will be helpful to companies to move forward and tackle their business challenges in a more strategy-driven and integrated way.

Conclusion

In this chapter we introduced the IVP process, with its different steps, how to compile information for the Executive IVP meeting into an Executive IVP dashboard. I introduced how to organize for IVP success, through the creation of a new role, the Chief Value Planning Officer or CVPO, which is running the IVP process, the underlying FSCP (Financial and Supply Chain Planning) process, which is running strategic planning and the Strategy-Driven Sustainable and Resilient Supply Chain Design, with a balancing financial metric like ROCE, and with key sustainability metrics as the compass. I discussed how organizing for IVP success leverages cross functional committees for key decisions, getting a 360° view, for instance when designing our service promises, or when defining inventory targets. It aligns with the suggestion of Henry Mintzberg to decentralize decisions in more organic organization structures, and use mutual adjustment as the primary coordinating mechanism. In other words, in our complex and dynamic worlds we need to put more trust into nimble cross-functional teams of managers and experts that make or propose decisions.

To make things practical and tangible, I have built an eight-stage IVP maturity model, that defines the different stages companies can go through. The case of Reckitt gives insight into how challenging this type of transformation is. With its ongoing planning transformation, Reckitt will brings its capabilities to a solid level 3 or 4, which is fantastic in the old Gartner world of 5 maturity stages, but is only halfway the eight maturity stages, when taking a 'systems' or 'business' or 'Integrated Value Planning' perspective.

At the end of the chapter, we were able to confirm that yes, Integrated Value Planning meets the requirements of tactical planning and steering in a fourth generation supply chain. We are still uncertain on how to unlock more investment and make people more ambitious and courageous in the planning transformations. Maybe being a level 1 or 2 on a scale of 8 will make it obvious to non-supply chain experts that something has to be done, but only time will tell!

Endnotes

1. B DeSmet. Integrated Value Planning Pentagon, 2024. https://www.bramdesmet.com/wp-content/uploads/2024/03/ReThinking_Template_IVP-Pentagon.pdf (archived at https://perma.cc/BAJ7-E9LQ)
2. B DeSmet. KPI dashboard template, 2024. https://www.bramdesmet.com/wp-content/uploads/2024/03/ReThinking_Template_KPI-Dashboard.pdf (archived at https://perma.cc/BTV7-ZF7R)
3. B DeSmet (2018) *Supply Chain Strategy And Financial Metrics: The supply chain triangle of service, cost and cash*, Kogan Page, London
4. B DeSmet (2021) *The Strategy-Driven Supply Chain: Integrating strategy, finance and supply chain for a competitive edge*, Kogan Page, London
5. H Mintzberg (1979) *The Structuring Of Organizations*, Prentice Hall, London
6. B DeSmet. Eight stage maturity model for Integrated Value Planning, 2024. https://www.bramdesmet.com/wp-content/uploads/2024/03/ReThinking_Template_8-Stage-IVP-Maturity.pdf (archived at https://perma.cc/6UEE-UYY6)

Conclusion

So, the world has changed. From the simple times of the 'Friedman doctrine', where increasing the shareholder value was the single objective of a company, we have entered an age where we have a responsibility for different sources of scarce capital, including social capital and environmental capital. Where we have a responsibility for a broader set of stakeholders, including the people and the societies we work with, and the future generations for which we need to preserve our planet. We have to become sustainable.

The world has changed, as it has become more volatility, and we need to become more resilient. If we don't do so, we will never be sustainable. As a lack of resilience puts pressure on our people, is wasting scarce resources and is increasing our carbon footprint.

If the world is changing, supply chain management needs to change as well. We need to embark on the fourth generation supply chain, which is five dimensional. It is not just about service, cost or cash or about financial metrics and capital, it is also about managing our social and environmental metrics and capital. Is about understanding and managing the harm and the good we can do.

In this book, I have tried to provide practical tools on how to manage that fourth generation supply chain, with proper fourth generation capabilities. On the strategic level, by including sustainability and resilience into our strategic trade-offs, and into our strategy-driven – sustainable and resilient – supply chain design. On the tactical level, through the new concept of Integrated Value Planning or IVP, that goes beyond supply chain and takes a broader business and ecosystems perspective, which requires rebalancing the power in the executive team, and takes decision making to a broader set of metrics.

Throughout this book I argued that supply chain is underinvested. There is a lack of urgency to improve our supply chain capabilities. I tried to clarify the impact of running a fourth generation supply chain with second generation capabilities. I may be naïve but I hope that a better understanding will increase the sense of urgency. I hope that the many exercises in the book will be the starting point of many intense discussions in as many executive teams and it will help in getting the ball rolling.

As illustrated with the eight-step maturity model for IVP, the road will be long and challenging for most of the companies, given our current level 1 or 2. Here again, by explaining what needs to be done and by revealing how far off we are, I hope it will clarify we need to move and we need to move now. I hope it will helping facing the brutal facts, as the start of a transformation.

This book is a snapshot of where I am in my personal journey. You will have thoughts, ideas and questions. You will see things and have perspectives that I haven't seen or discovered yet. So please reach out to me and let's have a discussion. Let's keep exploring and pushing the boundaries of supply chain thinking, together, for a greater good, for a broader and better impact.

INDEX

Note: Page numbers in *italics* refer to tables or figures.

Abeelen, Mark van 203–05
Afound 15–16
AI (Artificial intelligence) 87, 239
Air Wick 284
Amsterdam 33
AND-AND 6–7
APS (Advanced Planning System) 247
Arcelor Mittal 26
ARKET 15–16
Automotive Resin 94, 95–96, *95*, *96*

B corporations 185
B Lab 184
B2B companies 265–66
Backaert, Christian 98
Bakery Products (BP) 55
Bangladesh 103
Barcelona 33
Ben & Jerry's 181, 182
bike industry, case study 133, 137–42, *137*
  'assemble-to-order'(ATO) supply chain 139–42, *140*, *141*, *142*
  traditional 137–38, *137*
Bill-of- Materials (BOMs) 261, 270
biodiversity 25
blind forecast 103
Bloomberg 108, 197
Blue Ocean Strategies 160–61
Bluebell Capital Partners 121
The Body Shop 166, 167, 183
BOMs. *See* Bill-of-Materials (BOMs)
Brache, Alan 239–47, *240*, *246*
Bridgestone 69
Brussels 33
'bubble analysis' 97, *97*

Callebaut, Barry 182
Canada 47
Cannibals with Forks (Elkington) 1, 23
CAPEX 129, 132, 171, 176, 258, 275
CECONOMY 175
Central Africa 33
centre of excellence (CoE) 286
Chan Kim 160, 161
Changing World Order: Why Nations Succeed and Fail, The (Dalio) 119
ChannelX 175

Chief Sustainability Officer 176
'Chief Value Planning Officer' (CVPO) 273, 291–93, *293*, 303
Child Labor Monitoring and Remediation System (CLMRS) 180, 183
China 30, 47
Christopher, Martin 6
circular supply chain design 196–205, *200*
  Ricoh *195*, 201–05, 232–33
  R-ladder 198–99
Clockspeed (Fine) 134
CO_2 245–47, *246*, 270, 279–81, *280*, *281*, 287, 296
CO_2 emissions 19, 132, 133–34, 182–83
  Scope 3 emissions 133, 148, 149, 232
Collaborative Planning Forecasting and Replenishment (CPFR) 151
Colorado State University (CSU) 91
Colruyt Group 196, 220–23, 233
'concurrent engineering' 134–35
consumer packaged goods (CPG) 236–39
  integrated planning 249–51, *249*
  planning processes and systems ecosystem, lack of integration in 243–48, *244*, *246*
  supply chain and business, modelling 239–43, *240*
Consumer Price Index (CPI) 83–85
Corporate Governance 32
Corporate Sustainability Reporting Directive (CSRD) 2, 178
COS 15–16
'cost of goods sold' ('COGS') 245
Côte d'Ivoire 35, 180, 209, 232
Covid 2, 10–12, 137, 138, 251, 286, 288, 295
Covid paradox 81
CPFR (Collaborative Planning Forecasting and Replenishment) 120, 265
CPI. *See* Consumer Price Index (CPI)
Crawford, F 157, 159, 160, 224, 278
CRM (Customer Relationship Management) system 247, 261–62
CRM system CSCO 291
CSRD. *See* Corporate Social Responsibility Directive (CSRD)

Index

D&A 275
Dalio, Ray 83
Danfoss Climate Solutions 68, 74
Danfoss Power Electronics and Drives 68
Danfoss Power Solutions 68
Danone 55
Dettol 284
digitization 45
distribution centres (Dcs) 224, 225, 230
Doughnut Economics (Raworth) 1, 48
DRP engine 285
Drucker, Peter 148
Durex 284
Dutch 236

E2E connection 285
earnings before interest and taxes (EBIT) 1, 14, 258, 275
'earth overshoot day' 197
Egypt 87
electrification 45, 68
electronic data interchange (EDI) 148, 255, 265
electronics retail *See* MediaMarktSaturn
Elkington, John 1, 23–24, 37, 176–77
end-of-life products (EOL) 265
energy efficiency 68
Enfamil 284
English 236
environmental ceiling 44, 49, 60–61, 63
Environmental-Social-Governance (ESG) 5
ERP systems 149, 255–56, 261, 263, 270
Etihad Airways 206, 232
Europe 2, 30, 87, 101
European Commission, Green Deal 178, 199
European Supply Chain Conference (2022) 119
European Union (EU) 238
Every Day Low Price (EDLP) 170
executive teams 81
"experience electronics" strategy 174–75

fear of missing out (FOMO) 149, 302
Financial and Supply Chain Planning (FSCP) 235–36, 255, 258–60, 259, 262, 272, 275–77, 277, 296, 303
Financial Planning & Analysis (FP&A) 146, 245–47, 246, 257, 295–96
Fine,Charles 134, 232
Finish 284
5Ps, Sustainable Development Goals (SDGs) 126, 129
five-dimensional (5D) 2, 6–8, 6
FMCG companies 245, 265

'focal decision' 211–13, *212, 213*
FOMO. *See* fear of missing out (FOMO)
'forecast-to-availability' 221
fourth generation supply chain 125–54, *130*
  assemble-to-order bike supply chain *140, 141, 142*
  bike industry, case study 133, 137–42, *137, 140, 140, 141, 142*
  from second to fourth generation, processes and capabilities 129–31, 231–32, *231*
  from second to fourth generation, tactical planning perspective 144–53, *145*
  from second to fourth generation, strategic planning and design perspective 131–42, *131*
  lack of resilience, impact of 126–29, *127–28*
  nutrient additives manufacturer, case study 149–50
  outsourced manufacturing, case study 150–51
  retail VMI 151–52
  see also Supply Chain Triangle
Free Cash Flow 258
FSCP. *See* Financial and Supply Chain Planning (FSCP)

Gartner model 250, 298, 303
Gartner S&OP maturity model 235, 249, *249*, 254, 256–57, 259
Gattorna, John 6, 68, 136, 208, 210
Gaza 2, 92
Geneva 33
Germany 175
Ghana 35, 180, 209, 232
Giant Group 138
global warming 25, 91
GOOTDZ (Get Out Of The Danger Zone) 302
Gorillas 238
Grant, David 133
'green bonds' 238
Green Deal (Europe) 2, 87–88
'green financing' 238
green transition 68
Greenpeace 23, 35–36, *36*

Harpic 284
Healthcare pvdc 94
Henzen, Rozanne 196–99
'Homo economicus' 49
Hoshin Kanri 74
hybrid working 202

Index

IBP 258
Improving Performance: How to Manage the White Space on the Organization Chart (Rummler and Brache) 239
in-depth' trainings 221
Infineon 216–20, *217*
Inflation Reduction Act 178
Inflation Reduction Act (US) 2, 87–88
Institute for the Future (IFTF) 216
Integrated Business Planning (IBP) 144, 147
'Integrated Business Planning' (IBP) 254, 274, 295, 298
'Integrated Value Planning & Execution' (IVP&E) 256
'Integrated Value Planning' 235–36, 251–56, *252*, *253*, 270–71, 272–73, 305–06
  business planning processes 268–70, *269*
  Cross functional balance and the Chief Value Planning Officer 290–93, *293*
  dashboard 278–82, *279*, *280*, *281*
  financial and supply chain planning, integrating 256–60, *259*
  functional organizations and functional silos 287–90, *289*, *290*
  Integrating sales, marketing, product and resource planning 260–64, *264*
  key customers and key suppliers, integrating 265–68, *267*
  Organizing for complex and dynamic environments 293–303, *294*, *297*, *299*, *302*
  process 274–77, *276*
  strategy-driven Integrated Value Planning 283, *283*
Interface 166
International Committee of the Red Cross 40
International General Assembly (IGA) 33–34
'inverse fishbone' diagram 125, 126–29, *127–28*
IRA 30
Iran 87
Iranian Revolution (1978–79) 87
Iraq 87
Israel 87
'IVP'. *See* Integrated Value Planning'

JIT supply chains 102
Johnson Controls 158
Justice40 Initiative 178

Kaplan, Robert 66–67, 196, 224, 270
keep things simple, stupid (KISS) 99

'Keuringsdienst van Waarde' (TV programme) 179
Knoblich, Konstanze 216–20
KPIs 282
Kuik, Joeri 172–75

lack of resilience 125
  impact of 126–29, *127–28*
landfills 197
Linton, Erika 22–23
LIRP (Living Income Reference Price) 183
Lofvers, Martijn 236–39, *237*
London 119
Lysol 284

machine productivity 68
Make-To-Order (MTO) 99
Make-To-Stock (MTS) 99
Margarines, Culinary Oils and Fats (MCOF) 55
'Mastering the circular economy' (Weenk and Henzen) 196–97
Matthews 157, 159, 160, 224, 278
Mauborgne 160, 161
McGonigal, Jane 216
Médecins Sans Frontières (MSF) 5, 33–36
MediaMarktSaturn 156, 172–76, *173*, 192
Metro group 172
Metz, Jesper 16–19, 22–23
Mexico 47
MF5 195, 204–05
micro-electronics 10–11
Mill, John Stuart 49
minimum order quantities (MOQs) 110
Mintzberg, Henry 103, 273, 293–95, *294*, 303
Mondelez 55
MRP 255, 285
MRP calculation 140
MTO 292
Mucinex 284
Myanmar 103
Myth of Excellence, The (Crawford and Matthews) 157, *158*

National Centres for Environmental Information (NCEI) 91
National Oceanic and Atmospheric Administration (NOAA) 91
Nestlé 55
new product introduction (NPI) 99–101, 110–13, 145, 146, 265
New Product Introductions (NPIs) 99–101, 110–13, 145, 146, 265

Non-Financial Reporting Directive (NFRD) 52
non-profit supply chains 5
North Africa 103
North America 47
Norton, D P 196, 224
Nurofen 284
Nutramigen 284
nutrient additives manufacturer, case study 149–50

O'Leary, Michael 167
Observer, The (newspaper) 167
OEMs 210, 211
Oliver Wight IBP 254
'on shelf availability' (OSA) 152
one-dimensional (1D) 6
on-time in-full (OTIF) 170, 279–82, 281, 282
'Open Chain' initiative 181, 183, 208
OPEX 277, 291
OR-OR 7
outsourced manufacturing, case study 150–51

P&L 65
Paris 33
Patagonia 183, 198
    Common Threads Recycling Program 166
PESTELE 83, 212
Piao Jin 45–48
'planned obsolescence' 197
Porter, Michael 159, 185
portfolio complexity 99
post-Covid energy crisis 266
Primark 167
'process management' 239
'process thinking' 239
product breadth 159
product quality 159
Prosperity (Mayer) 1

quantum computing 87

R&D 139
Raworth, Kate 48–50
RCCP plan 263
Reckitt 284–87, 303
recycled PET 63
retail VMI 151–52
Return On Capital Employed 291
Ricoh 195, 201–05, 232–33, 279
R-ladder 198–99
ROCE 7, 13–15, 171, 183, 273, 295, 296, 303

Rombaut, Roeland 63–65
'Rough Cut Capacity Plan' (RCCP) 262
r-PET. *See* recycled PET
Rummler and Brache 287–88, 289, 290
Rummler, Geary 239–47, 240, 246, 287–88, 289, 290
Russia 83, 87, 90
Ryanair 167, 205, 206, 232

S&OP (sales and operations planning) 6, 274, 283, 295, 298
safety stocks 9–10
Saint Nicolas Day 224
Sales & Operations Planning (S&OP) 144, 146, 150, 174
sales, general & administrative (SG&A) 258, 275, 277
Sarker, Zaki 22
scenario management 211–23, 212, 213, 215
    Infineon 216–20, 217
Schneider Electric 210
Schneider Sustainability Essentials (SSE) 45
Scope 3 CO2 data 239
seconomic cycles 13
Segmenting markets and supply chains 136, 205–11, 207
Siemens Smart Infrastructure 157, 184–89, 186, 187, 188
social foundation 44, 49, 60–61, 63
Southeast Asia 30
Southwest 205, 206
SRM (Supplier Relationship Management) 247
strategic diamond 184–89, 186, 187, 188
Strategic Planning for Dynamic Supply Chains (Phadnis, Sheffi and Caplice) 211
strategic trade-offs 76
strategic value proposition 157–61, 158, 160
    extending, with sustainability and resilience 164–68, 164, 165
    mapping your 161–64, 162, 163
Strategy Driven Supply Chain, The 157, 161, 168, 202, 206
strategy-driven supply chain 168–71, 169
    MediaMarktSaturn 172–76, 173, 192
strategy-driven supply chain maps 196, 223, 224–30, 226, 227, 228, 229
strategy-driven sustainable and resilient supply chain design 176–91, 177
    complexity and variability 179–81
    iterate 184
    market analysis 176–79, 177

Siemens Smart Infrastructure 184–89, *186, 187, 188*
strategic value proposition 179
supply chain and product design 182–83
supply chain response 181–82
triple bottom line impact 183–84
Strategy-Driven Sustainable and Resilient Supply Chain Design 273
Strepsils 284
Suez Canal 2, 121
Supply Chain Magazine 236
Supply Chain Movement 236
Supply Chain Planning (SCP) 295–96
Supply Chain Strategy and Financial Metrics 157, 171
Supply Chain Triangle 249, *249*, 263, 283–84, 287–88, 302
  balancing of 12–15, *13*
  Covid-19 impacts on 10–12, *10, 12*
  ESG triangle 32–41, *33*
  H&M 5, 15–23, *17, 18, 20, 21, 22*
  impact across three triangles 28–31, *29, 31*
  MSF 33–40, *34, 35, 36, 38, 39*
  profit, people and planet triangle 23–27, *24, 25, 27*
  traditional imbalances 8–9, *9*
Supply Chain Triangle of Service 5
Sustainable Logistics and Supply Chain Management (Grant) 133
Sustainable Supply Chain Zone
  alternative models 65–67, *66*
  CSRD 52–53
  Danfoss 67–75, *69, 71, 72, 73*
  Doughnut Economics 48–50
  models to describe 5D supply chain 75–76
  Schneider Electric 44, 45–48
  Vandemoortele 44, 53–65, *54, 56, 61, 62, 63*
  see also fourth generation supply chain
Syria 87
'system view' 251, *252, 253*
  planning processes and systems ecosystem, lack of integration in 243–48, *244, 246*

Tactical Committee Food Retail (TCFR) 223
Teece, David J. 184–85
Tesla 158
Theory of Moral Sentiments (Smith) 49
3D printing 112
3D Concurrent Engineering (3DCE) 134
three-dimensional (3D) 2
3M 167–68, 206

TMS 255
Tony's Chocolonely 166, 167, 179–81, 182, 183, 184, 192, 199, 209, 232
Toyota 69
TPP (Trade Promotion Planning) system 247
trade-offs 7, 22
Transforming Supply Chains (Gattorna) 208
Treacy, T 159–60, *160*
Tricoire, Jean-Pascal 45
triple bottom line 24
Triple Triangle 5
Trump, Donald 83
Tschentscher, Alexander 184–89
Tunesia 103

Ukraine 2, 83, 87
United States 236
US (United States) 30, 47, 87

van de Keuken, Teun 179
Vandemoortele 278–79
Vanish 284
Vannier, William 36–38, 39–40
Vendor Managed Inventory (VMI) 266
Verstraeten, Jeroen 63–65
VICS (Voluntary Interindustry Commerce Solutions) 265
Victoria, Julio 34
VMI 287
volatility
  case study: fashion company 103–110, *104, 105, 106, 107, 109, 110*
  case study: high-tech company 110–19, *112, 113–14, 115, 116, 117, 118*
  drivers for resilience 98–103, *100*
  external drivers 82–88, *84, 85, 86*
  internal drivers 88–91, *90*
  resilience: sense, shift and steer 119–21
  Solvay 92–98, *92, 93, 94, 95, 96*
Vorrath, Frank 68, 69–74

Walmart 170
'Waste Electrical and Electronic Equipment' (WEEE) 197
'waterfall approach' 132–33
Wealth of Nations, The (Smith) 49
Weekday 15–16
Weenk, Ed 196–99
Western-Europe 236
Wiersema 159–60, *160*
Wight, Oliver 254
WMS 90, 255
World Economic Forum 32

Yom Kippur War (1973) 87

Looking for another book?

Explore our award-winning books from global business experts in Logistics, Supply Chain and Operations

Scan the code to browse

www.koganpage.com/logistics

More books from Kogan Page

SUPPLY CHAIN STRATEGY AND FINANCIAL METRICS
THE SUPPLY CHAIN TRIANGLE OF SERVICE, COST AND CASH
BRAM DESMET
ISBN: 9780749482572

THE STRATEGY-DRIVEN SUPPLY CHAIN
INTEGRATING STRATEGY, FINANCE AND SUPPLY CHAIN FOR A COMPETITIVE EDGE
BRAM DESMET
ISBN: 9781398600454

SUPPLY CHAIN NETWORK DESIGN
HOW TO CREATE RESILIENT, AGILE AND SUSTAINABLE SUPPLY CHAINS
NICK VYAS, DAS DASGUPTA, GREYS SOŠIĆ
ISBN: 9781398614918

MASTERING THE CIRCULAR ECONOMY
A PRACTICAL APPROACH TO THE CIRCULAR BUSINESS MODEL TRANSFORMATION
ED WEENK AND ROZANNE HENZEN
ISBN: 9781398602748

www.koganpage.com